What Mormons Really *Believe*

Isaiah Bennett

Inside Mormonism

What Mormons Really *Believe*

Catholic Answers
San Diego
1999

Copyright © 2001 by Catholic Answers

All rights reserved. Except for quotations, no part of this book may be reproduced or transmitted in any form or by any means, electronic or mechanical, including photocopying, recording, uploading to the Internet, or by any information storage and retrieval system, without written permission from the author.

Unless otherwise noted, Scripture quotations taken from the *King James Version* (KJV) of the Bible.

Other Scripture quotations taken from the *New American Bible* (NAB) © 1969–1986, Confraternity of Christian Doctrine, or from the *Revised Standard Version* (RSV) © 1946–1957, Division of Christian Education of the National Council of the Churches of Christ in the United States of America, from the *New International Version* (NIV) © 1973–1984, International Bible Society.

Published by Catholic Answers, Inc.
2020 Gillespie Way
El Cajon, California 92020
(888) 291–8000 (orders)
(619) 387–0042 (fax)
www.catholic.com (web)

Cover design by Kray Marketing
Printed in the United States of America
ISBN 1-8889932-06-9

Contents

Preface and Acknowledgments 11
Introduction 13

PART ONE: AN OVERVIEW OF MORMONISM

1. Early Mormon Stages 21
2. Recent Mormon Stages 38

PART TWO: MORMON LIFE

3. Mormon Organization 49
4. Mormon Ordinances 64
5. Sacraments and Ordinances, Valid and Invalid 84
6. Mormon Headquarters: A Look around Temple
   Square 108
7. Mormon Temple Work 112
8. All Is Well? 140

PART THREE: THE GREAT APOSTASY

9. Slipping from the Rock: The "Great Apostasy" 159
10. The Old Testament and the "Great Apostasy" 166
11. The New Testament and the "Great Apostasy" 172
12. Historical Arguments for Total Apostasy 193
13. "Specific Causes" of Apostasy 200
14. Charges of Catholic Misdeeds 215
15. The True Church of Christ 226
16. A Not Quite Total Apostasy? 245

Part Four: The Mormon Gods

17. Polytheism, Mormon Style 253
18. Mormon God Number One—A Glorified Man 267
19. Mormon God Number Two—Our Elder Brother . . . 280
20. Mormon God Number Three—Another Son 303
21. The True Godhead—The Blessed Trinity 311

Part Five: God in Embryo: The Mormon Doctrine of Man

22. Pre-Existence of Man 323
23. Fall Forward? Mormonism on Original Sin 336
24. Eternal Progression 344
25. Waiting for the End: The Intermediate State 353
26. Mormon Heavens 363

Part Six: Mormon Revelations and Scriptures

27. Mormon Revelations, Mormon Scriptures 381
28. Visions and Versions 384
29. The Book of Mormon 396
30. Arguments Made on Behalf of the Book of Mormon 412
31. Problems with the Book of Mormon 432
32. The Other Mormon Scriptures 456
33. Continuing Mormon Revelations 473

Conclusion 485

Appendices

I. Key Mormon Figures 491
II. Joseph Smith's Vision Accounts 495

III. "The Articles of Faith"	503
IV. Patriarchal Blessing	505
V. Resignation Letter	508

Bibliography	513
Scriptural Index	529
Subject Index	543

*This work is in reparation to
the Sacred Heart of Jesus*

Preface and Acknowledgments

On a visit to some black acquaintances, I learned from the father that his teenage daughter had begun taking instructions from Mormon missionaries. I was disappointed and curious. The father, sensing my impending question, said, "Oh, we know all about the former Mormon treatment of blacks. But the missionaries told us that that was all in the past."

"Have they informed you that their church still teaches that people born black are under the curse of Cain?" I asked. "That they believe black skin is a punishment?"

Neither daughter nor father had heard this, so they brought it up with the young "elders" when they called again. It elicited a typical Mormon reaction to criticism. At my next visit, I noticed two signs prominently displayed in the living room. One, in bold, colored letters, stated: "SATAN ♥'s CONTENTION." The other: "CONTENTION IS OF THE DEVIL." Both signs were framed by red-orange flames.[1] Mormons, Jehovah's Witnesses, and similar groups resort to a handy dodge when questioned too closely: They "demonize" their opponents. They seem incapable of acknowledging the sincerity of any critique. To them, all who fail to accept their novel beliefs are under Satan's sway, knowingly or not. Any opposition is seen as infernal.

This book is contentious in one sense: It contends for the true faith, once for all delivered unto the New Testament saints and, through them, to us. We are commanded to explain, defend, and, yes, contend for the faith.[2] This work aims to be a comprehensive presentation of Mormon teachings, accompanied by orthodox Catholic critique. I write from first-hand knowledge and

---

[1] See the Book of Mormon, Third Nephi 11:29.
[2] See Jude 3 and 1 Thessalonians 2:2.

experience. Why I have written this book is best summed up by Peter: "You therefore, beloved, knowing this beforehand, beware lest you be carried away with the error of lawless men and lose your own stability" (2 Pet. 3:17, RSV).

∼

I wish to thank the following for their contributions to this work. First, Karl Keating of Catholic Answers, whose kindness helped me return to the Church. My editor, James Akin, worked hard to deepen the analyses of many of Mormonism's false doctrines. Patrick Madrid provided the initial encouragement that helped me turn my dismay and self-condemnation into something that, I hope, will help others avoid my own foolishness. I would also like to thank Vidar André Eide and Edward Peters, JCD, who were helpful with the manuscript at several points.

During the past two years, I've had the blessing of corresponding via e-mail with others who have felt the sting of Mormonism in their families and relationships. Leonard, Lou, and Janet, in particular, have helped me with their comments and, especially, their prayers. If Nathan and Chad are any indication, the future of Catholic apologetics is bright. These young Internet friends display a maturity of faith and sensitivity to issues that will serve the Church well. They have also provided me their ideas and prayerful support. Finally, I thank my dear wife, Barbara. Through my own fault, I lost my priestly ministry. But I have received, from the good God, the grace of a holy marriage. Barbara's patience with her hermit-husband is matched only by my love for her.

Introduction

I'd been a practicing Catholic all my life. Some would say a devout Catholic. After high school I entered religious life and was ordained a priest. I knew, loved, and practiced my faith. There were no doctrines or moral precepts of the Church that I did not sincerely hold. You could say that I was "conservative," though I preferred the term "orthodox." I was convinced of the truths of Sacred Scripture and Tradition; I accepted wholeheartedly the teachings of the pope and the Church's magisterium. I preached and taught these to my congregation.

For reasons not clear to me, in the mid-1980s I picked up some literature about the Mormon church. I'd always been interested in comparative religion and had been, like most, contacted now and again by clean-cut Mormon missionaries. My curiosity developed into fascination, which in turn became something of an obsession. I could not read enough about this strange American religion.

"How could anyone believe this stuff?" I wondered. Plural gods? Plural wives? Plural wives in heaven? The more I read, the more curious I became. My collection of Mormon books and material filled two shelves and was growing. Most of the literature was written by those critical of Mormonism, generally Protestant Fundamentalists whose treatment ranged from analytical to sensational. This latter category reminded me of the lurid diatribes produced by some anti-Catholics.

The more I studied, the more convinced I became that Mormonism was not a Christian faith. While its outward "fruits" may have appeared good, they were produced and bought with counterfeit tender. Good works do not correct bad teachings.

These were the thoughts I brought to Salt Lake City in March 1992. Nothing I experienced during my five days in the heart of Mormonism changed my opinion. I returned to my New York parish where I was pastor and continued with my "hobby" off and on for the next year and a half. However, slowly a change of perspective began. As I got used to reading about Mormon teachings, they started to seem less bizarre to me. I intellectually realized how outside the historic Christian faith they were, but greater familiarity with them made them less shocking.

Particular facets of Mormonism, with its strong emphasis on family, spoke to my emotional needs on some level. I had "absentee" parents throughout my childhood. My father was rarely home. My mother was distant emotionally, and I never recall confiding in her, or anyone else, for that matter. When I was nine, my parents divorced, but since my father was rarely home, the divorce simply made that reality "official." Following my parents' divorce, I lost contact with my father and did not see him until a year before I left the Catholic Church. The meeting didn't go well. My father died soon after, and I lost the chance for reconciliation with him. My mother had died in a car accident a few years earlier and I had not handled her death well either.

Their dying fulfilled my worst fears. From my earliest memories, I had feared what would become of my parents at their deaths. This despair was unaffected even by the loving, sensible Catholic instruction I received, not only in grammar and secondary school, but in theology studies as well. I wouldn't let the peace of Christ and his Church penetrate my dark disposition. I was pessimistic and depressed, it seemed, by nature and I was reluctant to talk about it.

By the time I left the Church, I had lived with depression for years. Following a "breakdown" that required hospitalization and ongoing medication, Mormonism's false promise of easy salvation and eternally happy families affected me.

It's odd, but I never found myself denying my Catholic faith. It's just that my preoccupation with Mormonism was so great that it blocked all other considerations from view. I had become obsessed with it, and, like an addict, I hid my fixation. I did not discuss it with anyone except local Mormon leaders and missionaries. I didn't allow Mormon teachings to be cross-examined in the light of reason. I ignored my "head" in favor of my "gut feelings"—something Mormon missionaries encouraged. In fact, the basic principle of Mormon evangelism is: Trust your feelings, your "personal testimony," about the LDS faith.[1]

Mormons cite a passage from one of their scriptures, Doctrine and Covenants, that gives this criterion for determining truth: "[Y]ou must study it out in your mind; then you must ask me [Christ] if it be right, and if it is right I will cause that your bosom shall burn within you; therefore, you shall feel that it is right" (9:8).

Despite this promise, when I became more open to Mormonism, my bosom did not burn. I literally had stomach aches! I was forty-five years old, a life-long and committed Catholic and a priest. Would I now have to trade my Catholic truth for some other "truth"? I prayed about whether to leave the Church, but not convincingly. I told myself that the Lord wanted me to become a Mormon. The Mormons I consulted, of course, agreed with my assessment and assured me that the Holy Ghost had made the same thing known to them. My course was clear, though not easy. But I was certain that the Lord would make all things possible if this were his will.

I now can see that my prayer was not fruitful because it was not whole-hearted. I had let involvement with Mormonism become so extensive that I no longer saw options clearly. This is not to say that I consider Mormonism to be a cult set on brainwashing its members and deceiving potential converts. I don't. The weakness and fault were mine.

I didn't inform my superiors that I would be leaving the priesthood and the Catholic Church until I was certain in my own mind. This was typical of me: I rarely discussed personal struggles, preferring instead to resolve them myself. My superiors were sympathetic. They accepted my decision with surprise and sorrow but did not belittle it or try to coerce me in any way. I asked

---

[1] LDS is the preferred term Mormons use to refer to their religion, the Church of Jesus Christ of Latter-day Saints. Both it and "Mormon" will be used interchangeably in this book.

a woman who had been a long-time friend to marry me. My proposal came to her out of the blue, but she agreed. She took Mormon instruction, and we were both re-baptized in December 1993. We moved to Salt Lake City, where I taught in two colleges and in the church's Institute of Religion, a program for young adults usually found on or near secular college campuses.

My wife and I were active in the Mormon church, teaching and "giving testimony" about our conversion. We spoke, literally, to thousands and received warm feedback. Many Mormons said the Holy Ghost had touched them through our story and commented on how brave we were to face "the truth" and then make the difficult step toward it. We were destined to great things, they knew.

As I said, I never really denied the Catholic doctrines I had spent my life believing and teaching. Latter-day Saint doctrines simply shoved them aside. I also can say that I never spoke ill of the Church or my time in it. When questions arose about Catholic beliefs, I found myself giving my Mormon questioners responses that sounded convincing. Several times members thanked me for clarifying their misconceptions. A few were pleased that I did not "bash" my former faith, as some converts tend to do.

For nearly a year and a half, my wife and I participated as faithful and active members of the Mormon church. We were "temple worthy," and we received constant validation from our leaders and fellow members.

But there came stirrings of unrest, particularly with the temple and the Mormon church's moral teachings. Neither was as holy and righteous as we had come to expect. My wife, in particular, became increasingly disappointed with the lack of spirituality in Mormonism in general and in the temple ceremonies in particular. I had similar feelings but tried to talk myself out of them. My wife was more forthright.

Independently, we reached the conclusion that our "testimonies" supporting the Mormon church were no longer strong enough to maintain our membership. We uncovered deficiencies with Mormonism's permissive policies on abortion, contraception, and divorce. We longed for meaningful spiritual worship not available in the temple. We concluded that a church so wrong in such fundamentals could not possess the right to speak for God. We would leave the Mormon church, but where would we go? We both knew. Back to our Catholic faith, to the Church founded by Jesus Christ.

Catholic leaders have been forgiving and kind. We participate fully in the Church's sacramental life. Our marriage has been validated. I miss my ministry as a priest but have found in marriage a path to salvation equally beautiful and blessed. My prayer is that my experience and writings may stand in reparation for my acts against faith and charity. If they can enlighten readers to the beauty and truth of the Catholic faith and alert them to the dangers of Mormonism, then God will have brought something good from my sojourn. As Paul tells us, "We know that in everything God works for good with those who love him" (Rom. 8:28).

PART ONE

An Overview of Mormonism

1. Early Mormon Stages

Mormonism has passed through a number of theological stages in which its doctrine has changed, often suddenly and dramatically, due to supposed new divine revelations. The Mormon God seems to possess a rich imagination and a breezy resolve, characteristics he shares with his Mormon spokesmen.[1]

To help readers follow Mormon history, I have divided it into stages based on key revelations and events, a useful way of tracking major shifts in Mormon theology and culture. Names and numbers are assigned for convenience. Previewing the stages now will help us place in context theological discussions of succeeding chapters.

Stage 1: The First Vision Period (1820–1827)[2]

The man who founded Mormonism, Joseph Smith, Jr., was born in Sharon, Vermont, on December 23, 1805, but spent much of his youth in New York state. Smith's father embraced the universalist position that all people will eventually be saved. His mother eschewed all churches and trusted, instead, in her own interpretation of the Bible. Both sought a return to the New Testament-era church, purified of the "dross" that had accumulated over the centuries.

Smith's parents placed great faith in visions and dreams. Joseph Smith, Sr., is said to have had several visions, the contents of which

---

[1] Mormons teach a changeable God, one who progressed to godhood from an inferior, mortal state and who continues to grow as his children achieve their own divinity. A changeable God, therefore, is likely to produce changing, even contradictory, opinions.

[2] Dates assigned here to the First Vision stage and several others will correspond to the currently held position of the LDS church. The relevant chapters will show the impossibility of some of these dates.

his son appropriated for his own use. In 1811, the elder Smith learned in a vision that "all churches were in darkness," none of them professing the true Christian faith.[3] The Smith family based its understanding of the Lord's ways on visionary experience and personal enlightenment. They generally avoided organized religion, depending instead upon direct divine instruction —personal impressions not subject to independent verification since they were not attested by outward miracles, as was biblical revelation.

With this as his background, Joseph Smith, Jr., experienced a spiritual awakening at the age of fourteen. According to his later reports, he had been roused by the conflicting religious revivals near his home and sought the Lord's guidance in prayer: Which church, if any, was true? Should he join a church? The answer supposedly came to him in a vision, now called the First Vision. There are discrepancies about this vision, and at different times Smith gave different versions of it. In this chapter, we will follow the version currently approved by the Mormon church (an account that Smith gave in 1842), though in chapter 28 we will examine other versions.

According to the 1842 account, Smith saw God the Father and God the Son. The Lord (here meaning Jesus) told him that all churches were wrong and all who professed belief in them were corrupt.[4] He must not join any of them. Nonetheless, he attached himself to one of them in 1828. While he was "translating" the Book of Mormon, Smith joined a probationary class for membership in a Methodist church.[5]

Mormonism is not a Protestant church, but its foundations are Protestant in the sense that its founder depended upon his own divinely assisted interpretation of Scripture, saw traditional churches

---

[3] See H. Michael Marquardt and Wesley P. Walters, *Inventing Mormonism: Tradition and the Historical Record*, 49. This work is a good general source for information on the First Vision and Book of Mormon stages.

[4] Joseph Smith—History 1:19 (part of the volume Pearl of Great Price).

[5] See *Inventing Mormonism*, 54–55, 61.

as apostate and condemned their individual members for professing the historical creeds. Smith also assumed Protestant rather than Catholic theological principles as his base. According to Smith, he told his visionary experiences to several preachers who, incredulous, incited "a great persecution" against him. In fact, "all the sects" are said to have united to persecute Smith.[6]

The boy-prophet reportedly suffered this persecution for three years before a heavenly messenger (whom Smith called, variously, Nephi or Moroni) appeared to him four times in one day with the same message: All people would henceforth know of Smith and would call him either good or evil. The Lord had a work for him to do: find and translate a book written on gold plates that gave the account of America's former inhabitants. This book contained, in addition, the "fulness of the everlasting Gospel."[7]

Smith's father agreed that his son had experienced a visitation from heaven. He encouraged his son to pursue the angel's directions.

At age seventeen, Smith went to the hillside that the angel had described and found a large rock. Removing it and digging underneath, he found a stone box containing the gold plates, two stones set in bows like eyeglass frames (he called them the Urim and Thummim) and a breastplate. He tried to remove the treasure but was prevented by the angel, who told him he would not receive the plates for four more years. In the meantime, he was to return to the place once a year on that date for further instructions.

Stage 2: The Book of Mormon Period (1827–1835)

In southern New York and northern Pennsylvania, where Smith spent his teenage and young adult years, he enjoyed a reputation as a gifted "seer." In this he was joined by his father and two

---

[6] Joseph Smith—History 1:21–22.
[7] Joseph Smith—History 1:3–34.

older brothers, Alvin and Hyrum. Despite his divine election at the First Vision and the subsequent visitations by the angel, Smith avidly participated in "money digging," claiming he could find buried gold and silver. In this endeavor, he resorted to dowsing, or making use of a witch hazel rod; he would also consult a "seer stone."[8]

His performance could not always keep up with his promises and he was arrested on March 20, 1826, charged with being a "disorderly person and an impostor." Smith admitted to using his seer stone for several years to find lost property, but said he had given up the practice because it was straining his eyes. Smith was tried for the misdemeanor of "glass looking" and fined.[9]

The seer stone also played a role in the finding of the golden plates on which the Book of Mormon was written. Smith's account of the Book of Mormon's coming forth indicates he was directed to the burial site by the angel. The hill, now named Cumorah after a battle site in the Book of Mormon, had been the scene of a great deal of treasure digging even before Smith's discovery. Early Mormons said he found the plates by gazing into his "peep stone," the same stone he subsequently consulted in translating them.[10]

Smith obtained possession of the plates in September 1827, when he was twenty-one. The following months were a time of trial for Smith, who was involved in physical fights with local thugs and former money-digging partners seeking a share of his golden discovery.[11] Smith married Emma Hale the January before he received the golden plates. With a wife to support, Smith began "translating" the plates from a language he called "Reformed

---

[8] Joseph's personal stone was an egg-sized, smooth gray stone he found while digging a well. For a detailed discussion of Smith's controversial practices, see *Inventing Mormonism*, chapter four, and Jerald and Sandra Tanner, *Joseph Smith and Money Digging*.

[9] See Jerald and Sandra Tanner, *Mormonism—Shadow or Reality?* 32–39.

[10] *Inventing Mormonism*, 75.

[11] Joseph Smith—History 1:59ff.

Egyptian." In many cases, the plates were not even in the room when he dictated to various scribes a tale about ancient Hebrew immigrants building a civilization in the Americas. When finished, the book was over 500 type-set pages. In June of 1829, translation of the Book of Mormon was completed. Martin Harris, a local farmer of some means, agreed to finance the printing of 5,000 copies. The new scripture came off the presses March 26, 1830, though sales of the first edition were slow. No one had actually seen the plates from which the Book of Mormon was translated, though several men, called the Three Witnesses and the Eight Witnesses, are said to have seen them "with the eyes of faith" or in a vision. Some said they "hefted" the plates, though they were wrapped in cloth at the time.

Smith reported that the plates were taken from him when the translation was complete, though accounts differ as to how. One of the Three Witnesses said they were taken by an angel to a cave. Smith's brother William said the prophet was told to bury them again. Brigham Young and Orson Pratt, two of the earliest Mormon apostles, spoke of the Hill Cumorah opening up and Smith delivering the plates to a great repository of other, related ancient records.[12]

The current official revision of the account of finding and returning the plates has removed any mention of Smith's use of a seer stone and states only that the plates were taken away by the angel. While translating the Book of Mormon, Smith and his chief scribe, Oliver Cowdery, discovered that they must be baptized and receive proper priesthood power. On January 15, 1829, John the Baptist appeared to them, giving them the Aaronic priesthood and instructing them to baptize one another in the Susquehanna River, near Harmony, Pennsylvania.[13] Later that spring, Peter, James, and John appeared to Smith and Cowdery and conferred on them the greater, or Melchizedek, priesthood, giving them the power to act in God's name in all things.

---

[12] *Inventing Mormonism*, 104–105.
[13] See Doctrine and Covenants 13.

On April 6, 1830, Smith and five other men gathered at a home in Fayette, New York, and officially organized the "Church of Christ,"[14] which would evolve into the current Mormon Church.

Soon after, Smith began work on another volume of scripture, the Book of Moses, which is mostly a rewriting of the first several chapters of Genesis. The Book of Mormon and the Book of Moses contain a more-or-less traditional concept of God: He is one, eternal, all-powerful and unchanging.[15] Also at variance with later Mormon teaching is the Book of Mormon's forceful condemnation of polygamy (Jacob 2:23-24).[16]

By this time, Smith and his followers had moved to Kirtland, Ohio. In February 1832 he and former preacher Sidney Rigdon had a vision of the "three degrees of glory" or three heavens (now recorded in Doctrine and Covenants 76). Smith and Rigdon had been working on an "inspired revision" of the Bible which, when finished in mid-1833, contained no indication of plurality of gods that would later enter Mormon teaching.[17]

Smith produced the first version of the First Vision in his diary in 1832. He recounted how, in his sixteenth year, he saw in vision only one personage—the Lord Jesus.

On February 27, 1833, Smith reported a revelation known as the Word of Wisdom (Doctrine and Covenants 89). He had asked the

---

[14] See Doctrine and Covenants 20.

[15] I say "more-or-less" because the Book of Mormon tends toward modalism, an error completely opposite to the later Mormon heresy of, at least, tritheism.

[16] Some Mormon defenders are quick to point out that, just a few verses later, Almighty God leaves Himself a loophole: "For if I will, saith the Lord of Hosts, raise up seed unto me, I will command my people; otherwise they shall hearken unto these things" (Jacob 2:30). But that is precisely the point. On one hand, the Book of Mormon proclaims a confusing notion of an unchanging God (Who, in Smith's later writings, has continually evolved from a lesser being), while on the other hand it allows for major contradictory theological and moral positions.

[17] Though it appeared Smith was shrugging off his earlier mistakes of modalism.

AN OVERVIEW OF MORMONISM

Lord for advice after Emma complained about cleaning up the male members' (often missed) spittoons after their meetings.[18] Smith was given the revelation "not by commandment or constraint," but as advice or counsel, that henceforth, members should not use tobacco, alcohol or "hot drinks" (interpreted as coffee and tea). They should make ample use of grains and vegetables and eat meat only in winter and seasons of famine.

Observance of the Word of Wisdom was sporadic, even by Smith and other early leaders. By 1930, however, it had become more rigorously enforced, and those who fail to observe it now are denied entrance to a Mormon temple or Mormon priesthood.[19] Now it is enjoined "by . . . constraint" and not merely as advice.

The Book of Commandments, containing sixty-five "revelations" God made to Smith, was printed the same year the Word of Wisdom was promulgated. The Lectures on Faith were also composed and delivered at this time. These were instructions in theology composed by Smith and Rigdon and presented in the "School for the Elders" in Kirtland in 1834–35. They offer no hint of what would shortly appear as the Mormon teaching of polytheism, though the Lectures teach that the Godhead is made up of two personages, the Father and the Son, while the Holy Ghost is merely the "mind" of them both.[20] The Lectures on Faith were quietly dropped from the canon of Mormon scripture in 1921.

Divine revelations continued to accumulate, and in 1835 a work known as the Doctrine and Covenants was published. It incorporated the previous Book of Covenants, though some of the revelations now appeared in a severely altered form. Over time, Doctrine and Covenants (D&C) would be expanded to accommodate new revelations, some of which contradicted earlier pas-

---

[18] According to Brigham Young, *Journal of Discourses* 12:157–158.
[19] "Word of Wisdom," *Encyclopedia of Mormonism*, vol. 4. See also Leonard J. Arrington, "An Economic Interpretation of the 'Word of Wisdom,'" *BYU Studies*, vol. 1, No. 1, 40.
[20] See in particular Lecture Fifth.

sages. For example, D&C 101:4 states, "Inasmuch as this church of Christ has been reproached with the crime of fornication, and polygamy: we declare that we believe, that one man should have one wife; and one woman, but one husband." This condemnation of polygamy remained "on the books" until it was struck in 1876 and a new "revelation" was substituted, permitting the practice. (See D&C 132.)

Five years after the Mormon church was established, there were 8,800 Mormons and two "stakes" or ecclesiastical territories similar to small dioceses. The first Mormon temple was built in 1835. It was used for more mundane purposes than later temples —prayer, "the sacrament" (the Lord's Supper), preaching and a theology school. There were "preparatory" ordinances of washings, anointings and foot-washing.

Smith said the name of the newly restored true church was given to him by divine revelation. Apparently, God had a difficult time making up his mind about the new church's name. It was changed to "The Church of the Latter Day Saints" in 1834. It was changed to "The Church of Christ of Latter Day Saints" in 1836. Both changes were made at the Lord's command, Smith said. The Lord finally settled, in 1838, on "The Church of Jesus Christ of Latter-day Saints."

The church's name wasn't the only thing changing. In the February 1835 issue of the Mormon newspaper *Messenger and Advocate*, Cowdery declared that the First Vision had occurred in Smith's seventeenth year. Less than a year later, Smith gave another version, stating he was fourteen and had seen angels. By 1838, the angels were eliminated, two separate gods were described and Smith's age was fixed at fourteen. This has become the LDS church's current, official version.

Stage 3: The Polytheism and Polygamy Period (1835–1844)

The first five years of the Mormon church paint a picture of just one more Protestant sect with a "restorationist" bent—individuals trying to re-establish the faith and practice they thought existed in New Testament times. Still, it was a strange sect, with new revelations and some quirky ideas about the early Americas. As part of the restorationist trend, Smith re-created a number of roles from the early Church. By early 1835, twelve "apostles" had been appointed, together with the first quorum of "the seventy," a duplication of the offices that Mormons allege Christ intended his Church to maintain. (In actuality, there came to be more than twelve apostles in the apostolic period—Paul and Barnabas were not members of the twelve—and the seventy were a temporary evangelizing team that Jesus sent out and that did not remain together after their mission was finished.)

These early changes seem tame compared to what was coming. Mormon morality and doctrine were about to face serious alterations, novelties of belief and practice that put it well beyond the quirkiest forms of Protestantism.

In the summer of 1835, it was rumored that Smith had taken to himself a teenage girl who had been staying in the Smith home. Fanny Alger has been listed as the first of Smith's plural wives, a young lady who, when she was no longer able "to conceal the consequences of her celestial [i.e., carnal] relation with the prophet," was driven out by a furious Emma.[21] Over the next seven years, Smith is said to have added a dozen "wives," all sealed to him with or without Emma's knowledge.[22] Because Cowdery would not retract his opposition to Smith and Alger's relationship, he was excommunicated in 1838. This meant that all three of the original "witnesses" to the Book of Mormon plates had left or been excommunicated on charges of stealing, counterfeiting, lying, apostasy, and criticizing the Lord's prophet (Smith). The mandate for polygamy was first "revealed" by God on July 12, 1843, but was not formally announced until 1852. The revelation was canonized as Doctrine and Covenants 132 in 1876 and voted on by the general membership in 1880. (Mormons hold *pro forma* votes on

---

[21] See Linda King Newell and Valeen Tippetts Avery, *Mormon Enigma: Emma Hale Smith*, 65–67.

[22] Andrew Jenson, *Historical Record*, vol. 6, 233–234.

whether a revelation is of God or not.) God Almighty states, in D&C 132:2, that "all those who have this law revealed unto them must obey the same." No one can reject this "new and everlasting covenant" and enter into heavenly glory (verse 3). Permission is granted for a man to marry more than one wife (verses 44, 48, 61, 62). Also in D&C 132, Smith's first wife, Emma, is commanded by Christ to accept all the wives Smith already had taken, even if surreptitiously, or suffer destruction (verses 52, 54). Verse 61 requires the first wife give permission for the husband to take a second and additional wives.

Still, this revelation came in 1843, almost a decade after Smith first began living as a polygamist. How could this be explained? When confronted with the dilemma of an adulterous prophet or one who simply implemented the official church policy of polygamy years earlier than the rest of the membership, officials opted for the latter explanation. According to the current official heading for D&C 132, the principles and doctrines involved in this 1843 dictum "had been known by the Prophet since 1831," four years before the Alger affair.

Though this explanation allowed Smith to save face, there was at least one principle of the revelation he didn't seem to know. He knew enough to take more wives, but didn't know enough to ask Emma's permission.[23]

Of course, the 1843 polygamy "revelation" is dubious, since it came years after Smith had been acquiring polygamous unions. The revelation appears to have been introduced to justify previous behavior.

The same year Smith took his second wife, he bought several mummies and papyrus writings. Smith claimed that the papyri were writings from the hand of the great patriarch Abraham, and

---

[23] It has been concluded by some that Smith also asked for and received the lawful wives of other living men. See President Jedediah M. Grant, *Journal of Discourses* 2:14: "What would a man of God say, who felt aright, when Joseph asked him for his money? He would say, 'Yes, and I wish I had more to help to build up the kingdom of God.' Or if he came and said, 'I want your wife'? 'O yes,' he would say, 'here she is, there are plenty more.'"

he proceeded to miraculously "translate" them as the Book of Abraham, which he released in 1842. (The papyri were lost and were believed destroyed in a fire. But in 1967, the Metropolitan Museum of Art recovered them. Egyptologists concluded that the writings had nothing to do with Abraham, that they dated to early Christian times and that they were Egyptian burial texts—part of the Egyptian "Book of the Dead.")

Besides polygamy, today's Mormon church also seeks to distance itself from another doctrine Smith established: the idea that Negro blood is cursed. Like many people of his period, Smith harbored racist views. When he was growing up, his home state of New York was still a slave state. In an environment where slavery was tolerated, it was easy for Smith to look down on black people, and his disdain for them was incorporated as doctrine into the scriptures he "translated."

For example, many passages in the Book of Mormon speak of dark skin as a curse for sins, as opposed to the "white and delightsome" appearance of the righteous (2 Ne. 30:6; 1 Ne. 12:23, 13:15; 2 Ne. 5:21; Jacob 3:8–9; 3 Ne. 2:14–15; Moses 7:8, 12, 22). A passage in the Book of Abraham (1:26–27), which spoke of the Egyptian pharaohs as having Negro ancestry and thereby being disqualified from God's priesthood, was used by The Church of Jesus Christ of Latter-day Saints to deny Mormon priesthood and temple privileges to black people. These passages served as the basis for every Mormon prophet since Smith to teach that blacks were spiritually cursed for their supposed sins before earthly birth.[24]

Coinciding with Smith's practice of plural marriage was his new teaching on plural gods. The Book of Abraham proclaimed doctrines contrary to those of the Book of Mormon, the Book of Moses, the Lectures on Faith and the other early revelations. Abraham 3:22ff. teaches the pre-existence of human spirits. Abraham 4 reveals that a council of "gods" decided upon the means of organizing this world out of eternal matter. Smith had now broken with the historic Judeo-Christian faith in one true God and had become a polytheist. His polytheistic teachings were reinforced

---

[24] See John J. Stewart, *Mormonism and the Negro*, 8.

in what has been called "one of the Prophet's greatest sermons because of its comprehensive doctrinal teachings."[25] Man and God are one species, Smith said. If we could see God, we would see him as a man like ourselves. "God himself was once as we are now, and is an exalted man. . . . [He] dwelt on an earth, the same as Jesus Christ himself did. . . . [God] worked out his kingdom with fear and trembling."[26] Dwelling on some earth, growing and overcoming in order to become God—this implies a "previous" God to the one we call God the Father. Smith reinforced his new Book of Abraham teaching by claiming, "In the beginning, the head of the Gods called a council of the Gods; and they came together and concocted a plan to create the world and people it."[27]

Also more clearly delineated in the King Follett Discourse are the teachings concerning the potential divinity of men: "[Y]ou have got to learn how to be Gods yourselves, and to be kings and priests to God, the same as all Gods have done before you."[28]

The current Mormon prophet, Gordon B. Hinckley, has waffled on the issue, but Smith and his successors could not be clearer in stating God was once a man.

Because of local opposition, most of the Mormons left Kirtland, where the first Mormon temple was located, and, in 1839, settled in Illinois, on the banks of the Mississippi. Smith named the town Nauvoo, explaining that it meant "City Beautiful," a rough translation of an Old Testament Hebrew term.

In 1842, Smith joined the newly formed Nauvoo Masonic Lodge. At about the same time, he began composing the rituals and ceremonies for the newly introduced endowment and sealing rites of the Mormon temple. Smith maintained he was merely restoring practices observed centuries before in Solomon's Temple. The Lord, he said, inspired and directed him to compose the rites. They bear resemblance to Masonic rituals Smith learned.

---

[25] "King Follett Discourse," *Encyclopedia of Mormonism*, vol. 2.
[26] *Teachings of the Prophet Joseph Smith*, 345–347.
[27] Ibid., 349. Such ideas were unknown to the Book of Mormon.
[28] Ibid., 346. Also not found in the prophet's first works.

The divine ordinances of the LDS temple have been changed several times, most recently in 1990.

Because of conflict between Mormons and local settlers, the Illinois legislature granted the city of Nauvoo permission to retain its own militia, which had nearly 5,000 members at its peak.[29] Smith was appointed its lieutenant general. He also said that he possessed the title of king. According to Joseph Smith's *History of the Church*, witnesses heard him proclaim that "the kingdom referred to [in Dan. 2:44] was already set up, and that he was the king over it."[30] Perhaps his putative ordination as king was insufficient, for in 1844 Smith announced he would run for United States president. Rigdon was his running-mate, and Mormon elders electioneered for their success.[31]

Opposition to Smith's polygamy and his claims to kingship led former members and others to publish an independent newspaper in Nauvoo. The *Nauvoo Expositor* published one edition, June 7, 1844. Alarmed by the attack on his reputation and policies Smith, as mayor, had the newspaper proclaimed a "public nuisance" and ordered the presses and all copies destroyed.[32]

Following this, Smith was arrested and charged with treason (for his claims to kingship) and other crimes. He was jailed in Carthage, Illinois. On June 27, 1844, a mob including ex-Mormons overran the jail. He and his older brother Hyrum were killed in a shootout, in which, it is claimed, Smith shot and perhaps killed two of his attackers. He was thirty-eight years old.

At the time of his death, there were 26,000 Mormons.

---

[29] "Nauvoo Legion," *Encyclopedia of Mormonism*, vol. 3. The contemporary militia movement, particularly strong in the American West and Rockies, has had its share of Mormon sympathizers, though several have been excommunicated by the LDS church.

[30] *History of the Church* 6:568.

[31] *History of the Church* 6:322, 324–325.

[32] Some accounts state Smith had a revelation from the Lord directing him to do this. See *Mormonism—Shadow or Reality?* 258.

Stage 4: The Brigham Young Period (1844–1877)

The Latter-day Saints were split on Smith's successor. There was enough confusion to allow several men to step forward and claim the reins, and Mormon membership split into several factions. Rigdon, foremost Mormon theologian and Smith's first counselor and vice-presidential running mate, asserted authority but was excommunicated by the Council of the Twelve Apostles. Joseph Smith III, born in 1832, had supposedly been designated and anointed by his father to be prophet after Joseph Smith, Jr.'s, death and after having reached majority age. No provision had been made, however, for an interim "regent." Brigham Young, as president of the Quorum of the Twelve, promptly asserted his right to authority, and the majority of Mormon membership supported him.

Because the LDS church was in trouble in the East and Midwest, Young decided to relocate its headquarters to the "promised land" of the intermountain West. By July 14, 1847, the first Mormon pioneers entered the Great Salt Lake valley, and, by 1850, Young was governor of the territory, which was called Deseret, a name that allegedly meant "Honeybee" in an ancient Book of Mormon language (Ether 2:3). The name was later changed to Utah, after the Ute Indians who lived there.

Young and apostle Orson Pratt announced that some Mormons had been living in polygamous unions for a number of years. At the August 1852 church conference, they provided a rationale for the practice and its previously secret implementation: Righteous LDS men can produce more children with multiple wives, thus giving wholesome Mormon upbringing to spirits waiting for mortal bodies. The practice had been kept secret, and even denied, by Mormon officials because the majority of Mormons and the nation were not prepared to hear it.[33]

Four years later, Young made another attention-grabbing pro-

---

[33] See *Church History in the Fulness of Times*, 422ff.

nouncement. In the *Journal of Discourses* he asserted that there are some sins for which no forgiveness may be obtained, not even by Christ's atonement. Only if the sinner is killed in such a way that his blood is shed by another would he have any hope for redemption, according to this teaching (4:53).[34]

The following year, in September 1857, the Mountain Meadows Massacre occurred when Mormon forces attacked and killed nearly all 120 or so members of a non-Mormon band of men, women, and children traveling through southern Utah from Arkansas to California. Earlier, the Mormon territorial militia had been placed under martial law, in response to threats that the federal government was sending troops to Utah to address what Washington saw as civil disobedience and disloyalty. U.S. troops did enter Utah, but not for another year, and then peacefully.

In 1862, President Abraham Lincoln signed the Morrill Act, which prohibited the practice of bigamy. Because of the Civil War, the law was rarely enforced, and Mormons generally refused to obey. Young, throughout his tenure, promoted polygamy, saying, "Monogamy, or restrictions by law to one wife, is no part of the economy of heaven among men" (*Journal of Discourses* 9:322); "[Polygamy] is the only religion acknowledged there [in heaven]" (ibid., 9:319). He also asserted that Christian monogamy has been a fruitful source of "prostitution and whoredom."[35]

Young also underscored Mormonism's racist stand: "Any man having one drop of the seed of Cain in him cannot receive the priesthood. . . ."[36]

---

[34] Tenth Mormon prophet Joseph Fielding Smith further clarified: "Man may commit certain grievous sins . . . that will place him beyond the reach of the atoning blood of Christ" (*Doctrines of Salvation* 1:133ff). His son-in-law, Bruce R. McConkie, explains when the church will be able to implement this form of execution for such crimes as murder and apostasy from the LDS church: "This doctrine can only be practiced in its fulness in a day when the civil and ecclesiastical laws are administered in the same hands" (*Mormon Doctrine*, 93).

[35] *Journal of Discourses* 11:122–28; see *Mormonism—Shadow or Reality?* 225–27.

[36] Brigham Young, cited by Mormon apostle Matthias F. Cowley, in Jerald and Sandra Tanner, *Mormons and Negroes*, 10.

"Shall I tell you the law of God in regard to the African race? If the white man who belongs to the chosen seed mixes his blood with the seed of Cain, the penalty, under the law of God, is death on the spot. This will always be so."[37]

Young had other novel beliefs. At the April 1852 LDS church conference, he taught that Adam is God, saying, "Now hear it, O inhabitants of the earth, Jew and Gentile, Saint and sinner! When our father Adam came into the garden of Eden, he came into it with a celestial body, and brought Eve, one of his wives, with him. He helped to make and organize this world. He is MICHAEL, the Archangel, the ANCIENT OF DAYS! about whom holy men have written and spoken—HE is our FATHER and our GOD, and the only God with whom WE have to do."[38]

At the time of Young's death on August 29, 1877, the LDS church numbered 115,000 members dispersed among twenty stakes and 252 smaller wards and branches. The Nauvoo temple had been destroyed, and the Kirtland temple was in the hands of the Reorganized Church of Jesus Christ of Latter Day Saints, headed by Joseph Smith III. The first temple in Utah to be dedicated was in the southwestern town of St. George. Work was progressing on the temple in Salt Lake City.

Stage 5: The Taylor–Woodruff Period (1877–1889)

Former Methodist John Taylor was accepted as president of the Quorum of the Twelve at the October 1877 general conference. Three years later he was approved as president of the Mormon church.

In January 1879, the Supreme Court ruled anti-polygamy legis-

---

[37] Young, *Journal of Discourses* 10:109.

[38] *Journal of Discourses* 1:50; emphasis and punctuation as in original. In 1854, apostle Franklin D. Richards admitted Young had taught the doctrine and that "it is the word of the Lord." *Millennial Star*, August 26, 1854.

lation constitutional. This legislation had been used to disincorporate the Mormon church and jail several of its leading members. Congress passed the Edmunds Act in 1882 and strengthened it with the Edmunds-Tucker Act of 1887. These laws disenfranchised polygamists, barred them from holding public office and disqualified from jury service all who believed in polygamous marriages. Church property would also be confiscated if the Mormon church continued its illegal preaching of polygamy.

Because prosecution of polygamy greatly increased, many Mormons went into hiding. President Taylor joined a number of other members (including his successor, Wilford Woodruff) in attempts to evade capture and punishment. By 1885 and 1886, hundreds of Mormons had fled to Mexico and Canada. Taylor died in exile on July 25, 1887. Woodruff, still in hiding, assumed leadership of the church. By the time he was sustained (confirmed in office by the Mormon membership in a *pro forma* election) as the fourth president of the Mormon church in 1889 there were 183,000 Mormons in 388 wards or communities. Three temples, all in Utah, were operating.

2. Recent Mormon Stages

Stage 6: The Neo-Monogamy Period (1890–1950)

With polygamists' loss of the right to vote, Mormons found their cities falling to non-Mormon control. Attempts to influence Washington to grant statehood to Utah had proved fruitless. In August 1890, the government informed Woodruff that it intended to confiscate the temples in St. George, Manti, and Logan, Utah, because of the Mormon church's continued, illegal preaching of polygamy. President Woodruff wrote in his journal "that, after much anguish, prayer, and discussion with his counselors, he was prepared to act 'for the temporal salvation of the Church.'"[1] The Lord had revealed to him, he said, what would happen if polygamy continued: The temples would be confiscated, all saving ordinances for living and dead would end, church officials would be imprisoned, church and personal property would be forfeited and righteous leadership would be denied to the church and its families.

On September 24, 1890, Woodruff issued his "Manifesto." In it he noted that the highest court in the land had upheld laws that forbade polygamy. (In fact, it had done this more than ten years before.) He declared his intention to submit to those laws and to influence church members to do likewise. Further, he stated, "I now publicly declare that my advice to the Latter-day Saints is to refrain from contracting any marriage forbidden by the law of the land."[2]

Previously, Mormons lost their property, liberty and even lives

---

[1] *Church History in the Fulness of Times*, 440.
[2] "Official Declaration—1," published at the end of the Doctrine and Covenants.

to fulfill the God-given command of plural marriage. Henceforth, polygamists would be excommunicated from the LDS church.[3]

With their newfound obedience to the law of the land, Mormons recovered their confiscated property and their voting rights. The temples were removed from the threat of "Gentile pollution," and the Great Salt Lake temple was dedicated by President Woodruff in April 1893. Two years later, Utah approved statehood and was admitted to the Union on January 4, 1896. To prove its patriotism, the Mormon First Presidency[4] issued a statement in April 1898 that forbade selective pacifism by Mormons and supported all declarations of war made by a constitutional government.

Woodruff died September 2, 1898. By the turn of the twentieth century, the LDS church had 270,000 members. Woodruff's successor was Lorenzo Snow, who preached on the necessity of paying a full tithe.

With all the changes that the Mormon church experienced in its early stages, there were problems with "revelations" that contradicted each other. For example, the Pearl of Great Price, a volume that consists of a number of smaller works, had been canonized in 1880. It taught a plurality of gods and was given the title "scripture" alongside the Book of Mormon, which taught that there is only one God. The Lectures on Faith were still a part of the Doctrine and Covenants. These teachings of Smith's called the Holy Ghost merely the "mind" of God, not a person. The church had finally settled on an official version of the First Vision that revealed that God the Father and God the Son were two separate gods, each having a physical body. The Book of Mormon taught that God was a spirit. How could these problems be solved?

---

[3] Some Mormon theologians teach polygamy will be practiced again on earth after the Second Coming. See McConkie, *Mormon Doctrine*, 578.

[4] The First Presidency started during Smith's time. It consists of the president/prophet of the church, usually together with two men whom he appoints as his counselors. They are almost always from the quorum of the Twelve Apostles.

Beginning in Woodruff's term and extending through the first part of the twentieth century, several LDS authors reconciled conflicting teachings made by Mormon leaders throughout the church's first hundred years.

Apostles John A. Widtsoe and James E. Talmage, together with the Seventy's B. H. Roberts, reconstructed the Godhead for the Mormon in the pew. In sum, they created a god who was not the Creator but only the organizer of pre-existent matter, who was not omnipotent but subject to eternal, natural law. The Holy Ghost was declared to be a third "personage" of the Godhead, in the shape of a man but not having a corporeal body. Earlier theologians' speculations that the Holy Ghost was a "spiritual fluid" pervading the universe[5] were also dropped.

Joseph F. Smith, first counselor under Young and his supporter in the Adam-God doctrine, apparently changed his mind when he became president. In June 1916, he and his counselors issued "The Father and the Son: A Doctrinal Exposition." This official statement avoided the Adam-God teaching and has set the tone of all subsequent Mormon teaching on the Godhead.[6]

Official restructuring of Mormon doctrine necessitated revision and removal of standard Mormon scriptures. The Lectures on Faith were dropped from the Doctrine and Covenants in 1921. There was also at this time an addition to Mormon scriptures. On October 3, 1918, President Smith reported a vision of Christ's visit to the spirits of the righteous dead following the crucifixion, between Good Friday and Easter Sunday, during which he preached the "true" (i.e., Mormon) gospel to them. This revelation is now canonized as the 138th section of the Doctrine and Covenants. Thus far it is that scripture's final numbered section, though there have been two additional revelations added out of the numbered sequence, like appendices.

At Joseph F. Smith's death on November 19, 1918, there were almost half a million Mormons, in nearly 900 wards.

Heber J. Grant, who took the helm next, served one of the

---

[5] *The Essential Orson Pratt*, 199–200.
[6] See *Encyclopedia of Mormonism*, Appendix 4; also, *Adam-God Maze*, 236.

longest tenures as president. In 1919, he dedicated the first temple outside the United States in Oahu, Hawaii (before Hawaii was admitted to the Union). In 1923 he dedicated the first Canadian temple.

When Heber died in 1945, George Albert Smith assumed the presidency. During his five years in office, Mormon membership reached one million, with eight temples in operation.

Stage 7: The Standardized Missionary Period (1950-1978)

David O. McKay succeeded Smith in 1950. During his twenty years, efforts were made to strengthen the family life of members and begin an aggressive proselytizing program. A standardized system for presenting the Mormon gospel was devised in 1952 and has been revised several times. In 1961, Latter-day Saints were told that "every member [was to be] a missionary"—not only those called to a formal period of proselytizing. Each Mormon was expected to spread the Mormon church's message and work toward converting family and acquaintances. In 1963, membership reached two million.

By 1965, the church formally inaugurated a program it had been encouraging for years, a weekly evening families spend together. Mondays were set aside for this, and unlike most other days, there would be no church activities to split up families.

By this point, the Mormon canon of scripture was essentially in place. It contained four volumes: the King James Version of the Bible, the Book of Mormon, the Doctrine and Covenants and the Pearl of Great Price. This last book consists of the Book of Moses, the Book of Abraham, Joseph Smith—Matthew (Smith's rewriting of Matthew 24), Joseph Smith—History (his account of the First Vision and subsequent events) and the Articles of Faith (from a letter Smith wrote to John Wentworth, editor of the newspaper *Chicago Democrat*, in 1842; these 13 articles, he said, summarize the faith of Mormons).

Throughout the civil rights movement of the 1950s-1960s,

Mormon apostles continued to teach the LDS doctrine on people with African ancestry and other persons of color. Bruce R. McConkie maintained, "Negroes are not equal with other races" in spiritual matters and that this is God's law, not man's. The future prophet Spencer W. Kimball claimed that in just fifteen years from the time of their conversion he had seen Indian people who accepted the Mormon gospel become "white and delightsome."[7]

McKay's successor, Joseph Fielding Smith, explained that female spirits were created in "the image of a 'Mother in Heaven.' "[8] Every human was first given spiritual birth by the Heavenly Father and a Heavenly Mother.

Joseph Fielding Smith was succeeded by Harold B. Lee then Spencer W. Kimball.

In 1973, the Supreme Court granted women the "right" to abortion. Perhaps in response to this, the LDS church issued a statement on June 5, 1976, expressing the church's traditional opposition to the practice, though a number of startling exceptions are made to this opposition, as we will see later.[9] That same year President Kimball warned church members against disseminating doctrines not in accord with Mormon scriptures and that "are alleged" to have been taught by some previous general authorities (men who oversee the church's beliefs and practices). He specifically mentioned the Adam-God doctrine and concluded, "We denounce that theory and hope that everyone will be cautioned against this and other kinds of false doctrine."[10]

In this period, Mormon membership reached nearly four million, with 990 stakes in various countries. Seventeen temples were in operation, and the first temple in South America, located in São Paulo, Brazil, was scheduled to open in the fall of 1978.

---

[7] See Petersen, "Race Problems—As They Affect the Church," 4; McConkie, *Mormon Doctrine*, 1958 ed., 477; Kimball, *Improvement Era*, Dec. 1960, 922.

[8] *Answers to Gospel Questions* 3:142, 144.

[9] *1997-1998 Church Almanac*, 498.

[10] *Deseret News*, Church News Section, October 9, 1976, 11.

Stage 8: The Racially Open Period (1978–Present)

Mormon leadership acknowledged that many, perhaps most, of the converts to the church in Brazil had some degree of black ancestry. While their donations helped build the São Paulo temple, they were not permitted to attend it.

In the U.S., the NAACP brought discrimination charges against the Utah Boy Scouts for prohibiting a black member from assuming a senior patrol position. Athletes refused to play Brigham Young University teams. Boycotts were urged of Utah and Mormon Tabernacle Choir products, and groups protested at the church's twice-yearly conferences in Salt Lake City.[11]

In 1978, changes in social views on race and increasing consciousness of the evil of racism, coupled with Mormon evangelization in areas with large populations of racially mixed ancestry, led to a drastic reversal in Mormon belief and practice: Those with Negro blood would be allowed to attend the temple; worthy black men could hold the priesthood.[12]

Dated June 8, 1978, and released the following day, President Kimball's "Official Declaration—2" (as it is now called in the Doctrine and Covenants[13]) came after "extended meditation and prayer in the sacred rooms of the holy temple." He presented the changed doctrine to his counselors, the Twelve Apostles and other leaders, who approved it unanimously. The day has come, he said, when the Lord now grants to "every faithful, worthy man in the Church . . . the holy priesthood . . . [and] the blessings of the temple." The declaration was presented to the general membership and ratified *pro forma* on September 30, 1978.

---

[11] See *Mormonism—Shadow or Reality?* 262ff.

[12] No other race, regardless of skin color or features, had been excluded.

[13] This prophecy reversing the Mormon church's stand on race, together with the one reversing its stand on polygamy, appear at the end of Doctrine and Covenants, though curiously they are not numbered D&C 139–140 but as "Official Declarations" 1 and 2.

Though this opening of the priesthood to all races moved the Mormon church into a less racist position regarding its practice, Mormon teaching remained unaltered. The new "revelation" did not change the previous Mormon teaching that people are born black because of their sins in the pre-existence.

This latest change in Mormon doctrine contributed to the 1981 revision of the Book of Mormon, one in a series of changes made to the "divinely translated" work. Previously, 2 Nephi 30:6 noted that, once converted to the Mormon faith, the ancient dark-skinned Lamanites (ancestors of the American Indian) would become "white and delightsome." The new version was quietly changed to read "pure and delightsome."

In 1981, the Mormon church also added a subtitle to its banner scripture. They now give away thousands of copies a year of "The Book of Mormon: Another Testament of Jesus Christ." Concurrent with this addition are the sleek advertising spots in such American staples as Reader's Digest and network television. In 1997, the church began advertising free copies of the King James Version of the Bible, too.

Kimball died November 5, 1985. He was succeeded by Eisenhower's Secretary of Agriculture and ardent anti-Communist Ezra Taft Benson. At Benson's death, Howard W. Hunter became prophet, serving for nine months. Gordon B. Hinckley was elected president March 12, 1995.

During his presidency, Mormons have worked to portray themselves as Christians. Missionaries and members are urged to find common ground with Christians whom they seek to convert. Using much of the same terminology, professing faith in Jesus Christ and cultivating a reputation of traditional values, Mormons hope to convince investigators they are true Christians.

The embarrassing prophetic pronouncements that Adam is our God have been quashed. Conflicting teachings on the nature of God have been tidied up. The inconvenient practices of polygamy and priesthood that excluded blacks have been dissolved. At least for now.[14] The LDS positions on abortion, birth-control and di-

---

[14] The late Mormon apostle McConkie warned: "The Church of Jesus

vorce and remarriage have also been accommodated to the nation- and world-wide rejection of divine standards. The Mormon position now resembles that of most liberal Protestant churches.[15]

The Church of Jesus Christ of Latter-day Saints currently has ten million members (though not all are active, and membership rolls do not reflect those who leave Mormonism each year). There are more than 2,500 stakes and 25,000 wards, with more than half of the members living outside the United States. One hundred temples are in operation, but only a small minority of members, perhaps twenty percent, are considered worthy to attend them.

Mormonism's doctrinal transformations of the past give no confidence that there will not be equally drastic revisions to Mormon doctrine in the future. There may be more stages yet to come as Mormonism reinvents itself to fit the culture around it.

Shortly after Easter 1997, the *San Francisco Chronicle* printed an interview with Hinckley, who was asked, "[D]on't Mormons believe that God was once a man?"

"I wouldn't say that," the prophet responded. "There's a little couplet coined, 'As man is, God once was. As God is, man may become.' Now, that's more of a couplet than anything else. That gets into some pretty deep theology that we don't know very much about."[16]

There's something wrong here, as even Latter-day Saints admit. Hinckley appeared to dismiss the traditional Mormon belief that God was once a man by using the demeaning terms "little," "couplet" and "coined." What he failed to point out was that the couplet, coined by President Lorenzo Snow in the late nineteenth

---

Christ of Latter-day Saints is the Kingdom of God on earth.... For the present it functions as an ecclesiastical kingdom only. With the millennial advent, the kingdom of God [the LDS church] will step forth and exercise political jurisdiction over all the earth as well as ecclesiastical jurisdiction over its own citizens." *Mormon Doctrine*, 499-500.

[15] See *General Handbook of Instructions* 11-4; also, respective articles in *Encyclopedia of Mormonism*, vol. 1.

[16] "Musings of the Main Mormon," April 13, 1997, 3/Z1.

century, was a succinct summary of the doctrine taught by Smith, Young and the founding theologians of Mormonism.[17]

Since the interview, the Internet has been abuzz with speculation: Is Hinckley backing away from the traditional LDS doctrine that God was once a man who has now achieved perfection and divinity? If so, why? If not, then why did he cavil on this point? Only time will tell.[18]

The Mormon prophet, in the interview, discussed abortion, which he said his church permits in several circumstances, including for the mother's health. As we'll see later in the book, this also appears to be a change to a more liberal, politically correct position. When asked about euthanasia, Hinckley declared that "no, at this point at least, we haven't favored that." Mormons may well wonder if this leaves the door cracked open to future divine permission to kill their sick and elderly.

---

[17] See Doctrine and Covenants 130:22.

[18] An ironic twist: When asked how he receives divine revelation, to which he is entitled as God's prophet on earth, Hinckley said, "[W]e have a great body of revelation, the vast majority of which came from the prophet Joseph Smith. We don't need much revelation. We need to pay more attention to the revelation we've already received."

PART TWO

Mormon Life

3. Mormon Organization

Mormons say their church is the true church of Christ because, among other things, it is called by his name. The high claim is declared in its title—The Church of Jesus Christ of Latter-day Saints.[1] Jesus Christ is said to have revealed to Smith his intentions on the matter, "For thus shall my church be called in the last days, even The Church of Jesus Christ of Latter-day Saints" (D&C 115:3-4).

Apostle LeGrand Richards even claimed that, at the time of the founding of the Mormon church, no other church bore the name of Christ.[2]

The church, however, was not always known by its current title. In April 1830, the month of the church's founding, it was known as the "Church of Christ" (D&C 20:1). At that time, Smith noted in his *History of the Church*, "After prayer, the conference proceeded to discuss the subject of names and appellations, when a motion was made . . . that this Church be known hereafter by the name of 'The Church of the Latter-day Saints.' Remarks were made by the members, after which the motion passed by unanimous vote."[3]

Mormon scriptures first indicated the term "Church of Christ." Universal Mormon consent decided upon "The Church of Latter-day Saints." In a "revelation" of April 26, 1838, Jesus Christ himself gave the final decision as noted above in Doctrine and Covenants 115:3.

Though they offer no biblical support for the claim, Latter-day Saints assert that one sign of the true church is that it will bear Christ's name. Even if this claim could be backed by Scripture (which says nothing on the subject), the argument would

---

[1] Address of First Presidency, *Conference Report*, April 1907, 3-4.
[2] *A Marvelous Work and a Wonder*, 131-132.
[3] 2:63.

be inconclusive at best. A brief survey of U.S. Christian and pseudo-Christian groups reveals dozens of denominations bearing the names of Jesus or Christ in their titles.[4] There are even bodies using the same title Smith originally gave his church—"Church of Christ." But Mormons consider these religious bodies as reprobate as all the rest.

A further argument Mormons make in favor of their church concerns the names of its officers. The LDS church has chosen to call some of its leaders by the same titles as the early Church leaders. Thus, Mormons boast of "prophets," "apostles," "seventies," "elders," "bishops," "priests," "teachers," and "deacons," together with "high priests," "patriarchs," "evangelists," and "pastors."

This re-use of biblical terms is part of Mormon apologetics. Mormon missionaries will say, "See, our church has twelve apostles—that's a biblical concept. Our church has a prophet—that's a biblical concept. Other churches do not have these things, therefore, our church must be the biblical one."

But as we will see in this chapter and in the one on the validity of Mormon ordinances, the use of these terms is misleading. The titles do not fit the responsibilities undertaken by the men and boys holding those offices. Moreover, the Mormon offices bear little or no relation to the biblical offices of the same names.

The Organizational Structure of the Mormon Church

The Mormon church is serious about its hierarchy, however, and denies that its elements are of human invention. Mormonism's sixth Article of Faith states, "We believe in the same organization

---

[4] Consider, for example, two of the many splinter groups claiming Joseph Smith as their founder: "Church of Jesus Christ" (known also as the "True Church of Jesus Christ") and the "True Church of Jesus Christ Restored." See *The Encyclopedia of American Religions*, vol. 2, 206, 210.

that existed in the Primitive Church, namely, apostles, prophets, pastors, teachers, evangelists, and so forth."

Mormonism also claims to be an exact replica of God's own system of governing the heavens.[5]

We will now look in more detail at the offices of Mormon hierarchy.

General Authorities

Men holding office as general authorities oversee beliefs and practices of the Mormon church. Their jurisdiction is universal, provided it is exercised in obedience to their superiors. The highest office in the general authorities is that of prophet.

1. THE PROPHET AND PRESIDENT OF THE CHURCH

The current prophet is the highest figure in the Mormon church, who is also known as one of its presidents. His office is thought to share in equal authority and dignity with that of the biblical prophets. He is God's mouthpiece on earth (D&C 21:4–5). He has the right to inspiration and revelation from the Lord on behalf of the Mormon church, which he governs. The president is also a "seer," knowing the things of the past and the things to come. And he is thought to have power to translate documents miraculously, as Smith translated the Book of Mormon.

A man is chosen president upon the death of the preceding president. None have resigned in the institution's 170-year history, though depending on whose succession list is followed, more than one Mormon prophet may have been driven from office in the succession confusion following Smith's death.

The members of the Quorum of the Twelve Apostles must unanimously choose the next prophet, who in actuality is the senior apostle. This is a point of pride among Mormons: The Holy

---

[5] See John Taylor, *Journal of Discourses* 7:324.

Spirit has already made known his "choice" of the next prophet (by letting a particular candidate be the longest-serving surviving apostle), so the other apostles merely ratify the divine decision. At the time of this writing, Gordon B. Hinckley is president, attaining that office in 1995 at the age of eighty-four. He is the fifteenth Mormon prophet. (See appendix I for a list of the prophets.)

The prophet serves until death. In recent years, with the diminished mental abilities of elderly prophets, the Mormon church has come under criticism, often from its own members. They ask how a church founded on on-going revelation and direct inspiration of its leadership can exercise authority through a man who is clearly incapable of demonstrating the needed mental clarity such a burden entails. This criticism comes from both the "left" and the "right." Mormon "Fundamentalists" (belonging mostly to excommunicated polygamous sects) and Mormon "intellectuals" (dissidents) criticize a system that predictably promotes to its highest office a man who is advanced in years and declining in health.

But the Mormon church has a built-in safeguard—the First Presidency. It is strange that Mormonism has put itself at odds with its founding history by adopting a succession method guaranteed to produce elderly prophets. Smith founded the Mormon church in his twenties and died in his thirties. The current system of selecting the "longest-serving man" as the next prophet will never again produce a youthful president.

Aside from these succession matters, grave theological difficulties arise with the Mormon office of prophet and president. Mormons recognize that Peter was the chief apostle in the first century and they recognize that, since the earthly church needs an earthly leader, he is meant to have a successor, though they fail to recognize that Peter appointed the bishop of Rome (the pope) as his successor.

The theological problems with the Mormon concept of their prophet and president are far broader than this, however. First, the Mormon prophet is also called the church's president. First century Christians did not speak of Peter as the president of the

Church. The office of president is essentially a medieval concept, and the modern idea of a president as the highest officer in a governmental hierarchy is more recent.

Second, Peter was not viewed as "the prophet" of the Church in the New Testament. Neither the New Testament nor patristic literature portray him as such. Calling Peter "prophet" would be a demotion, since there were many prophets in the New Testament Church (Acts 11:27, 13:1, 15:32) who were inferior to the apostles (1 Cor. 12:28; Eph. 2:20, 4:11).

Third, the Mormon understanding of a prophet's role is inaccurate in several respects. In the Old and New Testament, the office of prophet: a) was not an institutional office involving successors, b) had its new members appointed by God alone, c) was possessed by many individuals at a time and d) was inferior to the office of apostle.

2. THE FIRST PRESIDENCY

According to Doctrine and Covenants 107:22, the highest governing body of the Mormon church consists not only of the prophet but also of his two counselors. Together, these three men constitute the First Presidency of the Mormon church. The two men are chosen by the president and usually come from the ranks of the apostles. In case of the incapacity of any one, the other two are authorized to continue the church's work. Each holds the title of "President." As of 1999, apostles Thomas S. Monson and James E. Faust are President Hinckley's counselors. President Monson, as senior apostle, is next in line to be prophet.

Some Mormon writers try to find a First Presidency among Peter, James and John.[6] But while Scripture supports the idea that Peter was uniquely commissioned to have a special office among the apostles (Matt. 16:18; Luke 22:32; John 21:15-17), there is no special office given to James and John. They are presented as

---

[6] See *A Marvelous Work and a Wonder*, 135-136.

apostles who were close to Jesus—within his inner circle, but not holding special offices.

3. THE QUORUM OF THE TWELVE APOSTLES

These twelve men collectively hold equal power with the First Presidency. They choose and ordain the prophet. When apostles die or are elevated to the First Presidency, new members replace them in the Quorum of the Twelve.

Mormons believe that this office and number of apostles should have been continued in the first century, but for some reason was not. As a basis for this claim, they cite Acts 1:20-26, which records the choice of Matthias to take the "bishopric" of Judas Iscariot. But the election of a replacement for Judas does not show that the twelve apostles were to maintain their identity as a group in the long term.

This is shown by the requirements that were set for Judas' successor: First, the man must have "companied with us [the Eleven] all the time that the Lord Jesus went in and out among us, beginning from the baptism of John, unto that same day that he was taken up from us" (Acts 1:21-22a). Second, the man must also be a witness to the risen Lord (Acts 1:22b). After the first generation of apostles, nobody could have fulfilled these conditions since there would not have been any further candidates who had traveled with the apostles from the time of Jesus' baptism to his ascension. This is confirmed by the later practice of the apostolic age. After Matthias, there were no new elections to replace members of the twelve as they died (for example, when James the son of Zebedee was martyred in Acts 12:1-2). Further, when God commissioned new apostles, such as Paul and Barnabas (Acts 14:14), they were not added to the twelve. The criterion for these new apostles was merely to have been a witness of the resurrected Lord (1 Cor. 9:1; Acts 9:1-16; Rom. 1:1; Gal. 1:15-16).

The apostles chosen by the Mormon president come from all walks of life. The present council is composed of men who have been active in education, politics, business, medicine, and research. But these men are not chosen because they are eyewitnesses of the risen Savior (Acts 1:22b; 1 Cor. 9:1-2), violating the key biblical requirement for membership among the apostles.[7] The Mormon concept of apostle is also defective in that their apostles are unable to issue binding, public revelation. Only the Mormon prophet is able to do that. Mere Mormon apostles, unlike the biblical apostles, are not capable of writing Scripture or receiving infallible, publicly binding revelation from God. Not surprisingly, they also lack the divine attestation God provided for the biblical apostles to show that they genuinely occupied the office they did. The New Testament expressly mentions that miracles—"signs and wonders and mighty works"—were performed as "the signs of a true apostle" (2 Cor. 12:12), which allowed people to separate true apostles from false ones. But Mormon apostles are not characterized by exercising such miraculous personal ministries.[8]

4. THE SEVENTIES

At one point in his ministry, Jesus appointed seventy men whom he sent on a preaching tour of the towns of Israel. In Luke 10:1 we read, ". . . the Lord appointed other seventy also, and sent them two and two before his face into every city and place. . . ." Though this body of men was a temporary group called together for one occasion, not kept in existence beyond that and mentioned only in one Gospel, Mormons have decided that it represents another fundamental office of Christ's Church and is one they have instituted in their church (D&C 107:25).

---

[7] Occasionally I heard remarks such as these: "Once a man is chosen to be an apostle, it is expected he will have a vision of the risen Lord." Of course, such an event is not verifiable.

[8] At least the Protestant Charismatics who claim to be apostles make a show of performing miracles to authenticate their claims. The "miracles" are not genuine but at least they recognize that an apostle is supposed to be personally attested by miracles.

However, the Mormon Seventy does not fit the biblical model. First, Mormons have more than one group of seventy. Second, the biblical seventy were sent out two by two and were accountable to Jesus. The Mormon Seventies, however, have their own internal structure, with an internal presidency of seven men, a body not found in the New Testament model.

Third, the biblical seventy was actually composed of seventy men. Not so the Mormon Seventies, which generally have only thirty to fifty men in each.

The Mormon Seventies are nothing more than "window dressing," groups created in an attempt to make the Mormon church "sound more biblical" but without corresponding to biblical precedent.

5. THE PRESIDING BISHOPRIC

The Mormon general authorities also contain a body that is absent from the New Testament and the early Church. Under the direction of the First Presidency, three "high priests" are set apart to administer the temporal affairs of the Mormon church. Together, they are known as the "presiding bishopric," and they are usually men who are accomplished in business and other worldly affairs.

It is impossible to compare them to a corresponding biblical model because there is no biblical equivalent of this group. However, we can point out ways in which the presiding bishopric model fails to correspond to the New Testament Church's ways of taking care of its temporal affairs. During Jesus' day, the common purse for Jesus and his immediate disciples was kept by one of the apostles. (It happened to be Judas Iscariot; John 12:4-6, 13:29.) Later the seven deacons took over administering the Church's charitable financial resources (Acts 6:1-6). After the Church became geographically diverse, apostles served as channels bringing financial offerings from some local churches to other local churches that were in financial need (1 Cor. 16:1-4; 2 Cor. 9:1-5; Gal. 2:10; Phil. 4:14-18).

If the Mormon church did not place such emphasis on its hierarchy's corresponding exactly to that used in the New Testament Church, this would not be an issue, for in real life financial arrangements and structures can change. But because Mormons claim their church is a mirror image of the early Church, they need to be what they claim.

~

The above four groups—the First Presidency, the Quorum of the Twelve Apostles, the Quorums of the Seventies, and the Presiding Bishopric—constitute the general authorities of the Mormon church. They are traditionally called the "Brethren," and they alone have the right to speak at general church conferences and have their words accepted as "scripture."[9] Whatever is spoken in general conferences is considered God's current teaching and will for his people. When such words are written down, Mormons treat them with the deference they give to their "canonized" scriptures.

The structure of the general authorities has evolved over the years.[10] Oliver Cowdery served as "assistant president of the church" from 1834 to his excommunication in 1837; Joseph's brother Hyrum served in the same capacity from 1841 to his death in 1844. Besides first and second counselors in the First Presidency, there were at one time "assistant counselors." Additionally, from 1941 to 1976, there was also a position entitled "Assistant to the Twelve."

---

[9] A member or two from the general presidency of one of the women's auxiliaries may also be invited to speak at these semi-annual conferences. Her words are not considered scripture.

[10] See D. Michael Quinn's exhaustive *The Mormon Hierarchy: Origins of Power*. Quinn, a historian who has been excommunicated by the LDS church, demonstrates the fluidity of such terms as "apostle," "prophet," "patriarch," "bishop," and others in the early days of Mormonism.

Does the LDS church replicate the church organization of New Testament times? Clearly not. While some of the names and offices used today may match those of the early Church, the similarities remain superficial.

Mormons have removed the New Testament offices of pastor and evangelist (Eph. 4:11), the latter being reworked and transformed into a non-New Testament position of patriarch: "An Evangelist is a Patriarch, even the oldest man of the blood of Joseph or of the seed of Abraham. Wherever the Church of Christ is established in the earth, there should be a Patriarch for the benefit of the posterity of the Saints, as it was with Jacob in giving his patriarchal blessing unto his sons."[11]

By prophetic fiat, Smith collapsed the two New Testament titles into that of patriarch.

Provision for certain non-biblical offices in the Mormon hierarchy is given in Doctrine and Covenants 107:98, "Whereas other offices of the church, who belong not unto the Twelve, neither to the Seventy, are not under the responsibility to travel among all nations, but are to travel as their circumstances shall allow, notwithstanding they may hold as high and responsible offices in the church."

Even with provision made for the coming and going of "minor" offices in the general authorities—offices not consisting of apostles or members of Seventies—one still wonders how Mormons can claim their hierarchy is a representation of the early Church or the hierarchy of heaven.[12] If the Mormon church's hierarchy is identical, even in its "major" offices, with that of the early Church, then when in Mormon history is its hierarchy identical? The "major" offices have changed over the years. Given the turbulence in the development of the Mormon hierarchy, even in its "major" offices, how can the Mormon church claim to have a

---

[11] *History of the Church* 3:381.

[12] The newest titles or offices created by the LDS church includes the so-called "Area Authority Seventies." See the Mormon-church published magazine *Ensign*, May 1998, 21.

hierarchy identical with that of heaven? Is the heavenly hierarchy continually undergoing revision and restructuring to match the Mormon church on earth? Or, if the earthly hierarchy is being adjusted to fit a changing heavenly hierarchy, where are the revelations directing this?

Regional and Local Authorities

In addition to general authorities, the Mormon church has regional and local authorities. The regional ones are a distinct "layer" of authority between the general and local authorities. These are men in charge of large geographical areas, which are in turn divided into smaller regions. Areas and regions, like Catholic dioceses, are generally based upon the Mormon population within their boundaries. Less than half of all Mormons are American. About twenty percent of Mormons live in Utah. Thus, most Mormons have little direct contact with a general authority, and the importance of local leaders is magnified. Members' faithfulness and worthiness are judged by their local stake president and ward bishop.

A stake is a non-biblical church unit comprising about six or eight smaller non-biblical units, known as wards (see below). A stake is headed by a president appointed by the First Presidency. He in turn chooses two counselors. All share the title of "president." These men oversee the general operation of the wards in their stake, assuring that church policy is promulgated and followed. They possess no "fuller" a priesthood than the rest of the Melchizedek priesthood-holders, but they function along the lines of a Catholic bishop of a small diocese.

The stake president's contact with stake members consists mainly in occasional talks at a Sunday meeting, the semi-annual stake conferences and the yearly meetings for temple recommend renewals. At these, one of the three presidents meets with a member, who has already met with his or her own bishop, to judge the member's worthiness to attend the Mormon temple for the next twelve months.

Twelve high councilors, chosen from the member wards, serve as an administrative and judicial body directed by the stake president. Besides helping to regulate the stake programs, these men serve in ecclesiastical trials of members brought before them.[13]

Mormon bishops are the central figures of the smaller church units, called wards, of which stakes are composed.[14] Wards correspond roughly with a Catholic parish, although they are generally smaller—perhaps 100 to 300 families. Members attend the ward in their area. The bishop is a high priest who has been approved by the First Presidency and appointed to his position for a customary five-year term.

Because he presides over the Aaronic priesthood in his ward, the bishop is responsible for the material welfare of the flock. This is understood to extend to all the people living within the geographical boundaries of the ward, including non-members.[15] The bishop also serves as a "common judge in Israel" (D&C 107:74). Through the gift of discernment, he must decide on a person's worthiness to advance to the next level of membership. He and his two counselors also determines an individual's readiness to attend the temple.

One feature of Mormon ward organization is the degree of involvement of the members. All those who want a "calling" or job and who are deemed worthy will be given one. Thus, the bishop is supported not only by his two chosen counselors but also by qualified men and women who lend their particular talents to the smooth running of the ward.

All workers, including bishops, serve without pay. This is a

---

[13] See *Mormon Doctrine*, 353.

[14] Church units that are not large enough to be wards are called branches and are headed by a branch president. His duties are similar to those of a bishop.

[15] Criticism is occasionally heard that Mormons "help only their own." It is true that the membership is, typically, open with both requests for and offers of help, and some maintain that it is difficult for a non-member to get a footing in some employment venues. But I witnessed instances in which non-members were given practical or financial aid.

source of pride for the Mormon church, which accuses the Catholic Church and Protestant groups of departing from the Lord's will by having a paid, professional clergy.[16]

Though having duties similar to those of a parish pastor, a Mormon bishop receives no formal training in the direction of souls or church units. He will occasionally speak in church but has not attended homiletics classes and is not required to be adept in spiritual matters. It is believed that with his appointment come the gifts and aid of the Holy Spirit. The Mormon understanding is that if a man has indeed been chosen by God for this office and has been set apart for it by one having the authority to do so, then God will supply the necessary talents.

The Mormon church attacks the Catholic priesthood on this point. Mormons think that a Catholic man decides he will be a priest, takes the necessary courses, graduates and gets himself ordained. The process is no different from, say, the manner in which a man becomes a high-school teacher. Mormons seem incapable of understanding that Catholic men are merely accepting Christ's invitation to priesthood. The period of training spent before their ordination is a period of reflection, as well, as they evaluate themselves and are evaluated by the Church to see if God really has called them to the ministry. When they are ordained, they are given gifts of the Holy Spirit to fulfill their office. This in no way contradicts their training, for, after all, the apostles, the original priests, were obliged first to learn at the Master's feet before they were sent forth to preach and baptize.

"Paid" and "professional clergy" are two Mormon bugaboos. While it is true that many "professional clergy" were early opponents of Joseph Smith's new religion, and many continue to speak and preach against the errors of Mormonism, neither their paid status nor their theological training is the underlying cause for the opposition. The novelty, inconsistency, and flagrant departure from orthodox, historical Christianity were ample cause for a pastor's concern. It is surprising, however, how often Mormons

---

[16] See "Clergy," *Encyclopedia of Mormonism*, vol. 1; *Mormon Doctrine*, 147.

say that the only reason Christian clergy attempt to dissuade their parishioners from joining the Mormon church is because they fear for their own livelihood.

Mormons frequently believe that Christian clergy treat their calling as just another job and that Catholic priests "call themselves" to the priesthood. This leads many Mormons to conclude that the Catholic clergy is invalid and corrupt. Thus, any attempt to convert Catholics to Mormonism is supposedly perceived as a threat to the priests' power and livelihood.[17] To point out the flaw in this argument, Catholics and other Christians might propose that the primary reason Mormons are so eager to obtain converts is to get their tithes. Both arguments have equal validity. (Which is to say, no validity.)

Mormonism's pride in its own unpaid clergy and scorn of other groups' paid clergy is unbiblical. The idea that a Christian minister must not be paid flatly contradicts several scriptural teachings. The Levites and priests of the Old Testament ministry were denied a portion of the territorial inheritance of the Promised Land. Instead, the Israelite tribes were to support these men and

---

[17] Some Mormon leaders have, however, attributed more "noble" intentions to our priests. Take, for example, this story repeated several times by Young: "I told the Elder that his argument seemed reasonable, but it made me think of the story about a Roman Catholic priest and a Jew. The priest was crossing on the ice, and on his way found a Jew, who had fallen through an air hole, clinging to the edge of the ice, unable to get out. He begged of the priest to help him out, but he would not, unless he first professed a belief in Jesus Christ. 'I cannot,' said the Jew. 'Then I will let you down [sic],' replied the priest, and let go of him. Still clinging to the ice, as the priest was about to leave, he again begged him to pull him out. 'I cannot, unless you believe in Christ.' 'I cannot believe,' said the Jew, and the priest let him go again. At length the Jew said, 'Take me out, I do believe in the Lord Jesus Christ with all my might.' 'Do you?' said the priest, 'then I think it is best to save you, while you are a Christian and strong in the faith,' and he shoved him under the ice." (*Journal of Discourses* 4:90.) Contemporary LDS leadership prescinds from such open calumnies, preferring a more indirect attack on the Catholic priesthood. McConkie's works illustrate this approach. See also the chapter on the Mormon temple ceremony.

their families while they devoted themselves to the Lord's service. (Numbers 18:21: "And, behold, I have given the children of Levi all the tenth in Israel for an inheritance, for their service which they serve, even the service of the tabernacle of the congregation.")

Likewise, Paul exhorted the Corinthian Christians to support those who ministered among them. In 1 Corinthians 9:1–14, he presents a sustained defense of the rights of clergy to receive their living in exchange for the ministry they perform. He concludes the discussion stating, "[T]he Lord commanded that those who proclaim the gospel should get their living by the gospel" (1 Cor. 9:14).

He further informs the bishop Timothy that "the labourer is worthy of his reward" (1 Tim. 5:18). In this he simply echoed the words of Christ, who sent forth his apostles to teach and preach, minister and heal. On one trip, the Lord specifically commanded them to travel light, taking nothing extra on their journeys and to rely upon God's providence as supplied by the communities they served. In so doing, he specifically made the point: "The labourer is worthy of his hire" (Luke 10:7–8). It is biblical for Christian ministers to receive their support from others.[18]

Finally, when Mormons criticize Catholic priests and other ministers for accepting the support of the parishes they serve, they seem to forget that their own general authorities are supported by LDS members. A man selected to such a calling within the Mormon church is expected to devote himself full time to the position. Since he is no longer able to work in his secular profession, he receives a living income from the Mormon church. Is this any different from the practice of supporting Catholic clergy, who also give up all other "career opportunities" to serve Christ and his people?

---

[18] See also 2 Timothy 2:6.

4. Mormon Ordinances

Andy's Story[1]

Andy was raised in a Catholic family. At eighteen, he is a freshman at Arizona State University. He's a popular young man and has been dating a few young women on campus. One of them is Joanne Gordon, a student who lives at home with her family. Several times, she has invited Andy to spend Sunday with her and her family, but Andy has so far declined.

Frankly, it didn't sound much fun. No sports were permitted, no traditional recreation and certainly no shopping. The more observant Mormon members, like the Gordons, would not watch television or listen to secular music. Besides going to church, they occupied themselves with reading Mormon scripture or other inspirational works, writing letters (Joanne had a girlfriend on a mission in Brazil), tracing family trees and talking. Sometimes there were additional meetings at the church later in the day. Joanne's brothers, Danny and Greg, for instance, were active in the Scouts; Greg was nearing completion of his Eagle award.[2]

One day, Andy decides to take Joanne up on her offer, at least to see what her church is like. The next Sunday he gets up early and goes to 7:00 A.M. Mass, then drives to Joanne's house. He arrives at 8:30, dressed in a sport jacket and tie. (She had already advised him of the dress code.) Andy, Joanne, her parents and two younger brothers pile into the car for the mile drive to the local Mormon chapel. The three-hour services begin at 9:00.

The first seventy minutes is called the "sacrament meeting." About fifteen minutes into the service, young boys, including

---

[1] This narrative is a composite account illustrating typical Mormon experiences.

[2] Mormons are major supporters of the Boy Scouts. It is not unusual to find a ward with a majority of the boys participating.

Joanne's thirteen-year-old brother, Greg, pass trays of bread and water along the pews. People take a bit of bread and a small plastic cup of water. Andy immediately identifies this as the Mormon equivalent of taking Communion. He is not surprised that Mormons use leavened bread (Andy already knew other churches do that), but he is stunned to see them using water instead of wine (or at least grape juice, like some Protestant churches). There is relative silence during the passing of the "sacrament"—at least compared with the buzz that occurs throughout the other parts of the service. Joanne tells Andy that he shouldn't partake of the sacrament—it's for members only.

Andy notices that the people sit the entire seventy minutes. The leaders on the stage are dressed in business suits, not vestments. There is no cross, nor are there holy pictures, statues, candles or other accouterments to indicate a spiritual place. There are four or five speakers, both men and women, including a young girl who looks about thirteen. Though some of the messages seem dry and perfunctory—the thirteen-year-old girl races through what seems to be a formulaic "testimony" to the truth of Mormonism—Andy is surprised that some of them are emotional, even tearful.

Finally, the sacrament meeting ends in the same manner as it began—with a hymn and a prayer offered by a member of the congregation.

While Andy found the service lengthy, he quickly learned that the Sunday "obligation" was not over. Joanne's two brothers went off to classrooms scattered around the building. Mr. and Mrs. Gordon, Joanne and Andy went to another classroom with most of the adult members for "Gospel Doctrine" class, or adult Sunday school.

This year's topic was the Book of Mormon. As far as Andy could tell, the teacher was going through a few chapters each week. Though many attending the class were quiet, some seemed to know more about the subject than did the teacher.

A bell rang, signaling the end of class. The men and teenaged boys assembled in the chapel. Andy didn't know where the women went. The leader (he was called a bishop, though nothing like a

Catholic bishop) spoke to the group about minor business matters: There was to be a clean-up of some lady's yard and volunteers were needed; the ward teachers' basketball team had beaten another chapel's team in yesterday's playoffs; Boy Scouts were recruiting sponsors for their annual trek to Lake Powell; thanks were extended to all the members who helped put up chairs in the stake center for that month's televised general conference. The usual announcements, Andy figured.

Afterward, the men broke again into smaller groups. Andy went with Mr. Gordon to something called the "elders' quorum," while Greg went to the "deacons" meeting. Passing along the hall to their next meeting room, Andy discovered the location of the young children. They were visible—and audible—during the sacrament meeting, but he hadn't seen any children under twelve since then. Now he was in a different section of the building and discovered classrooms containing pre-schoolers and older children being kept busy by teachers. He assumed Joanne's younger brother, Danny, was in one of the rooms. Mr. Gordon explained that these children made up what was called Primary, a program of instruction for young children that takes up the bulk of their Sunday meeting.

For the third meeting of the morning, Andy and Mr. Gordon sat with about thirty other men, mostly in their twenties, thirties and forties. One opened the meeting with a prayer and then turned the meeting over to another member who had prepared a lesson from some kind of manual. The day's topic was the Holy Ghost. The Holy Ghost is given, it was said, to all baptized Mormons. With this gift, each member can expect divine companionship and assistance in leading virtuous lives. Only with the gift of the Holy Ghost can a person return to God.

When the bell rang to end this forty-five minute meeting, Andy was relieved. After the meeting, he went to the Gordons' house for lunch. Joanne told the others about the presentation in the Relief Society[3] meeting about genealogy work. When Andy asked

---

[3] An organization of the adult women for their spiritual and temporal enhancement. It roughly corresponds to the men's priesthood organization.

what this had to do with going to church, Joanne explained that her parents were third-generation Mormons and had done a lot of research into their family trees. She herself had been to the Mormon temple in Mesa, Arizona, several times to perform baptisms for her deceased ancestors. That morning's pep talk had sparked a new interest, and she planned on going to the temple later that week. Andy was bewildered by the idea of being baptized for one's ancestors—especially in a Christian nation in which they had almost certainly been baptized themselves—but he kept quiet.

The main focus of discussion was Danny. He had turned eight just a few days before, and had requested baptism. This was to take place that afternoon in the stake center. Mr. Gordon would baptize Danny, as he had his other children when they turned eight.

At four o'clock the family assembled at the chapel, along with a few relatives and friends. After a brief talk and hymn, a sliding partition at the end of the room was opened to reveal a below-ground tank filled with water. Mr. Gordon and his son stood in the water, which rose nearly to Danny's shoulders. Both were dressed in white pants and long-sleeved shirts and were barefoot. Andy heard Mr. Gordon say: "Daniel Brent Gordon, having been commissioned of Jesus Christ, I baptize you in the name of the Father, and of the Son and of the Holy Ghost. Amen." With that, he immersed Danny in the water one time and immediately brought him up. The partition was closed and the people waited.

During the pause, Joanne told Andy that her brother would now be given the ordinance of confirmation, or the laying-on of hands. A few minutes later, Danny and his father came into the room, this time dressed in their Sunday suits. Danny sat on a chair in the front while Mr. Gordon and Danny's two grandfathers gathered around him, placing their hands upon his head. Mr. Peterson spoke the words of confirmation, "Daniel Brent Gordon, in the name of Jesus Christ, and by the holy Melchizedek priesthood which I bear, I confirm you a member of the Church of Jesus Christ of Latter-day Saints and say unto you, 'Receive the Holy Ghost.'"

Danny's father then spoke, blessing him to be a faithful church member, to grow to maturity in the Spirit, to receive and faithfully fulfill a mission call, to marry in the temple and to raise up righteous children and grandchildren.

The ceremony concluded with a hymn and a prayer. Family and friends gathered for a quiet party at the Gordons'. Danny received a few presents, chief among them a book of Mormon scriptures with colored marking pencils and a silver ring that had the initials "CTR" on it. Andy asked Joanne what they stood for. She told him it's a common Mormon motto, "Choose the Right," though sometimes moms tell their children it means "Clean Thy Room."

Andy was relieved when he got back to his dorm room. Though people had been pleasant to him at all of the events, there did at times seem to be something "forced" about their friendliness. He did, however, value the experience of the day for the information it provided.

Ordinances in General

During his visit to a Mormon church, Andy witnessed a number of ceremonies that Mormons call "ordinances." He saw the Mormon equivalents to the sacraments of baptism, confirmation and the Eucharist. In this chapter we will look at these and other ordinances.

Some Protestant churches use the term "ordinance" instead of "sacrament" because they do not believe sacraments are means of grace but are only symbolic ceremonies.

Mormons, also, do not teach the reality of sacramental grace. In their view, God may bless people who perform the ordinances (something even anti-sacramental Protestants believe), but the ordinances are not themselves means of grace. Rather, performing an ordinance—at least the ones needed for full salvation—is like contracting a covenant with God. This may put one in God's good graces, but it does not mean that grace is given to one in the sacrament itself. The most members can hope for is divine assistance after they have done all they can do for themselves.[4]

A disturbing feature of Mormon theology is that the validity of the ordinances is dependent on the worthiness of the one administering them. This is similar to a fourth century heresy known as Donatism that said the sacraments would not communicate grace if the priest administering them was not in a state of grace. The early Church recognized that if this were true, it would mean no one would be able to have confidence in the validity of the sacraments he had received.

Mormonism's reinvention of Donatism is all the more odd because Mormons do not believe the sacraments to be channels by which God gives us his grace. Nevertheless, it is clear in Mormon theology that the validity of the ordinance is dependent on the worthiness of the minister. Smith stated, "[T]he powers of heaven . . . may be conferred upon us, it is true; but when we undertake to cover our sins, or to gratify our pride, our vain ambition, or to exercise control or dominion or compulsion upon the souls of the children of men, in any degree of unrighteousness, behold, the heavens withdraw themselves; the Spirit of the Lord is grieved; and when it is withdrawn, Amen to the priesthood or the authority of that man" (D&C 121:36-37).

The Catholic Church recognizes and infallibly teaches that the sacraments work by the power and promise of God and not by the worthiness of the minister. Ultimately, it is God who performs the sacraments, not the minister, and it is on God's holiness, not that of his agent, that the sacraments depend. By stating the opposite, Mormonism throws a constant shadow of doubt over each of its ordinances. Suppose, for example, a young missionary elder who baptizes a new convert has secretly become skeptical of the Mormon gospel and the claim that we can become gods. Since he has only a couple of months left on his mission, he has decided

---

[4] 2 Nephi 25:23 states: "[W]e know that it is by grace that we are saved, after all we can do."

to "stick it out" and return home honorably rather than aborting his mission at the last minute in a dramatic apostasy. Would the convert's baptism have been valid? Or perhaps a man who performs "celestial marriages" in the temple happens to be a secret adulterer or a secret caffeine-drinker (either one of which would disqualify him from service in the temple). Are those he seals together still candidates for godhood? Smith stated, "If a man gets the fulness of the priesthood of God, he has to get it in the same way that Jesus Christ obtained it, and that was by keeping all the commandments and obeying all the ordinances of the House of the Lord."[5]

The gravity of the situation is illustrated by the example of a person who was baptized Mormon at the age of eight and who has now grown to adulthood. How can he ever know whether his baptism at age eight was performed by a minister who was in a worthy state? And if his baptism—the thing that made him a member of the Mormon church—was invalid, then so would be all the ordinances he has received since then. His priesthoods would be invalid, his sealing in the temple would be invalid, and all of the ordinances he has performed on others would be invalid, including the baptisms of his own children.

Not all ordinances are necessary in the Mormon view, but baptism and confirmation are, which is why Mormons practice them on behalf of the dead, believing that they will ultimately provide proxy ordinances for every individual who has ever lived.

The *Encyclopedia of Mormonism* distinguishes three classes of ordinances: (1) those necessary for entering celestial glory (i.e., the realm where God is), (2) those necessary for exaltation (i.e., for achieving godhood), and (3) those thought to contribute in some way to the physical, emotional or spiritual welfare of the recipient. Baptism and confirmation belong to the first category; ordi-

---

[5] *Teachings of the Prophet Joseph Smith*, 308. The *Encyclopedia of Mormonism* underlines this teaching: "The administration of all ordinances presupposes the worthiness of the administrator and the recipient." See "Administration of Ordinances," vol. 3.

nation to the priesthood, temple sealing and celestial marriage the second, and all other ordinances, including the Mormon versions of the Eucharist and the anointing of the sick, the third.

Unlike the Catholic Church, which has a definitive list of seven rites which meet the definition of a sacrament, the Mormon church does not appear to have a fixed list of ordinances. Nevertheless, it is possible to examine the three classes of ordinances. Afterward, we will evaluate them.

Particular Mormon Ordinances

Ordinances Contributing to Welfare

We will first deal with ordinances contributing to welfare since they are least important. They are thought to contribute to the welfare of Mormons but are not considered essential for achieving the celestial kingdom or godhood.

Although there is no official list of everything (and only those things) that could be referred to as ordinances, according to the *Encyclopedia of Mormonism*, the following belong to this category of ordinances: naming of children, patriarchal and paternal blessings, consecration of oil, dedication of buildings, dedication of graves, administering to the sick and "the sacrament" (the Lord's Supper, the Mormon equivalent of the Eucharist).

Except for "the sacrament," which may be conducted by holders of the Aaronic priesthood (typically boys in their early teens), these ordinances are administered by holders of the Melchizedek priesthood (ideally, any faithful adult male member). "The sacrament" has exact words that must be followed, but for other ordinances in this category, the prayer used is spontaneous, though it always begins by citing the person's priesthood authority and closes in the name of Jesus Christ.

The blessings done over inanimate objects (consecration of oil, dedication of buildings, dedication of graves) need not detain us, but let us look in more detail at those rites done over and with living people.

Naming of an Infant

There is an innate need in humans to turn their newborn children over to God, to ask his blessings upon them and to initiate them into the community of faith. In Judaism, this role was fulfilled by circumcision (in the case of boy babies). In historic Christianity, it is fulfilled by baptism, which Paul calls "the circumcision of Christ" (the Christian equivalent of circumcision; Col. 2:11-12).

In some of the newer Protestant sects, however, baptism is not given to infants, though the impulse to bless and (pseudo-)initiate one's children is filled by a "dedication" service, with baptism deferred until the child is older. Mormonism, which also refuses to baptize infants, fulfills the impulse in the same way, with a "naming" service for the infant.

In this service, a father, accompanied by several men, takes his newborn child to the front of the church. The men stand in a circle, one hand extended toward the child, the other resting on the shoulder of the man next to them. The father offers a spontaneous blessing, thanking God for the gift of the child, giving the child his official name and pronouncing a prayer for his health, happiness and a righteous life.

Patriarchal and Paternal Blessings

This naming ceremony may be the first but is not the last occasion when a person is given an extemporaneous blessing. For children, blessings are given at the beginning of a school year, before a trip or at a family crisis. Each husband and father is considered the patriarch of his family and, as such, may bestow family patriarchal blessings on his spouse and children. Often these blessings are written down or taped and kept as family records.

There are also special blessings given by the stake patriarch to church members under him. (For an example of a patriarchal blessing, see appendix IV.)

Administering to the Sick

This is the Mormon version of the anointing of the sick. In this, two Melchizedek priesthood holders officiate. One places a few drops of consecrated olive oil on the person's head while saying a simple prayer. The other then places his hands upon the ailing person's head and speaks a prayer of blessing. He is directed to speak whatever words the Holy Spirit gives him. Many Mormon men carry little vials of oil with them at all times in case they come upon an accident or are otherwise called upon to minister to the sick.

"The Sacrament"

This was the first ordinance Andy witnessed in his visit to a Mormon church, and it is a regular part of Mormon Sunday services. Despite this, and despite the fact that this ordinance alone is given the name sacrament, it is far less significant to Mormons and plays a far lesser role in their religious lives than the Eucharist does for Catholics.

The "sacrament service" in Mormon churches is not a liturgical worship service designed to capture the heart and mind and elevate them to the worship of God. Instead, it is based on Protestant Lord's Supper services that are designed to downplay, minimize and deny the Eucharistic Presence of Christ.

In contrast to even the simplest Catholic Mass, Mormon sacrament services have a Spartan simplicity of word and action. The desacralized "ordinariness" of the enterprise extends to the elements, which typically consist of pieces of supermarket bread and tap water.

At a Mormon sacrament service, several boys with the "Aaronic priesthood" go to the front of the chapel, where there is a simple table set to one side. On the table are trays covered by a white table cloth. After a hymn and an opening prayer, the bishop reads some announcements. After that, the "sacrament" hymn is sung. It typically deals with Christ's suffering and mentions bread and water.

The congregation sits during the hymn, while three teenaged priests stand in front of the table and remove the white covering, revealing the trays. Typically, these are stainless steel trays with handles, each with two slices of white bread. The boys tear each slice into pieces perhaps half an inch square. At the hymn's conclusion, one boy kneels and says the sacrament prayer over the bread:

> O God, the Eternal Father, we ask thee in the name of thy Son, Jesus Christ, to bless and sanctify this bread to the souls of all those who partake of it; that they may eat in remembrance of the body of thy Son, and witness unto thee, O God, the Eternal Father, that they are willing to take upon them the name of the Son, and always remember him, and keep his commandments which he hath given them, that they may always have his Spirit to be with them. Amen [Moroni 4:3].

Note that this does not even bother repeating Jesus' words of institution "This is my body," something that virtually all Protestant churches do, no matter how vigorously they deny the Real Presence of Christ.

The priests then hand the trays to younger "deacons," who spread through the chapel passing the trays along the aisles. Each member communicates himself, and even very young children receive pieces of the bread. When the deacons return, the trays are placed on the table while the teen priests pray over the water. Trays with compartments holding one-ounce plastic cups are used. The prayer is as follows:

> O God, the Eternal Father, we ask thee, in the name of thy Son, Jesus Christ, to bless and sanctify this water to the souls of all those

who drink of it, that they may do it in remembrance of the blood of thy Son, which was shed for them; that they may witness unto thee, O God, the Eternal Father, that they do always remember him, that they may have his Spirit to be with them. Amen [Moroni 5:2].[6]

Again, there is no reference to Jesus' words of institution—"This is . . . my blood."

The trays of water are then distributed in the same manner and are returned to the table. Afterward the priests re-cover the trays with the cloth and they and the deacons are dismissed to sit with their families.

Despite the absence of Jesus' words of consecration in the prayers over the bread and water, they must still be said word-perfect. If the boy makes a mistake, he has to start all over again because Mormons believe these prayers come from the words Christ used when he instituted the sacrament in the New World. Mormons can find no such wording in Christian Scripture, however, unless they advert to the Smith reworking of Matthew, which states, "[A]nd brake it, and blessed it, and gave to his disciples, and said, 'Take, eat; this is in remembrance of my body which I give a ransom for you'" (Matt. 26:26).

There is no notion of sacrifice in the Mormon sacrament. The LDS priesthoods are not ordered to the offering of sacrifice, nor do Mormons believe the bread and water to be anything but bread and water. The Catholic belief in the Real Presence is seen as just one more hellish doctrine introduced by an apostate church, despite the fact that it, like the sacrificial nature of the Eucharist, was the universal belief of the early Church and remained unquestioned for centuries.

---

[6] The original wording in the Book of Mormon specified wine, not water. Smith changed the ordinance, he said, because of an alleged divine revelation (given perhaps to accommodate the abstinence views common in 19th century American Protestantism, from which early Mormonism drew many members. See Doctrine and Covenants 27:2).

Ordinances Necessary for the Celestial Kingdom

We now examine those ordinances considered necessary to achieve the celestial kingdom—the third and highest Mormon heaven, where the most blessed go after death.

BAPTISM

Prior to a candidate's baptism, he is interviewed by a senior missionary who asks him questions, including about his compliance with the "Word of Wisdom."[7] For example, has he refrained from all alcohol, tobacco, coffee and tea? Has he lived chastely? Does he have a "testimony" of the Mormon gospel? And does he intend to live according to the teachings of Mormonism?

Mormons insist that the formal reception of baptism and confirmation are obligatory ordinances. No person can return to God in the celestial kingdom who has not received these rites from the hands of an authorized Mormon official. Even those who have died without receiving them must have the ceremonies done for them by proxy.[8]

Protestant critiques of Mormonism condemn the notion of there being ordinances necessary for salvation, but Catholics need

---

[7] This so-called "Word of Wisdom," a "revelation" Smith claimed came from the Lord, forbids certain products as harmful. The teaching fit with "temperance" movements in the 1800s. The instructions also counsel the consumption of grains and fruits and limit meat to the colder months, and then only sparingly (a practice no longer observed by Mormons.) Though the Lord is said to have protected his people from the ravages of alcohol, tobacco and caffeine, he was apparently not far-sighted enough to inform them of the dangers of sugar, salt or cholesterol. See Doctrine and Covenants 89.

[8] See chapter 7 on Mormon temples.

expend little concern in this area. Like all Christians until the Protestant Reformation, Catholics always have recognized that certain sacraments are necessary—at least normatively—for salvation. Historic Christianity has always pointed to passages such as John 3:5 ("Except a man be born of water and of the Spirit, he cannot enter into the kingdom of God") and 1 Peter 3:21 ("baptism doth . . . now save us"), as well as to the unanimous teaching of the early Church Fathers, as proof of this. (It is odd that Mormons fail to include "the sacrament" among their mandatory ordinances, given its prominent place in Scripture, rivaled only by baptism, and given the fact that Jesus explicitly affirmed it as necessary.[9])

Not all are given the chance to receive baptism and the Eucharist, and so, since the early Church Fathers, Catholics have recognized that God allows "baptism of desire" and "baptism of blood" to supply for those who cannot receive the sacrament itself. (By extension, one might speak of a "Eucharist of desire"—more commonly referred to as a spiritual act of Communion—which supplies for those who cannot receive the Eucharist due to circumstances.) This is why certain sacraments can be said to be normatively, though not absolutely, necessary for salvation. God acknowledges the desire for the sacraments in place of their actual reception for those who are unable to receive them.

Mormonism, as on so many other points, rejects the historic

---

[9] "I am the living bread which came down from heaven: if any man eat of this bread, he shall live for ever: and the bread that I will give is my flesh, which I will give for the life of the world. The Jews therefore strove among themselves, saying, How can this man give us *his* flesh to eat? Then Jesus said unto them, Verily, verily, I say unto you, Except ye eat the flesh of the Son of man, and drink his blood, ye have no life in you. Whoso eateth my flesh, and drinketh my blood, hath eternal life; and I will raise him up at the last day. For my flesh is meat indeed, and my blood is drink indeed. He that eateth my flesh, and drinketh my blood, dwelleth in me, and I in him. As the living Father hath sent me, and I live by the Father: so he that eateth me, even he shall live by me" (John 6:51–57).

Christian teaching and does not acknowledge the spiritual reception of the sacraments—at least not without someone receiving them on one's behalf. Thus baptism and other necessary ordinances end up being practiced for the dead. The Mormon church views the reception of these sacraments as absolute necessities for the celestial kingdom and godhood.

Mormons insist that baptism be performed by an authorized Mormon male, and they reject the practice of infant baptism. Denying original sin, they consider a child absolutely sinless. This is largely because Mormons are reacting to the Protestant theological base from which Mormonism sprang. In Protestant circles there is a persistent misunderstanding of original sin that holds that infants are not simply born deprived of God's sanctifying grace on account of Adam's sin,[10] but that they are held personally and gravely culpable for Adam's sin, so that each child would be doomed to eternal suffering in hell through no fault of his own.

The Catholic Church recognizes that this is not the case. It would be unjust of God to condemn one to eternal suffering for something one did not do. While we may be born deprived of the grace that would allow us to have union with God in the next life, we are not condemned to eternal suffering except through our own sins.

Mormonism, reacting against the Protestant notion of original sin, throws out the entire concept and, consequently, throws out infant baptism. It fails to recognize that, even though the child does not yet have personal sins, he is deprived of the sanctifying grace baptism gives. As the Church has historically explained, in-

---

[10] Original sin consists of the deprivation of sanctifying grace due to Adam's sin. If Adam had retained the state of original grace, sex would have operated in a manner that would have transmitted grace to the offspring. Since he did not retain the state of original grace, he could not pass this grace on to his offspring, and so today we are born deprived of sanctifying grace. The fallen nature that accompanies original sin and which leads us to commit actual, personal sins is known as the "stain" of original sin (i.e., the stain in our nature caused by being deprived of grace), but is not the same thing as original sin.

fants need to be baptized not on account of personal sins (which they lack), but on account of their being deprived of grace.

Rejecting infant baptism, Mormons instead require "believer's baptism." For this reason, only children who have reached eight years of age may present themselves for baptism.

Among Mormons, any person with the rank of priest in the Aaronic priesthood (usually sixteen- and seventeen-year-old boys), or any member of the Melchizedek priesthood, may conduct baptism.

Though Mormons eschew most formal prayers, the prayer said at baptism has been prescribed by the LDS authorities and must be repeated exactly. Its text comes, with some variations, from several passages in Mormon scripture (3 Nephi 11:25; D&C 20:73). God is understood "to pour out his spirit upon them [the baptized], redeem them from their sins, raise them in the first resurrection, and give them eternal life" (Mosiah 18:7–10; D&C 20:37).[11]

While Mormons admit that baptismal symbolism represents the candidate's belief in the Lord's death and resurrection, there is little consideration of a death to one's own sins, at least on the part of the young children who receive the ordinance. Its main significance is in admitting the person into the Mormon church and placing upon him the obligations and privileges of this membership.

Mormons do not believe that baptism makes an indelible mark in the recipient's soul.[12] Consequently, it may be received more than once. In earlier years members received baptism frequently as a sign of renewed faith and commitment, or as a way of showing repentance after sin. Today, re-baptism is generally reserved to those who have been excommunicated and then wish to return.

---

[11] "Baptism," *Encyclopedia of Mormonism*, vol. 1.

[12] The same is true of the other two Mormon ordinances that mirror the Catholic sacraments of holy orders and confirmation.

Confirmation

Confirmation is given after baptism. During the ceremony, several men will typically gather around the recipient and place their hands upon his head. The one administering the ordinance then says the words of confirmation which, as with baptism, are a fixed formula. Confirmation is regarded as conferring the gift of the Holy Ghost, which includes the right to receive the Holy Spirit's help and blessing. This laying-on of hands by one bearing the proper priesthood authority is considered the second essential ordinance for entering the celestial kingdom, so it also is performed for the dead.

Ordinances Necessary for Godhood

We now move to the ordinances considered necessary to achieve godhood. Not all who go to the celestial kingdom will go on to become gods of their own planets. Only those who receive the three ordinances known as temple endowment, celestial marriage and (in the case of men) priesthood ordination may qualify as gods in the age to come.

Because temple endowment and celestial marriage are performed only in Mormon temples, rather than in ordinary Mormon churches, we will leave them to chapter 7. Here we will discuss the priesthood ordinations, which may be received even if a Mormon never enters a temple.

Priesthood Ordinations

One of the key claims of the Mormon church—indeed, part of its justification for its existence—is the idea that it alone has divinely authorized priesthoods. No other church, according to Mormon theology, had retained valid priesthoods, and so God started the Mormon church to return his priesthoods to the earth.

Notice we have referred to priesthoods in the plural. This is because Smith asserted the existence of two priesthoods in the Mormon church: the Aaronic and the Melchizedek.

Aaronic Priesthood

According to Doctrine and Covenants 107:13-14, the Aaronic priesthood was first conferred by the Lord upon Aaron, the brother of Moses, and his seed throughout their generations. It is the "lesser" or preparatory priesthood and was held, according to D&C 84, by John the Baptist. According to Mormons, this priesthood was for repentance, baptism and the remission of sins.

Though purporting to be a restoration of the former Aaronic priesthood, the LDS version is conferred upon all worthy males aged twelve and older. Adult male converts receive the Aaronic priesthood ordination immediately after baptism and confirmation.

The ordination is done by the authority of the greater, or Melchizedek, priesthood. The Aaronic priesthood is considered a preparatory priesthood in that it prepares the recipient for the Melchizedek priesthood. There is no set formula of words for Aaronic ordination.

There are several groups (called "quorums") within this priesthood, each with its own leader or president and counselors. To be ordained to either priesthood, or to any group within a priesthood, a person must be a baptized and confirmed Mormon male and must have demonstrated personal worthiness. The offices in the Aaronic priesthood are:

1. *Deacon:* Boys twelve years of age may be ordained deacons. These youngsters usually pass the bread and water at the Mormon Sunday "sacrament meeting" and help collect offerings from the members. They may also be called upon to help with the general upkeep of church property.

2. *Teacher:* Boys fourteen years of age may be ordained teachers. They prepare the bread and water for the sacrament meeting. Together with an adult male, they make monthly visits to mem-

bers' homes to share some insight into Mormon beliefs. This fulfills their role as "teacher."

3. *Priest:* Boys sixteen years of age may become priests. Three significant responsibilities are given them: A priest may baptize (either a child or a convert); he prays over the bread and water at the sacrament meeting; and he may ordain other priests, teachers and deacons.

4. *Bishop:* The bishop is actually an adult high priest who has been assigned to preside over the Aaronic priesthood of his ward (local church unit). He is responsible for the temporal needs of the members, interviews the members to determine their worthiness, issues temple recommends (passes) and so forth.

Melchizedek Priesthood

Ordination to the Melchizedek priesthood (for males who are eighteen or nineteen years of age, or for adult male converts after a period of probation) is an ordinance required not only for entrance into God's presence but for eventual godhood. The greater priesthood, together with endowment and temple marriage, are the only means by which any person can become a god. Ordination is done by the authority of the Melchizedek priesthood, and there are no set words for this ordination.

Strangely, Mormons do not claim to know when the Melchizedek priesthood was restored. There is no date given for its alleged return, supposedly conferred upon Smith and Cowdery by Peter, James, and John. One would think that so momentous an occurrence as the restoration of full priesthood power would have registered as strong an impression as the restoration of the lesser priesthood, for which we have an exact date.[13]

Mormons describe the character of this priesthood as the power and authority to act in the name of God. The adult male mem-

---

[13] While D&C 27:12 is cited to show that the Melchizedek priesthood had been restored by the summer of 1830, this portion was not in the original version (called the Book of Commandments) when it was published in 1833.

ber displays his worthiness for this priesthood by his integrity, chastity, and obedience to the church's laws of tithing and health.

Having received the Melchizedek priesthood, the man is ordained to an office within that priesthood, generally elder.[14]

It is these nineteen-year-old "elders" who do most of the Mormon church's evangelizing. They are the ones with white shirts, ties, and dark pants, pedaling bicycles and wearing nametags that identify them as "Elder Smith" or "Elder Jones."

---

[14] See "Melchizedek Priesthood," *Encyclopedia of Mormonism*, vol. 2.

5. Sacraments and Ordinances, Valid and Invalid

The Mormon church does not recognize the sacraments or ordinances of any other church as being valid before God. If any other church had valid ordinances then it would prove the true Church had survived from the first century, and Smith would not have needed to institute the Mormon church in 1830.

Mormons can be especially harsh regarding the practice of infant baptism, calling it idol-worship or even Satanic. Joseph Fielding Smith considered non-Mormon baptism as idolatrous.

"[T]housands grow up with the belief that in infancy they were made Christians—they speak of 'Our Savior' and go now and then to church," he wrote. "That they are not Christians never enters their heads. . . . But the lie is upon their forehead and in their heart. They perish, sacrificed to infant baptism and membership, as completely as are the crushed worshipers of Juggernaut sacrificed to their idols."[1]

Lamenting the perversions of the so-called general apostasy, James E. Talmage noted the corruption of this primary ordinance was a signal of further diabolical assaults.

"[T]he rites of baptism were perverted," Talmage wrote. "The sacrament was altered; public worship became an exhibition of art; men were canonized; martyrs were made subjects of adoration; blasphemy grew apace, in that men without authority essayed to exercise the prerogatives of God. Ages of darkness came upon the earth; the power of Satan seemed almost supreme."[2]

Along with the idea that Christian baptism was lost to the earth shortly after the death of the original apostles, Mormon scripture advances the conviction that Christian baptism was practiced in

---

[1] Joseph Fielding Smith, *The Way to Salvation*, 201.
[2] *Articles of Faith*, 200–201.

pre-Christian Old Testament and Book of Mormon times. Adam was supposedly baptized by the Spirit of the Lord. (See Moses 6:64–66.)

Subsequently, all "gospel dispensations"[3] are said to have had a clear understanding of Jesus Christ, were led by a prophet who held full priesthood authority and were given Christian (i.e., Mormon) baptism.

The Catholic view is nowhere near as harsh as the Mormon view. The Catholic Church recognizes that it was founded by Jesus Christ and, in accordance with his promise that the gates of hell would not prevail against it (Matt. 16:18), it has endured and remains the true Church of Christ. Catholics also recognize that God gives his grace to those who are, through no fault of their own, outside his true Church. It is possible for them to be saved so long as they would be willing to follow God if they knew the truth concerning him and his Church. Even the sacraments of other Christian churches may be valid.

Because the Catholic Church does not simply dismiss the sacraments of other churches, but evaluates them on a case-by-case basis, it is necessary to look at the Mormon "ordinances" individually and see if they are valid or not.

Sacraments, Sacramentals, and Ordinances

Mormonism does not distinguish between rites that the Catholic Church refers to as sacraments and those it refers to as sacramentals. A sacrament is a rite that was instituted by Jesus Christ and

---

[3] As Mormons use the term, a dispensation refers to an era in the world's history during which God directly reveals the message of his saving plan in the name of his son, Jesus Christ. Each dispensation is headed by a prophet bearing full authority. Dispensations were presided over by Adam, Enoch, Noah, Abraham, Moses, the Twelve Apostles and finally, in the last dispensation of the fullness of times, Joseph Smith. In each era the saving knowledge of Jesus Christ was revealed, together with the essential ordinances supposedly restored in the latter-days. See Robert L. Millet, "The Eternal Gospel," *Ensign*, July 1996, 48–56.

which has a divine promise that, whenever the rite is correctly celebrated and received, God will use it as a means to confer his grace on the recipient. Sacraments are backed by a divine promise.

The Church also recognizes the existence of sacramentals, rites founded by the Church and used to bless and consecrate people and things. God also uses them to provide his blessings, but they are not backed up by the same kind of divine promise that the sacraments are. They operate through the intercession (prayer) of the Church rather than by the institution and promise of Christ.

Particular Mormon Ordinances

One difference between the Catholic view of sacramentals and the Mormon view of the equivalent ordinances is that Mormons believe that certain of these—notably patriarchal and parental blessings—are frequently (even ordinarily) occasions on which God will inspire the person performing the blessing to utter words of prophetic significance.

Catholics acknowledge that God can use blessings to impart prophetic information. He did it in the case of Jacob's and Moses' final blessings on the Israelites, for example (Gen. 49; Deut. 33). But it is not frequent and not to be expected. Private revelation, when it occurs, is also likely to be detached from blessings. One reason is that the Catholic prayers used for blessings are more set (though they do still allow for variation) than those for the equivalent Mormon ordinances. More fundamentally, however, God simply does not give private revelation with the kind of frequency Mormons imagine.

To the extent the term "validity" can be applied to sacramentals, the Mormon equivalents of them would not be valid. The reason is not that the sacramentals require a properly ordained priest to perform them. Many do not and can be performed by lay people (for example, parents blessing their children; Book of Blessings, "General Introduction" 18). Instead, the reason is that the sacramentals operate through the intercession of the Church, and Mormons are not relying on the intercession of the Catholic Church to work through these rites.

This is not to say that God may not bless the innocently ignorant child of a Mormon couple. It simply means that the Mormon equivalent of sacramentals would have no more "weight" than the private prayers of an individual person. How God would respond to those prayers would depend on the state of the Mormon's soul and how culpable he is for embracing the false beliefs of the LDS church.

Mormon Baptism

Though the Catholic Church has not definitively settled the question of the validity of Mormon baptism, it currently assumes that they are valid. According to the *Canon Law Society of Great Britain and Ireland Newsletter*, "A letter from the Congregation for the Doctrine of the Faith dated March 31, 1992 states that on February 15, 1991 the Holy Father confirmed to the Prefect that 'there are insufficient grounds to change the current practice not to contest the validity of Mormon baptism.' . . . The letter of 31/3/92 goes on to say that there may be irregularities in individual cases, that each case needs to be examined, and that conditional baptism of converts from Mormonism may continue."[4]

For a baptism to be valid, several conditions must be met: a) the proper form (the Trinitarian baptismal formula, ". . . baptize you in the name of the Father, and of the Son, and of the Holy Ghost [Spirit]") must be used, b) the proper matter (water) must be applied to the recipient in some fashion, c) the minister must intend, on a general level, to bestow the sacrament of baptism, and, in the case of those who have the use of reason, d) the

---

[4] *Canon Law Society of Great Britain and Ireland Newsletter*, no. 110 (June 1997), 32. See also *Canon Law Digest* VIII:677–678 on the presumption of regarding Mormon baptisms as valid for purposes of determining marriage cases.

recipient must intend, on a general level, to receive the sacrament of baptism.

Does Mormon baptism meet these four conditions?

There is no dispute that Mormons use the proper form and matter.

Regarding the minister's intent, the Catholic Church has been clear that only a minimal, general intent is necessary for baptismal validity. Because baptism is so essential to the ordinary reception of eternal life, it potentially can be performed by anyone, even a non-Christian.

The current *Directory for the Application of the Principles and Norms of Ecumenism* states, "The minister's insufficient faith concerning baptism never of itself makes baptism invalid" (1993 *Directory on Ecumenism* 95b).

For validity, the same level of intent is required on the part of the recipient that is required on the part of the minister. This is why the baptisms of many Protestant groups are valid. Some groups, such as Baptists and Pentecostals, as well as many Presbyterians, do not believe that baptism is anything more than a symbolic ritual. In their view, it does not impart grace. Nevertheless, because these individuals are attempting to follow Christ by doing what he instructed, their baptisms are valid. It does not matter that they do not understand the grace of baptism or the purposes for which Christ instituted it. They recognize that Christ did institute baptism and did command his followers to receive it, so they obey.

The same is true of those who have even graver departures from the correct understanding of Christian doctrine. Aquinas said, "[R]ight faith is not necessary in the one baptized any more than in the one who baptizes, provided the other conditions [form, matter] are fulfilled which are essential to the sacrament" (ST III: 68:8).

He added, "Even he who has not right faith on other points, can have right faith about the sacrament of baptism, and so he is not hindered from having the intention of receiving that sacrament. Yet even if he think not aright concerning this sacrament, it is enough, for the receiving of the sacrament, that he should have a general intention of receiving baptism, according as Christ instituted, and as the Church bestows it" (ibid., ad 3).

Aquinas also noted, however, that there is a difference between validly receiving a sacrament and receiving it in such a way that it is profitable to one's salvation. Specifically, in the case of baptism, one may validly receive it in such a way that the permanent baptismal mark or "character" is imprinted on one's soul, but due to unrepentance one may fail to receive the sanctifying (saving) grace that is meant to accompany baptism.

A person who is culpably clinging to heretical, even gravely heretical, beliefs thus could validly receive baptism but fail to receive sanctifying grace. Aquinas said, "Just as the sacrament of baptism is not to be conferred on a man who is unwilling to give up his other sins, so neither should it be given to one who is unwilling to renounce his unbelief. Yet each receives [i.e., validly receives] the sacrament if it be conferred on him, though not unto salvation" (ibid., ad 4).

It would appear that Mormon baptism may be valid, meaning that Mormons would carry the mark of baptism on their souls, despite holding un-Christian and even anti-Christian beliefs. Whether they receive the grace that accompanies baptism would depend on their individual level of accountability for holding Mormonism's gravely heretical teachings.

Mormon Marriage

The other sacrament that does not require a validly ordained priest to be performed is matrimony because it is performed by the two spouses through their exchange of matrimonial consent.

At Catholic marriages, a priest or deacon officiates, but does so as the Church's witness to the union, not as the person who brings the sacrament of matrimony into existence. Catholics are required by canon law to observe the Catholic form of marriage or to get their bishop's permission if they wish to be married outside the Church. Failure to do this results in the marriage being invalid.

Since canon law is not binding on those who have never been members of the Catholic Church (Canon 11), and since those who have left the Catholic Church by a formal act of defection are not bound to observe the Catholic form of marriage (Canon 1086 §1), it is not required that a Catholic priest or deacon officiate at weddings of non-Catholics. Consequently, the Catholic Church recognizes the validity of marriages between non-Catholics.

In the case of a couple where one or both of the parties are unbaptized, the Church recognizes that they have a valid natural marriage. However, if both parties are baptized, the Church recognizes them as having a valid sacramental marriage. Among the differences between a natural and a sacramental marriage is that the latter carries with it sacramental grace; when a sacramental marriage is consummated, it becomes indissoluble by anything except the death of one of the parties (Rom. 7, 1 Cor. 7).

Since the Catholic Church presumes that Mormon baptisms are valid, it presumes that Mormon marriages are valid and sacramental. Thus when a Catholic marriage tribunal is adjudicating an annulment case, marriages between two Mormons or between a Mormon and another baptized person are assumed sacramental.[5]

They can be rendered invalid, however, through particular circumstances, most notably polygamy. In the Western Plains states, where Mormonism is common, and especially in Utah, there are many "Fundamentalist" Mormons living in polygamous unions. Though these unions are not legal nor valid in the eyes of the state, there are many Mormon men who attempt to take multiple wives at the same time. The Mormon church does not condone this, but it frequently turns a blind eye to these situations, with many Mormon leaders feeling the anti-polygamy laws are unenforceable. According to Catholic teaching, a baptized person cannot validly enter more than one marriage. If a Mormon man's first marriage was valid, the marriages to all of his subsequent "wives" would be invalid.

In addition to the unique complications presented by the con-

---

[5] See *Canon Law Digest* (VIII:677–678).

tinuing, though unofficial, practice of polygamy in Mormon circles, their marriages can also be invalid through the same set of invalidating conditions that can strike at non-Mormon marriages.

All of what we have said applies to "regular" Mormon marriages. There is also a special kind of marriage done in Mormon temples. Mormon couples who are considered worthy may go to a temple and there be "sealed" to one another in marriage, supposedly for all eternity. This is known as having a "celestial marriage."

Whereas ordinary Mormon marriages can be valid from a Catholic point of view, these "celestial marriages" definitely are not valid sacraments. Mormon claims to the contrary, they were not instituted by Christ. The premise on which they are based—that a couple can be united together in marriage for all eternity—is flatly against Christ's teaching. When challenged by the Sadducees (who did not believe there would be a resurrection) to say whose wife a woman would be if she had been married and widowed more than once, Jesus replied, "The children of this world marry, and are given in marriage: But they which shall be accounted worthy to obtain that world, and the resurrection from the dead, neither marry, nor are given in marriage: Neither can they die any more: for they are equal unto the angels; and are the children of God, being the children of the resurrection" (Luke 20:34–36).

Mormons have to go through a great deal of exegetical squirming to get around this teaching.

MORMON ORDINATION

As for priestly ordination, Mormonism stakes its right to exist on the claim that it alone has a valid priesthood, all other churches having lost by apostasy a divinely authorized priesthood.

One way to address this claim is by pointing out that the promises of Christ (Matt. 16:18) indicate that there would never be an apostasy sufficient to destroy Christ's Church. Since the Catholic Church is the organic extension of the Church Christ founded in the first century—since the Catholic Church is that Church—and since it is protected by Christ's promises from apostasy and from losing its authority as Christ's representative (and his mystical body) on earth, it continues to have a valid priesthood, passed down through the apostolic succession of the bishops, who were originally ordained by the apostles. God had no need to start a new priesthood in the 1800s under Joseph Smith, therefore he did not.

The only way Mormons could have a valid priesthood is if they had obtained valid holy orders from one of those churches that has it (for example, one of the Eastern Orthodox churches), but this they have not done.

Even if they had done so, they would not have been able to pass on holy orders, since they have a fundamentally different and invalidating understanding of the priesthood. Pope Leo XIII made clear, in his letter *Apostolicae Curae*, that the Anglicans—who originally did have valid orders—lost them through changing their rite of ordination and concept of priesthood to one incompatible with historic Christian theology. As has always been recognized, the concept of priesthood is inextricably linked to the idea of offering sacrifice to God. Without a system of sacrifice, there is no priesthood, and when Anglicans changed their rite of ordination to eliminate the idea of a Christian priesthood dedicated to the Eucharistic sacrifice, they lost the priesthood itself. Since the Mormon concept of priesthood is devoid of the idea of offering sacrifice, they too would be incapable of transmitting valid holy orders, even if they had gotten them from somewhere.

A final way to show the absurdity of the Mormon claim to having a valid priesthood—indeed, the only valid one on earth—is to compare their system of offices with that found in the Bible. The two do not match up. Mormons apply a lot of terms from the Bible to the offices in their church, but anyone with even the most rudimentary understanding of the corresponding biblical offices has to laugh at the idea that the modern Mormon offices bearing their names are in any way re-institutions of what we find in the Bible.

Biblical Priesthood

Outside of Israel there were a variety of priests serving the true God. Among them was Melchizedek, the priest-king of the city now known as Jerusalem. He is mentioned only twice in the Old Testament: Once, when Abraham visited him (Gen. 14:18-20), and once in the Psalms, where another priestly king is compared to him (Ps. 110:4). At the time Abraham visited Melchizedek, Israel was not even a nation. In a sense, Abraham himself was the nation, for he did not yet have any descendants (Gen. 15:2). When the nation did arise, God guided Israel into developing its own priesthood, just as other nations had. In fact, there continued to be true priests to the true God outside of Israel, even after it developed a priesthood. For example, Moses' father-in-law, Jethro, was a Midianite priest who offered sacrifice to God (Ex. 18:11-12).

In Scripture, we find that the Israelite priesthood, from the earliest days, was three-fold. The lowest level of the priesthood, which in theological terms is known as the general or universal priesthood, is possessed by all God's people. Thus God told Israel: "And ye shall be unto me a kingdom of priests, and an holy nation" (Ex. 19:6). Members of this general, universal priesthood were qualified to offer "spiritual sacrifices," such as the sacrifice of prayer (Ps. 141:2), thanksgiving (Ps. 107:22), a broken spirit and contrite heart (Ps. 51:17). They were not allowed to offer the sacrifices that belonged to the second kind of priesthood, theologically referred to as the ministerial priesthood.

Even before Aaron was consecrated as high priest, there were ministerial priests in Israel. This is seen, for example, from Exodus 19:21-22, 24, where Moses warned the people *and* the priests to stay away from the sacred mountain where he met with God. In Exodus 28 the ministerial priesthood was transferred to the line of Aaron, creating what is biblically called the Levitical priesthood (Heb. 7:11), though Mormons prefer "Aaronic" priesthood. Members of this priesthood had to be a son of Aaron, (Ex. 28:1), and thus of Levi's tribe (Heb. 7:5). When others tried to function as Aaronic priests, God punished them (Num. 16; 2 Chron. 26:16-21). As long as the Levitical priesthood endured, it consisted only of those men belonging to Aaron's line (1 Chron. 23:13). Only these priests could offer incense, grain and other tangibles.

Under the New Covenant, with the tearing of the Temple veil, Christ abolished the Old Covenant priesthood and became the new high priest (Heb. 3:1). Yet Christ was of Judah's tribe, which Moses had not authorized to produce priests (Heb. 7:13-14). When Christ took his place as the new and superior high priest, he received the office from God without a priestly genealogy, as did the non-Jewish priest Melchizedek (Heb. 7:3, 15-17). Thus there was a change in the system of priesthood (Heb. 7:12). The Levitical priesthood was abolished (Heb. 7:18) and replaced by the Christian priesthood (Heb. 7:19).

This system, also, is three-fold. It has a high priest (Christ) and a general or universal priesthood of all Christians. The New Testament applies to Christians the same words that were applied to the children of Israel: "a royal priesthood, an holy nation"[6] (1 Pet. 2:9; Rev. 1:6, 5:10). This universal priesthood is authorized to offer "spiritual sacrifices" (1 Pet. 2:5), including our praise (Heb. 13:5), faith (Phil. 2:17), finances (Phil. 4:18) and very lives as living sacrifices (Rom. 12:1).

In addition to the New Testament high priesthood and universal priesthood, there is also a ministerial priesthood authorized to offer the Eucharistic sacrifice. Paul explicitly refers to the Eucharist as "the table of the Lord" (1 Cor. 10:21), which is another way of saying "the *altar* of the Lord." (See Malachi 1:7, 12, where the phrase refers to the altar in the Temple.) He parallels our eating of the Eucharist (1 Cor. 10:17) with the Jews' eating of the sacrifices offered on their altar (1 Cor. 10:18) and even with the

---

[6] The King James Version does not render this in such a way to make the connection with Exodus 19:6 as clear as possible. In that passage, the translation is "a kingdom of priests and an holy nation." Here we have "a royal priesthood, an holy nation," but Peter is quoting Exodus.

sacrifices eaten by pagans in their temples (1 Cor. 10:21 and 7:19 with 8:7–10). The Eucharist thus is a sacrifice, and it is offered by those in the ministerial priesthood—those who have the duty of preaching the gospel and performing other "priestly services" (Rom. 15:16[7]). As writings of early Christians confirm, offering the Eucharist was not something every Christian could do.[8]

The Christian priesthood seen in the early Church mirrors the Old Covenant pattern of priesthood—a high priest at the top (Aaron before, Jesus now), a ministerial priesthood in the middle (Aaron's sons before, Christian priests now), and a universal or common priesthood at the bottom (Jews before, Christians now).

The Mormon Caricature of the Priesthood

Mormonism's two priesthoods—Melchizedek and Aaronic—fail to capture the biblical system of priesthood in the Old or New Testament.

The Levitical priesthood was limited to Aaron's descendants and if one could not prove one's descent by genealogical records, one was not allowed to serve as priest (Ezra 2:61–63). This priesthood was eliminated by Christ's coming as the new high priest. The idea that Mormon males today, in no way descendants of Aaron, could be validly appointed to a no-longer-valid priesthood is absurd.

---

[7] The King James Version, translated under the anti-priestly bias rampant in Elizabethan and Jacobean English, deliberately mistranslates the Greek of this verse, for in it Paul says that he does the work of a priest, something not conducive to the anti-priestly agenda of the KJV translators. The Revised Standard Version renders the verse better. Paul says that he has been given the grace "to be a minister of Christ Jesus to the Gentiles in the priestly service of the gospel of God, so that the offering of the Gentiles may be acceptable, sanctified by the Holy Spirit."

[8] Ignatius of Antioch (d. 110), was explicit on this point: "Let no one do anything of concern to the Church without the bishop. Let that be considered a valid Eucharist which is celebrated by the bishop or by one whom he appoints" (*Letter to the Smyrnaeans* 8:1).

Mormons might assert that their ever-mutable God has changed the rules again, but this would undercut their claim to embody a re-institution of the biblical offices. An *Aaronic* priesthood that is not limited to the sons of *Aaron* is not an *Aaronic* priesthood at all! The distinguishing characteristic of the Levitical priesthood was who belonged to it. There were other priests of God—like Melchizedek—who were distinguished from the Levitical priests because they were *not* from the line of Aaron.

The Mormon understanding of the so-called "Melchizedek priesthood" is equally groundless from a biblical perspective.

According to the Order *of Melchizedek?*

English translations of the Bible have ill served us in their rendering of the Hebrew word *dibra* as "order" in Psalm 110:4b, which is commonly translated something like: "You are a priest for ever after the order of Melchizedek." Today the term "order" can have a technical, ecclesiastical meaning signifying an organized group of priests or religious (the Franciscan order, the Dominican order). Consequently, moderns reading the passage may think Melchizedek belonged to a particular order of priests, parallel to the Levitical priests (who *were* a definite, organized group of priests). This is not the case.

The term *dibra* simply means "cause," "reason" or "manner." It does *not* denote an ecclesiastical order in Hebrew. The term, and its Aramaic counterpart, appears seven times in Scripture (Job 5:8; Ps. 110:4; Eccles. 3:18, 7:14, 8:2; Dan. 2:30, 4:17), and it *never* has the sense of an ecclesiastical order.[9] All the phrase in Psalm 110 means is that, by the special command of Yahweh, the one being

---

[9] The following are the seven verses where *dibra* and its Aramaic counterpart appear. The phrase translating *dibra* has been italicized and the term inserted in brackets. Job 5:8 ("As for me, I would seek God, and to God would I commit *my cause* [*dibra*]"); Psalm 110:4 ("The Lord has sworn and will not change his mind, 'You are a priest for ever *after the order* [*dibra*] of Melchizedek'"); Ecclesiastes 3:18 ("I said in my heart *with regard to* [*dibra*] the sons of men that God is testing them to show them that they are but beasts"), 7:14 ("In the day

addressed is a priest *like Melchizedek was* in that he is not subject to the restrictions of the Levitical priesthood, needing no genealogy and having no fixed term in office (Heb. 7:3). The New American Bible renders the verse well: "The Lord has sworn and will not waver: 'Like Melchizedek you are a priest forever.'"

The same is indicated in the New Testament, where the word used for "order" is *taxis*, which means "an arrangement," "a sequence," "an orderly condition," "a civic post," "character," "fashion" or "style." The term appears in nine verses, and in none does it have the sense of an ecclesiastical order. Three of the nine verses with *taxis* are outside the book of Hebrews, and none indicates an ecclesiastical order.[10]

Of the six occurrences in Hebrews, three of them (Heb. 5:6,

---

of prosperity be joyful, and in the day of adversity consider; God has made the one as well as the other, *so* [*dibra*] that man may not find out anything that will be after him"), 8:2 ("Keep the king's command, and *because* [*dibra*] of your sacred oath be not dismayed"); Daniel 2:30 ("But as for me, not because of any wisdom that I have more than all the living has this mystery been revealed to me, but *in order* [*dibra*] that the interpretation may be made known to the king, and that you may know the thoughts of your mind"), 4:17 ("The sentence is by the decree of the watchers, the decision by the word of the holy ones, to *the end* [*dibra*] that the living may know that the Most High rules the kingdom of men, and gives it to whom he will, and sets over it the lowliest of men"). These citations, and those below dealing with the Greek term *taxis*, are taken from the Revised Standard Version for easier reading.

[10] The three occurrences outside Hebrews are: Luke 1:8 ("Now while he was serving as priest before God when his division was *on duty* [*taxis*]"); I Corinthians 14:40 ("but all things should be done decently and in *order* [*taxis*]"); Colossians 2:5 ("For though I am absent in body, yet I am with you in spirit, rejoicing to see your good *order* [*taxis*] and the firmness of your faith in Christ"). The last two are using *taxis* in the sense of an orderly condition. Though it is not apparent from the RSV rendering above, Luke 1:8 is using it in the sense of an arrangement or succession. A more literal translation of the verse would be, "Now while he was serving as priest before God according to the sequence (or arrangement) of his division . . ." Zechariah was one of the twenty-four courses of Levitical priests, which took turns serving in the Temple according to a definite sequence or arrangement.

7:17, and 7:21[11]) are quotations of Psalm 110:4. In these the term *taxis* is being used to translate the Hebrew term *dibra*, so we must select the meaning of *taxis* that is closest to the meaning of *dibra*. Since the latter term's basic meaning in Psalm 110:4 is "manner," the meanings "character," "fashion" or "style" would be most appropriate. The quotations of Psalm 110:4 in Hebrews need to be understood in the same sense as the original, and thus they indicate a manner, likeness or character of priesthood, but not an ecclesiastical order.

The remaining three verses containing *taxis* (Heb. 5:10, 6:20, 7:11) are built on the quotations from Psalm 110:4, so the proper understanding of that passage must inform them as well. Since the original psalm is speaking of a manner of priesthood, as are the quotations of it in Hebrews, we must understand the subsequent, contingent verses as doing the same.[12] The bottom line: All of these verses speak of being a priest *like* Melchizedek or *in the manner of* Melchizedek. They do not speak of an ecclesiastical "Melchizedek order."

This is reinforced by passages like Hebrews 7:12–16, where the core of the argument is presented. The problem that the author of Hebrews is solving for his audience is how Jesus Christ can be our high priest when he is not from the tribe of Levi, and thus is not a Levitical priest:

---

[11] In most manuscripts, the phrase "after the order [*taxis*] of Melchizedek" does not appear in Hebrews 7:21. Instead the quotation ends after "You are a priest forever . . ." Since Mormons use the King James Version, which does have the phrase about Melchizedek, we are including the verse here.

[12] Here are the three verses with the term "manner" substituted for "order": Hebrews 5:10 ("being designated by God a high priest after the manner of Melchizedek"), 6:20 ("where Jesus has gone as a forerunner on our behalf, having become a high priest for ever after the manner of Melchizedek"), 7:11 ("Now if perfection had been attainable through the Levitical priesthood—for under it the people received the law—what further need would there have been for another priest to arise after the manner of Melchizedek, rather than one named [i.e., appointed] after the manner of Aaron?").

(12) For when there is a change in the priesthood, there is necessarily a change in the law as well. (13) For the one of whom these things are spoken belonged to another tribe, from which no one has ever served at the altar. (14) For it is evident that our Lord was descended from Judah, and in connection with that tribe Moses said nothing about priests. (15) This becomes even more evident when another priest arises in the likeness of Melchizedek, (16) who has become a priest, not according to a legal requirement concerning bodily descent [Heb. 7:12–16a].

There has been a change in the law (v. 12b), allowing a change in the priesthood (v. 12a). Under the previous dispensation, the only valid priests for Israel were the Levitical ones. But now Christ, of the tribe of Judah, has become our high priest (vv. 13–14). How can this be? The answer is evident when we look to the case of Melchizedek. *Not all* priests of God were Levitical. There were also priests like Melchizedek, who did not have to be descended from Aaron. Consequently, it is evident that there has been a change in the law (and the priesthood) when "another priest arises in the likeness of Melchizedek" (v. 15), who does not gain the priesthood "according to a legal requirement concerning bodily descent" (v. 16a).

This is the heart of the argument concerning Jesus' claim to priesthood, and it stresses that he is *like* Melchizedek. The word rendered "likeness" is the Greek word *homoiotes*, and it here serves the same summary function that *taxis* and *dibra* do elsewhere. Christ is a priest in the *likeness* (*homoiotes*), the *character/quality/style* (*taxis*), the *manner* (*dibra*) of Melchizedek. And Melchizedek is himself seen as a prefigurement of Christ. Hebrews 7:3 states that he "is like" (*aphomoioo*) the Son of God.

Mormonism's "Melchizedek Priesthood"

The "Melchizedek priesthood" of Mormonism thus turns out to be as unbiblical as its "Aaronic priesthood." There *was no* "Melchizedek priesthood" in the Bible. Melchizedek was simply *one of many* non-Jewish priests who worshipped the Lord before the time of Christ. When Christ comes as our new high priest, despite the fact that he is not from the tribe of Levi, the author of Hebrews points back to Melchizedek as an example of a genuine priest, acceptable to God, who was *not* from Levi. If there could be non-Levitical priests back then, before the Mosaic Law, there can be non-Levitical priests now, after the Mosaic Law has been superseded. Thus Christ's belonging to the tribe of Judah is not a barrier to his being high priest.

Again, Mormonism lifts a term from the Bible—in this case, "Melchizedek"—and pays no attention to how it is used. Yes, there was a Melchizedek, and yes, he was a priest. But there was no "Melchizedek priesthood."

Neither Mormon priesthood can claim to be remotely biblical. They were invented, with a biblical name slapped on to give them an air of credibility. Because Mormon priesthoods are unbiblical, they are invalid. We established this through Mormonism's lack of apostolic succession. Mormonism's defective intent for the priesthood and the unbiblical nature of the "Melchizedek" and "Aaronic" priesthoods merely underline their falsity.

Mormon Sub-Divisions

If the only connection the Mormon priesthoods have with the Bible is the terms used for them, the same is true of their subdivisions. In the previous chapter, we noted that the "Aaronic priesthood" is divided into the sub-offices of "deacon," "teacher," "priest" and "bishop," while the "Melchizedek priesthood" is likewise divided into "elders" and "high priests." But there is little or no correspondence between Mormon offices and their biblical counterparts.

For Mormons, "deacons" are typically twelve- or thirteen-year-old boys who pass out the bread and water at Mormon "sacrament meetings." This does *not* reflect the biblical concept of deacon. The biblical foundation for the office of deacon is found in Acts 6:

> Now in these days when the disciples were increasing in number, the Hellenists murmured against the Hebrews because their widows were neglected in the daily distribution. And the twelve summoned

the body of the disciples and said, "It is not right that we should give up preaching the word of God to serve tables. Therefore, brethren, pick out from among you seven men of good repute, full of the Spirit and of wisdom, whom we may appoint to this duty. But we will devote ourselves to prayer and to the ministry of the word." And what they said pleased the whole multitude, and they chose Stephen, a man full of faith and of the Holy Spirit, and Philip, and Prochorus, and Nicanor, and Timon, and Parmenas, and Nicolaus, a proselyte of Antioch. These they set before the apostles, and they prayed and laid their hands upon them [Acts 6:1–6, RSV].

Deacons were originally needed to oversee the Church's temporal affairs so that higher ministers could devote themselves to praying and preaching. This is not the way twelve-year-old boys are used in the Mormon church. They may mow lawns or occasionally do "meals on (bicycle) wheels," but it is not the same as having authority over the charitable distributions of a church with thousands of members (as the Jerusalem church had at the time). Furthermore, the text specifies that those to be appointed deacons are to be "men" (6:3). The Greek word here is *anar*, which indicates an adult man rather than a boy. In his first letter to Timothy, Paul details the requirements for being a deacon:

> Deacons likewise must be serious, not double-tongued, not addicted to much wine, not greedy for gain; they must hold the mystery of the faith with a clear conscience. And let them also be tested first; then if they prove themselves blameless let them serve as deacons. The women [i.e., their wives] likewise must be serious, no slanderers, but temperate, faithful in all things. Let deacons be the husband of one wife, and let them manage their children and their households well; for those who serve well as deacons gain a good standing for themselves and also great confidence in the faith which is in Christ Jesus [1 Tim. 3:8–11, RSV].

Paul eliminates any doubts about the age requirement when he speaks of a deacon's wife and children.[13]

---

[13] Paul is not saying that deacons *are required* to have a wife and children. He was a celibate bachelor and highly recommended it to others (1 Cor. 7), yet he held a position far higher than that of deacon. Paul is saying *if* a deacon is

Next, Mormon boys become "teachers" when they are fourteen. As Mormons will admit, the kind of teaching a fourteen-year-old boy can do is limited. Others must prepare or closely review the lessons before he gives them publicly.

When they are two years older, Mormon boys may be called to the "Aaronic priesthood," but unlike biblical Aaronic priests, these teens do not place slaughtered bulls and goats on an altar of burnt offering. If one correctly objected that Christ did away with animal sacrifices, then one would have to conclude that either: (a) the Aaronic priesthood was eliminated (the *correct* answer) or (b) Jesus instituted a replacement sacrifice for Aaronic priests to offer, though Mormons don't have one. The bread and water that Mormon boy priests pray over at "sacrament meetings" is not viewed as a sacrifice. Neither do Mormon "Aaronic priests" offer anything beyond the "spiritual sacrifices" of prayer, praise and a contrite spirit, all of which could be offered by the universal priesthood and that were not restricted to and thus not characteristic of the Aaronic priesthood.

In the New Testament, the term "bishop" was often used as a synonym for the term "elder." By the late first and early second century, however, it had become more fixed in meaning and was applied exclusively to those men who appointed elders—men like Titus and Timothy, who in the New Testament tend to be called "evangelists" (2 Tim. 4:5).

This is logical since bishop means "overseer." Because, in early Church history, the term became more specific in application, we will not fault Mormons for applying the term "bishop" to an office distinct from "elder." Latter-day Saints consider their bishop to be the presiding officer in each ward's Aaronic priest-

---

married then he must have only one wife (and since neither Jews nor Greeks were polygamous at this period, he means that a deacon must have had only one wife, *period*). Similarly, *if* he has children, he must manage them well. Infertile deacons or those with barren wives would not be barred from serving, nor would unmarried deacons. Paul is indicating deacons are to be of marital (adult) *age*, as illustrated by the fact he makes requirements for those deacons who are married and have children.

hood, though the bishop himself is always taken from the ranks of the "high priests." Their idea of what a bishop is supposed to do and be may be problematic, but we will not fault them on this terminological ground with regard to the office of bishop.

An elder is the basic office of the "Melchizedek priesthood," which Mormon boys may gain at eighteen. It is difficult to imagine an eighteen-year-old as an "elder," and Mormon missionaries wearing their nametags saying "Elder Smith" or "Elder Jones" tend to get a lot of chuckles. An "elder" is someone who is expected to be a mature adult, at least in the Bible's view. Consider Paul's instructions to Titus concerning the ordination of elders: "This is why I left you in Crete, that you might amend what was defective, and appoint elders in every town as I directed you, if any man is blameless, the husband of one wife, and his children are believers and not open to the charge of being profligate or insubordinate. For a bishop, as God's steward, must be blameless; he must not be arrogant or quick-tempered or a drunkard or violent or greedy for gain, but hospitable, a lover of goodness, master of himself, upright, holy, and self-controlled; he must hold firm to the sure word as taught, so that he may be able to give instruction in sound doctrine and also to confute those who contradict it" (Tit. 1:5-9, RSV).

As with deacons, elders are expected to be men of the age to have wives and well-trained children (children obviously older than toddlers, since no toddler could be accused of being profligate or culpably insubordinate).[14] The assertion that an elder must be hospitable also indicates that he is capable of receiving guests in his house. The passage suggests anything but an eighteen- or nineteen-year-old unmarried boy who has not even completed his schooling, much less embarked upon a career and begun raising a family.

The Mormon office of "high priest" presents, perhaps, the most serious problem of all from a terminological point of view. There

---

[14] Again, these conditions do not *require* an elder to have a wife and children, as the requirements on deacons did not. However, they do indicate the age and maturity level expected of elders.

is only one high priest (*perhaps* two) at any time in Scripture because he serves as leader and focal point of the other ministerial priests. Mormons, however, have not one, not two, but thousands of "high priests," since each Mormon who serves as a bishop, on a high council, in a stake presidency, or as one of the general authorities must be ordained a high priest.[15]

A final problem within Mormonism's priesthoods is that up to the level of elder, the sub-offices should be held by every adult Mormon male. Unless a Mormon male makes himself unworthy (for example, by drinking tea), he should progress through and possess the sub-offices of deacon, teacher, priest, and elder.[16] This is another point on which the Mormon view flies in the face of Scripture. Any unbiased person who reads the New Testament and studies the way in which these offices are discussed cannot help but come away from the text with the realization that these offices are not meant to be held by all Christian men, even in the ideal.

The office of deacon, for example, was created to assist the apostles by overseeing the Church's charity system. It was *not* envisioned that *all* Christian men in Jerusalem would become overseers of this system. The apostles limited to seven the number of deacons serving in that church. They did not envision ordaining to the diaconate the more than 1,500 men in the Jerusalem church. Nor when we turn to the epistles do we find the institution of the diaconate different in other New Testament churches. The impression is reinforced that deacons are supposed to stand out from other Christian men in terms of their spiritual maturity and life situation. Not even this ostensible "worthiness" is sufficient to qualify them for office, for Paul declares, "Let them also be

---

[15] *Encyclopedia of Mormonism*, vol. 2, "High Priest." The position of "high priest" may also be granted to older or more influential members of the LDS church.

[16] In the Mormon view, one does not lose the previous office when one adds to it a new office. Thus a deacon who becomes a teacher remains a deacon, though he has added a new, higher sub-office as well.

tested first; then *if* they prove themselves blameless let them serve as deacons" (1 Tim. 3:10, emphasis added). The diaconate is not something every Christian man should have unless he disqualifies himself through sin. It is something only a special few who are called to it should have.

The office of "elder" is equally select in the New Testament. The first reference to Christian elders in the New Testament—Acts 11:30—speaks of churches in outlying regions sending relief to the church in Jerusalem, where it is received by the elders of that church from the hands of Paul and Barnabas. This conveys the idea that the elders were the leaders of the Jerusalem church, not just its average, worthy male members.

Likewise, in the next mention of Christian elders, we see elders as men specially appointed *for* the benefit of individual congregations: "And when they [Paul and Barnabas] had appointed elders *for them* [i.e., the laity] in every church, with prayer and fasting they committed them to the Lord in whom they believed" (Acts 14:23, RSV, emphasis added).

The instructions Paul gives Titus for appointing elders speak just as clearly as the instructions regarding deacons: These are positions for people of special spiritual distinction, not just men who aren't in the Mormon equivalent of mortal sin.

This becomes clearer when one realizes that in the pastoral epistles, the term "bishop" is applied to the office of elder:

> The saying is sure: If any one aspires to the office of bishop, he desires a noble task. Now a bishop must be above reproach, the husband of one wife, temperate, sensible, dignified, hospitable, an apt teacher, no drunkard, not violent but gentle, not quarrelsome, and no lover of money. He must manage his own household well, keeping his children submissive and respectful in every way; for if a man does not know how to manage his own household, how can he care for God's church? He must not be a recent convert, or he may be puffed up with conceit and fall into the condemnation of the devil; moreover he must be well thought of by outsiders, or he may fall into reproach and the snare of the devil [1 Tim. 3:1–7].

Here we are told that serving as elder ("bishop") is a *noble* task, requiring one to be above reproach, displaying many virtues and no vices, knowing how to manage his own family well, not being a recent convert and having a good reputation with non-Christians. It is without credibility to claim that this suggests that the office should be held by the average believing male who is not in gross sin.[17]

When we come to the term "priest," we find the scriptural disconnect mentioned earlier, under which Mormons fail to recognize the three-fold system of priesthood used in Old and New Testaments. In Mormonism, the sub-office of "priest" within the Aaronic priesthood should be held by all worthy boys of sixteen, but this is too restrictive to be equal to the Bible's universal priesthood and too broad to be the equivalent of the ministerial priesthood, which is *never* conceived of as something that should be held by all worthy men among God's people.

Finally, the Aaronic priesthood's sub-office of teacher is also meant to be universally held by Mormon males meeting the age and minimal worthiness requirements. But this is at odds with the biblical concept of a teacher. James says, "Not many of you should become teachers, my brothers, for you realize that we will be judged more strictly" (Jas. 3:1, RSV[18]).

Paul also indicates that God does not call all to be teachers when he writes, "And his [God's] gifts were that some should be apostles, some prophets, some evangelists, some pastors and teachers" (Eph. 4:11).

Elsewhere, Paul reiterates that only *some* are called to and given the gift of teaching, and he makes his point that these offices and

---

[17] Mormons may object to this last citation since the term "bishop" is used rather than "elder," and they may wish to interpret it as a reference to one of their own "bishops." However, we have already seen the term "bishop" being used as a synonym for "elder" in the pastoral epistles in Titus 1.

[18] The KJV inaccurately renders the term "teachers" as "masters." The Greek, however, is clear: The word is *didaskoloi*—the plural of *didaskolos*, which is the Greek word for *teacher*.

gifts are *not* universal by asking rhetorical questions: "And God has appointed in the church first apostles, second prophets, third teachers, then workers of miracles, then healers, helpers, administrators, speakers in various kinds of tongues. Are all apostles? Are all prophets? Are all teachers? Do all work miracles? Do all possess gifts of healing? Do all speak with tongues? Do all interpret?" (1 Cor. 12:28–30).

Not only do Mormons fail to have valid holy orders, they hold to an untenable caricature of the biblical idea of priesthood. The terms they give to the sub-offices within their "priesthoods" fail to correspond to the way Scripture uses the terms.

REMAINING MORMON "SACRAMENTS"

Because Mormonism is devoid of valid holy orders, it is unable to dispense those sacraments that depend on possession of a valid priesthood, namely, confirmation, the Eucharist, penance, and anointing of the sick.

Mormons do not claim to have an ordinance equivalent to the sacrament of penance (reconciliation).[19] They do, however, have simulations of the remaining three sacraments—confirmation, called this or "the laying-on of hands;" the Eucharist, called "the sacrament;" and anointing of the sick, called "administering to the sick."

None of these are sacramentally valid, nor are the remaining ordinances—temple endowment and sealing and ordinances for the dead—which have no biblical equivalent sacrament or sacramental. Since they were not instituted by the Church, they are not sacramentals, and since they were not instituted by Christ, they are not sacraments. They are Mormon inventions.

---

[19] Mormons guilty of various sins, from breaking the Word of Wisdom to adultery and murder, are expected to confess to a priesthood leader. The leader often confers with his counselors and superiors to determine corrective action. There is no "seal of the confessional" within Mormon "confession."

6. Mormon Headquarters: A Look around Temple Square

I first visited Temple Square in spring 1991, before I became Mormon. I had studied Mormonism for years and had found it to be a seriously deficient faith system. Its fundamental beliefs were implausible and, well, weird. But it presented a fascinating study and had become something of a "hobby" for me, which led to my trip to Salt Lake City. I wanted to put some "meat" on the bare bones of my reading and study.

About ten of us gathered at the designated spot on Temple Square for the forty-five-minute tour. A young sister missionary from Samoa, teeth chattering in the March cold, was our guide. I didn't know any of the others on the tour; I assumed they had come to Salt Lake City as pilgrims, tourists or skiers.

The grounds, though not yet fully awakened from winter, showed signs of planting. The Mormon church's April conference was upcoming, and the square would be filled with flowers as Mormons from all over converged on Temple Square to listen to their leaders.

Scattered along the walkways of the ten-acre square were relics or replicas of the Mormons' early travails. One metal statue depicted the famous pioneer handcart, piled high with family possessions and pulled by the father. Another monument contained a bell brought by Mormons from Nauvoo, Illinois. The Seagull Monument was erected to honor the flock of birds that "miraculously" appeared and prevented crickets from destroying the early Utah settlers' harvest.

The sister missionary led us into the Mormon Tabernacle. Built by the Utah settlers under the direction of Brigham Young, this oval auditorium seats over six thousand persons. It is home to the famous choir and is used for large gatherings of Mormon faithful.

The acoustics are legendary: While our group stood in the back, an assistant stood on the stage and dropped a pin. Without the aid of any amplifying device, we heard it fall to the table.

At opposite corners of the walled square, visitors' centers welcomed a steady stream of both pious and curious. Inside one, there was a diorama of the Book of Mormon story. Several other exhibits portrayed the early years of the Mormon church, with special emphasis on the alleged persecution from a skeptical public. We were invited to sign a guest book and were told we could receive a free copy of the Book of Mormon if we requested it.

The lavish square, the unique architecture and the professional presentations made a big impression on the group. Many gushed with praise over the Tabernacle, its turtleback roof and its marbleized pine furnishings. Some wanted to learn more about the Book of Mormon. A few asked about the difficulties faced by the first settlers in the Salt Lake Valley.

I was particularly curious about the gray, granite Mormon temple. Though a good portion of the exterior was scaffolded for cleaning, it was still impressive. It was not as large as I had imagined; many Catholic cathedrals are larger. But it was *the* most important Mormon temple. While not the first to be built, it is the one in which Mormon leaders meet weekly to conduct the affairs of the LDS church, and in it, Mormons believe, Jesus Christ has appeared.

From my reading, especially of writers critical of Mormonism, I had a good idea of the ceremonies that went on inside. I could not go in and witness them myself, of course. Throughout the world, no non-Mormons and perhaps no more than twenty percent of Mormons are permitted to enter LDS temples. The work done inside is said to be "too sacred" to be revealed to the unworthy. The vast majority of Mormons are considered unfit to enter "the Lord's house."

Beside the temple is the Joseph Smith Memorial Building, a white, brick structure, which is again open for business in the Utah capital. Since 1987, this former Hotel Utah serves as an important cell in the beehive of buildings where the Mormon church conducts business. It contains offices overseeing church hosting, public relations, church materials distribution and genealogy research. It also contains a video presentation center and banquet and meeting rooms.

The sumptuous lobby, with its marble columns, crystal chandeliers and stained-glass ceilings creates an almost reverent tone, one that is augmented by frequent live musical offerings. Though it could be said that the beauty of this space easily rivals that of the "celestial room" in the temple opposite, this area is open to all people, including lax Mormons and non-Mormons. A statue of Joseph Smith is the lobby's focal point. Standing a good deal larger than life and with his back to the temple, Smith's statue surveys the thousands who pass through Temple Square each day.

Some, including many non-Mormons, visit the square to do genealogical research, either in the building named after Smith or in the Family History Building a block away. The Mormon church oversees the largest genealogical research project in world history and is custodian of an estimated one billion names gathered from parish, personal, and governmental sources throughout the world.

Other visitors get a ticket for one of several movies produced by the LDS church and shown in the Memorial Building's 500-seat theater. A favorite is "Legacy," a fictionalized account of early Mormon history (not unlike other movies that use historical fiction to give people a sense of life during a particular period).

Many of those passing Smith's statue are professional church workers going to jobs in buildings adjacent to Temple Square. From these offices the Mormon church directs the religious affairs of its more than ten million members, preparing study lessons for the youngest child to high priests, receiving and recording tithes and donations and appointing local leaders. From here the church announces, enforces and revises its doctrines and practices and assigns and deploys its missionaries. Sometimes exceeding 50,000, the missionaries march to all but the most intransigent areas of the world. (Moslem nations are perhaps the most difficult to pierce.)

These proselytizers exempt no group from their efforts. Catholics, in particular, are sought as good potential converts.

It is from these offices, too, that Mormon leaders hold counsel, deciding on matters as essential as temple rites and as seemingly inconsequential as the color of carpet in a new Mormon chapel in Hong Kong.

Some visitors can be seen carrying small suitcases on their way to the temple. These are the "temple-worthy" Mormons who have been approved for entrance into any of the more than fifty Mormon temples throughout the world. In the valises they carry special robes that they will don during a secret ceremony in which only the elect may participate.

And then there are the many backsliders, "Jack Mormons" as they are sometimes called by other LDS members. Though nominally Mormon, these individuals have drifted away from either the doctrine or, more usually, the discipline, preferring a cigarette or a cup of coffee to active participation in the Lord's "one true church." Or maybe they refuse to tithe, observe personal chastity or attend church meetings. In any case, the temple is closed to them.

Finally, "the Gentiles" (all non-Mormons, including Jews) cannot avoid coming under the gaze of the prophet's statue. In this capital city, the population of which is estimated to be only fifty percent Mormon, the upswing in the non-Mormon population is disconcerting to many church members. For their part, newcomers often tire of the perceived restraints on their accustomed pleasures. (Utah has strict, though workable, laws governing smoking and the sale of alcohol.) There is also a growing incidence of robbery, gang-related violence and white-collar crime. To the faithful member, the steady rise in the non-Mormon and Jack Mormon population serves as adequate explanation.

7. Mormon Temple Work

Some Mormons are offended by detailed discussions of the particular rites used inside a Mormon temple, considering them too sacred to be discussed among the unworthy. In this chapter, we will respect these sensibilities by not discussing the details of particular rites. We will, however, discuss material that is commonly acknowledged by Mormons, even the "unworthy," to take place in their temples (such as baptisms for the dead).

There is very little in the temple endowment ceremony that cannot be gleaned from Mormon scriptures and other LDS writings. Aside from the confidential handshakes, arm gestures and code words—which we will not discuss—the well-informed patron would find nothing new or startling.[1] No new doctrines, just different packaging.

Mormons often hold out to their members the experience of going to the temple as the height of Mormon spirituality, and they ask their members to make an investment of significant effort and commitment before allowing them to gain an understanding of what goes on in the temple. In the interest of "truth in advertising," we will present a fuller picture of what it is like inside a Mormon temple than some might feel comfortable with. We will write with discretion, attempting to respect Mormon preferences.

Brett's Story[2]

Brett Ramsey is a typical "cradle" Mormon. He has just turned twelve and has been ordained a deacon. He's preparing to go to

---

[1] Several texts and videos about the temple have been produced by LDS church critics. Some material alleges that sexual misconduct or satanic rituals occur in the temple. Neither charge is true.

[2] This narrative is a composite account illustrating typical Mormon experiences.

a Mormon temple for the first time. Before he can do this, he must obtain a "temple recommend" from his bishop, so he makes an appointment and meets with the man. At this meeting, he is asked to testify to his personal worthiness to enter the temple. The prescribed questions ask if he has: believed in God, Jesus Christ and the Holy Ghost; had a firm testimony or conviction of the Mormon gospel; sustained (or supported) the president of the Mormon church and other general and local leaders; lived chastely and honestly; affiliated with any individual or group opposed to the Mormon church; attended all required meetings and performed all his duties; obeyed the rules, laws and commandments of the Mormon church; paid a full tithe;[3] kept the Word of Wisdom; behaved honorably with his family and others; and considered himself worthy to enter the temple and participate in its ordinances.[4]

Brett's acceptable answers establish his suitability to enter the temple. He declares that he is worthy to be received by the Lord.[5] The bishop writes out a "recommend slip," indicating that Brett has permission to go to any Mormon temple and perform baptisms for the dead. Temple recommends are valid for one year, after which the interview process must be repeated and new passes issued.

Early the following Tuesday, Brett and his older sister, Kathy, dressed in Sunday clothes, drive to the Arizona temple in Mesa, a vaguely classical, cream-colored structure fifty-five feet tall, dedicated in 1927. They present their recommends to a male volunteer at the front desk. He checks them for proper signatures and expiration dates and then invites them to proceed to the baptismal font dressing rooms.

---

[3] This applies to children as well as adults. A twelve-year-old would have to pay ten percent of his allowance, of money he earned, etc.

[4] For members who have already attended the temple and received their endowments, additional questions ask if they are faithful to the promises made in the temple and if they wear the prescribed undergarments day and night.

[5] Compare this with the Catholic's confession before receiving the Lord: "O Lord, I am not worthy to receive you. . . ."

It's 6:30 in the morning, and the temple is already busy. As Brett and Kathy are led to the clothing counter, they notice about a dozen high-school boys and girls ahead of them. They have come to "do" baptisms for the dead before they begin their school day.

All Mormon temples contain a large font of water resting on the back of twelve sculpted oxen, meant to call to mind the "brazen sea" constructed for Solomon's temple (1 Kgs. 7:23–26). The fonts are set below ground level, and the baptisms for the dead are done in them. Large mirrors are placed on opposite walls so that the font's reflection may be repeated "into infinity," symbolizing the eternal nature of the work done there.

As Brett's turn to be baptized arrives, he recognizes the process and wording are identical to that used at his own baptism, except that this ordinance is done by him serving as a proxy for a deceased person who had never been a Mormon. He doesn't know any of these people, though some of them are his long-dead ancestors, whose names he got from family records. Others are complete strangers.

After the baptisms, Brett, Kathy and the others serve as proxies for church "confirmation" by the laying-on of hands. Brett notices that none of the names correspond with those he had heard when he was being baptized. This is common. Members and professional researchers scour records from various institutions (including the baptism and marriage records of Christian churches) and submit their findings to the temples. These names are then computerized and made available to temple patrons who do not bring their own family names for processing.[6] The only requirement for doing the proxy work for the deceased is that the ordinances

---

[6] Some of the women in the Ramsey's ward, for example, obtained death records of Civil War soldiers. They "extracted" the names, along with as much other information as they could find (such as dates of birth and death, marriages if any, parents, siblings, and children), and placed them in the approved format required by the Mormon church. The names were then presented to the temple. On their regular trips to the temple, the teenaged boys of the ward would ask for these names and be baptized on behalf of the deceased soldiers.

be done in order. Thus, baptism must precede the laying-on of hands, and both must precede the endowment and sealing. All the ordinances for a deceased person need not be performed by the same living member.

Brett and Kathy leave the temple, and Brett feels satisfied knowing that the dozen or so people for whom he was baptized and confirmed now will have the opportunity of joining the Mormon church in the spirit world. Assuming that the spirit missionaries have already contacted them and convinced them of the truthfulness of Mormon doctrine, these candidates have the choice of accepting or rejecting the proxy work done in their behalf. Brett prays that all will embrace the work he has done for them. In doing so, they will free themselves from "spirit prison" and enter "paradise," to await the resurrection and return to the Father.

Brett and Kathy continued attending the temple over the course of the school year. On one occasion, Brett was baptized and confirmed for nearly forty persons, first being dunked forty times in a row, then being confirmed forty times in a row. Since his own parents had been somewhat delinquent in their genealogy work,[7] Brett himself had started working on his family tree. With the help of Kathy, he learned to use the local Mormon family history center. Brett began piecing together a comprehensive list of ancestors going back over four generations. To keep track of the information, Brett got a Mormon genealogy program for his home computer, which made it easy to place the data in "temple-ready" format.

Baptism for the Dead

Now let's back up and observe this process. Brett attended the temple for the first time, receiving baptism and the laying-on of hands for a dozen or so men who are long dead. None had been members of the Mormon church while they lived on earth. If they

---

[7] Mormons are expected to research and do the temple work for their families back at least four generations.

had died before 1830, there was no Mormon church for them to belong to. Others may have heard of it but gave it no thought. Still others may have had some contact with Mormon missionaries but refused to convert.

Mormonism teaches the absolute necessity of baptism, confirmation and the other essential ordinances for heaven for every person who has ever lived or will ever live. Since Mormonism does not have the concept of baptism by desire, and since it does not wish to simply condemn all non-recipients to hell, it advocates the idea of baptism (and the other necessary ordinances) by proxy. No one in world history is thought to be exempt, and Mormons intend (at least during the millennium) to do "proxy work" for everyone in world history.[8]

Mormons cite a single biblical passage to support baptizing members on behalf of dead persons, "Else what shall they do which are baptized for the dead, if the dead rise not at all? Why are they then baptized for the dead?" (1 Cor. 15:29).

Noting that the Mormons are alone in providing baptisms for the dead, the ninth president of the church, David O. McKay, said, "The pseudo-Christian world, unenlightened by revelation, has stumbled over the meaning of this simple text."[9]

Mormons believe that their church has missionaries in the "spirit world" who are busy spreading the Mormon gospel to dead people who have not yet received it. Should any of these dead people want to convert to Mormonism, they are required to abide by all its rules, one of which is water baptism.

Mormons infer that in 1 Corinthians, Paul speaks approvingly of living Christians receiving baptism on behalf of dead non-

---

[8] Some members have researched Catholic "lives of the saints" to gather sufficient family information about our canonized saints. They then prepare these names for the temple and are systematically doing proxy work for them. The same has been done with the names of victims of the Holocaust, though recent Jewish pressure has led the Mormon church to reformulate its public policies of temple work for non-family persons.

[9] *Gospel Ideals*, 18.

Christians; however, the context and construction of the verse indicate otherwise. The Greek phrase rendered by the King James Version as "for the dead" is *huper ton nekron*. This phrase is as ambiguous in Greek as it is in English. The preposition *huper* has a wide semantic range and can indicate "for the sake of," "on behalf of," "over," "beyond" or "more than." Like the English preposition "for," it does not have a single meaning and does not require the Mormon idea of being baptized *in place of* the dead. Such a reading would be unlikely given the more plausible interpretations available, and even if *huper* were taken to mean "in the place of," it doesn't mean Paul endorses the practice.

First Corinthians 15 is a key chapter for Paul's teaching on the resurrection of the body. He makes no statement on baptism for dead persons except to note that some group he identifies as "they" practice it. While the rest of his teaching in chapter fifteen refers to "we," his Christian followers, "they" are not further identified. Who this group was may not be available to us today, but there are some reasonable interpretations:

1. Some commentators assume this verse refers to the practice of giving newly baptized children the names of deceased non-Christian relatives, with the hope that the dead might somehow share in the Lord's mercy.

2. Another interpretation envisions the baptism of catechumens who have witnessed the persecution and martyrdom of their Christian predecessors. With their belief that the dead do rise, the Christian candidates come forward boldly and accept both the Faith and its consequences.

3. A related view holds that the group consists of those baptized in connection with a dead Christian loved one. In the first century, many families were split religiously, as only one or two members may have converted to Christianity. When it came time for these new Christians to die, they no doubt exhorted their non-Christian family members to consider the Christian faith and to embrace it so that they could be together in the next world. After the deaths of their Christian loved ones, many family members no doubt *did* investigate the Christian faith and were baptized so

that they could be reunited with their loved ones in the afterlife. At the time, many pagans had at best an unclear idea of what the afterlife was like, and there were a large number of sects promising immortality to those who went through their initiation rituals.

A pagan husband mourning the death of his Christian wife might thus have an unclear idea of what her religion was all about, but still have it fixed in his mind: "If I want to be with her again, I need to become a Christian, like she was, so I can go where Christians go in the afterlife." This, then, could prompt him to investigate Christianity, learn its teachings about the afterlife and the resurrection, and embrace faith in Christ and receive Christian baptism for the sake of being united with his dead loved one. The same is true, by extension, for other family relations as well, such as parents and children, grandparents and grandchildren. Even today deathbed exhortations to live the Christian life are not uncommon. People still undertake resolutions to live as Christians in order to please dead loved ones, honor their memories and be united with them in the next life. The difference is that, today, most of those being exhorted have already been baptized.

4. Others advance the possibility that Paul was referring to the practice of a heretical cult that existed in Corinth. On this theory, Paul was not endorsing the practice of the group, merely citing it to emphasize the importance of the resurrection.

A contemporary Catholic speaker could exactly reproduce this last application. Consider what the pastor of a Catholic parish in Salt Lake City might preach in his Easter Sunday homily:

> Today we commemorate the truth of the resurrection, both the resurrection of our Lord and Savior, Jesus Christ, and the resurrection that awaits us at the end of time. Eternal life has been a constant theme throughout the religious strivings of mankind. Lives have been lived and lost in the hope of gaining eternal life. Devout people of nearly every faith have been willing to pay any price in exchange for God's promise of heaven.
>
> Look at the early martyrs, beaten and brutalized; look at the desert ascetics, withdrawing from this world to live for the world to come; look at the saintly lay people, religious, and clergy who sacrificed their comforts to serve the poor and unwanted. All were impelled

by a love for God and for others and by a hope for everlasting joy.

Why, even the Mormons pay attention to the afterlife! See the multimillion-dollar temples they build. Observe the constant stream of patrons passing through the temple doors. They are willing to do what they believe is necessary, not only for their own salvation, but for their dead relatives, as well. The human heart universally testifies to the reality of the afterlife, which we know involves resurrection, as Christ Jesus showed us. But if there is no resurrection of the dead, then our faith and works are in vain.

The Utah Catholic listening to this homily need not be reminded that Mormon temple practices are not Christian or that Mormon proxy work does not really secure the salvation of their dead. That's not the point. The priest uses their practice as an illustration of belief in the afterlife and the resurrection.

There is no other evidence in the Bible or the early Church Fathers' writings of baptism being practiced on the living in place of the dead. Some Mormon writers assert that some Christian commentators have discussed the possibility of a kind of "baptism for the dead" among some in the Corinthian community in Paul's time. But these commentators do not suggest that the practice was accepted or mainstream.[10] Given the silence of Scripture

---

[10] The Mormon authors of *Offenders for a Word* actually liken baptism for the dead to the Catholic doctrine of purgatory and prayers offered on behalf of the deceased. This is a mistake. Catholics know that those who are undergoing purgatorial cleansing are already saved and will enjoy the Lord's presence forever. We cannot change the *destiny* of those who have died, only help their transition into heaven. Their eternal dwelling place has been determined by their lives of faith and charity while on earth. The same authors also assert that the Montanist sect ("whose chief sin was admitting post-biblical revelation") also practiced this baptism. The writers call them "universally recognized as Christian" (52, 108–110). But this is untrue. Montanism is recognized as an early heresy, and Montanists were not considered Christians "in good standing" by their orthodox counterparts.

This is not surprising considering what Montanists believed. They claimed that Jesus Christ and the Holy Spirit spoke in the voices of the leader, Montanus, considered the Paraclete, and his two prophetesses, Prisca and Maximilla.

and tradition,[11] we conclude rightly when we see this behavior as another aberration within a community of believers already soundly scolded by Paul for its lack of charity, its factionalism, its immorality, its abuse of the Eucharist and other matters.

Brett's Works toward Godhood

Mormon prophets have made it clear that every young Mormon male is to live worthily, that he may be called on a mission. Brett, now almost nineteen, dreads the thought of leaving his girlfriend, Amy, for such a long time, but he also knows how proud she would be to have a "missionary boyfriend." Before he can go on a mission he must receive the Melchizedek priesthood and his "temple endowments," ordinances necessary for missionary work and for eventual godhood.

Before he received the Melchizedek priesthood, he had to have another interview with his bishop to answer the same questions he had been asked prior to his temple recommend for baptism for the dead. He also answered that he considers himself worthy to receive the Melchizedek priesthood. The following Sunday,

---

Unconditional faith and absolute obedience to their orders were demanded. The world would end shortly upon Maximilla's death. Marriage was forbidden and martyrdom encouraged. Believers were not to avoid persecution. Severe asceticism was required of all members. Montanus asserted his superiority over Scripture. Some of the Church's earliest synods were convened in Asia Minor, and at them the Montanists were excommunicated. Pope Zephyrinus (199–217) condemned the movement, as did his successors, including Pope Innocent I (401–417). We are left to wonder in which "universe" the Montanists were recognized as Christian. (See *Encyclopedia of the Early Church*, vol. 1, 570–571.)

[11] James E. Talmage asserts in *The House of the Lord* that this form of baptism was "evidenced by numerous passages in the writings of the early Christian Fathers, and by later authorities on ecclesiastical history" (78). Yet the article "Baptism for the Dead: Ancient Sources" in the *Encyclopedia of Mormonism*, vol. 2, admits that there is no other New Testament or early Christian evidence to support the orthodoxy of proxy baptism.

during the elders' quorum meeting, Brett was ordained to this higher priesthood and set apart as an elder. The procedure was simple: Several men laid their hands on his head while the bishop pronounced a blessing. Brett was an elder, though that title was usually reserved to missionaries and general authorities. For now, he would continue to be called "Brother" rather than "Elder."

The Temple Endowment

Finally, Brett had another recommend interview, this one concerning his temple endowments. It occurred in two parts. He spoke first with the bishop, who asked the same questions as before. Then Brett met with the stake president, who asked the same questions once more, then pronounced Brett worthy to enter the temple to receive his endowments. He gave him two temple recommends; the first permitted Brett to receive his own temple ordinances, while the second—valid for one year—permitted him to enter any Mormon temple and do proxy work for the dead.

Since his family was planning to go to Salt Lake City on vacation, Brett went along to visit Mormonism's best-known temple for his first time "through" a temple. He and his family made the ten-hour drive to Salt Lake on a Wednesday. Brett was scheduled to receive his endowments at the 10:30 morning session the following day, though he was instructed to be at the temple by 9:00.

He had asked his father to be his "escort," and the two left the hotel at 8:45. Both were fasting and would eat nothing until after the ritual. Mrs. Ramsey, Kathy and Brett's two younger brothers would meet them later at the temple.

The Salt Lake temple, completed in 1893, dominates the ten-acre Temple Square. Brett and Mr. Ramsey approached the outer gate of the massive, walled square, passed through a turnstile and entered a small outer lobby of the temple annex. Several children and a few adults sat quietly on the couches along the wall. Three or four older men, assigned to verify the temple recommends of patrons, stood behind the lobby counter. After Brett and Mr. Ramsey were approved, they passed into a larger interior lobby, decorated with several paintings of Christ and religious scenes. Brett noticed a chapel off to the left; it was empty except for an organist quietly playing a hymn.

The women workers, most of them his grandmothers' age, all wore long, lacy white dresses that covered them to the neck, wrists and ankles. They wore white slippers as well. Everything was hushed.

His father led Brett downstairs to the men's locker room. There, he instructed Brett to remove all his clothes and put them in a locker. Brett was given a large, white "shield," a poncho-style covering to wear during the first part of the rituals. Barefoot and holding the shield closed at the side, Brett was taken to a small, curtained cubicle, where a worker washed and anointed various parts of Brett's body. Everything was done with modesty and reserve.[12]

Then, Brett was handed his temple garments. He was to put them on for the first time and would be required to wear them throughout his life.[13] Before leaving for Salt Lake, Brett had gone to a Beehive Clothing center, run by the Mormon church and located near the Mesa temple. There he had purchased several sets of undergarments, along with the white outer clothing and robes he would wear during the endowment ceremony.

These "garments," as they are called, are made of white fabric (cotton, nylon or polyester) and are similar to a man's tee-shirt and boxer shorts with legs that reach to the knees. (The woman's top is a kind of camisole.) This was the first time Brett had the garments out of their plastic bags.

Before coming to the temple, Brett had learned that the garments copy those the Lord had fashioned for Adam and Eve after their fall in the Garden. Endowed Mormons wear them out of obedience to God and as a way of demonstrating their faithfulness to the promises they make in the temple.

---

[12] Some anti-Mormon works obsess on this part of the temple ritual and portray it as a lurid rite. My own experience contradicts the graphic imaginings of such literature.

[13] Except when taking baths, etc.

Brett noticed a few small "embroidered" white markings on the shirt. One looked like a backwards capital L over the right breast; the other looked like a V over the left breast. Near the navel there was a straight line—and the same symbol appeared on the shorts over the right knee. Brett expected he would learn more about the symbols later in the temple. (He would, but only a little.)[14] Brett was also given the "new name," taken either from the Bible or the Book of Mormon, which he must keep sacred and tell no one until directed to do so.

Dressed in his temple undergarments, Brett returned to his locker where he found Mr. Ramsey waiting. The two got dressed in their temple outer clothing: White pants, shirt, tie, socks, and slippers. Afterward, they were brought to a small meeting room where about five other young men, with their escorts (probably their fathers), were waiting. Brett and the other young men wore paper nametags that indicated they were going through the endowment ceremony for the first time.

Soon, a distinguished-looking gentleman entered and introduced himself as President Andersen, a member of the temple presidency. He spoke to the group for about twenty minutes, reminding them of the sacred nature of the temple and the rites that take place in it and stressing that nothing concerning the temple ordinances may be discussed outside the temple walls.[15] He went on to urge them to be alert and attentive to the sights and sounds, explaining the temple practices to be the university of the Lord,

---

[14] We'll see that many changes have occurred over the years in temple practices. One practical change is the modification of the temple garments. Formerly, they were in the style of union suits with sleeves to the wrists and legs to the ankles for both men and women. Change in secular dress styles provides an impetus to such alterations. In *The Mysteries of Godliness: A History of Mormon Temple Worship*, David John Buerger details the several alterations made to the temple garments, along with other changes in temple ordinances. See in particular 133–171.

[15] While others use the term "secret," Latter-day Saints prefer "sacred" in referring to their temple rituals. "Sacred" things are not meant to be given to the unworthy. (The "sacred" Book of Mormon, however, is shared with anyone who asks for or accepts it.)

where he teaches his people all those things necessary for them to return to their heavenly home. He claimed that some have actually seen Jesus Christ within this, his house. Perhaps they, too, President Andersen stated, would prove worthy of a similar blessing.[16]

The temple is to be "a house of prayer, a house of fasting, a house of faith, a house of learning, a house of glory, a house of order, a house of God" (D&C 88:119).[17] President Andersen explained that temples are the holiest places on earth. They are built to last until the Second Coming of Jesus Christ and through his millennial reign. It is expected that when the Savior returns, the temples will be filled with patrons around the clock, since by God's plan the names of the dead previously unavailable will be made known and their temple work done.

At the conclusion of the president's talk, the candidates and their escorts were shown into the first of the rooms through which they would pass. This one had painted walls depicting land and water scenes. In it were about one hundred fifty seats, like those in a theater. The men silently sat on one side of the center aisle, the women on the other.

Throughout the ceremony, the words of the endowment were presented verbatim. The patrons were reminded again of the secrecy expected of them, and were told that the endowment ceremony would impose on them sacred obligations.

Brett was told that he was about to receive an endowment or

---

[16] Several accounts of supernatural sightings have been reported. In addition to alleged appearances of Jesus Christ, the U.S. Founding Fathers reportedly appeared in the temple to President Wilford Woodruff to ask him to have their temple work done for them (see "United States of America," *Encyclopedia of Mormonism*, 1496).

[17] "Let me give you the definition in brief. Your endowment is, to receive all those ordinances in the House of the Lord, which are necessary for you, after you have departed this life, to enable you to walk back to the presence of the Father, passing the angels who stand as sentinels, being enabled to give them the key words, the signs and tokens, pertaining to the Holy Priesthood, and gain your eternal exaltation in spite of earth and hell" (Brigham Young, *Discourses of Brigham Young*, 416).

"outpouring" of power from on high, characterized especially in the imparting of additional knowledge and intelligence.[18] His spiritual potency would be heightened by learning about the gods' eternal plan of creation and redemption and man's eventual divinization.

The process of the world's creation was presented, followed by an explanation of God's plans to redeem men and have them reach eternal exaltation. In the Salt Lake temple, this is communicated to the attendees by a stage performance with live actors representing God the Father, Jesus, the Holy Ghost, Adam, Eve, and Lucifer. In most temples a video is used.

The play's message is straightforward and greatly contradicts Scripture. Elohim, Jehovah, and Michael replace the Father, Son, and Holy Spirit as creators. Michael, taking on mortality, becomes Adam. Adam and Eve are given two contradictory commandments: Don't eat the fruit, yet be fruitful and multiply (Mormons allege that one had to be transgressed in order to fulfill the other, meaning that God put Adam and Eve in a double-bind situation). They choose to disobey one that they may fulfill the other and bring pre-existent spirits into the world. The result of their transgression is banishment from paradise and a life of toil.

By heeding the heavenly messengers sent by Elohim, the first parents and all their descendants may make their way through this lone and dreary world and return to the Heavenly Father. There, they will continue to progress, becoming gods themselves, creating, populating and ruling over their own worlds. To accomplish this eventual exaltation, faithful members make covenants and surround their promises with handclasps, gestures and code words that are to be kept sacred and secret.

During the endowment, the participants don various ritual garments and receive and repeat four special "names, signs, and tokens" of the Mormon priesthoods. The signs and tokens are various handclasps and arm gestures. Before the more recent changes in the ordinance, Mormons would also make verbal oaths and

---

[18] *Encyclopedia of Mormonism*, vol. 4.

various hand movements swearing to have their lives taken if they should reveal any of these secrets to outsiders.[19]

The climax came when Brett successfully duplicated all the names and handclasps he had been taught. He was thereby found worthy to enter the Lord's presence. The veil to the "celestial room" was parted and an actor representing the Lord took him by the hand and drew him through.

The celestial room resembles the lobby of a better hotel, with pale colors, chandeliers, vases containing artificial flowers, painted molding, wall mirrors and many stuffed chairs and couches. After they have been admitted to the celestial room, patrons sit or stand quietly in small groups. Voices are kept to a whisper. Mr. and Mrs. Ramsey passed through the veil shortly after Brett, eager to hear his reactions. There is no set time to remain in the celestial room. Some patrons spend a minute or two and then return to their lockers; others stay longer.

Mormons hope and expect that Brett's first-time experience in the temple will be positive and compelling. Having once partaken of the beauty and sacred character of the endowment presentation, Brett should be eager to return often and go through the same ceremony on behalf of the dead. Many LDS members make it a point to attend the temple regularly—monthly or even weekly. Those who live at a great distance from a temple may plan their annual vacations around a visit to one.

Reactions to the temple endowment vary greatly. On the one hand, the Mormon member has become used to the rather stolid "worship" that takes place at Sunday meetings. There is no liturgy, no adornment of either the chapel or the presider, no feast days.[20] All are allowed to these meetings, and only non-members

---

[19] Prior to 1990, the character playing Lucifer told how he would "buy up" not only priests but popes to use in his work of turning men from God's true church.

[20] Mormons attend church on Christmas only if it falls on a Sunday. Moreover, Mormons do not attend church on Easter Sunday if it falls on the first Sunday of April, since the church's annual conference is held that weekend.

and those under church discipline are forbidden the bread and water. On the other hand, only the "worthy" are allowed entrance into the temple. There they find a series of rituals—words, gestures, and clothing—revealed, Mormons believe, by the Lord to Joseph Smith and subsequent prophets. Some find this contrast surprising and puzzling.

Before the 1990 changes in the temple ordinances, some Mormons were disturbed by elements in the endowment ceremonies. These included the gestures (and, before 1927, words)[21] of slashing one's throat, chest, and abdomen as penalties for revealing temple secrets; portraying Christian ministers as the hirelings of Satan; and the "five points of fellowship."[22] These were eliminated in 1990. Though the LDS church claims that it does nothing without members' consent, the above changes were made by the First Presidency and Quorum of the Twelve Apostles, without consultation of the Mormon laity. The rank and file learned of the changes when they attended temples in late April 1990.

Though these most troubling aspects were removed (some claim as a result of non-Mormon pressure), I personally was disturbed by the rote repetition of the teachings, the solemn promises not to reveal any of the tokens, names, and signs, and the general lack of worship. My reaction after my own endowment, and after the dozen or more sessions I later attended, was always the same: "So what? Is that all there is?"

Throughout the first year of my membership, Mormon friends had extolled the temple as the holiest place on earth. "Wait and see," they promised. "When you go, you'll feel like you're at

---

There is no Advent, Lent or any other liturgical season. Holy Thursday and Good Friday are not observed. (This is not to say, however, that Latter-day Saints ignore the realities these feasts commemorate.)

[21] See Buerger, 141.

[22] Before 1990, all patrons who spoke with "the Lord" through the veil were required to make contact with him at five points on the body: inside of right foot to "the Lord's" right foot, inside of knee to inside of knee, breast to breast, hand to back, and mouth to ear. Some patrons, particularly women, found this upsetting.

a Solemn High Mass! The rooms are ornate, the different ceremonies breathe holiness and the spiritual splendor is beyond compare!" I believed it, expected it. And I was terribly disappointed.

The temple ceremonies are neither as vile as their detractors allege nor as spiritually nourishing as their proponents promise. Frankly, they're boring, even silly at times, and in past years they could be shocking.

James E. Talmage captured the official stand of the LDS church, "No jot, iota, or tittle of the temple rites is otherwise than uplifting and sanctifying" (*The House of the Lord*, 84).

If this were the case, why has the ceremony been revised so many times? Was the former agreement to have one's tongue, heart, and bowels ripped out an uplifting and sanctifying component? If so, why has it been removed? Formerly, Satan promised to pay the Christian minister several thousand dollars a year to preach "orthodox religion" and thus lure souls away from God. Why has that part been removed if it contributed to the holiness of Latter-day Saints? Why are women no longer required to press their bodies against those of unknown men if such a practice served to elevate the spiritual sensitivities of the participants?

No Mormon believes that receiving his endowment and learning the handgrips, arm gestures, and code names is sufficient to enter God's eternal presence. Righteous living and perseverance in the LDS faith are equally important. But not more important, since those not endowed will never return to the Heavenly Father, regardless of their sanctity. The "sacred secrets" learned in the temple are as necessary to eventual salvation as is a holy and faithful life. Yet the endowment ritual places great emphasis on never revealing the secret tokens, names, and signs of the Mormon priesthoods. I could only wonder why there was so much insistence on what, objectively, seemed inconsequential.

The only prayer offered during the endowment generally focuses on a brief thanksgiving and a lengthy request for divine blessings. I can't remember any time when the prayer included pure praise of God or simple contrition for sin. This latter, perhaps, can be explained by the fact that those who attend the temple are considered worthy to stand in God's presence and serve him.

"It is not proper to go to the temple for the purpose of getting the strength to live righteously, but rather to acquire the strength and determination to live the commandments so that there can be total worthiness when you go to the temple," according to *The Teachings of Spencer W. Kimball* (536).

God does not appear to be the focus of temple work. The participant is. A member goes first to the temple for himself, to insure that he receive the equipment necessary to make it to the celestial kingdom and eventual godhood. Subsequent visits focus on dead ancestors. Going to the temple is not about worshipping God, which may not be surprising. (Who would want to worship a God that makes entrance into his presence contingent on knowing secret handshakes and passwords?) But such work is a necessity for achieving one's own godhood, as made clear by Joseph Fielding Smith (note the superlatives):

> Salvation in behalf of the dead is the binding or sealing of the hearts of the fathers and children, the welding link. . . . It is the most glorious subject belonging to the everlasting gospel. . . . It is the greatest responsibility in this world that God has laid upon us—to seek after our dead. . . . It is obligatory to man. . . . Without it the whole earth and its inhabitants would be smitten with a curse. . . . If we neglect it, it is at the peril of our own salvation. . . . Through it we become saviors on Mount Zion, and may save multitudes of our kin. . . . We, without our dead, and our dead without us, cannot be saved with a perfect salvation. . . . We cannot lightly pass this doctrine over as pertaining to our salvation [*Doctrines of Salvation* 1:268].

Over ninety percent of temple endowments are performed in behalf of the dead. Members who thus become their "saviors"[23]

---

[23] See Doctrine and Covenants 103:9; Obadiah 1:21. Also see *Doctrines of Salvation* 2:157 and *Journal of Discourses* 18:213.

are encouraged to follow the rituals carefully because the rites have become familiar. The hope is that the patrons who receive temple ordinances for the dead will be reminded of and strengthened in their own temple covenants.

Some critics of Mormon temple rituals assert that the ceremonies are rife with satanic influence, sexual debauchery, and anti-Christian propaganda.[24] Aside from the pre-1990 depiction of all Christian churches as minions of Satan (admittedly a grave error of both fact and public relations), there is no basis for any of these assertions.

Rather, the most grievous defect of the temple is found in its misrepresentation. Members had assured me, "We know the sacrament meetings can get noisy and distracting. Yes, the talks are often poorly prepared and boring. And yes, it seems like the same things are said repeatedly. That's because Mormons have a 'plain-Jane' religion. We don't have any decorations in our churches, no candles, no incense; our leaders wear no special vestments; we concentrate on encouraging one another to be faithful to the Mormon religion. But wait till you go to the temple! It will be so different. It's the closest to Heaven you can come in this life. You'll be overwhelmed by its beauty and significance. You'll never be the same!"

This was false advertising, even if unintentional. By force of will I brought myself to the temple over a dozen times, each time hoping that I would find the spiritual nourishment I had craved since my Mormon baptism. I fasted and prayed before attending the temple sessions, wanting to make myself receptive to the enlightenment promised me there. I was not conscious of any sin or failing that would block the influences of the Lord while I was in his house. But each time I left the temple with the same feeling:

---

[24] Such, for instance, is the contention of Edward Decker in his inflammatory *The God Makers* series of books and videos. Decker is an excommunicated Mormon who became a Fundamentalist Protestant. His work receives acceptance by those who share his conspiratorial and sensationalistic notions. His research is shallow and he twists the facts to suit his point of view.

"This does not speak to me of Christ. This is not spiritual. This is not enough."

When asked for my reactions to the temple, I gave a safe answer: "It's something that you have to let sink in." The more I attended, though, the more I came to realize that I couldn't do this for the rest of my life. If this was the best the Mormon church could offer to feed my soul, I would starve. And this marked the beginning of my doubts.

That the temple experience could be the spiritual summit of Mormonism is conceivable only if nothing else were available to Mormons. The temple rituals are no match for even the simplest Catholic Mass offered with faith and reverence. Aside from the infinite value of the Eucharistic Sacrifice, there is an enormous difference between these respective "pinnacles" of worship.

For the Mormon, temple work is undertaken as a means to advancement, for oneself or for a dead person. The central figure is the patron. He has declared himself worthy and has been deemed such. For about an hour and a half, the patron listens to the instructions, makes the prescribed responses and promises, receives and gives the required hand signals and names and dons the ritual clothing. In return for proper performance, he is promised exaltation as a god. He contemplates this eternal delight by being brought through a veil (curtain) and into the celestial room.

How different the liturgy or "work of the people" at Mass, the central act of worship for Catholics! Here, Christ and his Father are the focus. The Lord is the center, the source and goal of worship. Imperfect, striving members come to the Eucharist, confessing their sinfulness to God and one another. In this house of prayer for all people, praise is raised together in adoration of the one Lord. It is to *his* service that the congregation dedicates itself. The only perfect participant is the Sacrifice himself, whom all adore and to whom all submit. In place of self-aggrandizement is the Lord's self-abasement. The Catholic is finally sent forth from Mass, not to contemplate his virtue, but to remember his need; not to enjoy his own excellence, but to love and serve the Lord and his people.

Temple Sealings

The final temple ordinance is sealing. Should Brett persevere as a faithful Mormon, and if he chooses Amy or another suitable Mormon woman, he and his fiancée will enter into what the Mormons call the "new and eternal covenant" of celestial marriage. Only endowed members with valid recommends may be married in the temple "for all eternity."

The ceremony is a simple one and takes place in one of the small rooms clustered about the celestial room. Bride and groom generally go through an endowment session first; usually it is for the bride's own endowment. Dressed in their temple robes, the couple enters a sealing room. These may hold anywhere from ten to fifty persons. There is a small, upholstered "altar" in the center, surrounded by a kneeler. Only those family members and close friends who have temple recommends may attend.

In each temple several male workers have been officially designated as sealers. They are additionally given authority by the state to join the couple in a legal marriage. These men bind the couple in a marital union that, Mormons claim, survives death and endures throughout eternity. At the resurrection, if they have been faithful Mormons, they will be clothed in glory and will be given kingdoms, powers, and exaltations. They will be gods.

The sealing of one spouse to the other is also performed for the dead. Just as a living person may serve as proxy and be baptized, confirmed, washed, anointed, ordained, and endowed on behalf of the deceased, a man and woman may also kneel at the altar in the sealing room and be "married" for all eternity in behalf of dead ancestors or others. This is a common practice among Mormons who do work on their family trees extending back to the generations who lived before the church was formed. While the dead being sealed to each other were usually husband and wife on earth, those serving as proxy for the sealing need not even know each other. Remember, unless a person has been sealed in the everlasting covenant of celestial marriage, he or she cannot enter into the highest heaven and progress to eventual godhood. It is thus incumbent on the living to see that their deceased ancestors receive eternal spouses, even if the spouses did not know each other in life or even live during the same period.

A second form of sealing is that of children to parents. Children born to a couple after the couple's temple marriage need not be sealed to their parents. They are considered "born under the covenant." Those born to parents who were not sealed at the time of the child's birth, but who later were married in the temple, must be sealed to their parents. The child is brought, dressed in white, to the sealing room, where an invocation is made and he is sealed to his parents.

Children are sealed to deceased parents, as well. Thus, once my deceased father and mother had been baptized, endowed, and sealed by proxy, I could have sealed myself to them and have had them sealed to their parents, provided my grandparents' temple work had also been done. The Mormon plan is to seal the generations one to another, joining all within the family of man back to Adam and Eve.

All of this is either unnecessary or ineffective. Sealing of parents to children is unnecessary because, in reality, a person always remains the child of his parents and will not be separated from them in heaven unless he or they fail to attain heaven. No special sealing has to be done to keep parents and children together in the afterlife. The parties simply need to be saved. Sealing of spouses to each other is ineffective because Jesus explicitly stated that marriage is an institution pertaining only to this life, "The children of this world marry, and are given in marriage: But they which shall be accounted worthy to obtain that world, and the resurrection from the dead, neither marry, nor are given in marriage: Neither can they die any more: for they are equal unto the angels; and are the children of God, being the children of the resurrection" (Luke 20:34-36).

In the next life, there will be no marriage—and no reproduction (the principal end of marriage). Instead, humans will exist in an immortal state like that of the angels, where reproduction (and thus marriage) is not necessary to "perpetuate the species." Just as Jesus had a gender in his resurrected body, yet remained celibate, we will still have our genders in our resurrected bodies, but we will no longer need to use them to reproduce.

Mormons attempt to get around this teaching of Christ by saying it applies only to those who were not sealed in celestial marriages, but Jesus said no such thing. His statement was prompted by a question of whose wife a particular (hypothetical) woman would be at the resurrection, and if some humans *would* be married at the resurrection, he would have said, "It depends. Was she 'sealed in the temple' to a husband or not?" Instead, he gave a universal reply concerning all humans in heaven.

Marriage is specifically indicated to be an institution of *this world*, for Jesus contrasts "the children of *this world*" with "they which shall be accounted worthy to obtain that world, and the resurrection from the dead." He tells us that "The children of *this world* marry" but "the children of the resurrection" neither "marry nor are given in marriage."

Jesus is making categorical statements about the children of this world and the children of the next. He is not talking about just one set of people in the next, and, in particular, he is not talking about a set of unfortunate people who were lucky enough to get into the next world by the skin of their teeth, yet were unlucky (or unworthy or unmotivated) enough that they never entered into a celestial marriage. Indeed, he stresses *the worthiness* of the people in question, saying that they are those "which shall be accounted *worthy* to obtain that world, and the resurrection from the dead" and noting that they are now "equal unto the angels, and are the children of God, being the children of the resurrection."

Mormon temple marriages are thus ineffective rites that do nothing regarding the next world. They merely insult the teaching of Christ, which promises a state more blessed than that of marriage. Spouses who are in heaven will still be together, and they will love and be loved by each other more intensely than they ever did on earth, but they will have been elevated to a higher state, being the children of the resurrection, where marriage and reproduction are no longer needed.

The Masonic Connection

Freemasonry is a naturalistic religion claiming about six million members. Though perhaps known today mainly as a fraternal and philanthropic fellowship, the Masonic Lodge couches its beliefs and practices in vague religious discourse unamenable to fundamental Christian beliefs. Throughout its modern history, lodges have also been active in anticlerical and anti-Christian movements.

Some critics of Mormonism place heavy emphasis on what they imagine are the obscene and devil-inspired rites of the temple. For instance, on the exterior of some temples there are carvings of the sun, moon, and stars. Extremist opponents of the LDS faith take the sunstones, or carvings of the sun with a face superimposed, to be representations of the ancient pagan god Baal, while they see in the inverted stars the face of the devil.[25] Neither has the sinister meaning such critics imagine.

The features that draw the severest denunciations, however, are those supposedly imported from Freemasonry. I have found many of the claims overblown. The link between Mormonism and Freemasonry is much looser than many "conspiracy theorists" in Fundamentalist circles would lead one to believe. Nevertheless, there are Masonic elements in Mormonism, especially in its temple rituals.

McConkie stated that the essential portions of Mormon temple worship have existed throughout human history. When the church was restored by Joseph Smith, the Lord revealed these sacred elements to him.[26] Smith also claimed to "translate" portions of the temple rituals from the same papyri that he said contained the patriarch Abraham's writings.[27]

If Smith received the contents of the temple endowment by divine revelation, what's the reason for the strong similarities between those rituals and Masonic temple practices? A comparison

---

[25] Chuck Sackett, *What's Going on in There?* 61.
[26] *Mormon Doctrine*, 779.
[27] See the chapters on the Book of Mormon and other Mormon scripture.

of the tokens, names, signs, and former penalties reveals a similarity too close to be coincidental. Both ceremonies employ the symbols of compass, square, and ruler. Aprons and other vestments are worn in both. There are differences between rituals used in a Masonic Lodge and those used in Mormon temples, but that is to be expected since Masonry and Mormonism are separate institutions.[28] The number of similarities, however, is so striking that Mormons do not attempt to claim they are due to mere coincidence.

Faithful Mormons claim that the Masonic rituals are a shadowy copy of true temple worship, which Smith restored. Believing the temple ceremonies to be as old as mankind, Mormons claim that the version used by the Masons is a corrupted form of that used in Solomon's Temple and others. Just as the Catholic Church is a perverted version of Christianity, now corrected and restored by Smith, so the Masonic rites are an adulterated rendition of the divine temple ritual corrected and restored by an inspired American prophet.

Others—including active Mormon thinkers—note Smith's own involvement with Masonry as the likely source for some temple material. On March 16, 1842, Smith noted, "I was with the Masonic Lodge and rose to the sublime degree."[29] Several of his close associates, including his brother Hyrum, had been long-time Masons. Less than two months later, the prophet introduced the temple endowment ceremony.[30]

---

[28] The article "Freemasonry and the Temple" in *Encyclopedia of Mormonism*, vol. 2, however, notes, "The philosophy and major tenets of Freemasonry are not fundamentally incompatible with the teaching, theology, and doctrines of the Latter-day Saints." This is not surprising, since the founder of Mormonism and many early Mormons were Masons.

[29] *History of the Church*, 4:552.

[30] According to the Mormon publication *Times and Seasons* (July 15, 1844), Joseph and Hyrum "were both Masons in good standing" at the time of their deaths. Other Mormon authors acknowledge that Joseph, immediately preceding his death at the hands of a lynch mob, gave the Masonic signal of distress by raising his arms and crying, "O Lord, my God, is there no help for the widow's son?" See *Mormonism—Shadow or Reality?* 484-485 for references.

Mormons who admit these facts offer an explanation. While Smith was working out the details of the endowment, he drew on his knowledge of Scripture and Masonry. So what if he adopted elements from the Masonic rites? That could only mean that these rituals were the best way he knew to convey Mormonism's deeper, more spiritual teachings.

This is not unreasonable. The explanation does, however, seem to contradict the more prevalent Mormon belief that Smith "received" the endowment through divine revelation.[31] In any case, the presence of Masonic elements within the Mormon temple is sufficient to convince some that Mormonism draws its power from non-Christian, malevolent forces.

It also puts Mormons in the uncomfortable position of being unable to dismiss Masonic claims to antiquity. Mormons are compelled to accept some of Masonry's more tongue-in-cheek claims regarding the origins of its rituals. Freemasonry originated in the eighteenth-century Enlightenment as a men's club that mocked established religion and jokingly claimed an ancient, secret heritage for itself.

Later Masons often took these claims at face value, and Smith, as a man purveying his own allegedly ancient secrets, bought into the idea of Masonry as an authentic transmitter of ancient ritual. He then incorporated into Mormonism's most sacred ceremonies elements of what was originally a set of parody rituals intended to mock solemn religious ceremonies. This puts Mormons today in a difficult position since they neither wish to acknowledge that their most sacred rituals are partly based on satires of religious ceremonies nor to acknowledge that their founder was taken in by phony claims to antiquity of an organization that so recently appeared.

Consequently, the *Encyclopedia of Mormonism* is forced into the embarrassing position of suggesting that the origins of Freema-

---

[31] The same quandary is presented in the descriptions of how Smith "translated" the Book of Mormon. Was he given the translation perfectly and directly, as he and others claimed, or did he have to "work at it," making the most of his own knowledge and insight? See the chapters on Mormon scripture.

sonry are ancient and downplaying the actual, eighteenth-century origins of the movement: "There is no universal agreement concerning when Freemasonry began. Some historians trace the order's origin to Solomon, Enoch or even Adam. Others argue that while some Masonic symbolism may be ancient, as an institution it began in the Middle Ages or later" (op. cit.).

The Catholic Church opposes Masonry, a stance that was reaffirmed by Cardinal Joseph Ratzinger, Prefect of the Congregation for the Doctrine of the Faith, in 1983:

> [T]he negative position of the church in regard to Masonic associations remains unchanged, since their basic principles have always been considered irreconcilable with the teachings of the church, and consequently, membership in them remains forbidden. The faithful who belong to Masonic associations are in a state of grave sin and may not receive Holy Communion.[32]

In evaluating what goes on in a Mormon temple, some writers, especially Fundamentalists, go to great lengths to look for salacious elements in the endowment ceremony or to identify occult, satanic or Masonic elements in the rituals. Most claims are without foundation, though we have noted that there are some Masonic elements in the rituals. At the most basic level those who obsess about such things are missing the forest for the trees, since the critic doesn't *need* to scrutinize every detail of the text or rituals in an effort to unmask the grave theological problems with the rituals.

The flaws within Mormon theology itself condemn the entire premise on which the temples are built. In reality, there is one God, not three. The Son of God is not a mere messenger or "gofer" for the Father. Michael was not a pre-existing spirit son of God who became Adam. The first parents were not given impossible and contradictory commands by the Father. Peter, James and John did not have a separate existence before their human conception, as they are depicted in the temple endowment ceremony. To enter

---

[32] *Declaration on Masonic Associations*, Nov. 26, 1983. See Brother Charles Madden, O.F.M. Conv., *Freemasonry*.

his presence, God requires lives of faith and obedience, not the perfect repetition of code words and secret gestures. Men, even perfected men, do not become gods. At death, God judges each person and his eternal dwelling is decided. No one, no matter how sincere, can change or affect that just decision by performing ordinances on behalf of the dead.

No matter how they are marketed, the doctrines of Mormonism oppose the truth. *That's* what needs to be shown. One does not need to spend a lot of time tracing obscure connections and so end up "majoring in the minors."

8. All Is Well?

A signature hymn of Mormon churches is "Come, Come, Ye Saints." The Mormon Tabernacle Choir includes it in many of its album recordings. It's often heard on the LDS Sunday morning broadcast, "Music and the Spoken Word." The refrain "All is well, all is right" is repeated throughout, like a form of divine affirmation of the rectitude of the Mormon church.

Neither Christian Scripture, nor two millennia of historic Christian teaching, nor even earlier Mormon scriptures and teachings support the beliefs and practices of the contemporary Mormon church.

Still, the appeal Mormonism makes for itself in the contemporary world is not based on a sober exposition of Scripture, theology or history. To the degree those are brought into Mormonism's missionary outreach at all, they are secondary. The primary way in which the Mormon church tries to reach out to contemporary culture is by creating a public persona characterized by family values, neighborliness, and patriotism. This makes it appropriate for us to take a brief look to see if "all is well" among the Mormons, as the hymn declares. Do the facts support the public image the Mormon church tries to project?

Before we begin, it is important to state that by discussing the failings of the Mormon church and its members, we are in no way suggesting their sins are unique among the world's religions. Nor is it implied that Catholics outshine Mormons or others in the ethical areas cited.[1] The point is not to place blame on individual Mormon lay people.

---

[1] Indeed, the fault can be *graver* among Catholics, since they have a clearer moral standard. Mormons who practice contraception, who commit abortion and who divorce and remarry may be doing so with their church's approval. Catholics who do the same things do so in violation of the Church's teachings, making them more accountable for their behavior.

There are two points this chapter makes: (1) Mormon moral theology comes up lacking. When faced with a changing world, the Mormon response is not to continue proclaiming God's unchanging moral truth, but to revise, reword, and accommodate —to appear righteous while holding to doctrines of iniquity.[2] (2) The Mormon church is being deceptive when it tries to create a pro-family image that suggests Mormon family life is superior to that of average Americans. Despite the slick Mormon television and radio advertisements, the rule of the day should be *caveat emptor*—let the buyer beware.

Abortion

The Mormon church ostensibly asserts that abortion—the elective termination of pregnancy—is "one of the most... sinful practices of this day."[3] In commenting on Doctrine and Covenants 59:6 ("thou shalt not kill"), former church president Spencer W. Kimball observed, "Abortion, the taking of life, is one of the most grievous of sins. We have repeatedly affirmed the position of the Church in unalterably opposing *all abortions*.... Abortion is a calamity... one of the most revolting and sinful practices of this day.... This Church of Jesus Christ opposes abortion and counsels all members not to submit to nor participate in any abortion, in any way, for convenience or to hide sins.... Those encouraging abortion share guilt."[4]

Ezra Taft Benson, Kimball's successor, stated that the Lord does indeed teach his people in these days against such a "damnable practice" as abortion. In responding to nonmembers and dissident members of the Mormon Church, President Benson scolded, "[T]hey do not believe that God reveals His will today to the Church through prophets of God.... All objections, whether they be on abortion... or other subjects, basically hinge on

---

[2] See Matthew 23:27-28.
[3] *General Handbook of Instructions*, 11-4.
[4] *Teachings of Spencer W. Kimball*, 189; emphasis added.

whether Joseph Smith and his successors were and are prophets of God receiving divine revelation."[5]

Prolific writer and current LDS apostle Neal A. Maxwell noted that abortion is an "obvious manifestation" of "[i]ndifference, insensitivity, and cruelty"[6] and aptly described abortion as "that Buchenwald for babies."[7]

Current Mormon prophet, seer, and revelator Gordon B. Hinckley has noted that life is a gift that "is sacred under any circumstance."[8]

Abortion is just such a heinous crime because it attacks the gift of life given by the Lord, and the Mormon church does at least *publicly* declare the sanctity of human life, citing Scripture and the teachings of its prophets and apostles in support of its position.

For example, when prospective and current members are taught from the church-published text *Gospel Principles* (1992), they read, "If a child is conceived by those who break the law of chastity, they may be tempted to commit another abominable sin: abortion" (251).

Church members preparing for a temple, or celestial, marriage read in their student manual the words of President James E. Faust, "One of the most evil myths of our day is that a woman who has joined hands with God in creation can destroy that creation because she claims the right to control her own body. Since the life within her is not her own, how can she justify its termination and deflect that life from an earth which it may never inherit?"[9]

The teaching is clear. Mormon prophets, apostles, and theologians recognize that the unborn child is, in fact, a "child" (Kimball, 188), a "human" (Benson, 296); that the child's life is a gift from the Lord; and that the taking of such life is a "heinous crime" (Kimball, 274), "a serious sin" (Kimball, 189), a "damnable prac-

---

[5] *Teachings of Ezra Taft Benson*, 539, 61.
[6] *Wherefore Ye Must Press Forward*, 79.
[7] *Notwithstanding My Weakness*, 93.
[8] *Improvement Era*, Dec. 1970, 72.
[9] *Achieving a Celestial Marriage*, 144.

tice" (Benson, 539). The current *General Handbook of Instructions* for Mormon leaders calls abortion "one of the most revolting and sinful practices of this day" (11-4).

It is a credit to Mormons in Utah that their state has a low abortion rate. According to the Alan Guttmacher Institute, a national abortion advocacy and monitoring group, Utah has only nine abortions per year per thousand women (age 15-44), compared to a national average of twenty-six.[10] We wish to do nothing but praise Utah's low abortion rate, and we wish the people of Utah all possible success in eliminating abortion in their state.

But the rate in Utah might be even lower if not for church teachings that *endorse* abortion in particular situations. These teachings are not publicly advertised by Mormon leaders, but they are privately discussed with people in "problem pregnancy" situations.

The point we wish to make is not a statistical one, but a theological one. It is also moral, for the Mormon church opens itself to the charge of grave hypocrisy when it presents itself to the public as unabashedly pro-family and pro-life. There is an underside to this righteous self-portrait, and further examination of the same sources cited above yields evidence of serious cracks in Mormonism's pro-life foundation.

Yes, Presidents Kimball, Benson and Hinckley condemn the practice of abortion, stating that the LDS church decries it. Except . . .

The Mormon church places itself in an untenable position: It opposes abortion because abortion takes the life of an innocent human child, a gift from the Lord, making abortion a selfish, cruel act, comparable to murder in gravity. Yet Mormon leadership consistently allows for exceptions. These exceptions are spelled out by the leaders cited above. *Gospel Principles*, a manual of belief and practice published by the Church of Jesus Christ of Latter-day Saints, stated in its 1979 and 1988 editions, "There is no excuse

---

[10] From the monograph "Contraception Counts: State-by-State Information," Alan Guttmacher Institute, 1998.

for abortion unless the life of the mother is seriously threatened" (243 and 241, respectively).

Benson and Hinckley, apostles and presidents when these two editions were approved, apparently also gave their permission to the much more permissive stand presented in the 1992 version, which reads, "There is seldom any excuse for abortion. The only exceptions are when: 1. Pregnancy has resulted from incest or rape. 2. The life or health of the woman is in jeopardy in the opinion of competent medical authority; or 3. The fetus is known, by competent medical authority, to have severe defects that will not allow the baby to survive beyond birth" (*Gospel Principles*, 1992, 251).

Men and women faced with any of the above circumstances may submit to or cooperate in abortion only after consulting with each other and their bishop or branch president and receiving divine confirmation through prayer. (See *General Handbook of Instructions* [30943], 11-4.) This 1992 policy change liberalizes those of earlier years, so it turns out that Mormon theology and history are not the only areas revamped to suit contemporary standards. Now, while outwardly trying to maintain a pro-life image, the Mormon church ends up collaborating with the call for liberal abortion "rights" and becomes complicit in the performing of abortion, since its bishops and branch presidents are brought into situations to approve abortions—and with "inner witness" from the Holy Spirit, no less!

This apparently includes late-term and "partial-birth" abortions. No distinction is made in the relevant documents concerning the stage of pregnancy or the method by which the child is killed. A Mormon parent's "health" may not exhibit alarming distress until late in the pregnancy. Or a fetal exam may have been delayed, revealing only in the last few months the presence of some "fatal" illness. Or perhaps the Lord was late in answering the prayers of the sincere Mormon importuning him for advice about whether or not to kill the child.[11]

---

[11] We must assume the Lord would answer prayers about abortion in the same way he answers prayers concerning the truths of the Book of Mormon

An unborn child is an innocent human, regardless of the circumstances of his conception, and this is what makes abortion so grave a crime against humanity. Though tragic, the crimes of rape or incest are only exacerbated, and the mother's anguish only intensified, by adding the crime of abortion. Since LDS authorities admit that the unborn is human, regardless of the "quality" of his or her pre-born life, no alleged deficiency in this "quality" can justify killing him or her. The same applies to the so-called "either/or" dilemma, in which the mother's life is *supposedly* in danger.[12] One is never justified in doing evil that good may come of it (Rom. 3:8).

It should be noted that the Mormon position allows for abortions in cases where the mother's "health" is in jeopardy. But what health? Physical only? Or emotional as well? What is the definition of "jeopardy"? All mothers know that pregnancy inevitably brings "health" problems, if nothing more than nausea, varicose veins, weight gain and other forms of discomfort. The "mother's health" loophole is the greatest entrée to abortion.

Before the infamous 1973 Supreme Court decision *Roe v. Wade* legalized abortion in the United States, such "mother's health" clauses were routinely used by pro-abortion physicians and psychologists as a legal pretext to give abortions to women whose health was in no actual jeopardy. There were informal "old-boy networks" among physicians and psychologists whereby a woman seeking an abortion could be referred for a "second opinion" to a physician or psychiatrist who could be counted on to rubber-stamp the application for an abortion on "health" grounds.

In some cases (such as the Supreme Court case *Doe v. Bolton*,

---

and the LDS church: The seeker just *feels* his decision is right and righteous.

[12] The number of cases in which (1) the unborn's presence poses a significant risk to the mother's health, (2) the problem can be detected early enough and (3) the unborn cannot be safely delivered is small. Almost always either (1) the risk is exaggerated by doctors not schooled in a pro-life ethic, (2) the problem cannot be detected before it is too late (thus most tubal pregnancies are not detected before the child is so large that a rupture occurs), or (3) the baby can be given a premature but safe delivery—or at least a delivery which does not directly and intentionally kill the child.

released in 1973 as a companion case to *Roe v. Wade*), "health" was even defined so broadly as to include the mother's *financial* health! What guarantee do the shifting sands of Mormonism give that individual bishops and branch presidents (let alone future apostles and prophets) will not so interpret the "health" exception as the Mormon church continues its slide to conform to contemporary non-Christian morals and attitudes?

The theological foundations of Mormonism's ostensible opposition to abortion are so shaky that Mormons will say that the point at which the spirit enters the body is not certain, that it has not been revealed by God, making it possible for some future Mormon prophet to whisk away all opposition to abortion by defining the point of ensoulment as birth or afterward.

Even today, without a "revelation" about the point of ensoulment, Mormon leaders are acting in bad faith by permitting abortion. They admit that the child either has or may well have a soul, yet they permit killing him anyway! The Mormon position on abortion is disingenuous. At least most "liberals" who favor abortion have the tactical sense to convince themselves and others that the unborn is a non-human blob, a thing of no consequence.

The Mormon church claims to provide contemporary man with clear moral guidance. However, its leaders do not have the power of biblical prophets, who roused men to repent and reform. As the Mormon church's many doctrinal flip-flops indicate, Mormon "prophets" base their "revelations" on the collective opinions of their internal governing authority, on social pragmatism and on political astuteness. They are no different from those in our society wanting to water down and revise morals so that they may call evil good.

A statement made by the LDS First Presidency under David O. McKay, "which continues to represent the attitude and position of the [LDS] church," claimed that "no definite statement has been made by the Lord one way or another regarding the crime of abortion."[13]

---

[13] Quoted in *Sacred Truths of the Doctrine and Covenants*, vol. 1, 290.

The Catholic Church, however, has known and taught the mind and will of the Lord concerning abortion for two thousand years. One can only turn away in disgust from the Mormon church's dithering on the necessity of protecting unborn humans. How much more clear and forthright is the Catholic Church's stand on the right to life: "Human life must be respected and protected absolutely from the moment of conception. From the first moment of his existence, a human being must be recognized as having the rights of a person—among which is the inviolable right of every innocent being to life" (*Catechism of the Catholic Church* 2270).

This states unambiguously what God has revealed concerning the sanctity of the unborn. There is no possibility of finessing this statement to jibe with modern, secular mores. The right of the unborn to life exists from the moment he exists—that is, conception. It is absolute and inviolable.

Supported by Scripture and tradition, the Catholic Church has faithfully believed in and taught the personhood of the unborn (see Luke 1:41; Jer. 1:5; Job 10:8-12; Ps. 22:10). The Church Fathers, even from the time of the apostles, proclaimed the sin of abortion (*Didache*, 2:2 [c. A.D. 80]; Hippolytus, *Refutation of All Heresies*, 9:12 [A.D. 222]; *Letter of St. Basil the Great*, 188:8 [A.D. 374]).

Far from compromising its divine commission to speak the truth in season and out, the Catholic Church continues to raise its voice in the wilderness of moral collapse. It is not ashamed of testifying to its Lord and his commands. It knows that it must speak the things men need to hear, whether they are "popular" or "politically correct."

All righteous men and women should take heed of Paul's command, "Do not be conformed to this world but be transformed by the renewal of your mind" (Rom. 12:2). Mormon authorities seeking to appease the spirit of the age particularly need to heed Paul's warning, "[T]he time is coming when people will not endure sound teaching, but having itching ears they will accumulate for themselves teachers to suit their own likings, and will turn away from listening to the truth" (2 Tim. 4:3).

Shortly after I had left the Mormon church, I received a letter from a Mormon convert from Catholicism, praising me for the testimony tape I had made earlier for the Mormon church. Apparently, she had not heard that I had returned to the Catholic faith. Since she included her telephone number, I called to explain why I was no longer a Mormon. The woman, in her late sixties, informed me she was leaving in two weeks to begin serving a mission in England.

When I asked her the Mormon standpoint on abortion, she answered, "We're very much against it. Only if the mother's life is in danger." I then cited the actual LDS position. She was incredulous. While she did not call me a liar, she said she would have to check for herself with her priesthood leaders. Though noticeably shaken by her church's "updated" liberal position on abortion, she could not tell me if that were enough to affect her testimony and deter her from urging others to embrace Mormonism.

Another Mormon couple from Nevada wrote after hearing my tape, "Interview with an Ex-Mormon." Though they still attempt to maintain a testimony of the Book of Mormon, after they discovered the Mormon church's policy on abortion, as they later wrote to me in a letter, "[We] knew immediately that the General Authorities were not following their conscience and God. We have written to Pres. Hinckley and he has said the Church will not change this policy."[14]

These two members, who support such pro-life groups as Priests for Life and American Life League, say that they expect

---

[14] Some Mormon leaders argue they have received no revelation from the Lord concerning the life of an unborn child or the intrinsic evil of abortion. Absent such divine enlightenment, their church's policy conforms to the assumed will of the American majority. It's useful to compare this "We have no word from the Lord" position on abortion with the positions taken by the church on drinking a cup of coffee, attending Sunday meetings or wearing the prescribed undergarments. On these, the Lord has spoken clearly. On the most vital and divisive issue of killing the unborn, the Lord remains uncommunicative.

to "resign or get excommunicated" because they question the inconsistency of an institution with an imposing front door marked "pro-family and pro-life" and several unadvertised back doors marked "exceptions, exceptions, exceptions."

The Mormon church's values on abortion, as with so many other issues, are unreasonable, even irrational. While drinking a cup of tea may keep a Mormon from attending the temple, procuring an abortion may not.[15]

Divorce

The Mormon church distributes, free of charge, thousands of copies of the Book of Mormon each year. In response to modern tastes, it also gives away slickly produced videos that present the more bland teachings of the faith. "Family First" is a current favorite. It extols the virtues of married love, respect and kindness among family members and family unity built around sharing an evening a week together. A number of television spots proclaim the same message and promise that families can remain together forever. Countless talks given by general authorities at the church's general conferences underscore the theme of righteous family living. The Mormon church projects the image of its members as belonging to large, happy, and close-knit families.

The reality of Mormon family life, however, is somewhat different. Statistics indicate that Mormon families are not happier, more well-adjusted or more stable than other American families. In fact, the Utah divorce rate (4.7 per thousand persons per year) is actually slightly higher than the national average (4.6 per thousand persons per year).[16]

The Mormon church's teachings on divorce do not differ sig-

---

[15] The same is true with artificial contraception. The 1998 *Church Handbook of Instructions* states the current, official position: "The decision as to how many children to have and when to have them is extremely intimate and private and should be left between the couple and the Lord. Church members should not judge one another in this manner."

[16] *The American Almanac 1996-1997*, 107. Compare Mormon Utah's 4.7 with Catholic Rhode Island's 3.2 and even New York's 3.3. The divorce rate

nificantly from American Protestant churches,[17] where divorce and remarriage is discouraged or disapproved, but permitted. The Mormon church "officially disapproves of divorce but does permit both divorce (the legal dissolution of a marriage bond) and annulment (a decree that a marriage was illegal and invalid) in civil marriages and 'cancellation of sealing' in temple marriages."[18]

Early Utah laws were quite lenient in granting divorces. Brigham Young, in particular, made it easy for wives (especially in polygamous relationships) to dissolve their marriages ("Divorce," *Encyclopedia of Mormonism*, vol. 1).

Today, Mormon bishops and other priesthood leaders are urged to help members strengthen their marriages but, "when necessary, to permit divorce and to determine whether disciplinary action should be taken against any spouse guilty of moral transgression."[19] Sometimes, the divorce (and subsequent remarriage) is permitted and even, it's been alleged, encouraged when one spouse is a non-Mormon who shows no interest in converting.

Though the Mormon church creates an image as a family-friendly institution that builds strong families who stay together, the reality is that Mormon family life does not prove to be all that it's advertised—*literally*—to be.

---

for the combined Mountain states (where most American Mormons live) is 5.8, compared with New England's 3.0 and the mid-Atlantic's 3.2.

[17] The Catholic Church recognizes that Catholic spouses may obtain a civil divorce—that is, a divorce in the eyes of the state—but does not recognize this as dissolving the marriage in God's eyes. Jesus was explicit in teaching that Christian marriages are indissoluble. In the Catholic view, for a Christian whose former spouse is still living to be able to remarry, it must be shown that their marriage was not valid in God's eyes from the very beginning. If their marriage was valid then, as Paul says, they must either remain chaste or be reconciled to each other (1 Cor. 7:11).

[18] "Divorce," *Encyclopedia of Mormonism*, vol. 1. Note that the "sealing" of marriages in the temple is the mechanism by which Mormons claim to unite spouses for eternity in the next life. Here it is indicated that such sealings can be canceled while still in this life.

[19] Ibid.

Drugs, Depression and Suicide

Mormon prophet Joseph Fielding Smith stated, "Saints [i.e., Mormons] are the best people. We are, notwithstanding our weaknesses, the best people in the world. I do not say that boastingly, for I believe that this truth is evident to all who are willing to observe for themselves. We are morally clean, in every way equal, and in many ways superior to any other people."[20]

Mormons would have us believe Mormonism is divinely ordained to lift mankind toward God and be an example to the whole world. Some observers might be lured by the press copy, sophisticated advertising and aggressive missionary efforts, but the data suggest otherwise. While the consumption of alcohol and illicit drugs is low in Utah, the state ranks third in prescription drug expenditures (255)[21] and sixth in over-the-counter drug abuse treatment admissions for 1992 (311).

Several explanations have been offered to account for these facts. Many members, especially women, express a constant urgency in their daily duties. The Mormon mother is expected to keep house, keep a journal, keep a garden, and keep a year's supply of food and other necessities on hand. Working outside the house is discouraged. She is to bear and rear a good number of children, keeping them clean, pure, active, industrious, and obedient. She is to receive counsel from her husband and obey him as the patriarch of the family. She is to participate in Sunday meetings, weeknight activities, visiting teaching and all her children's groups. She is to attend temple often. Some find they are unable to meet the demands of their religion and become depressed.

Several middle-aged wives and mothers in my LDS Institute classes confided to me their frustrations in not living up to the

---

[20] Joseph Fielding Smith, *Doctrines of Salvation* 1:236.
[21] All citations are from *Gale State Rankings Reporter*, 2nd edition, Helen Fisher, ed., 1995. Unless otherwise indicated, statistics are for 1993; page numbers are in parentheses.

demands they (and, I believe, their church) made on themselves. As of April 1, 1993, the United States average for all suicides was 12.1 per one-hundred thousand persons. The Utah average was 14.[22]

Child Abuse

David O. McKay declared, "Go into any Latter-day Saint home, and there see if you can find anything that is not uplifting and ennobling."[23]

Despite his confident invitation (almost challenge), some *have* gone into Mormon homes and found things that are not uplifting and ennobling. The *Deseret News*, owned by the Mormon church, reported on May 27, 1989, that the Utah Division of Family Services investigated 11,235 reports of child abuse and neglect during 1988, reflecting a thirty-two percent rise in the number of victims from the previous year. Most non-sexual child abuse and neglect was committed by parents, and three-fourths of all abuse was at the hands of someone living with the child (12–D).

In 1993, according to the *Gale Reporter*, Utah ranked 24th in substantiated reports of child abuse and neglect (1324). Utah's high divorce rate also puts its children at risk.

Crime Rate

In 1994, the U.S. average for forcible rape was 39.2 per one-hundred thousand persons. Utah's average was 42.2,[24] with Utah ranking second in arrests for those sex offenses excluding forcible rape and prostitution.[25]

Some Mormons equate material prosperity with spiritual blessing. Given their propensity to "trust their own," they may fall victim to white-collar fraud and other schemes which, unknow-

---

[22] *The American Almanac*, 98.
[23] David O. McKay, *The Improvement Era*, March 1965, 188.
[24] *The American Almanac*, 202.
[25] *Gale Reporter* for 1993, 1361.

ingly, some Mormon church leaders may have actually supported. This has led some to call Utah the "scam capital of America." Salt Lake City's dubious distinction has been recognized for years. A front page *Wall Street Journal* report labeled Salt Lake a "stock fraud center."[26] United Press International said, "Major reasons for the success of scams in Utah are the highly organized, tightly knit structure and trust-oriented doctrines of the Mormon Church."[27]

Utah ranked first in arrests for larceny and theft in 1993.[28] It was also first in property crimes arrests (1360), second in vandalism arrests (1362–1363), ninth in motor vehicle theft arrests (1358) and fourteenth in arrests for fraud (1356).[29]

The Hofmann Cover-up

Fraud and deceit extend well beyond the unheralded mutations of Mormon doctrine and history. In the 1980s, the nation's attention was grabbed by the Mark Hofmann scandal. An accomplished forger, Hofmann was a privately disaffected Mormon who used his abilities to embarrass the Mormon church and make money in the process.

During the early 1980s, he claimed to have discovered several old documents which he knew the Mormon church would want. The so-called "Salamander letter" was a forgery of a letter from Book of Mormon witness Martin Harris to early Mormon leader W. W. Phelps. In it, Harris wrote that Smith told him the angel who had led him to the gold plates had transfigured himself from a white salamander and had struck him three times. Another document purported to be a blessing by which Smith designated his son, Joseph Smith III, as his rightful successor to the presidency and office of prophet upon Smith's death.

Either document could, if authentic, destroy the credibility of

---

[26] February 25, 1974.
[27] Quoted in *Utah Holiday*, October 1990, 27.
[28] *Gale Reporter*, 1357.
[29] Note that "arrests" is not the same as "convictions." See note 34, below, for information regarding the interpretation of numbers of arrests.

the Utah Mormons. In particular, the blessing to Joseph III would seem to legitimize the prophetic succession as found in the Reorganized Church of Jesus Christ of Latter Day Saints (which *was* organized under Joseph Smith III and in which Emma Smith died) and to deny the authenticity of the Utah (or Brighamite) Mormons.

The Mormon hierarchy began a cover-up. After having the excellent forgeries authenticated,[30] the LDS hierarchy purchased the documents and kept their existence a secret.

Hofmann's forged documents, unpaid loans and intrigues eventually grew unwieldy, and he feared exposure. His solution was to kill those who could uncover his fraud. Package bombs claimed two victims. When a third bomb exploded in his car and injured him, Hofmann fell under suspicion. He was ultimately convicted and is serving a life sentence in a Utah state prison.

Church leaders would not have arranged for enormous sums to be paid for suspected forgeries. That they *believed* the Salamander letter, the Joseph III blessing and other documents were real is seen in their subsequent purchase and hiding of the papers, as well as in their contradictory statements given throughout the Hofmann investigation.[31]

Some have bluntly labeled what the Mormon hierarchy did "lying for the Lord." Excommunicated Mormon historian D. Michael Quinn used the term "theocratic ethics" to explain the hierarchy's behavior. This term covers not only lying but also a host of other legal and ethical violations done in the name of promoting the Mormon religion.

Illegal and unethical practices in the service of Mormonism go back to the time of Smith. In 1835, and without legal authority

---

[30] One photo shows then-president Spencer W. Kimball with President Gordon B. Hinckley and Mark Hofmann carefully examining the forger's work. Kimball and Hinckley had received the "keys" of prophecy and discernment, meant, in part, to protect the Mormon church from such deception.

[31] Several works are available on the Hofmann case and the church's attempted cover-up. See *Salamander* by Linda Sillitoe and Allen D. Roberts. For a more benign version, see *Victims* by faithful Mormon Robert Turley.

to do so, he performed a marriage between Newel Knight and a woman who was already married and who had not been divorced. At the time, Smith declared, "I have done it by the authority of the holy Priesthood and the Gentile law has no power to call me to an account for it. It is my religious priviledge [sic], and the congress of the United States has no power to make a law that would abridge the rights of my religion. . . ."[32]

This ethical independence permitted changes in scripture and reversals of doctrines, explained marriage and other sexual irregularities, allowed denials of actual events, threats and attacks against dissenters or other alleged enemies, bribery of government officials and unethical business practices.[33]

Certainly there are bright spots on the Utah cultural scene—most notably the low abortion rate, which would be lower if not for horrific exceptions Mormon theology makes to the defense of unborn humans. However, in other ways Utah turns out to be just an average state—as its slightly higher-than-median child abuse rate indicates—and far worse than average in some respects, as suggested by the high arrest rates for various crimes. Some studies (hotly disputed by some in Utah[34]) have suggested that Utah's crime rate is higher than New York City's.[35]

In any event, it is clear that Mormon family life is not all that it's advertised to be.

---

[32] D. Michael Quinn, *The Mormon Hierarchy*, 88.

[33] Ibid., 89, 327ff.

[34] Some might argue that high arrest rates indicate that Utah police are extraordinarily efficient. However, it is quite implausible that Utah cops are so much better than average American cops that it could account for the dramatically high Utah arrest rates. It is more plausible that Utah police officers are significantly *less* efficient than average American police officers, not through their own fault, but because they are geographically required to police a large, rural, thinly populated, mountainous state. Utah has been famous since the Old West days for providing ideal places for criminals to hide, and rural states tend, if anything, to have a significant problem with *underreporting* in crime statistics, as many crimes go undiscovered and uncounted in statistical surveys.

[35] Cf. "Utah's crime rate is sky-high—or is it?" by Mark L. Reece, *Deseret News*, July 27, 1997.

PART THREE

The Great Apostasy

9. Slipping from the Rock: The "Great Apostasy"

"I have more to boast of than any other man had," Joseph Smith declared. "I am the only man that has ever been able to keep a whole church together since the days of Adam. A large majority of the whole have stood by me. Neither Paul, John, Peter, nor Jesus ever did it. I boast that no man ever did such a work as I. The followers of Jesus ran away from Him; but the Latter-day Saints never ran away from me yet."[1]

But in the early years of the Church of Jesus Christ of Latter-day Saints, the majority of apostles left Smith, along with other Mormon leaders and most "witnesses" to the golden plates. Some were instrumental in Smith's death. From the Mormon church's founding in 1830 to Smith's death in 1844, many splinter groups broke from the larger Mormon assembly.[2] After his death, there was a power struggle in which Smith's son, his purported successor, was denied the leadership of the Mormon church, which passed instead to Brigham Young. One might wonder whether this was a running away from Smith, since several men claimed the succession and excommunicated those who would not follow them.

Mormons nonetheless emphatically contend that there has been a falling away of all other Christian churches. There would be no need for Smith to "restore" God's church to the earth if there already was a healthy and functioning Christian church. To justify creating his own church, Smith had to assert that something was wrong in Christendom. He explained that it had been revealed to him that all Christian churches were in darkness. None had the

---

[1] *The History of the Church* 6:408-409.
[2] Gordon H. Fraser, *Sects of the Latter-day Saints*, 10.

true gospel. There had been a massive falling away from Christ's teachings, which Mormons call the "Great Apostasy." As a result, no church in Smith's day was preaching Christ's message. Without this claim, the Mormon church would have no reason for its existence.

Among the general Mormon membership, today at least, very little is made of the Great Apostasy. It's taken for granted. The average member cannot cite any scriptures "proving" it. Instead, he reverts to his testimony on the truthfulness of the First Vision and Smith's prophetic call. If Smith said that Christ condemned all churches as corrupt, and if the Mormon can *feel* that Smith was a prophet, then it is true.

While Mormons exhibit civility and outward respect, they believe the Catholic Church and all others calling themselves Christian are utterly lost. Christ himself told Smith that all churches were wrong, all creeds were abominations, and all those who professed them were corrupt. Apostle James E. Talmage, in *The Great Apostasy*, spoke for all his Mormon brethren.

"If the alleged apostasy of the primitive Church was not a reality," Talmage wrote, "the Church of Jesus Christ of Latter-day Saints is not the divine institution its name proclaims."[3]

Mormon writers are fond of using superlatives in connection with their beliefs. In chapter 28 we note that a prophet stated the Mormon church stood or fell on the truthfulness of the First Vision. Here, an apostle depicts the apostasy as Mormon theology's pivotal point. The same will be said about the Book of Mormon's authenticity, Smith's character as a true prophet of God, the practice of polygamy or temple ordinances. We agree. If any one of these assertions, or a dozen others like them, should be proved false, Mormonism is false. They are essential components of the Mormon claim, and they reveal the anti-Catholicism of Smith and the Mormon church.

---

[3] *The Great Apostasy*, iii.

The Great and Abominable Church

It's not enough for the LDS church to teach a falling away of the true Church. It must also account for the persistence of at least the semblance of Christian religion from the earliest times. When the primitive Christian Church fell away, it was replaced, according to Mormons, by the "great and abominable church," or "church of the devil." The Book of Mormon, predicting that such an impostor would arise, states, "And the angel said unto me [Nephi, an ancient prophet in the Americas]: Behold the formation of a church which is most abominable above all other churches, which slayeth the saints of God, yea, and tortureth them and bindeth them down, and yoketh them with a yoke of iron, and bringeth them down into captivity.... And I saw the devil that he was the founder of it" (1 Nephi 13:5, 6).

Beyond the torment to which it subjects the true children of God, this devilish church has perverted the Bible: "For behold, they [the abominable church] have taken away from the gospel of the Lamb many parts which are plain and most precious; and also many covenants of the Lord have they taken away" (1 Nephi 13:26).

This explains in large measure why, when confronted with clear biblical teaching contrary to their doctrine, Mormons will counter that Scripture has been butchered from the earliest centuries after Christ. Because the biblical testimony is no longer reliable, mankind needs new, contemporary revelation to supply for the loss of the original teachings.

Bruce R. McConkie, formerly a member of the Quorum of the Seventy, was appointed an apostle of the Mormon Church in 1972. One of his most widely read and influential works is *Mormon Doctrine*,[4] a compendium of LDS theology. In this book,

---

[4] Faced with McConkie's testy theology and embarrassing etiquette, some Mormons are quick to distance themselves from his works. He was, however, a general authority for over thirty-eight years and an apostle at the time of

first published in 1958, McConkie dogmatically declared, "It is also to the Book of Mormon to which we turn for the plainest description of the Catholic Church as the great and abominable church. Nephi saw this 'church was most abominable above all other churches.' . . . He 'saw the devil that he was the foundation of it,' and also the murders, wealth, harlotry, persecutions, and evil desires that historically have been part of this satanic organization" (314-315).

Such characterizations of the Catholic Church were allowed to remain until a revised edition was issued in 1966. Then, direct references to the Catholic Church as the church of Satan were removed, allegedly at the order of the First Presidency and the Twelve Apostles. Nevertheless, McConkie continued to make his point. In this best-seller, we find listed as cross references for the apostasy articles on celibacy, christening, Eucharist, extreme unction, inquisitions, infant baptisms, priestcraft, shrines, sign of the cross, and worship of images. Though more generous in his amended treatment of the abominable church (he now included any organization other than his own church), McConkie was unable to resist the low road of insinuation, though he simply was taking his cue from earlier Mormon authorities. Apostle Orson Pratt, for instance, wrote in *The Seer*:

Q. Who founded the Roman Catholic Church?

A. The Devil, through the medium of Apostates, who subverted the whole order of God by denying immediate revelation, and substituting in the place thereof, tradition and ancient revelations as a sufficient rule of faith and practice [*The Seer*, 205].

Latter-day Saints often complain that they are misunderstood and, therefore, easily subject to persecution for their religious be-

---

his death. Aside from rumors that the First Presidency scolded him for the anti-Catholicism of his first edition of *Mormon Doctrine*, I can find no indication that McConkie was considered anything but a credible proponent of authentic Mormon teachings. His works continue to be published and sold by church-owned companies.

liefs. Their eleventh Article of Faith proclaims, "We claim the privilege of worshiping Almighty God according to the dictates of our own conscience, and allow all men the same privilege, let them worship how, where, or what they may."

One wonders how hard they try to understand and respect others' religious beliefs. Smith began the battle of words when he asserted that all Christian churches were wrong in God's sight. And it was Smith's nephew, Joseph F. Smith, the church's sixth president, who impugned the faith of all Christians who celebrate the Lord's resurrection when he proclaimed,

> Today, April 8, 1917, throughout the world, the people of the various Christian denominations are assembling in their churches because it is Easter Sunday. They have not assembled there because they have faith in the literal resurrection of the Lord; they have not assembled there because they believe in the literal resurrection of all mankind through the atonement of our Lord, and they have not assembled because they accept him as the Son of God. (I want to make honorable exceptions, because there are some who have done so, but I speak generally.)
>
> They have assembled there for a very different purpose—because it is the custom, because in many cases, among the sisters, they want to show their millinery and the styles of their clothing, their dress. They are there more in the nature of a social function and fashion show than to worship the Lord, and I say this not withstanding the expression that appears in one of our morning papers to the effect that anybody who expressed this kind of an idea is cynical and expresses a perverted opinion [*Doctrines of Salvation* 3:287–288, under the heading, "The Apostate World"].

It takes great effort to respect the honesty and good will of an institution with leaders so misinformed and contemptuous. However, the Mormon church's current policy is to maintain cordial relations with the Catholic Church and others. It advises its representatives, including young missionaries, to be cautious and controlled in their speech. For instance, in *Missionary Pal, a Reference Guide for Missionaries and Teachers* (73–74), we read, "CAUTION!!! Missionaries, be careful in your use of the information above, or you may hurt someone's feelings, and may even lose an interested investigator."

The "information above" referred to the "Great and Abominable Church," citing scriptures that are believed to be prophetic descriptions of this church of the devil. Lest anyone wonder which institution is meant, immediately following the caution is a lengthy excerpt from a publication entitled "The Truth about Catholics" (no author, date or place of publication given). The excerpt concerns the Catholic Church's determination of the sacred canon of Scripture. (A favorite Mormon accusation is that the Catholic Church, in the course of determining the canon, removed "many parts, which are plain and most precious" from the original Old and New Testaments. Naturally, those items supposedly removed would have "proved" Mormon claims to the truth.)

Because attacks on orthodox Christianity continue in many Mormon circles, at the church's April 1995 general conference, new President Gordon B. Hinckley addressed members in the irenic tone currently promoted by the Mormon Church, saying, "I plead with our people everywhere to live with respect and appreciation for those not of our faith. There is so great a need for civility and mutual respect among those of differing beliefs and philosophies.... We can and must be respectful toward those with whose teachings we may not agree."[5]

Later that same day, apostle Dallin H. Oaks, apparently not heeding the counsel of his prophet, delivered a blast against Catholic doctrine in a talk entitled "Apostasy and Restoration." He adverted to the notion presented in 1 Nephi that Scripture as we now have it was tainted by the corrupting influence of the abominable church. Additionally, Oaks misrepresented the bedrock doctrine of the Holy Trinity, a belief essential to the Catholic profession of faith. Portraying it as a hybrid of pagan views and primitive Christian teaching, he said, "In the process of what we call the Apostasy, the tangible, personal God described in the Old and New Testaments was replaced by the abstract, incomprehensible

---

[5] "This is the Work of the Master," *Ensign*, May 1995, 71.

deity defined by compromise with the speculative principles of Greek philosophy."[6]

He makes the common mistake of confusing "incomprehensible" with "unknowable," claiming that Catholics and others who believe in the Trinity have substituted a "philosophical abstraction" for a personal, compassionate God. Granted, God is incomprehensible in the technical sense—that is, he cannot be fully comprehended; we cannot plumb the depths of the infinite "three-personed God." But that is not to say that we can know nothing about him or his attributes. To the extent that we are open to grace's influence and our fallible minds permit, we can, by God's self-revelation in Scripture and tradition, attain a saving knowledge of the Lord, his nature and his will.

When addressing Catholics, Mormons will draw upon two sources to substantiate their claims that the Catholic Church (and, derivatively, all Protestants) apostatized from the Lord's truth in the early centuries. The first source consists of Bible verses they allege support their claim. The second consists of certain events in Church history. In the next two chapters we will address the scriptural basis Mormons offer for a total apostasy and the historical indications that the Church of Christ was absent from the earth for all these centuries. Afterward, we will give a Catholic response to the Mormon teaching on the apostasy, together with solid evidence that the Catholic Church was and has always been the one, true Church of Christ.

---

[6] *Ensign*, May 1995, 84–87.

10. The Old Testament and the "Great Apostasy"

The following Bible passages that Mormons cite as evidence of the Catholic Church's total apostasy are from the King James (or Authorized) Version, the only one Mormons accept. The reader may find it useful to compare that translation with a more easily understood, Catholic translation.

When reading the biblical attacks Mormons and others make against the Catholic Church, it is wise to remember Christ's warning, "Beware of false prophets, which come to you in sheep's clothing, but inwardly they are ravening wolves" (Matt. 7:15).

Vincent of Lerins noted that part of the "sheep's clothing" false prophets use are the words of the true prophets and apostles.

> [W]henever false apostles, false prophets, or false doctors quote passages from the Bible—in an attempt to support their errors with the aid of wrong interpretations—they are obviously imitating the cunning machinations of their master," he said. "Satan certainly would never have invented them if he had not known that there was no easier way to deceive people than by pretending to the authority of the Bible when wicked errors were to be fraudulently introduced [*Commonitories* 25].

Generally, the verses Mormons cite are easily refuted by noting that the passage in question describes only a partial falling away, the unfaithfulness of individuals or groups. Not a single passage points to the total abandonment of the Christian faith by the entire Church.[1]

---

[1] Catholics, along with other Christians and Mormons, have long made the proper distinction between the "person" of the Church and the "personnel" of the Church. See Jacques Maritain, *On the Church of Christ*.

Isaiah 24:3–5: "*The land shall be utterly emptied, and utterly spoiled: for the Lord hath spoken this word. The earth mourneth and fadeth away, the world languisheth and fadeth away, the haughty people of the earth do languish. The earth also is defiled under the inhabitants thereof; because they have transgressed the laws, changed the ordinance, broken the everlasting covenant.*"

In his treatment of the phrase "the everlasting covenant," Talmage asserted that it must point to a future disruption of the Lord's commands, since "the Mosaic law is nowhere called an everlasting covenant."[2] He concluded, as do all Mormons, that the covenant cited is a future one, established by Christ. Thus, they say, apostasy by the early Church ensued when it broke the laws and ordinances regarding this "everlasting covenant."

However, in Genesis 17, the phrase "everlasting covenant" is used three times to describe the covenant of circumcision, and in 1 Chronicles 16:17, the phrase is used to describe the covenant giving the Jews the land of Canaan. The passage in Isaiah speaks of the land and the sins of the people, making the obvious interpretation of the passage not a reference to the New Covenant (which is not tied to a particular land or people) but to God's land covenant with the Jews. He promised to protect and defend them in their land if they would keep his commandments (circumcision included). But now they have broken this covenant and sinned against him, so he is punishing the land by "turning it upside down, and scatter[ing] abroad the inhabitants thereof" (Is. 24:1) by sending them into foreign exile. Thus, "The land shall be utterly emptied, and utterly spoiled [i.e., plundered by armies]" (Is. 24:3).

The ancient Near Eastern military-political situation is also dealt with in the next passage Mormons use to support a total apostasy in the Christian age.

---

[2] *The Great Apostasy*, 25.

Isaiah 29:13-14: "*Wherefore the Lord said, Forasmuch as this people draw near me with their mouth, and with their lips do honour me, but have removed their heart far from me, and their fear toward me is taught by the precept of men: Therefore, behold, I will proceed to do a marvellous work among this people, even a marvellous work and a wonder: for the wisdom of their wise men shall perish, and the understanding of their prudent men shall be hid.*"

Mormons would like to see in this passage another reference to a Christian apostasy. However, the text refers to the Jewish nation that Isaiah was addressing. In response to their sins, God declared that he was sending a judgment on Israel—a judgment involving bringing a "multitude of all the nations" to fight against Israel (Is. 29:8) and bringing the plans of Judah's leaders ("the wisdom of their wise men . . . the understanding of their prudent men") to nothing against the invading armies.

When Isaiah speaks of "this people" he is referring to the Jewish people, which is confirmed by Christ, who cites this passage when condemning the hypocrisy of the Pharisees by saying, "Ye hypocrites, well did Esaias prophesy of you, saying, This people draweth nigh unto me with their mouth, and honoreth me with their lips; but their heart is far from me" (Matt. 15:7-8).

From no less an authority than the author of Scripture himself do we have the correct application of the Isaian passage.[3]

Isaiah 60:2: "*For, behold, the darkness shall cover the earth, and gross darkness the people: but the Lord shall arise upon thee, and his glory shall be seen upon thee.*"

Mormonism has wrested this radiant Messianic verse, proclaimed in the Church each Advent, and has applied it to the hypothesis that the earth lay in darkness and error for centuries between the death of Christ and the call of Joseph Smith. Yet the next verses

---

[3] Even the LDS version of the Old Testament cites Matthew 15:8 in a footnote to Isaiah 29:13.

provide the context, noting that the Gentiles and kings will come to the Lord, bringing dromedaries laden with gold and incense.

The darkness conquered here is the darkness of sin that covered Israel in Isaiah's day, as the preceding verses indicate. Isaiah speaks to the Jews of his day and says, "Behold, the Lord's hand is not shortened, that it cannot save; neither is his ear heavy, that it cannot hear; But your iniquities have separated between you and your God, and your sins have hid his face from you, that he will not hear. For your hands are defiled with blood and your fingers with iniquity" (Is. 59:1-3a).

This is to change, however, as Isaiah says, "And the Redeemer shall come to Zion, and unto them that turn from transgression in Jacob, says the Lord" (Is. 59:20).

It is the coming of the Redeemer, the birth of Christ in Zion, that dispelled the darkness that had covered the land and that brought light to all. Indeed, Christ's ministry in Israel is the fulfillment of more than one of Isaiah's prophecies of light dispelling darkness in Israel. As the Gospels declare, "And leaving Nazareth, he [Jesus] came and dwelt in Capernaum, which is upon the sea coast, in the borders of Zabulon and Nephthalim; That it might be fulfilled which was spoken by Esaias [Isaiah] the prophet, saying, 'The Land of Zabulon, and the land of Nephthalim, by the way of the sea, beyond the Jordan, Galilee of the Gentiles; The people which sat in darkness saw a great light; and to them which sat in the region and shadow of death, light is sprung up.' From that time Jesus began to preach, and to say, 'Repent; for the kingdom of heaven is at hand'" (Matt. 4:13-17, citing Is. 9:1-2).

Amos 8:11-12: "Behold, the days come, saith the Lord God, that I will send a famine in the land, not a famine of bread, nor a thirst for water, but of hearing the words of the Lord: And they shall wander from sea to sea, and from the north even to the east, they shall run to and fro to seek the word of the Lord, and shall not find it."

Amos, preaching to the northern kingdom of Israel about 760 B.C., explains to the people that, since they have not heeded the word of the Lord as delivered to them by the prophets, they will be delivered into the hands of their enemies (the Assyrians). At that time, they will seek frantically for a word of comfort from the Lord, but will not find one.

Again, the context points to an immediate fulfillment of the prophetic warning, as can be seen in the next two verses, which read, "In that day shall the fair virgins and young men faint for thirst. They that swear by the sin of Samaria, and say, 'Thy god, O Dan, liveth'; and, 'The manner of Beersheba liveth'; even they shall fall, and never rise up again" (Amos 8:13-14).

"The sin of Samaria" was the golden calf worshipped in the ancient city of Samaria. This calf idol was worshipped by the ten tribes of Israel, Dan included, and idolatrous pilgrimages were made to Beersheba in ancient Israel. Constantly, we are pointed to situations of the prophet's own day, not of some far later period, where none of these things holds true.

Micah 3:5-7: "Thus saith the Lord concerning the prophets that make my people err, that bite with their teeth, and cry, Peace; and he that putteth not into their mouths, they even prepare war against him. Therefore night shall be unto you, that ye shall not have a vision; and it shall be dark unto you, that ye shall not divine; and the sun shall go down over the prophets, and the day shall be dark over them. Then shall the seers be ashamed, and the diviners confounded: yea, they shall all cover their lips; for there is no answer of God."

A prophet to the southern kingdom of Judah, Micah wrote in about 710 B.C. The circumstances were similar to those of Amos' time. God again is silent, in judgment of his disobedient people. This is again evident from the immediate context. The condemnation of false prophets is the middle strophe in a three-strophe prophecy of judgment. In the first strophe (vv. 1-4), Micah prophesies against the princes of Judah and Israel, who have denied justice to the people. In the second strophe (vv. 5-8), he condemns the false prophets who have erroneously prophesied that there will be peace in Judah, when in reality God is going to bring a

THE GREAT APOSTASY

war upon it in judgment. And the third strophe (vv. 9-12) rebukes not only Judah's political leaders and its prophets, but its priests also.

Again, this fits the social and political situation of the prophet's own day, when princes, prophets and priests were the stock elements of Israel's national life. It does not fit the later Christian age, by which time the prophets had disappeared as a national institution and no longer advised kings about whether there would be war or peace.

All the Old Testament verses Mormons offer to indicate a general apostasy of the future Christian Church really refer to the spiritual darkness and disobedience of the Hebrew people and their consequent punishments, before the time of Christ. Only by unreasonable Scripture stretching can the Mormon church apply the above passages to the Christian age.

11. The New Testament and the "Great Apostasy"

Mormons also try to enlist New Testament passages to support their claim that there was a total apostasy of the early Church.

Matthew 7:15: *"Beware of false prophets, which come to you in sheep's clothing, but inwardly they are ravening wolves."*

As noted earlier, this is good advice from the Lord for all people, for all times. There is nothing here pertinent to our subject, unless it is taken as a warning to Catholics to avoid being fooled by Mormon masquerading. Jesus does not speak of a great apostasy. He indicates that there will be at least some false prophets in some ages of the Church, but he does not say that they will destroy his Church by their false teaching.

Matthew 21:43: *"Therefore say I unto you, The kingdom of God shall be taken from you, and given to a nation bringing forth the fruits thereof."*

Ezra Taft Benson interpreted this passage as predictive of the general apostasy.[1] This Mormon prophet, to whom were accredited the gifts of revelation and inspiration, perhaps missed the previous verses. Jesus was telling the "parable of the tenants." The chief priests and elders of Judah were his audience (v. 23). In the parable, a landowner left his vineyard to the care of his workers. At harvest time, the owner sent servants to collect his share of the produce. The workers killed them. He then sent his son, thinking the workers would respect and obey him. But the son also was killed. The owner then returned, destroyed the wicked workers and rented his vineyard to others more trustworthy. The Lord

---

[1] *The Teachings of Ezra Taft Benson*, 85.

concludes his admonition to the self-righteous Jewish leaders by the verse cited above. The mighty are put down, the dispossessed raised up. Clearly, Jesus Christ, the creator of the story, is its best interpreter. As we investigate the isolated verses propounded by Mormon missionaries and others, we see that context plays an enormous role in determining their true meaning. Here, Jesus is speaking of how the Jewish authorities of his day would put him —God's Son—to death and how the kingdom would be taken from Israel (Acts 1:6) and given to the Christian Church.

In fact, even the chief priests and Pharisees recognized that Jesus was talking about them, for Matthew tells us, "And when the chief priests and Pharisees had heard his parables; they perceived that he spake of them" (Matt. 21:45).

Acts 20:30: "Also of your own selves shall men arise, speaking perverse things, to draw away disciples after them."

We certainly have no argument here. Christ's Church has had enemies from the very beginning, often originating from within its own membership.[2] But again, nothing in this verse implies a total falling away. No religion is immune from dissidents whose flattering rhetoric draws followers away from the truth.

Recall, for instance, that most of Smith's apostles rebelled against him or were excommunicated by him, and the movement he founded has split into a number of different groups, which drew away members into their own circles (the Reorganized Church of Latter Day Saints, the Strangites, the Temple Lot Mormons, the True and Living Church of Jesus Christ of the Saints of the Last Times, etc.). Even Smith's son became the prophet of an opposing Mormon sect.

---

[2] See Andrew C. Skinner, "Apostasy, Restoration, and Lessons in Faith," in *Ensign*, December 1995, 26. "This may be the most pointed and succinct description in all scripture of how the great apostasy of the early Church came about." Skinner teaches at church-sponsored Brigham Young University.

Galatians 1:6–9: "*I marvel that ye are so soon removed from him that called you into the grace of Christ unto another gospel: Which is not another; but there be some that trouble you, and would pervert the gospel of Christ. But though we, or an angel from heaven, preach any other gospel unto you than that which we have preached unto you, let him be accursed. As we said before, so say I now again, If any man preach any other gospel unto you than that ye have received, let him be accursed.*"

Mormons try to use this verse to bolster their assertions that the primitive Church early on lost the pure doctrine of Christ and substituted "another gospel." Once more, we must study the context: Paul is condemning some members of the church in Galatia for being duped by so-called "Judaizers," Hebrews who had become Christian but continued to practice the Mosaic rituals and insisted that all other Christians do so as well. Particularly, they asserted that one must be circumcised and keep the Mosaic Law in order to be saved. This was the "other gospel" that was present in Paul's day, and it *lessened* as time went on and more Gentiles came into the Church.

Paul's warning that we must cling to the historic Christian gospel even if an angel from heaven should bring us a different one is something that early Mormons should have taken to heart. It was the angel Moroni that supposedly brought Smith the Book of Mormon, which is claimed to be "Another Testament of Jesus Christ."

Ephesians 4:11–14: "*And he gave some, apostles; and some, prophets; and some, evangelists; and some, pastors and teachers; For the perfecting of the saints, for the work of the ministry, for the edifying of the body of Christ: Till we all come in the unity of the faith, and of the knowledge of the Son of God, unto a perfect man, unto the measure of the stature of the fulness of Christ: That we henceforth be no more children, tossed to and fro, and carried about with every wind of doctrine, by the sleight of men, and cunning craftiness, whereby they lie in wait to deceive. . . .*"

Mormons note that in the first part of this passage, as with similar ones, early Christians were called saints. Because they also call themselves saints, many Mormons argue, they must be the true Christians. Of course, anyone can call himself anything he likes, but that doesn't create the reality. In the passage's latter portion, Paul notes the danger in his age, as in every other age, that is presented by false teachers who try to deceive. But in the middle section of the passage, he notes the provision God has made to counter this problem—he has given his Church leaders to help the people, especially in the apostolic era of doctrinal change, grow into a proper understanding of Christ. If anything, this passage predicts a growth of orthodox understanding of Christ, not an apostasy from that understanding.

2 Thessalonians 2:1–4, 7–8: "Now we beseech you, brethren, by the coming of our Lord Jesus Christ, and by our gathering together unto him, That ye be not soon shaken in mind, or be troubled, neither by spirit, nor by word, nor by letter as from us, as that the day of Christ is at hand. Let no man deceive you by any means: for that day shall not come, except there come a falling away first, and that man of sin be revealed, the son of perdition; Who opposeth and exalteth himself above all that is called God, or that is worshipped; so that he as God sitteth in the temple of God, shewing himself that he is God. . . . For the mystery of iniquity doth already work: only he who now letteth [hinders] will let, until he be taken out of the way. And then shall that Wicked be revealed, whom the Lord shall consume with the spirit of his mouth, and shall destroy with the brightness of his coming."

Here Paul warns the community that the day of Christ (the Second Coming) is not at hand, even if a letter purportedly from him states that it was. Rather, other events must happen first. Specifically, there will be a great rebellion against God and the "man of sin" will appear. Mormon scriptorians equate the "man of sin" with Satan and say he is the head of the historic Christian Church.[3] More plausibly, the man of sin is an earthly king who, like many of the pagan Roman emperors, claimed to be divine. One of them

---

[3] Kent P. Jackson, "Early Signs of the Apostasy," *Ensign*, December 1984, 9. Jackson is a professor at BYU.

—Caligula—even tried to have a statue of himself placed in "the temple of God" in Jerusalem. This may be a foreshadowing of an event that will occur just before the Second Coming. For Paul, a first-century Jew, the phrase "the temple of God" would most naturally refer to a Jewish temple in Jerusalem, and the idea of one appearing in this temple and displaying himself as a divinity would suggest a pagan king claiming divine honors for himself.

The idea that Satan, who already ruled the nations (Matt. 4:9), would *invisibly*—out of sight to the earthly Church—"show himself" in the (spiritual) temple of God, and that we in the visible world would be able to clearly discern this as a sign of the Second Coming, does not fit the passage. In fact, Paul *contrasts* the man of sin with Satan in the very next verse of the chapter, where he says that the man of sin's "coming is after the working of Satan, with all power and signs and lying wonders" (2 Thess. 2:9). If the man of sin's coming is "after the working of Satan"—that is, caused by the power of Satan, who is spoken of in the third person—then the man of sin must not be Satan, but one of his minions. Paul continues the pagan king theme by discussing what will happen to those who follow the man of sin, saying that all will "be damned who believed not the truth, but had pleasure in unrighteousness" (2:12). "Pleasure in unrighteousness" is a more apt description of the excesses of pagan worship and culture than the strictures of Christian discipline in the early centuries.

This passage does speak of a falling away from the faith. However, to Paul, in a first-century context, this would mean people leaving the Christian Church, denying faith in Christ, and returning either to Judaism or paganism. It would not refer to people remaining in the Church, continuing to profess faith in Christ, yet simplifying their faith by collapsing the Father, the Son and the Spirit into a single God and forgetting about all other gods.

The Mormon use of this text fails in two points. First, it nowhere states that there will be a total falling away. In his discussion of the Second Coming in 1 Thessalonians, Paul had specifically indicated that the falling away would not be total but that some would remain faithful to the Second Coming (1 Thess. 4:17).

Second, the Mormon use of the text fails because it does not take into account that the two signs of the manifestation of the man of sin and the falling away are signs that Paul presents as indicators of the Second Coming. If these two signs had occurred beginning in the apostolic age, as Mormons claim the Great Apostasy did, then it would scarcely be an indicator to Paul's Thessalonian readers that the Second Coming was still in the future. Furthermore, if the text did indicate a total falling away as an indicator of the Second Coming, then there would not be room for a period in which the true gospel resurges and triumphs. Otherwise, the apostasy would not be a sign of the Second Coming, merely an intermittent event.

1 Timothy 1:6–7: "From which [i.e., the faith] some, having swerved, have turned aside unto vain jangling; Desiring to be teachers of the Law; understanding neither what they say, nor whereof they affirm."

Here Paul indicates that some people have, not surprisingly, turned aside from the faith, something that happens in every age. Paul does not prophesy a great future falling away in this passage. Neither does he say that it was a massive falling away in his own age. His comments indicate otherwise, since he says that the people he is talking about fell away "desiring to be teachers of the Law." This indicates that he is talking about those early Christians who had erroneous theories about Jewish law ("understanding neither what they say, nor whereof they affirm"), such as those who taught the Galatians that Gentiles must become Jews in order to be saved. This group died out, nullifying this verse as a prophecy or a confirmation of a mass apostasy. All one can draw from this passage is a salutary warning that one must not turn aside from faith, from charity or from a good conscience. This warning is necessary at all times and in all places, for Paul also warned Timothy to "preach the word; be instant in season, out of season; reprove, rebuke, exhort with all long suffering and doctrine" (2 Tim. 4:2). Timothy was to persist, whether or not it was convenient, in teaching the true faith and in encouraging his flock to follow God's teachings.

Had Paul not believed in the efficacy of his own exhortation, he would not have insisted on Timothy's determined cooperation.

It is interesting that Mormons do not quote 1 Timothy 1:6–7 with the immediately preceding verses, which say, "As I besought thee to abide still at Ephesus, when I went into Macedonia, that thou mightest charge some that they teach no other doctrine, Neither give heed to fables and endless genealogies, which minister questions, rather than godly edifying which is in faith: so do. Now the end of the commandment is charity out of a pure heart, and of a good conscience, and of faith unfeigned" (1 Tim. 1:3–5).

Paul indicates the direction in which some have wandered from the faith when he tells Timothy to make sure people do not teach non-Christian doctrine and give heed to fables and endless genealogies, which only cultivate speculation rather than godly edification in the faith. The genealogies Paul is here talking about could be the genealogies of the Old Testament or the heavenly genealogies of some Gnostics. It is no surprise that Mormons fail to quote these verses, considering the Mormon church operates the largest genealogical library in the world, dwarfing anything that anyone was doing with genealogies in the first century.

1 Timothy 4:1–4: "Now the Spirit speaketh expressly, that in the latter times some shall depart from the faith, giving heed to seducing spirits, and doctrines of devils; Speaking lies in hypocrisy; having their conscience seared with a hot iron; Forbidding to marry, and commanding to abstain from meats [i.e., foods], which God hath created to be received with thanksgiving of them which believe and know the truth. For every creature of God is good, and nothing to be refused, if it be received with thanksgiving. . . ."

Here we have a second passage that mentions a future apostasy. When interpreting it in his book, *The Great Apostasy*, Talmage relied on the works of a number of anti-Catholics to guide this interpretation.[4] Besides exhibiting poor scholarship by relying on such questionable works, the Mormon apostle's dependence on

---

[4] Among them are the eighteenth-century former Catholic and anti-Christian Edward Gibbon (*The Rise and Fall of the Roman Empire*); and three anti-

THE GREAT APOSTASY

these authors' anti-Catholic views led him into serious misunderstanding of the Catholic Church. His enthusiastic use of the polemic indicates unwillingness to research more unbiased histories and commentaries.

For example, from Clarke's *Commentary* on 1 Timothy 4:1-4, he quoted, "Speaking lies in hypocrisy: Persons pretending not only to divine inspiration, but also to extraordinary degrees of holiness, self-denial, mortification, etc., in order to credit the lies and false doctrines which they taught. Multitudes of lies were framed concerning miracles wrought by the relics of departed saints as they were termed" (*The Great Apostasy*, 38).

Some Mormons confuse the reference to "forbidding to marry" with the Catholic Church's requirement for priestly celibacy for its Latin rite priests. Additionally, they cite this passage against the Catholic practice of abstaining from meat on some Fridays of the year. The passage concerns neither. Paul is referring to radical ascetics, such as those in later centuries, who claimed *all* marriage and procreation was wrong and that certain foods should *never* be eaten. Paul had nothing against celibacy for some—he even practiced it himself. Nor did he have anything against the biblical practice of abstaining from certain foods (including meat; Dan. 10:2-3) for a time. It was the total prohibition of marriage or of certain foods that he was concerned with—saying that these things are *intrinsically wrong*.

And therein lies a profound irony, for it is Mormons who claim that some foods are intrinsically wrong and should not be consumed. Thus Mormons are commanded to abstain from all alcohol, coffee, and tea. If they do not abstain from these foods, then they are not "temple worthy" and are excluded from the most important rituals of their religion.[5] This contradicts Paul and counts as one of the "doctrines of demons" he speaks of.

Catholics: J. L. von Mosheim, an eighteenth-century German historian (*Ecclesiastical History*); Joseph Milner, an English historian (*History of the Church of Christ*); and Adam Clarke, British commentator (*Bible Commentary*).

[5] Oddly, the Word of Wisdom's prohibition of meat in most circumstances is consistently ignored and Mormons are counted "temple worthy" even if

Toward the Second Coming ("in the latter times") there will be many who fall away from the Christian faith by "giving heed to seducing spirits," thus embracing "doctrines of devils." However, the Catholic Church, which has existed since the time of Christ, does not make either prohibition that Paul mentions. The Mormon church, which openly declares itself to be a "Latter-day" church, *does* forbid certain foods, and does so on the basis of a supposed revelation. If anything, it is the Mormon church that is part of the last times apostasy, that has given in to seducing spirits and thus forbidden certain foods.

2 Timothy 1:15: "This thou knowest, that all they which are in Asia be turned away from me; of whom are Phygellus and Hermogenes."

Mormon apologists delight in this verse and attempt to use it as a statement that all the Christians of Asia had already apostatized, in spite of the work of the apostle to the Gentiles. They then argue that, if such a massive apostasy was underway at so early a date, a worldwide falling away would soon occur.

But is the premise of this argument true—that all Christians in Asia had fallen from the faith? In the New Testament, "Asia" refers to a small Roman province (Asia Minor or Anatolia) at the western tip of what is now Turkey. It did not indicate the continent of Asia that we speak of today, so the scale is not nearly as large as the Mormon argument would suggest in modern language.

Did the Christians in this province all fall away from the faith? No. The city of Ephesus is in the province, and in the very next verse Paul praises the family of Onesiphorus, who often helped and comforted Paul in the latter's trials (2 Tim. 1:16-18). Onesiphorus is from Ephesus (1:18; 2 Tim. 4:19 with 1 Tim. 1:3).[6] These Asians had not turned away from Paul.

---

they eat meat in circumstances where the Word of Wisdom rejected it. Meat is such an important part of the modern American diet that Mormons ignore this part of the alleged revelation.

[6] Cf. *The Navarre Bible: Thessalonians and Pastoral Epistles*, 139-140.

We also know that there were solidly Christian churches not only in Ephesus, but in other places in Asia Minor as well, for the book of Revelation begins with letters to seven of them. In the letters, Christ addresses the spiritual states of the churches and, while he mentions faults in all but two of them (what church *couldn't* be improved?), he also *praises* all but one of them, indicating that they were true Christian churches.

Paul never suggests that they had fallen from the Christian faith. He says that they had "turned away *from me*"—that is, from Paul, not from Christ.

What is Paul speaking of in this passage? The answer is found, as always, by looking at the passage in its context. We know that this was a lonely time for Paul. He was in Rome, awaiting trial for the second time there, and knew that his life was coming to a close (2 Tim. 4:6). He was away from his home and his family, and many of his friends and colleagues in ministry had forsaken him. In this loneliness, he writes to Timothy,

> Do thy diligence to come shortly unto me: For Demas hath forsaken me, having loved this present world, and is departed unto Thessalonica; Crescens to Galatia, Titus unto Dalmatia. Only Luke is with me. Take Mark, and bring him with thee: for he is profitable to me for the ministry. And Tychicus have I sent to Ephesus. . . . Alexander the coppersmith did me much evil: the Lord reward him according to his works: Of whom be thou ware also; for he hath greatly withstood our words [2 Tim. 4:9–15].

Only Luke was with Paul during his second captivity in Rome, so Paul asks Timothy to come to him and bring Mark, too. All of his other noteworthy companions have left him or have been sent elsewhere by Paul.[7] Particularly stinging to Paul was his sense of aloneness at his first legal defense hearing ("my first answer"), concerning which he writes, "At my first answer no man stood with me, but all men forsook me: I pray God that it may not be laid to their charge. Notwithstanding the Lord stood with me,

---

[7] Tychicus, for example, was absent because Paul had sent him on a mission and is thus "absent with excuse." The same may be true of Crescens and Titus, whose absence Paul merely mentions, without criticizing or explaining it.

and strengthened me; that by me the preaching might be fully known, and that all the Gentiles might hear: and I was delivered out of the mouth of the lion" (2 Tim. 4:16-17).

This is precisely the kind of abandonment Paul spoke of when he wrote, "This thou knowest, that all they which are in Asia be turned away from me; of whom are Phygellus and Hermogenes" (2 Tim. 1:15). It is not a reference to a mass apostasy in Asia but to the personal abandonment Paul feels in his second Roman imprisonment and trial. He was hoping that others would back him up at his defense and stand with him, but none did—or at least, the ones he wanted to (including Phygellus and Hermogenes) did not.[8] Some colleagues that Paul had counted on either did not come from Asia to defend him or returned to Asia without helping in his hour of need, and this pained Paul.

2 Timothy 3:1-5: "This know also, that in the last days perilous times shall come. For men shall be lovers of their own selves, covetous, boasters, proud, blasphemers, disobedient to parents, unthankful, unholy, Without natural affection, trucebreakers, false accusers, incontinent, fierce, despisers of those that are good, Traitors, heady, highminded, lovers of pleasures more than lovers of God; Having a form of godliness, but denying the power thereof: from such turn away."

First, Paul writes that "in the last days" these problems will beset the Church. He does not say that the Church as a whole will collapse or lose its divine authority.

Second, Joseph Smith—History 1:19 quotes 2 Timothy 3:5 in describing the Catholic Church and other Christian groups of his time: They have "a form of godliness, but they deny the power thereof." Even the most rabid anti-Catholic must admit that the

---

[8] We should not assume, for example, that Luke did not stand with Paul but that Luke was not one of those Paul had in mind, since Luke's testimony may not have been relevant to Paul's case. The evidence indicates that Luke wrote his Gospel and the book of Acts during Paul's previous Roman imprisonment, as part of an effort to help Paul.

Catholic Church has existed prior to the "last days." This passage, as with all the others, will find its fulfillment only in the end times preceding the Second Coming of the Lord.

Third, this passage is not a prophecy of a general Christian apostasy. Paul warns Timothy that "in the last days perilous times shall come," suggesting that the problem is much broader in society than just a falling away of Christians. People in the general population, not the ostensibly Christian population in particular, will have the evil vices Paul lists. They may appear to be religious (Paul does not say which religion they will have—it may be Jewish, Christian or pagan, cf. Acts 17:16, 22), but they do not know the morally transforming power of God. The context would suggest that the men Paul is talking about are *not* Christian, for he indicates that some people in his own day (as opposed to "the last days") were of this kind.

"For of this sort are they which creep into houses," Paul continues, "and lead captive silly women laden with sins, led away with divers lusts, Ever learning, and never able to come to the knowledge of the truth. Now as Jannes and Jambres withstood Moses, so do these also resist the truth: men of corrupt minds, reprobate concerning the faith. But they shall proceed no further: for their folly shall be manifest unto all men, as theirs also was" (2 Tim. 3:6-9).

House-to-house evangelism was common in the ancient world, done by Christian and Jewish missionaries and adherents of the pagan mystery religions as well. In the *Republic*, Plato mentions Orphic missionaries who went from house to house and left a "heap of treatises" (2:364b-e). And Plutarch, in chapter 19 of his *Precepts for Newly Married People*, advises new brides not to let in missionaries who want to leave literature, for it may alienate their husbands. Jews also were heavy proselytizers in this period (Matt. 23:15). Given these facts, we cannot assume that Paul is speaking here of professedly Christian missionaries. The evidence would suggest that they were *not* Christians since Paul says that they or their victims are "ever learning" (a phrase fitting Greek religious and philosophical speculation) yet "never able to come to the knowledge of the truth"—that is, never coming to know Jesus Christ. Similarly, he states that "as Jannes and Jambres withstood Moses, so do these also resist the truth." According to ancient writers, Jannes and Jambres were two of the pagan magicians in Egypt who used their magic to withstand Moses before Pharaoh (Ex. 7-8), suggesting that the missionaries Paul speaks of were non-Christian teachers opposing the preaching of Christ. We see nothing at all in 2 Timothy 3:1-9 predicting a general apostasy of the Christian Church, much less one in the first century.

2 Timothy 4:3-4: "For the time will come when they will not endure sound doctrine; but after their own lusts shall they heap to themselves teachers, having itching ears; And they shall turn away their ears from the truth, and shall be turned unto fables."

This passage speaks of a future time when men will not put up with sound doctrine. How far in the future? Read in context of the same epistle (2 Tim. 3:1-5) and the companion epistle (1 Tim. 4:1-4), the time will be in the last days, before the Second Coming, not during Paul's own day. He also does not say that it will be a total apostasy, merely a widespread one.

Further, read in context of the previously discussed material, it would not be a falling away into a kind of pseudo-Christianity but a complete repudiation of the Christian faith, either back to Judaism or paganism. This is indicated by Paul's statement that men "shall be turned unto fables." The word in the Greek text that is rendered "fables" is *mythoi*—i.e., "myths." In the technical sense in Greek, myths were stories about the gods, though Paul also used the term to refer to "Jewish myths," which he linked with the "endless genealogies" (1 Tim. 1:4; Tit. 1:14). He also speaks of some myths as profane (lewd) old wives' tales (1 Tim. 4:7). This would fit the model of pagan myths, which were known for containing gross sexual immorality.

In either case, Paul is not saying that people will fall into a pseudo-Christianity but that when they refuse to put up with sound doctrine, they will turn to myths like those in first-century Judaism and Greco-Roman paganism. This presents Mormons with two problems. First, if any church today could be said to be preoccupied with stories about gods, involving sexual intercourse[9] and "endless genealogies," it would be Mormonism, not historic Christianity. Second, it would be difficult to suppose that Mormonism was the original Christianity that then fell away into myths and endless genealogies when it became historic Christianity. Historic Christianity is not known for myths or long genealogies. It doesn't really care about either, and if Mormonism had been the original Christianity then the switch to historic Christianity would be a *de*-mythologization, not a *re*-mythologization.

2 Peter 2:1–3: "But there were false prophets also among the people, even as there shall be false teachers among you, who privily shall bring in damnable heresies, even denying the Lord that bought them, and bring upon themselves swift destruction. And many shall follow their pernicious ways; by reason of whom the way of truth shall be evil spoken of. And through covetousness shall they with feigned words make merchandise of [exploit] you: whose judgment now of a long time lingereth not, and their damnation slumbereth not."

Just as many people followed false prophets in Israel, so "many shall follow" the ways of false teachers who pretend to speak for the Church. But not everyone will be deceived. The presence of false prophets in Israel did not cause a total apostasy of Israel. It remained God's institutional, religious presence on earth. Indeed, God sent *true* prophets to combat the false ones. So Mormons will not be able to use the parallel case of Israel and the Church to prove a total apostasy. Quite the opposite. If the parallel proves anything, it proves too much—that the Church, the New Israel, will remain faithful despite false teachers, and that God will send

---

[9] Such as God the Father's impregnation of the Mormon version of the Virgin Mary, who was betrothed to another man.

true teachers to combat them when they appear. The Mormon cannot find in this passage a prophecy of total apostasy for any stage of Church history.

2 Peter 3:3: "*Knowing this first, that there shall come in the last days scoffers, walking after their own lusts, And saying, Where is the promise of his coming?*"

Men will continue to deny the blessed return of the Savior to judge the living and the dead. This will be the case even in the face of the evidence amply provided in "the last days." It is amazing that Mormons use this passage, because it clearly refers not to a pseudo-Christianity but to a totally non-Christian skepticism that denies that the Second Coming will take place—something that historic Christianity has never done. Peter is talking about non-Christian scoffers, not people who still profess to be Christians.

Jude 3–4: "*Beloved, when I gave all diligence to write unto you of the common salvation, it was needful for me to write unto you, and exhort you that ye should earnestly contend for the faith which was once delivered unto the saints. For there are certain men crept in unawares, who were before of old ordained to this condemnation, ungodly men, turning the grace of our God into lasciviousness, and denying the only Lord God, and our Lord Jesus Christ.*"

There are warnings against individual, personal apostasy, but Jude in no way predicts a mass falling away. He merely states that there are *some* false teachers in the Christian community, which God foresaw. Yet God continues to provide the remedy—our "common salvation"—which flows from the good news handed on by the apostles and their successors, "the faith which was once delivered unto the saints." It is a faith that is the same in every age, common and available to all men and all times in Christian history. Because it was *once* (Greek *hapax*, "once for all") delivered, it does not have to be re-delivered all over again eighteen-hundred years later.

Jude 18: "How that they told you there should be mockers in the last time, who should walk after their own ungodly lusts."

In this parallel passage to 2 Peter 3:3,[10] we have the same prophecy of skeptics in the last days. As before, there is no prophecy of an apostasy into a pseudo-Christianity. The repudiation of the faith is total, rejecting the promise of Christ's Coming, something historic Christianity has never done, meaning historic Christianity cannot be seen as a fulfillment of this passage.

Revelation 12:1–5: "And there appeared a great wonder in heaven; a woman clothed with the sun, and the moon under her feet, and upon her head a crown of twelve stars: And she being with child cried, travailing in birth, and pained to be delivered. And there appeared another wonder in heaven; and behold a great red dragon, having seven heads and ten horns, and seven crowns upon his heads. And his tail drew the third part of the stars of heaven, and did cast them to the earth: and the dragon stood before the woman which was ready to be delivered, for to devour her child as soon as it was born. And she brought forth a man child, who was to rule all nations with a rod of iron: and her child was caught up unto God, and to his throne. . . ."

Mormons declare that the woman represents the Church, which was forced to flee from the world, and the man child represents the true priesthood, which God took back to heaven in order to protect it from Satan's onslaughts. A fuller and more customary

---

[10] This section in Jude structurally parallels part of 2 Peter. It is not certain whether Peter wrote using Jude, whether Jude wrote using 2 Peter, or whether both depended on some other source (written or oral), but the striking series of parallels in the two books has been noted for centuries, and each helps shed light on what the other is discussing. In this case, 2 Peter 3 sheds light on Jude 18.

interpretation acknowledges that the woman may be the Church, the people of God, who were first protected in the wilderness from the rage of Pharaoh.[11] After the Lord's ascension (the man child's being taken up to the throne of God, where he now sits at his right hand), the Church must again turn to the desert of faith, where it will find intimate union with Christ, be fed and protected by him and continue its difficult sojourn to the end of time.

The passage does not say that the woman is taken to heaven by God. Instead, it indicates that she remained on earth:

> And when the dragon saw that he was cast unto the earth, he persecuted the woman which brought forth the man child. And to the woman were given two wings of a great eagle, that she might fly into the wilderness, into her place, where she is nourished for a time, and times, and half a time, from the face of the serpent. And the serpent cast out of his mouth water as a flood after the woman, that he might cause her to be carried away of the flood. And the earth helped the woman, and the earth opened her mouth, and swallowed up the flood which the dragon cast out of his mouth [Rev. 12:13–16].

God gave the woman the ability to escape the dragon by going into the wilderness. And when the devil unleashed a flood of persecution against her, she was *not* swept away by it, but the land absorbed the flood. In both cases, the woman remains protected and on earth.[12]

---

[11] See *The Navarre Bible: Revelation*, 97–99. The symbol of the woman has four references—Israel, the Church, Eve, and Mary. Like Israel, she is associated with the sun, moon, and twelve stars (Gen. 37:9–11); like the Church, her other offspring are Christians (Rev. 12:17); like Eve, the woman and her Seed are involved in a conflict with the serpent (Gen. 3:15, Rev. 20:2); and like Mary, she is the mother of Jesus, the child who will rule the nations with a rod of iron (Rev. 19:11–16).

[12] A plausible historical fulfillment of this prophecy may be found in the flight of the early Christians from Jerusalem during the Jewish War of the 60s. Jesus had told the apostles to "flee to the mountains" when "ye shall see Jerusalem compassed with armies, [for] then . . . the desolation thereof is

There is not a total apostasy during the period of the woman's desert sojourn, which is indicated by the fact that when the dragon fails to kill the woman, he must content himself with killing only *individuals* among her children: "And the dragon was wroth with the woman, and went to make war with the remnant of her seed, which keep the commandments of God, and have the testimony of Jesus Christ" (Rev. 12:17).

The devil is prevented from destroying the Church, which remains safely on earth.

Revelation 13:7: "And it was given unto him [the beast from the sea] to make war with the saints, and to overcome them: and power was given him over all kindreds, and tongues, and nations."

The reference here is to the persecution endured by the early Christians at the hands of the Romans. We know that the Church of Christ has faced persecution from its beginning. No person or people, no matter how holy, is exempt from such torment. In the verse, "him" refers to the beast that John sees rising from the sea (13:1). The symbolism of this beast is based on a vision of the prophet Daniel (Dan. 7). In it, Daniel saw four beasts, representing four kings that would oppress God's people (Dan. 7:17), rising from the sea. The beast that John sees rising from the sea incorporates elements of Daniel's four beasts (compare Rev. 13:1–2 with Dan. 7:4–8), indicating that this beast is a sequel to those four kings—a king of the same kind, one who will persecute God's people. The waters from which the beast rises represent the Gentile nations—"peoples, and multitudes, and nations, and tongues"

---

nigh" (Luke 21:20–21). In the 60s, Vespasian invaded Israel and surrounded Jerusalem with armies. Suddenly, Vespasian was called away to become emperor when the current emperor died, and Jerusalem was spared for the moment. Recognizing the sign, the Christians in Jerusalem fled, ultimately settling in Pella in Peraea. In 70, however, the armies did surround and sack Jerusalem. The Christian community was protected because they had fled, and the land absorbed the flood of destruction unleashed by the pagan army.

(17:15; Dan. 7:2-3 with 17). Thus the persecuting king will be of Gentile origin. In the first-century context in which John was writing, there could be no doubt about the identity of that king. Since we are told that "power was given him over all kindreds, and tongues, and nations," he can be none other than the Roman emperor, the ruler of the known world.[13] It is no surprise, then, that we are told his name adds up to 666 (Rev. 13:18). As has been often pointed out, the name of one of the Roman emperors—Nero—*did* add up to 666.[14] That this was understood in the first century is confirmed by a textual variant that gives the number as 616.[15]

This enables us to understand Revelation 13:7. Daniel had seen a persecuting Gentile king who "made war with the saints [i.e., the Jewish nation], and prevailed against them" (Dan. 7:21) and was even allowed to "wear out the saints of the most High" (Dan. 7:25) and kill many of them until "judgment shall sit, and they shall take away his dominion, to consume and to destroy it unto

---

[13] It is, of course, true that there were small places in the known world of the time that the emperor did not rule—the area that is now Scotland, for example—but these were not counted in ancient speech, and it was idiomatic to refer to the Roman emperor as ruling the whole world and all its peoples. A slight exaggeration, but one that was an established mode of speech in the ancient world.

[14] In Hebrew, the name "Caesar Nero" (NRWN QSR) adds up to 666: N (50) + R (200) + W (6) + N (50) + Q (100) + S (60) + R (200) = 666. The values given for the letters here are the standard ones for the Hebrew alphabet. Before the introduction of modern, Arabic numerals, letters of the different alphabets (Hebrew, Greek, Latin) doubled as numbers. They had standard numerical values which everyone knew, making it possible for John's original audience to calculate the number of the most famous persecuting Gentile king of the day. Nero's name could be spelled more than one way in Hebrew, which led to an early textual variant in the book of Revelation. (See next note.)

[15] A few early manuscripts give the number as 616. This is based on a variant Hebrew spelling of "Caesar Nero" (NRW QSR), which adds up to 616: N (50) + R (200) + W (6) + Q (100) + S (60) + R (200) = 616. These two numbers, based on variant spellings of the same first-century Gentile king who persecuted Christians and Jews, reveal the first-century identification of the beast with Nero.

the end" (Dan. 7:26). This king (who in history was Antiochus IV—called Antiochus Epiphanes—who ruled the Seleucid kingdom from 175 to 164 B.C.) was able to persecute and kill many of God's people, but only for a time, and not to destroy them utterly. He also was unable to force God's people to apostatize *en masse* from the faith. He did force some Jews to renounce Judaism and embrace Greco-Roman paganism, but God kept the bulk of the Jews faithful to him.

Paralleling this, the Roman emperor—the new Gentile king who persecuted God's new people, the Christians—also had it "given unto him to make war with the saints, and to overcome them" (Rev. 13:7, virtually a direct quote of Dan. 7:21). He thus persecuted and killed many Christians for a time, but was not able to destroy them. He was unable to force Christians to apostatize *en masse* from the faith. He did force some Christians to renounce Christianity and to embrace Greco-Roman paganism, with its emperor worship (Rev. 13:4), but God kept the bulk of Christians faithful to him. Indeed, the Church grew despite the emperors' efforts to destroy Christianity.

There is no basis for seeing in Revelation 13:7 a prophecy of mass apostasy from the Church, much less a mass apostasy into a pseudo-Christianity. To the biblical authors, apostatizing meant going back to Judaism or paganism, not continuing to profess a corrupt form of Christianity.

Revelation 14:6: "And I saw another angel fly in the midst of heaven, having the everlasting gospel to preach unto them that dwell on the earth, and to every nation, and kindred, and tongue, and people. . . ."

Mormons attest that an angel would not need to preach the "everlasting gospel" to mankind if it had been present all along. Thus, they say, this restoration of the gospel implies its original loss. This is a gratuitous assumption. No matter when in history this passage is referring to—shortly after Christ's First Coming or shortly before his Second Coming—it is simply an announcement of the gospel and in no way implies that there were not others announcing the gospel.

This is especially clear when we look at what the angel says and at what then happens:

> And I saw another angel fly in the midst of heaven, having the everlasting gospel to preach unto them that dwell on the earth, and to every nation, and kindred, and tongue, and people, Saying with a loud voice, Fear God and give glory to him, for the hour of his judgment is come: and worship him that made heaven, and earth, and the seas, and the fountains of water. And there followed another angel, saying, Babylon is fallen, is fallen, that great city, because she made all nations drink of the wine of the wrath of her fornication. And the third angel followed them, saying with a loud voice, If any man worship the beast and his image, and receive his mark in his forehead, or in his hand, The same shall drink of the wine of the wrath of God [Rev. 14:6-10].

There has never been a time, since the creation of the world, when the gospel preached by the first angel has not been preached among men. God has always had people preaching the need to fear and glorify God and worship him as creator of the world. The only difference here is that the angel proclaims the hour of God's judgment.[16] In its proper context, then, the passage does not discuss the "bringing back" of the gospel after a long absence, but rather the "bringing to account" of the peoples of the world.

Even a casual reading of this passage, as with the others we have examined, reveals that no general or total apostasy of the Christian Church from its Founder and Head was prophesied. This holds true for the Old and New Testaments. Quite the contrary, Christ promised to remain with his Church till the end of the world (Matt. 28:20) and that the gates of hell would not prevail against his Church (Matt. 16:18).

---

[16] Whether this is God's judgment on the ancient Roman world at the beginning of the Christian age or his judgment on the whole world at the end of time is a matter that may be debated.

12. Historical Arguments for Total Apostasy

The Mormon misunderstandings reported in previous chapters highlight the confusion Latter-day Saints have interpreting Catholic Church history and doctrine. This brings us to the second source from which Mormons infer a general apostasy: Catholic Church history from post-apostolic times to the present.[1] But Mormons do not appraise history objectively. Instead, they begin with the Mormon teaching of a total apostasy, which taints their reading of early Christian history. The Mormon church first *concludes* that the Catholic Church can't be the true faith and *then* rummages through its two-thousand-year history to find "corroborating evidence."

Persecution of the Early Church

Mormon apostle Talmage proposed the following hypothesis to account for the alleged apostasy of the early Church:

> In the fierce battle between Christianity and its allied foes—Judaism and heathendom—the strong men who stood for Christ were the first to fall. And with their fall, the traitors within the Church, the ungodly and the rebellious, those who had crept in unawares, and whose sinister purpose it was to pervert the gospel of Christ, were relieved of restraint, and found themselves free to propagate their heresies and to undermine the foundations of the Church. Persecution, operating from without, and therefore essentially an external cause, served to set in motion the enginery of disruption

---

[1] For the treatment of so-called historical causes of the "Great Apostasy," see B. H. Roberts' *The Falling Away*, a book long out of print. Roberts was a member of the Seventy.

within the Church, and therefore must be treated as an effective element contributing to the great apostasy [*The Great Apostasy*, 56].

This is a strange understanding of the effects of persecution, considering Talmage inherited his religion from a community whose prophet (Joseph Smith) and patriarch (Hyrum Smith) had been "martyred" in a shootout. Talmage also held fresh memories of the persecution of those Mormons who refused to comply with the federal government's (and eventually the Mormon church's) outlawing of polygamy.[2] Yet all this "persecution" had not led to the collapse of Mormonism or its apostasy into a fundamentally different faith from what its founder taught.

True, most of the early leadership—the apostles and others—fought with Smith over various issues and either left the Mormon church voluntarily or were excommunicated. And true, at the prophet's death, several men stepped forward, claiming to have received the prophetic mantle of leadership, leading to the establishment of splinter churches.[3] But Mormons believe that the jailing and shooting of the leaders resulted in exquisite inspiration, most useful for proselytizing.

So it was with the early Church. "The blood of the martyrs is the seed of Christians," Tertullian wrote.[4] We know that, rather than vitiating the power and witness of the Church, the precious deaths of the early martyrs strengthened the resolve of true Catholics as they struggled under *real* persecution by the Roman empire.

---

[2] He wrote *The Great Apostasy* in 1909; polygamy had been officially suspended by the Mormon church in 1890.

[3] The largest of these churches claiming priesthood succession from Joseph Smith and, therefore, divine authority, is the Reorganized Church of Jesus Christ of Latter Day Saints. This church, with headquarters in Independence, Missouri, has over 200,000 members and was led, until the mid-1990s, by a direct descendant of Smith. The RLDS maintain that Brigham Young usurped control of the church at Smith's death.

[4] *Apologeticus* 50:13

The Emperor Constantine and the "State Church"

For the first three Christian centuries, faithful Catholics suffered deprivation and death at the hands of the Roman government, though, for the first two hundred years, this persecution was not as organized as it came to be. Instead, anti-Christian violence was fostered by grass-roots agitation and denunciation by anonymous informers.[5] Consequently, Christians had time to recoup their strength, reaffirm their faith and regroup with their bishops. The torments were officially sanctioned by the emperors in the third century. Large numbers of weaker members apostatized, though many tried to return to the Church when the persecutions ceased. Septimius Severus, Maximin, Decius and Diocletian sent to their deaths succeeding generations of Catholic leaders, including Pope Fabian and Pope Sixtus, with his deacon, Lawrence. Yet the list of popes, uninterrupted from Peter through the centuries of persecution, manifests God's unfailing hand choosing and supporting his elect. The measures taken to stamp out Christianity had the reverse effect. The number of Christians continued to grow; their courage and resistance evoked wonder and admiration.[6]

Talmage, and other Mormon writers, have an inaccurate view of what happened at the close of the age of persecutions:

> The Diocletian oppression was the last of the great persecutions brought by pagan Rome against Christianity as a whole. . . . A stupendous change, amounting to a revolution, now appears in the affairs of the Church. Constantine, known in history as Constantine the Great, became emperor of Rome A.D. 306 and reigned 31 years. Early in his reign he espoused the hitherto unpopular cause of the Christians and took the Church under official protection. . . .
>
> It is held by many judicious historians that Constantine's so-called conversion was rather a matter of policy than a sincere acceptance

---

[5] José Orlandis, *A Short History of the Catholic Church*, 16–17.
[6] Joan O'Grady, *Early Christian Heresies*, 74.

of the truth of Christianity. The emperor himself remained a catechumen, that is, an unbaptized believer, until shortly before his death, when he became a member by baptism. But whatever his motives may have been, he made Christianity the religion of state, issuing an official decree to this effect in 313. "He made the cross the royal standard; and the Roman legions now for the first time marched beneath the emblem of Christianity" (Myers).

Immediately following the change there was great competition for church preferment. The office of a bishop came to be more highly esteemed than the rank of a general. The emperor himself was the real head of the Church.[7]

Talmage did not bother to cite even his anti-Catholic sources in this dismissive indictment of Constantine. Did the emperor sincerely esteem Christianity? Talmage said "many judicious historians" think not (though he quoted none), seeing in his postponement of baptism a tepid spirit or a shrewd political strategist.

We, however, can cite those who accord the emperor both Christian temperament and motives, including O'Grady, who wrote, "It seems that the moral strength of the Christians and their higher standards of morality impressed Constantine, so that he was almost certainly sincere in his admiration for Christianity and, indeed, he had his children educated as Christians."[8]

Deferral of baptism until the end of life did not indicate a lack of devotion. In Constantine's age, it was a common practice, since the sacrament of penance was administered less frequently. Among Christians, in accord with the teaching of the New Testament (Acts 2:38; Rom. 6:3-4; 1 Pet. 3:20-21), it was universally acknowledged that baptism blotted out all sin prior to its reception, and since reception of the sacrament of penance, following baptism, was less frequent, many devout individuals chose to postpone their baptism until late in life. Thus, as historian Lietzmann wrote, "Constantine could look forward to receiving baptism and with it the forgiveness for all his sins. His enemies, in any case,

---

[7] *The Great Apostasy*, 75-76.
[8] *Early Christian Heresies*, 75.

have never accused him of hypocrisy, but of a conscience genuinely troubled by sin. Hence the logical inference, however reluctantly drawn [by some], is that he was a genuinely religious man."[9]

Talmage further erred in stating that Constantine made Christianity the official state religion by a decree in 313. Christianity was not the official religion of the empire until long after Constantine's time. Talmage seems to be referring, in a confused manner, to the Settlement of Milan, made in common with Licinius, the ruler of the eastern part of the empire. This agreement granted tolerance and religious freedom for Christians. Confiscated land was returned to Christians. But Constantine did not force on others his belief in God. When Constantine defeated Licinius and consolidated the empire under one head in 324, he recommended his Christian beliefs to all, but was emphatic that no one should be compelled; each was to live in accord with his own convictions.[10]

Calling Constantine head of the Catholic Church is an eccentric charge, found only in the works of the uninformed. The only precedent for the role of a Christian emperor was that of the Old Testament kings, who were involved in maintaining peace and pure religion, but who did not govern Israel's religious institutions, such as the temple. That task belonged to priests, and when one king, Uzziah, tried to usurp the priestly office by offering incense in the temple, God struck him with leprosy (2 Chron. 26:16–21).

Constantine understood that his relationship with the Church was one of temporal protector rather than spiritual ruler, just like the Old Testament kings. At a banquet Constantine told bishops in attendance, "You have been installed bishops for the inner affairs of the Church, and I have been installed bishop by God for its outer affairs."[11]

Constantine never usurped ecclesiastical authority; he respected

---

[9] Hans Lietzmann, *A History of the Early Church*, vol. 2, 161.
[10] Ibid., 152–154.
[11] Eusebius, *The Life of Constantine* 3:12.

and deferred to it. This is evident in his social policy, which changed established practices to agree with Christian morals. The shedding of blood was declared illegal, gladiator combats were forbidden, and pagan temples, no longer subsidized by the state, were left to crumble from lack of use. Slaves, children, widows and orphans were treated more humanely.[12] And, though he did not make Christianity the state religion, Constantine explained to pagans in his empire how the error of polytheism had led the peoples into darkness and moral chaos, and how Christ brought justice and peace to the world.[13]

One final charge against Constantine and his "state church" claims that Church leaders were under his heel, mere toadies. He forced his will, so the accusation states, on bishops and councils alike. The truth is quite the opposite.

"Though it was the Emperor who summoned [the councils] and who chose the subjects they were to discuss," O'Grady wrote, "the councils tended to encourage rather than to diminish the independent attitude of the Christian bishops. The councils were the first [ecclesiastical] representative deliberating bodies that had ever existed. The Church appeared as the opponent of state absolutism rather than its supporter."[14]

After Constantine's death, and throughout the decline of the empire in the fourth century, the Church continued to gain in popular favor and official standing. The Church gradually became the only true bastion of freedom within the totalitarian Roman state.[15]

Rather than being lords and masters of the Catholic Church, the emperors, Constantine included, acted as its servants and protectors, just as the Israelite kings of old had for the institutions God had ordained for Israel. The Church, as the New Israel, received similar protection, again by God's design.

---

[12] Thomas Bokenkotter, *A Concise History of the Catholic Church*, 39.
[13] *A History of the Early Church*, 157–158.
[14] *Early Christian Heresies*, 76.
[15] *A Concise History of the Catholic Church*, 56.

It is ironic that in their drive to think up confirming rationales for their prior belief that the early Church apostatized, Mormon writers are willing to make the most twisted arguments. First, we saw the assertion that it was persecution that led to a total Church apostasy. Then, we saw the argument that, because Christians were so successful, a calculating emperor realized political advantage in converting, and *that* supposedly led to a total apostasy. Thus it is paradoxically asserted that both persecution and also the conversion of the persecutors led to apostasy! Mormon writers have constructed an interpretive grid such that *any* evidence brought forward from the early centuries can be twisted into an accusation of apostasy.

13. "Specific Causes" of Apostasy

In addition to general charges of apostasy due to persecution and the conversion of the persecutors, Talmage and other Mormons make specific charges that Christ's Church was dying from three mortal wounds—the introduction of pagan philosophy, changes in its "ordinances" (sacraments), and changes in its organizational structure. Talmage writes:

> Among the more detailed or specific causes of this ever widening departure from the spirit of the gospel of Christ, this rapidly growing apostasy, the following may be considered as important examples:
>
> (1). The corrupting of the simple principles of the gospel by the admixture of the so-called philosophic systems of the times.
>
> (2). Unauthorized additions to the ceremonies of the Church, and the introduction of vital changes in essential ordinances.
>
> (3). Unauthorized changes in Church organization and government.[1]

We will deal with church organization and government in other chapters, so here let's look at the first two charges.

Ancient Philosophy

Talmage listed the importation of ancient philosophical ideas as the "[f]irst among the specific causes of disturbance operating within the Church, and contributing to its apostasy."[2] He then catalogues heretical and allegedly heretical ideas that he asserts were introduced into the Christian community through the philosophies of

---

[1] *The Great Apostasy*, 90–91.
[2] *The Great Apostasy*, 96.

the day. This catalogue suffers from grave problems in proving a total apostasy. Much of what Talmage says deals with heretical ideas that existed for a time and then passed from the scene, never becoming accepted by mainstream Christianity. Since the ideas were not embraced by historical Christianity, they cannot be used to prove that historical Christianity is in an apostate state.

Consider an example on the level of individuals: If Bill and Johnny are both Christians and Bill becomes an apostate, the fact that Johnny refuses to go along with Bill does *not* prove that Johnny is an apostate. It is irrelevant to cite Bill's apostasy as proof of apostasy by Johnny. Thus much of Talmage's recitation of early heresies (Gnosticism, Sabellianism, Docetism, Arianism) is irrelevant to proving an apostasy of mainstream, historical Christianity. It is as irrelevant as using the fracturing off of the numerous Mormon sects from the LDS church to prove the LDS church is in apostasy from Joseph Smith.

The second general problem with Talmage's catalogue is that much of it is factually inaccurate. Consider, for example, a statement he makes about Judaism in this period: "The perversion of true theology thus developed within the Church is traceable to the introduction of both Judaistic and pagan fallacies. Indeed, at the opening of the Christian era and for centuries thereafter, Judaism was more or less intimately mixed with pagan philosophy, and contaminated with heathen ceremonies."[3]

For anyone who knows anything of Judaism's history in this period, Talmage levels a baseless charge. It is preposterous to assert that in this period "Judaism was more or less intimately mixed with pagan philosophy." Judaism, in this period as in every other, has been staunchly anti-pagan. Pagans of the period viewed Jews as an obstinate people who insisted on clinging to their own views rather than going along with those of the rest of the world. One might identify a few groups of Jews (such as the Hellenistic Jews) who had a measure of non-Jewish influence, but the assertion that Judaism itself was intimately mixed with pagan ideas is devoid of credibility.

---

[3] Ibid., 97

There are also numerous statements that suggest wishful thinking by Talmage. In describing Judaism at the time, he writes, "There were numerous sects and parties, cults, and schools, each advocating rival theories as to the constitution of the soul, the essence of sin, the nature of Deity, and a multitude of other mysteries."[4]

It is true that there were a significant number of Jewish groups at this time (the Pharisees, Sadducees, Essenes, Zealots, and Hellenists being the most well known). One could claim also that the schools had disagreements about what is and is not a sin, and some had different conceptions of the soul. The Sadducees did not believe it to be immortal, for instance.

But Talmage would be wrong to suggest that there was serious controversy at this time about "the nature of Deity" among Jews. It would be apologetically advantageous for him, as a polytheistic Mormon, to assert that the Judaism from which Christianity sprung had an unclear understanding of God—one perhaps allowing the existence of other gods—but such is not the case. The complete rejection of polytheism is one of Judaism's key tenets, and was at this period.

Talmage eventually turns from his recitation of early heresies and states, "The moral effect of the potent spirit of apostasy operating through the first three centuries of the Church's existence and nourished by the contributions of heathen philosophy, proved, as was inevitable, highly injurious and evil. Some of the most pernicious of these effects it becomes our duty to consider."[5]

Talmage then criticizes three specific "effects" of pagan influence on Christian morals: asceticism, celibacy, and lying.

---

[4] Ibid., 97
[5] Ibid., 105.

Asceticism

"A result of this grafting in of heathen doctrines was an abundant growth of hermit practices," Talmage said, "by which men sought to weaken, torture, and subdue their bodies, that their spirits or "souls" might gain greater freedom. Many who adopted this unnatural view of human existence retired to the solitude of the desert, and there spent their time in practices of stern self-denial and in acts of frenzied self-torture. Others shut themselves up as voluntary prisoners, seeking glory in privation and self-imposed penance. It was this unnatural view of life that gave rise to the several orders of recluses, hermits, and monks."[6]

In every age, some people have gone to extremes—Mormons included—and so a case cannot be made for a mainstream apostasy by citing the behavior of those on a group's fringe. Excesses of ascetical behavior have never been mainstream in Christian history. Even so, Mormons are wrong to criticize moderate asceticism, for it is endorsed in Scripture. Paul says, "I do not run aimlessly, I do not box as one beating the air; but I pommel my body and subdue it, lest after preaching to others I myself should be disqualified" (1 Cor. 9:26–27, RSV).

Of course, Paul does not mean that he literally pommels his body (though the Greek word is *hupopiazo*, which means "to beat black and blue"), but he does mean that he practices biblical asceticism. This asceticism took forms such as wearing sackcloth (rough cloth worn to abrade and irritate the skin), fasting, weeping and humiliating oneself by sitting on ashes and putting dust on one's head. While not for everyone, at all times, in all cultures, this form of behavior was approved and even commanded by God, as the following quotations (taken from the Revised Standard Version) illustrate:

---

[6] Ibid., 105.

- The Lord, Yahweh Almighty, called you on that day to weep and to wail, to tear out your hair and put on sackcloth [Is. 22:12–13].

- O daughter of my people, gird on sackcloth, and roll in ashes; make mourning as for an only son, most bitter lamentation; for suddenly the destroyer will come upon us [Jer. 6:26].

- Then I [Daniel] turned my face to the Lord God, seeking him by prayer and supplications with fasting and sackcloth and ashes [Dan. 9:3].

- Gird on sackcloth and lament, O priests, wail, O ministers of the altar. Go in, pass the night in sackcloth, O ministers of my God! [Joel 1:13].

- When you fast, do not look somber as the hypocrites do, for they disfigure their faces to show men they are fasting. I tell you the truth, they have received their reward in full. But when you fast, put oil on your head and wash your face, so that it will not be obvious to men that you are fasting, but only to your Father, who is unseen; and your Father, who sees what is done in secret, will reward you [Matt. 6:16–18].

- Now John's disciples and the Pharisees were fasting. Some people came and asked Jesus, "How is it that John's disciples and the disciples of the Pharisees are fasting, but yours are not?" Jesus answered, "How can the guests of the bridegroom fast while he is with them? They cannot, so long as they have him with them. But the time will come when the bridegroom will be taken from them, and on that day they will fast" [Mark 2:18–20].

- Come near to God and he will come near to you. Wash your hands, you sinners, and purify your hearts, you double-minded. Grieve, mourn, and wail. Change your laughter to mourning and your joy to gloom. Humble yourselves before the Lord, and he will lift you up [Jas. 4:8–10].

- And I will give power to my two witnesses, and they will prophesy for 1,260 days, clothed in sackcloth [Rev. 11:3].

When Mormons criticize Catholics for doing things of this sort, they are criticizing biblical behavior. One wonders whether by mounting such criticism Mormons are not elevating the physical form and promoting a "cult of the body," something that also may come out in the next criticism.

Celibacy

The Catholic Church is charged also with bowing to Gnostic demands by implementing a system of "unnatural" asceticism, with clerical celibacy its centerpiece. This, its enemies hold, denies the goodness of the human body and sex and institutionalizes the Gnostic hatred of material creation.[7] Talmage writes, "An unmarried clergy, deprived of the elevating influences of home life, fell into many excesses, and the corruption of the priests has been a theme of reproach throughout the centuries. 'The Lord said, It is not good that the man should be alone. . . .' An apostate church decrees that its ministers shall be forbidden to follow the law of God."[8]

It's not surprising that Mormons would have problems with the idea of celibacy. A life of consecrated celibacy flies in the face of the Mormon exaltation of marriage. Only married men will become gods, and one who would deliberately forego a spouse and children is suspect. You would expect opposition to celibacy from a religion that makes the bearing and begetting of children

---

[7] See Lowell L. Bennion, *An Introduction to the Gospel*, 57–58.
[8] *The Great Apostasy*, 106–107.

essential to godhood and declares that polygamy in heaven is essential to it as well.

Moreover, Mormons have their facts wrong. They don't recognize that celibacy is a mandatory discipline only for priests in the Catholic Church's Latin rite. The Church's Eastern rites have married clergy, and in the Latin rite, deacons are married and there is a growing number of married priests (former Protestant ministers who have converted and been ordained to the Catholic priesthood).

Consecrated celibacy is a biblical practice. Marriage, sex, and procreation are good in and of themselves, and useful for propagating the human race, but they are not the highest vocation in life. Ultimately, it is our destiny to be celibate in heaven, as Jesus declared (Mark 12:25). Those who are given the gift of celibacy in this life are given a blessed vocation, receiving a degree of conformity to our ultimate spiritual destiny. Just as Jesus was celibate and remains so (any Mormon ideas to the contrary notwithstanding; see pp. 300–302), those who are called to consecrated celibacy in this life are following in their Master's footsteps.

Since the clergy represent Christ and stand *in persona Christi*, it is not surprising to find Paul recommending celibacy to Timothy, specifically as something advisable to clergy.

"Thou therefore endure hardness," Paul says, "as a good soldier of Jesus Christ. No man that warreth entangleth himself with the affairs of this life; that he may please him who hath chosen him to be a soldier" (2 Tim. 2:3–4).

The "affairs of this life" include marriage and a family. Paul did without these for the sake of his ministry, and there is no doubt that this was included in his recommendation to Timothy, especially given Paul's recommendation of celibacy even to the laity.

"Now concerning the things whereof ye wrote unto me: It is good for a man not to touch a woman," he says, "Nevertheless, to avoid fornication, let every man have his own wife, and let every woman have her own husband" (1 Cor. 7:1–2).

Notice that Paul considers it *good* for a man to abstain from sexual relations. That is the preferred situation he presents, only conceding the general practice of marriage because most people do not have the self-control needed to live continently, a point he returns to in his discussion when he says, "Defraud ye not one the other, except it be with consent for a time, that ye may give yourselves to fasting and prayer; and come together again, that Satan tempt you not for your incontinency. But I speak this by permission, and not of commandment" (1 Cor. 7:5–6).

Paul states that he is *not* commanding that spouses engage in sexual relations, but only recommending that they should in order to prevent temptations to infidelity. Consecrated celibacy—celibacy undertaken to devote oneself to fasting and prayer—is still the ideal situation he presents, even within marriage. While Paul acknowledges that not all have been given the gift of being able to live celibately, he views this as preferable, adding, "For I would that all men were even as I myself. But every man hath his proper gift of God, one after this manner, and another after that. I say therefore to the unmarried and widows, It is good for them if they abide even as I. But if they cannot contain, let them marry: for it is better to marry than to burn" (1 Cor. 7:7–9).

Marriage, then, is presented as a preferable alternative to living a life of unfulfilled, burning passion, but it is *not* preferable in Paul's view to a life of celibacy. One reason for this is the trouble that having a family can bring in this life, as Paul notes when he says, "Art thou bound unto a wife? seek not to be loosed. Art thou loosed from a wife? seek not a wife. But and if thou marry, thou hast not sinned; and if a virgin marry, she hath not sinned. Nevertheless such shall have trouble in the flesh: but I spare you" (1 Cor. 7:27–28).

In particular, being married can divide one's loyalties so that one does not follow Christ with an undivided heart.

"He that is unmarried careth for the things that belong to the Lord," Paul writes, "how he may please the Lord: But he that is married careth for the things that are of the world, how he may please his wife. There is difference also between a wife and a virgin. The unmarried woman careth for the things of the Lord, that she may be holy both in body and in spirit: but she that is married careth for the things of the world, how she may please her husband. And this I speak for your own profit; not that I may cast a snare upon you, but for that which is comely, and that ye may attend upon the Lord without distraction" (1 Cor. 7:32-35).

Paul thus believes that people can be happier if they do not marry—if they have been given the gift of living celibately—and he indicates this judgment to be formed under the guidance of the Holy Spirit, saying, "The wife is bound by the law as long as her husband liveth; but if her husband be dead, she is at liberty to be married to whom she will; only in the Lord. But she is happier if she so abide, after my judgment: and I think also that I have the Spirit of God" (1 Cor. 7:39-40).

Paul's view of marriage and celibacy is irreconcilable with the Mormon view, as illustrated in his treatment of the case of a man betrothed to a virgin. Should they marry or not? Paul writes, "But if any man think that he behaveth himself uncomely toward his virgin, if she pass the flower of her age, and need so require, let him do what he will, he sinneth not: let them marry. Nevertheless he that standeth stedfast in his heart, having no necessity, but hath power over his own will, and hath so decreed in his heart that he will keep his virgin, doeth well. So then he that giveth her in marriage doeth well; but he that giveth her not in marriage doeth better" (1 Cor. 7:36-38).

Statements like 1 Corinthians 7:38—rendered in more modern translations as "he who marries his betrothed does well; and he who refrains from marriage will do better" (RSV)—are unimaginable on the lips of Mormon leaders. But this *is* the biblical view, and opposition to it underscores Mormonism's unbiblical nature.

Lying

In one of the strangest historical disconnects conceivable, Talmage asserted that the early Church came to regard lying as a virtue, claiming, "As early as the fourth century, certain pernicious doctrines embodying a disregard for truth gained currency in the Church. Thus, it was taught that it was an act of virtue to deceive and lie, when by that means the interests of the church might be promoted. Needless to say, sins other than those of falsehood and deceit were justified when committed in the supposed interests of church advancement, and crime was condoned under the specious excuse that the end justifies the means. Many of the fables and fictitious stories relating to the lives of Christ and the apostles, as also the spurious accounts of supernatural visitations and wonderful miracles, in which the literature of the early centuries abound, are traceable to this infamous doctrine that lies are acceptable unto God if perpetrated in a cause that man calls good."[9]

The sweeping nature of this charge, coupled with the lack of citations showing early Church Fathers endorsing lying and deception, make it difficult to respond to this charge. It is so out of touch with historical reality that one does not know where to begin. The early Church Fathers, like Christians of every age, have regarded lying as an objective, grave sin. It has never been viewed as acceptable to fabricate information, stories, or miracles in the service of Christianity. The early Christians were willing to die for the truth of their faith, to die rather than lie and say they did not worship Christ, and the idea that Christians came to view lying and deception as a virtue lacks all historical credibility.

Changes in Ordinances

The Church's true "ordinances" (the term Mormons use instead of "sacraments" and "sacramentals") were abandoned by making "unauthorized" changes in them, according to Talmage.

"As one of the effective causes leading to the apostasy of the Primitive Church we have specified: Unauthorized additions to the ceremonies of the church, and the introduction of vital changes in essential ordinances."[10]

---

[9] Ibid., 107.
[10] *The Great Apostasy*, 113.

One can make this statement, if one wishes. One can say that there were changes in the sacraments and that these changes were unauthorized, but it is another matter to back up these charges with evidence.

Mormons don't do so well in that regard, as illustrated by Talmage's condemnation of the use of incense.

Incense

"The burning of incense," Talmage said, "at first abhorred by Christian assemblies because of its pagan origin and heathen significance, had become common in the Church before the end of the third century."[11]

This observation is typical of the shallow scholarship behind such assertions. No references are given for a Christian disdain for burning incense to honor the Lord. Is it possible that the Mormon apostle overlooked the entire Old Testament practice of sacrificing incense to God as a sign of adoration? Did he disregard the wise men's gift to the Christ Child? Did he forget the practice of the angels in heaven, who offered incense mingled with the prayers of the saints before the throne of the Holy One (Rev. 8:3–4)? How could early Christians abhor incense as a pagan custom when it was commanded by God to be used in the Jewish temple in Jerusalem? God even had his own formula of temple incense with the ancient equivalent of a patent! Nobody else was allowed to make it or to use it for secular purposes (Ex. 30:34–38).

In making the charge, Talmage is fabricating historical claims in order to justify the *Mormon* change of an ordinance by *abandoning* the historic Christian use of incense. His charges of falsification in the service of one's religion, as well as his charges of changes in ordinances, actually apply to *his* religion.

---

[11] Ibid., 115.

The Eucharistic Sacrifice

On a far more important note, Talmage dismissed as erroneous "the notion of the eucharist . . . as a real sacrifice" (114). In so doing, he ignores testimonies of the earliest Christians.[12] He may deplore the rites and ceremonies that have developed in the celebration of the Eucharist, but these do not affect its nature.

History has shown that these secondary features of a rite may be changed without altering basic character or validity. Indeed, the Mormon temple ceremonies, thought to have been given directly by God, have been corrected by the Mormon hierarchy several times since they were first performed—and without the prescribed authorization. Only excommunicated, "Fundamentalist" Mormons deny their church's right to make such changes.

Infant Baptism

The full wrath of Mormondom, however, is reserved for the change in what they claim was the true form of baptism: immersion of believing members by those having authority. Even a Book of Mormon prophet, in the final chapters, is made to take up the cause.

"Behold I say unto you, that he that supposeth that little children need baptism is in the gall of bitterness and in the bonds of iniquity, for he hath neither faith, hope, nor charity; wherefore, should he be cut off while in the thought, he must go down to hell" (Moroni 8:14).

Except for chapter eight of Moroni, infant baptism is not mentioned in the Book of Mormon. When his opinion was sought to solve this perennial concern, Smith wrote into his work the definitive Mormon position: Catholic, Orthodox, and many Protestant

---

[12] See the writings of Clement of Rome, A.D. 80, the *Didache*, A.D. 60, and Justin Martyr, A.D. 148, among others, in *The Faith of the Early Fathers*, vol. 1.

churches are condemned to hell.[13] Yet the apostles' testimonies show that infants were, in fact, baptized in the earliest years of Christ's Church. Refer to Acts 16:15, 33, 18:8; and 1 Corinthians 1:16, where the baptism of entire households is conducted. In any ancient culture, the practice of household baptism was certain to include infants. Early Christian writers also declared infant baptism to be of apostolic origin. Origen (*Homilies on Leviticus* 8, 3) and Augustine (*On Baptism* 4, 24, 31) both called infant baptism a tradition received from the apostles.

As with so many other areas, Mormons fail to get their facts straight when examining historic Christianity. McConkie, for example, said, "Those churches in modern Christendom which practice infant baptism do so because of the false notion that all children who die are eternally damned unless they have been baptized."[14]

This is an entrenched misunderstanding in the Mormon church. The Catholic Church has never taught the damnation of any unbaptized infant.[15] Neither do Protestant churches who practice infant baptism.

Immersion

Baptism by affusion ("pouring") is still another "proof" of the apostasy. Latter-day Saints reject all baptism but their own, which is by immersion only. The Mormon *Doctrinal Commentary on the*

---

[13] McConkie, not surprisingly, pushes his predecessors' point to the absurd: "Few heresies have been more firmly lodged in the minds of large segments of fallen man than that of infant baptism. Some even say that because original sin begins not with birth but at conception itself [the Catholic teaching], baptism is required not only for every aborted fetus, but even for a blood clot that has yet to take upon itself an embryonic form. The traditional sectarian phrase in many of the sermons of the past was that the road to hell was paved with the skulls of unbaptized infants...." *A New Witness for the Articles of Faith*, 101.

[14] McConkie, *Doctrinal New Testament Commentary*, vol. 1, 550.

[15] See George J. Dyer, *Limbo: Unsettled Question*.

New Testament states, "As every informed person knows, Jesus was baptized by immersion. Baptism means immersion."[16]

Neither of these claims is true. Baptism does not *mean* immersion. In Mark 7:4, Christ condemns the hypocrisy of the Pharisees, saying, "And when they come from the market, except they wash [*baptizontai*], they eat not." A full immersion is suggested by neither the context nor the actual custom of the day. What is meant here is the ritual ablution of pouring water over one's hands and arms, thus "purifying" oneself from the taint of the marketplace.

The Savior, yearning to fulfill his Father's will and redeem the world, exclaims, "I have a baptism [*baptizma*] to be baptized with; and how am I straitened till it be accomplished!" (Luke 12:50.) No immersion in water or anything else is implied here. Instead, the Lord refers to the spiritual urgency of the work before him.[17]

Mormon author B. H. Roberts wrote, "It was early in the third century that the form of baptism began to be changed. Up to this time it had been performed only by immersion of the whole body."[18]

However, Paul was baptized in the house of Ananias (Acts 9:17–18). Peter performed baptisms in the house of Cornelius (Acts 10:47–48). And three thousand Jews were baptized at one time in Jerusalem (Acts 2:41). Archeologists have shown that there was no sufficient supply of water for immersing all these converts. The method must have been by pouring or sprinkling.[19]

The *Didache*, dating from around the year 70, presents the authentic, Trinitarian formula for baptism and explicitly allows pouring, stating, "In regard to baptism, baptize thus: After the foregoing instructions, baptize in the name of the Father, and of the Son, and of the Holy Spirit, in living [i.e., running] water. If you have not living [running] water, then baptize in other water;

---

[16] *Doctrinal New Testament Commentary*, vol. 1, 124.
[17] See also Matthew 28:19; Romans 6:3; 1 Peter 3:21.
[18] *The Falling Away*, 55.
[19] See the Catholic Answers pamphlet, "Baptism: Immersion Only?"

and if you are not able in cold, then in warm. If you have neither, pour water three times on the head, in the name of the Father, and of the Son, and of the Holy Spirit" (*Didache* 7:1–3).

The pictures in the catacombs reinforce the practice of pouring. In fact, catechumens are frequently shown standing in water while being baptized by having water poured on their heads. Even Christ's baptism is so depicted.

Scriptural evidence and the earliest Church writings are conclusive. Pouring was not a late, un-Christian practice, but was an acceptable means of baptizing from the Church's earliest days.

14. Charges of Catholic Misdeeds

Realizing, perhaps, the weaknesses of the argument they make from Scripture for a total apostasy, Mormon theologians cast about for any indication of weakness in the Catholic Church to disprove that it (and, by extension, its Protestant "daughters") has valid claim to be Christ's Church. The theme most often employed is that the "persecuted" Church of the first century degenerated into the "persecuting" Church of the Dark and Middle Ages. Three "proofs" that are commonly given are the Crusades, "the Inquisition," and the Galileo case.

Catholics need to consider several things when presented with allegations of past injustices done by or in the name of the Church. Is the source of the allegation dependable and dispassionate? Mormon theologians, historians, and apologists almost universally quote only anti-Catholic histories and interpretations when discussing the apostasy. Worse, they make assertions and cite no supporting literature. Uncited sources or unreliably cited sources as the basis for charges amount to nothing more than historical gossip and cannot be given credence.

Are the reported events atypical of their times or do they display typical modes of thought and behavior for the period? People must be judged relative to the period in which they live. We would not expect a person from Abraham's time to have all the doctrinal development of Moses' time or a person from Moses' time to have all the development of a person from Jesus' time. God's revelation is progressive, as is his guidance of the Church. Practices must be judged in their historical context.

What do the issues raised have to do with the point under discussion? The idea that some Catholics, even some Catholic leaders, have done bad things in the past would prove only that they individually were at fault. It would not prove a general apostasy. Mormon individuals and Mormon leaders, too, have done bad things in the past, but that is not taken by them as evidence of a general apostasy on their part. This leads to the final question one should ask.

Are there parallel cases in Mormon history that would equally prove a *Mormon* "Great Apostasy" during or since the time of Joseph Smith? If Mormons are going to count certain kinds of historical misdeeds as evidence of a "Great Apostasy," then they, too, must be willing to subject their history to the same scrutiny to see whether *they* have also been the subjects of such an apostasy.

The Crusades

The Crusades are a favorite target of Mormons. Consider, for example, how Thomas S. Monson—First Counselor in the First Presidency and currently the man next in line as prophet—has answered the question, "Where and how should we begin a search for Jesus?"

"Some," said Monson, "have attempted to answer these questions by turning to idols, others by burning incense or lighting candles. In times past, great throngs journeyed in the crusades of Christianity, feeling that, if only the Holy Land could be secured from the infidel, then Christ would be found in their lives. How mistaken they were. Thousands upon thousands perished. Many others committed heinous crimes in the very name of Christianity. Jesus will not be found by crusades of men."[1]

Observe the subtle manipulation of terms in the first sentence: burning incense (an activity of true worship for both Jews and Christians, as seen in both Testaments) and lighting candles (a harmless practice) are equated with turning to idols. In the next breath, Monson mentions the Crusades. The implication is that they are of the same nature as all the other "idolatrous" practices of the Catholic Church.

---

[1] *Conference Report*, October 1965, 142.

Too often, Mormons, like Fundamentalists, refer to the Crusades in a talismanic manner, as if mentioning the very word were sufficient to prove one's point. However, vague allusions to the Crusades do not prove anything and tend to be made by those who lack an understanding of what the Crusades even were. In the popular mind, the Crusades are often thought of as attempts by Christians to forcibly convert Moslems and Jews to the Christian faith. Nothing is further from the truth.

The Crusades were part of a long-term defensive strategy to protect Christendom from Moslem encroachment and conquest. The conflict began in the seventh century, when Moslem conquerors came out of Arabia and began forcibly subjugating half of Christendom. Moslem forces conquered the Holy Land, pushed west and conquered North Africa, then pushed north and conquered Spain. They also spread north from the Holy Land and gained territory in Eastern Europe. For a time, matters looked very desperate for Christendom, and it appeared that all of Europe might fall to Moslem invaders.

The conflict with Moslem forces lasted for centuries, with Christendom defending itself as best it could. As with any long-term conflict, the battle lines changed many times. Spain was not permanently liberated until the fifteenth century, and Christendom did not finally reach a state of security until the battle of Lepanto in 1571, when Christian forces beat the Ottoman Empire's naval forces, ending the threat of Turkish naval supremacy in the Mediterranean. The Crusades were just one period in Christendom's defensive campaign, when Christians tried to liberate territory that was symbolically important (just as any attacked power wants to secure and/or liberate its capital and other principal cities). Ultimately, that set of campaigns failed, but they were campaigns that were part of a larger, centuries-long defensive effort.

Did bad things happen in the Crusades? Certainly. Bad things happen in every war, but that does not mean that the war itself is unjust, and we do no service to memory or history if we allow the Crusades to be painted as wars of aggression in which Christians went out to conquer those who were in no way threatening them. Christ's Church would have survived, even if all of Christendom had fallen. The Church would have simply returned to the underground status it had during the Roman persecutions, but immeasurable damage would have been done, a tidal wave of human suffering would have washed over Europe, and millions of souls would have been lost to the gospel.[2]

Mormons also should not be too quick to cite the use of military force as proof of a church's apostasy, for they have had more than a share of it in their short history. For example, in 1838, leaders in the Mormon church organized a band which came to be known as the "Danites," whose purpose was to use force against the enemies of the LDS church.

Mormon historian B. H. Roberts provides information about the purpose of the Danites. In testimony given by Dr. Avard, the leader of the group, it was disclosed that "the original object of [the group] was to drive from the county of Caldwell [Missouri] all those who dissented from the Mormon church; in which they succeeded admirably and to the satisfaction of all concerned."[3]

Nor was violence a staple only of Smith's tenure. The second Mormon prophet, Brigham Young, boasted, "And if the Gentiles [i.e., non-Mormons] wish to see a few tricks, we have 'Mormons' that can perform them. We have the meanest devils on earth in our midst, and we intend to keep them, for we have use for them, and if the Devil does not look sharp, we will cheat him out of them at the last, for they will reform and go to heaven with us" (*Journal of Discourses*, 6:176).

Young's willingness to use force of arms against non-Mormons led to events such as the Mountain Meadows Massacre. As explained by the *Encyclopedia of Mormonism*, "The massacre occurred between September 7 and 11, 1857, when a group of Mormon settlers in southern Utah joined with nearby Indians in killing all

---

[2] Cf. Warren H. Carroll, "The Crusades," *Reasons for Hope*, 206–212.
[3] Roberts, *Comprehensive History of the Church*, 1:501.

but some of the youngest members of a group of non-Mormon emigrants en route to California."

This action was taken because Young and other Mormons perceived a threat to their territory. Mormons try to defend what happened at the Mountain Meadows Massacre, arguing that it was an accident, that the innocent travelers going west should not have been harmed, but the fact remains that this was one instance in a larger conflict in which Smith, Young, and other Mormon leaders were actively in favor of the use of armed, organized force to protect Mormon territory from perceived threats. This, plus the history of Mormon use of force in general, makes it impossible for Mormon apologists to cite the Crusades as examples proving the apostasy of the Christian Church without their own history proving the apostasy of the Mormon church.

The Inquisition

The various inquisitions that have occurred in Christian history are an even more favorite target of Mormon apologists.

"During the Christian era," McConkie wrote, "hundreds of thousands have been burned and hanged as heretics while millions have been slain in wars fomented, instigated, commanded, and led by religious leaders. We make no attempt to recount these deeds of brutality and butchery, libraries are filled with histories that preserve the ugly and revolting details. There are ample accounts of the dark deeds of the Spanish Inquisition, of the papal crusades against the Albigenses, of the unspeakable atrocities wrought upon the Protestants in the Netherlands in the sixteenth century, of the massacre of St. Bartholomew, and so on."[4]

Unfortunately, the inquisitions are even less well understood than the Crusades. Two common fallacies are that the Church killed people (not true; the Church merely evaluated the status of a person's beliefs; penal consequences were the domain of the

---

[4] McConkie, *A New Witness for the Articles of Faith*, 677–678.

state) and that vast numbers of people were killed. One of the wildest anti-Catholic claims is that as many as ninety-five million people were killed, more than Europe's population at the time.

There is also a misperception that there was just one inquisition, the Spanish Inquisition. Actually, there were a number of inquisitions, in various locations, spread over six hundred years. Still, it is the Spanish Inquisition that is most talked about and most vilified, even though it was quite meticulous, especially compared to secular tribunals in Protestant and Catholic countries during this period. There are even records in Spain of people blaspheming in civil court in order to get their case transferred to the Spanish Inquisition, where they knew they would get a fairer and more careful hearing.

The Spanish Inquisition also occurred at a unique point in history. It was created just after Spain had been liberated from Moslem hands, when there were still many non-Christians in the country. For security reasons (to make a re-conquest more difficult), non-Christians were deported. In the process, some Moslems and Jews decided to convert to Christianity, but given the tense political situation, the Spanish government was concerned about insincere conversion and possible treason. The state, therefore, asked the Church to investigate the faith of individuals who might, for religious reasons, give their loyalty to potential invaders.

Even so, the Spanish Inquisition was careful in evaluating evidence regarding the accused. This is why, for example, witch hunting was virtually unknown in Spain, yet ran rampant in Northern Europe's Protestant countries and, later, in America. The ecclesiastical officials in charge of the Spanish Inquisition insisted on the presentation of evidence, not just rumor, for conviction, and there was no evidence of large-scale witchcraft (i.e., pre-Christian paganism).

The same carefulness was applied to those accused of practicing other non-Christian religions. Significant evidence was demanded, and the person was allowed to speak for himself concerning his religious beliefs. Even if convicted, he was given the opportunity to repent. Only if this failed was his case remitted to the state. Consequently, serious historians of the Spanish Inquisition have shown that there were not millions of people sent to their deaths. At most there were perhaps a few thousand death sentences carried out, and these were stretched over several centuries. Given the severity of the penal systems of the time and willingness to use capital punishment in those days, it is difficult to see the Spanish Inquisition as anything but one of the most moderate and careful tribunals of the period.[5]

It is not advisable for Mormons to point to cases of force or even capital punishment in religious cases, since their own history includes such things. Indeed, Mormon prophet Young preached a doctrine of "blood atonement," which taught that the only way consequences of certain sins could be remitted was if the person's own blood was shed. In such cases, execution was not looked on as a last resort given only to dangerous members of society who refused to repent, but as a positive good to be given *even to those who had repented!* In fact, Young argued that it was an act of generosity to shed another's blood so that he might be freed from sins:

> Now take a person in this congregation who has knowledge with regard to being saved in the kingdom of our God and our Father, and being exalted, one who knows and understands the principles of eternal life, and sees the beauty and excellency of the eternities before him compared with the vain and foolish things of the world, and suppose that he is overtaken in a gross fault, that he has committed a sin that he knows will deprive him of that exaltation which he desires, and that he cannot attain to it without the shedding of his blood, and also knows that by having his blood shed he will atone for that sin, and be saved and exalted with the Gods, is there a man or woman in this house but what would say, "Shed my blood that I may be saved and exalted with the Gods"? All mankind love

---

[5] A brief and cogent treatment of the Inquisition is in Karl Keating's *Catholicism and Fundamentalism*, 290–300. See also *Catholic Dossier*, Nov.-Dec. 1996. For a detailed, scholarly treatment, see Edward M. Peters, *Inquisition* (Berkeley: University of California Press, 1989).

themselves, and let these principles be known by an individual, and he would be glad to have his blood shed. That would be loving themselves, even unto an eternal exaltation. Will you love your brothers or sisters likewise, when they have committed a sin that cannot be atoned for without the shedding of their blood? Will you love that man or woman well enough to shed their blood? That is what Jesus Christ meant [*Journal of Discourses* 4:219].

Some Mormons try to argue that Young's doctrine of "blood atonement" was never put into practice. If this were true, then Mormons would be in a problematic position, because they would be denying the fullness of salvation to those who had committed the sins that could be expiated only by shedding the person's own blood. However, "blood atonement" *was* practiced in early Mormonism. This can be established from a variety of sources, but we will cite only one. Gustive O. Larson, a Mormon church history professor at Brigham Young University, explained,

> To whatever extent the preaching on blood atonement may have influenced action, it would have been in relation to Mormon disciplinary action among its own members. In point would be a verbally reported case of a Mr. Johnson in Cedar City who was found guilty of adultery with his stepdaughter by a bishop's court and sentenced to death for atonement of his sin. According to the report of reputable eyewitnesses, judgment was executed with consent of the offender who went to his unconsecrated grave in full confidence of salvation through the shedding of his blood. Such a case, however primitive, is understandable within the meaning of the doctrine and the emotional extremes of the [Mormon] Reformation [*Utah Historical Quarterly*, Jan. 1958, 62, n. 39].

Note how, like an inquisition, this is an ecclesiastical review of church members' alleged wrongdoings. Unlike the European inquisitions, however, the point of inquiry was not whether the person was ostensibly practicing one religion while secretly practicing another. Nor was it inquiring about the teaching of heresy or other religious crimes. The inquiry concerned matters such as adultery and other "garden variety" sins. Also unlike the European inquisitions, it was the bishop's tribunal which *itself* handed down sentence. The case was not remanded to the secular court for sentencing. Unlike the European inquisitions, the convicted was not given the chance to repent and avoid the sentence. And, finally, unlike the European inquisitions, the sentence was viewed as a favor to the convicted—something he should be grateful for —not simply as an undesirable but needed means of protecting society.

Galileo

Mention is made of the Galileo controversy by those who would disprove the Church's claim to divine, infallible guidance. Unlike the two examples above, the issue here involves a direct attack on the Church's teaching office.

"Galileo, in June of 1633, was condemned to renounce, in the presence of a tribunal, the truths he had maintained as a result of his discoveries," said current Mormon apostle Neal A. Maxwell. "The Christian 'astronomy' that then triumphed, however, proved as unreliable as some of what then passed for 'theology.' "[6]

A more tendentious note was struck by Heber J. Grant, seventh president of the Church (1918-1945): "You know when Galileo announced that the earth revolved," Heber claimed, "they passed the sentence of death upon him."[7]

Not true. The Italian astronomer was sanctioned for teaching as a fact something for which he had not laid a proper, scientific foundation. Though we now know that the earth revolves around the sun, not the sun around the earth, we do not know it from Galileo's reasoning. Among his unsuccessful guesses were that the earth is moved by the tides, and the planets travel in circles rather than ellipses, and that the sun is not just the center of the solar system but of the *entire universe*. Galileo was right about one thing, but wrong about a lot, too. Had the Church rushed to embrace his theories, it would have ended up with egg on its face. For

---

[6] *A Wonderful Flood of Light*, 5.
[7] *Gospel Standards*, 321.

this reason, the Church historically has encouraged the sciences (the Holy See played a key role in the development of modern astronomy and currently operates an observatory), but does not endorse particular scientific theories.

There is a lot of misinformation about the Galileo case. Galileo was only suspected of heresy, never condemned for it. No papal intervention superseded the hearings. No infallible office pronounced on the matter. In fact, Pope Urban VIII stated in 1624, "The Holy Church had never, and would never, condemn it [Galileo's theory of heliocentrism] as heretical."[8]

Robert Bellarmine, who conducted one of the investigations, did not consider Galileo a heretic. Pope Paul V especially admired the astronomer. After a subordinate congregation of the Holy Office declared him "vehemently suspect of heresy" in 1633, the Pope commuted the recommended penalties. Throughout the entire affair, it is certain that no pope ever promulgated the idea that Galileo's teachings were heretical. The accusation that the Catholic Church once taught as heretical a proven scientific fact is false.

Mormons, for their part, have not always been as ready to embrace the results of certain scholarly research, either. And they, too, have taken sanctions against researchers who produced "problematic" results. There have been a variety of Mormon scholars—especially historians—who have been charged with apostasy, excommunicated, or disfellowshipped for their publications. Specially noteworthy is the case of Mormon historian D. Michael Quinn, who has even received anonymous death threats since ecclesiastical action was taken against him.[9] The perceived problem with the writings of Quinn and others is not that they teach false theological doctrines (a church is certainly within its purview in regulating theological matters), but that the scientific results pro-

---

[8] William G. Most, *Catholic Apologetics Today*, 168–169; Jeffrey A. Mirus, *Reasons for Hope*, 213–218; Jacques Maritain, *On the Church of Christ*, 200–211.

[9] Cf. *Salt Lake City Tribune*, Oct. 2, 1993, Oct. 18, 1993.

duced—via the science of historical research in this case—are embarrassing to the Mormon hierarchy.

A Catholic should, therefore, have no qualms about raising cases where Mormon scholars have had ecclesiastical action taken against them for their non-religious opinions. If the Galileo case were to prove an apostasy on the part of the Catholic Church (which, of course, it does not), the multiple Mormon scholars who have been disciplined in this century alone would equally prove an apostasy on the part of the Mormon church.

15. The True Church of Christ

Catholics are supreme realists. We recognize and acknowledge that false teachers and abuses have assailed the Church, from within and without, throughout the centuries. They will continue to do so. But standing face to face with any individual's or group's sinful teaching or behavior, or with any cumulative listing of offenses, is the Lord Jesus Christ's promise to establish his Church firmly, to be its head and to lead it into all truth. The Catholic Church may point to a clear scriptural pattern to support its claims to be Christ's indefectible Church. We look at that evidence now.

*Scriptures Indicating the
Permanent Establishment of the Church*

Catholics may offer the testimony of Scripture presented below when dealing with anyone who declares that the Catholic Church is not the true Church or that Christ's Church is not to be identified with a visible organization. Our applications here, however, are to the discussion at hand, namely, that there was in the Savior's mind the establishment of a Church that would preach his truth throughout all human history. This divine intention was made a reality during the years of Christ's ministry and was constituted to last until he comes again in glory. Therefore, the Church has disappeared from the earth with neither a bang nor a whimper. No persecutions, no philosophical systems, no state entanglements, and no degree of internal abuse or sinfulness could nullify the Lord's promise. Scripture, the early Church Fathers and the entire working out of God's plan of salvation point to the Catholic Church as the one established by Christ to be his Body, to continue to sanctify, teach and rule all mankind. The Church as Jesus founded it during his ministry has continued faithful and true throughout human history. Supporting references are reported in four groups.

GROUP ONE: CHRIST PROMISED HIS PERPETUAL PRESENCE

Matthew 16:18: "I say also unto thee, That thou are Peter, and upon this rock I will build my church; and the gates of hell shall not prevail against it."

Not only does this passage declare that the Church, founded by Christ to last forever, will not fail, it also serves in establishing the primacy of Peter and his successors, the popes. This will be treated in a later section. The importance of this verse for establishing the continuity and survival of the Church cannot be overstressed. Every Catholic dealing with Mormons should make this his first piece of scriptural proof that Christ's Church did not, indeed, *could not* apostatize. Christ himself said that it would not. Hell did not, will not, and cannot prevail against it.

Matthew 28:20b: "Lo, I am with you always, even unto the end of the world. Amen."

Mormon theologians like to fancy that they alone treat the Bible seriously and interpret it validly, but they refuse to accept those clear passages that state the opposite of current Mormon doctrine. This verse is a good example. One Mormon apostle put the official spin on the verse, stating that it indicates "that when his kingdom should be set up in the latter days that he would be with his servants until the end of the world."[1] But this is not what the verse says. Jesus Christ—Emmanuel, God with us—who was first promised at the very beginning of Matthew's Gospel (1:23), now promises his continuous presence here at the end of the same Gospel. The Greek translated in the King James Bible as "alway"

---

[1] LeGrand Richards, *Conference Report*, October 1959, 33.

[sic] is rendered "all the days," meaning an ongoing, constant, uninterrupted period of time "unto the end."

Jesus Christ, the omniscient Lord, surely would have been aware of a pending apostasy, were there to be one. Jesus Christ, God without deceit, would not have pledged his perpetual presence if he knew he would soon withdraw it. And Jesus Christ, the omnipotent Ruler, could not fail to fulfill his promises.

John 14:16, 26; John 16:13: "And I will pray the Father, and he shall give you another Comforter, that he may abide with you forever. . . . [H]e shall teach you all things, and bring all things to your remembrance, whatsoever I have said unto you."

McConkie acknowledged that the Comforter was given at the first Pentecost.[2] Catholics take comfort from the Lord's words heard at each Mass: "I leave you peace, My peace I give you." We know that, though we may prove at times unfaithful, the Lord will look upon the faith of his Body, the Church, and will honor his promise of peace. For he gives "not as the world giveth." It is no different with the Holy Spirit of Promise (Luke 24:49; Eph. 1:13). The Paraclete, once sent, remains forever with his people, the Church. Isaiah 55:11 promises, "So shall my word be that goeth forth out of my mouth: it shall not return unto me void, but it shall accomplish that which I please, and it shall prosper in the thing whereto I sent it."

These few verses set the stage for a fuller presentation of the Catholic doctrine of the perpetuity of the Church. From the above passages we recognize that Christ promised to be with his Church until the end of time. He is its builder, its head, its soul. In the New Testament, favorite images of the Church include "the body of Christ" and "the household of God." We turn to these descriptions for further proof that the Lord's "faithfulness is unto all gen-

---

[2] *Mormon Doctrine*, 181.

erations" (Ps. 119:90). It is Jesus Christ who planned his Church, who instituted and established it, and upon whom it is founded.[3]

Group Two: Christ Established and Animates His Church

Luke 14:28–30: "*[Jesus speaking to the disciples:] For which of you, intending to build a tower, sitteth not down first, and counteth the cost, whether he have sufficient to finish it? Lest haply, after he hath laid the foundation, and is not able to finish it, all that behold it begin to mock him, Saying, This man began to build, and was not able to finish.*"

Jesus, the Master Teacher, could certainly be expected to "practice what he preaches." Wouldn't God, intending to found the Church, first foresee the weakness of unaided men and hence supply for it? Yet the Mormon Christ didn't foresee the falling away of his own creation or wasn't able to prevent it or foreknew the apostasy but made idle promises to his apostles nonetheless. In any event, he is not a God to inspire confidence and trust.

Matthew 7:24: "*Therefore whosoever heareth these sayings of mine, and doeth them, I will liken him unto a wise man, which built his house upon a rock.*"

The "foolishness" of God is wiser than the wisdom of man. If we, with all our sins, can still be expected by Christ to build our faith on solid rock, how much more will he, the divine architect, build his own house on an unshakeable foundation?

---

[3] For a valuable treatment of some of the following points, see Patrick Madrid, "In Search of the 'Great Apostasy,'" *This Rock*, March 1992.

Mark 3:27: "*No man can enter into a strong man's house, and spoil his goods, except he will first bind the strong man; and then he will spoil his house.*"

If we admit that the Lord is the builder of his Church, as the following passages show, then this verse, again from Christ's lips, assures us that he can't be bound nor his Church spoiled.

The following passages stress similar themes.

> [Paul speaking to the bishop, Timothy:] But if I tarry long, that thou mayest know how thou oughtest to behave thyself in the house of God, which is the church of the living God, the pillar and ground of the truth [1 Tim. 3:15].

> [Abraham] looked for a city which hath foundations, whose builder and maker is God [Heb. 11:10].

> Wherefore also it is contained in the Scriptures, Behold, I lay in Sion a chief corner stone, elect, precious: and he that believeth on him shall not be confounded [1 Pet. 2:6].

> For other foundation can no man lay than that is laid, which is Jesus Christ [1 Cor. 3:11].

> [The angel Gabriel speaking to Mary about her Son:] And he shall reign over the house of Jacob for ever; and of his kingdom there shall be no end. He shall be great, and shall be called the Son of the Highest: and the Lord God shall give unto him the throne of his father David [Luke 1:32–33].

> Unto him [the Father] be glory in the church by Christ Jesus throughout all ages, world without end. Amen [Eph. 3:21].

From the above citations, we conclude: Christ established his Church; Christ is the foundation and life of this Church; Christ protects his Church;[4] this Church is destined to offer praise to

---

[4] 1 John 4:4: ". . . greater is he that is in you, than he that is in the world." The attacks of the world, the flesh, and the devil are no match for the power of Jesus Christ. Neither heresy nor moral laxity can confound the divine plan.

the Father throughout all time and all eternity; and this Church is the visible, earthly source of saving truth.

The intimate, inviolable bond between the Lord and his Church is perhaps best seen in Christ's own self description: "I am the good shepherd; the good shepherd giveth his life for the sheep" (John 10:11). Paul, in like vein, entreats the leaders of the early Christian community to feed and defend "the church of God, which he hath purchased with his own blood" (Acts 20:28). Bought at an incomparable price, the Church will be sustained and protected throughout all time by its founder and head. This leads us to a third group of Scripture references, those depicting the Church as the "body of Christ."

GROUP THREE: THE CATHOLIC CHURCH IS CHRIST'S MYSTICAL BODY

Not only did Christ found and promise to protect his Church, the Church represents his mystical body on earth, and he is its head.

> So we, being many, are one body in Christ, and every one members one of another [Rom. 12:5].

> And he is the head of the body, the church: who is the beginning, the firstborn from the dead; that in all things he might have the preeminence [Col. 1:18].

> And [the Father] hath put all things under his feet, and gave him to be the head over all things to the church [Eph. 1:22].

> [Paul, speaking to married Christians:] For no man ever yet hated his own flesh; but nourisheth and cherisheth it, even as the Lord the church [Eph. 5:29].

Biblical testimony declares that the Church is the mystical body of Christ. As such, it is upheld and treasured by its head. The word of the Lord is living, active, and fruitful. It accomplishes its purposes. The Church that the Lord planned and built, which he heads and feeds, for which he bled and died, and to which he promised the perpetual presence of the Holy Spirit, could not fail, for the Lord can neither deceive nor be deceived. For Christ's Church to apostatize or be exterminated from the earth would be for Christ's own mystical body to apostatize or be exterminated, which he has promised will not happen.

GROUP FOUR: OLD TESTAMENT PASSAGES INDICATING THE LORD'S ETERNAL LOVE AND CARE FOR HIS PEOPLE

Mormon apologists rely in part on Old Testament passages as cited in chapter 4 for proof of a general apostasy. We have seen how each of those passages really predicts the fall of Israel or Judah, or the rigors to be endured at the end of time. For their part, Catholics may celebrate the loving faithfulness of the Father not only as revealed in his Son, but also as affirmed in his earlier covenants. Only a sample can be given here:

Isaiah 9:6–7: *"For unto us a child is born, unto us a son is given: and the government shall be upon his shoulder: and his name shall be called Wonderful, Counsellor, The mighty God, The everlasting Father, the Prince of Peace. Of the increase of his government and peace there shall be no end, upon the throne of David, and upon his kingdom, to order it, and to establish it with judgment and with justice from henceforth even for ever. The zeal of the Lord of hosts will perform this."*

The LDS footnotes to this passage admit that it refers to Jesus Christ. In that case, it must also be admitted that the government he brings—the Church—will have no end, that it is established "henceforth even for ever." It cannot apostatize.

Jeremiah 32:37–41: *"Behold, I [God] will gather them out of all countries . . . and I will bring them again unto this place, and I will cause them to dwell safely: And they shall be my people, and I will be their God: And I will give them one heart and one way, that they may fear me for ever, for the good of them, and of their children after them: And I will make an everlasting covenant with them, that I will not turn away from them, to do them good; but I will put my fear in their hearts, that they shall not depart from me. Yea, I will rejoice over them to do them good, and I will plant them in this land assuredly with my whole heart and with my whole soul."*

God the Father is speaking, assuring his wayward people of his eternal love. He abides by his covenant with them. The clear sense of this divine promise is that God remains faithful; once he has chosen a people for a singular blessing, he proves worthy of trust. Mormons are fond of saying that Jesus Christ does only what he has seen his Father **before** him do. If that is the case, then Christ's own promises of fidelity are equally valid and potent.

Daniel 7:13–14: "I saw in the night visions, and behold, one like the Son of man came with the clouds of heaven, and came to the Ancient of Days, and they brought him near before him. And there was given him dominion, and glory, and a kingdom, that all people, nations, and languages, should serve him: his dominion is an everlasting dominion, which shall not pass away, and his kingdom that which shall not be destroyed."

Catholic and Mormon writers often apply these verses to the end times, at which Jesus Christ will present his kingdom pure and without spot to God the Father. By extension, however, we may properly apply this passage to the Church of Christ, indestructible from its institution.

That the Church is to be identified as the kingdom of God is taught in the New Testament passages listed above. Moreover, in Matthew 10:7, the Savior tells us that "the kingdom of heaven is at hand." It is here, and it already enjoys the promises made to it.

The Church enjoys perpetuity from its founding by Christ through its ultimate fulfillment at the end of time. Here is how.

The Primacy of Peter and the Popes

Unlike most Protestants, Mormons recognize the supremacy of Peter's position among the apostles, as writer Parley Pratt makes clear, noting, "And by this means the great Apostle of the Father chose and ordained the Twelve Apostles of the Jews, and gave the keys or presidency of the Kingdom to Peter."[5]

Reading into the apostolic organization of the Church their own latter-day system, Mormons call Peter, James, and John the "first presidency," with Peter the "president of the Church" and the others his counselors.[6] The demands of a general falling away require the Mormon to say that this divinely constituted government, with apostles at the head of the Church, disappeared in the early years of Christianity. Catholics can demonstrate the contrary using testimony from Scripture and Church history.

PETER WAS GIVEN A UNIQUE ROLE BY CHRIST

Matthew 16:18: "*And I say also unto thee, That thou are Peter, and upon this rock I will build my church. . . .*"

Smith, in his *Teachings*, said that the "rock" was "revelation" (p. 273). Commenting on his brief statement, Mormon theologians explain that the rock on which Christ built his Church was the revelation Peter received from the Father, namely that Jesus is the Son of God. This interpretation is incorrect for two reasons. First, it fails to address the significance of Simon Bar-Jona's new name, given by the Lord. Protestants are quick to point out the Greek *petros*, given to Peter, means a small stone, movable and not permanent. The Greek *petra*, upon which Christ will build his Church, means a massive, immutable rock. This anti-Catholic

---

[5] Parley Pratt, *Key to the Science of Theology*, 69.
[6] See *Doctrines of Salvation* 3:152.

argument is premature in its linguistic revelry. Christ and his apostles spoke Aramaic. The Aramaic for "rock" is *kepha*; the Aramaic for "Peter" is *kepha*. Not Christ, not Peter's faith, and not a heavenly revelation are called *kepha*. Only Peter is. Name changes in the Bible are not made casually or to no purpose. Jesus named Peter "Rock" because he meant him to be the rock.[7]

Second, asserting that "rock" refers to "revelation" ignores the basic pattern that a noun phrase modify the noun nearest it. In this instance, "this rock" must refer to "Peter." "Revelation" is adverted to only indirectly, and then only in a different verse.[8]

John 21:15–17: "So when they had dined, Jesus saith to Simon Peter, Simon, son of Jonas, lovest thou me more than these? He saith unto him, Yea, Lord; thou knowest that I love thee. He saith unto him, Feed my lambs. He saith to him again the second time, Simon, son of Jonas, lovest thou me? He saith unto him, Yea, Lord; thou knowest that I love thee. He saith unto him, Feed my sheep. He saith unto him the third time, Simon, son of Jonas, lovest thou me? Peter was grieved because he said unto him the third time, Lovest thou me? And he said unto him, Lord, thou knowest all things; thou knowest that I love thee. Jesus saith unto him, Feed my sheep."

Jesus Christ is the Good Shepherd who never leaves his flock untended. Both Testaments are rich in shepherd/flock imagery describing the Lord and his people. Jesus Christ gave not only his authority to Peter, but here, at the end of his earthly stay, he gives Peter the office and title of pastor even over the other apostles ("lovest thou me more than *these?*"). Peter, the Vicar of Christ, takes up the Shepherd's staff.

Matthew 10:2 (see also parallels at Mark 3:2, Luke 6:14, and Acts 1:13): "Now the names of the twelve apostles are these; The first, Simon,

---

[7] For a detailed look at the structure of the passage and why it requires Peter to be the rock, see J. Akin, "Peter the Rock," *This Rock*, November 1998, 33.

[8] *Catholicism and Fundamentalism*, 208.

who is called Peter, and Andrew his brother; James the son of Zebedee and John his brother. . . ."

In every listing of the twelve apostles, Peter's name comes first. The words "the first," with respect to Peter, do not merely indicate his place on the list. None of the rest are given a number. Nor can "the first" indicate the order in which the men were called by Christ, for Andrew was chosen before Peter. Neither can "the first" refer to foremost in the Lord's affection, since John repeatedly called himself "the disciple whom Jesus loved." The only explanation is Peter is first among the apostles in rank or primacy of jurisdiction. (Peter is given more attention by the Gospel writers than all the other apostles combined. Reference is made to him one hundred and seventy-nine times; reference to all the others, one hundred and forty-nine times.)

Peter's Exercise of His Office

As the New Testament also shows, Peter exercised his unique role and was accepted as leader by the apostles. He often spoke on behalf of all the apostles (Matt. 18:21; Mark 8:29; Luke 12:41; John 6:69). He first preached to the Jews gathered on the day of Pentecost (Acts 2:14). He received into the Church the first Jewish and first Gentile converts (Acts 2:41, 10:44–49). He performed the first miracle in the Church (Acts 3:6–7). He called for the election of a replacement for Judas Iscariot (Acts 1:15–23). He defended the apostles before the Jewish tribunal (Acts 4:8–12). His opinion prevailed at the first council of the Church (Acts 15:6–12). And Paul, after his miraculous conversion and calling as an apostle of Christ, regarded it his duty to present himself to Peter (Gal. 1:18[9]).

Peter was chosen by Christ to be the visible, sure foundation of the Church on earth. He was the second chief shepherd, the

---

[9] See J. Akin, "Peter in Galatians," *This Rock*, May 1998, 33.

vicar of him who governs and guides infallibly from his heavenly place. Peter knew it; the other apostles confessed it.

THE TESTIMONY FROM CHURCH HISTORY

Peter's successors, the bishops of Rome, have always exercised supreme power in the Church; that power has been acknowledged from the beginning of the faith. Consider the following:

1. John the Apostle likely was alive and active in the faith, working in Ephesus, when problems arose in the Church at Corinth. There were disagreements among the leadership of that local church, and recourse was made, not to the last living original apostle, but to Peter's successor in Rome, Clement, to seek Rome's verdict. Clement did not have to explain or assert his right to intervene; it was assumed. Clement responded, in *The Epistle to the Corinthians*, in about the year 80.[10]

2. In about 190, Pope Victor commanded the people of Asia Minor to conform to the Roman usage in the celebration of Easter. Those who resisted were threatened with excommunication. Though other bishops, including Irenaeus, asked the Pope for gentler treatment of those who resisted his order, they did not dispute Victor's right to proceed with due discipline throughout the Church.[11]

3. About 255, Pope Stephen forbade bishops of North Africa to rebaptize apostates returning to the Church and excommunicated those who disobeyed.[12]

4. When Athanasius, the great defender of the Holy Trinity, was deposed by the emperor, an Arian sympathizer, in the mid-fourth century, Pope Julius I reinstated and protected him.[13]

5. In 431, before the Council of Ephesus, Cyril of Alexandria traveled to Rome to receive a decision from the pope about the

---

[10] *The Faith of the Early Fathers*, vol. 1, 6–13.
[11] Ibid., 106.
[12] Francis Spirago, *The Catechism Explained*, 224.
[13] Charles Poulet, *A History of the Catholic Church*, vol. 1, 249.

Eastern heresy of Nestorianism. The pope sent delegates to the Council who asserted without contradiction, "There is no doubt, it has been known to all centuries, that the holy and blessed Apostle Peter, the prince and head and pillar of the faith and foundation of the Catholic Church, received the keys of the kingdom from our Lord Jesus Christ. . . . He [Peter] lives even to this time, and always in his successors gives judgment."[14]

Pope Celestine had admonished his legates: "We enjoin upon you the necessary task of guarding the authority of the Apostolic See. . . . If it comes to controversy, it is not yours to join the fight, but to judge of their opinion."[15]

6. In 451 the Council of Chalcedon dealt with another Eastern heresy, that of Eutyches. Pope Leo (the Great) sent his decision that Christ has, indeed, two natures. When the Pope's letter had been read, the bishops exclaimed, "This is the faith of the Fathers, this is the faith of the Apostles. We all believe thus. . . . Peter has spoken through Leo."[16]

Further Testimony of Church Fathers

The early Church was careful in keeping succession records to demonstrate the connection between the earliest apostles and the bishops they ordained, guaranteeing the various lines of apostolic succession. Particular attention was paid to the succession of the Roman See, since it was here that Peter finished his life during the persecution by Nero and here that he left his successor as head of the Church as a whole. This is illustrated in the various early succession lists for the See of Rome, only a few of which are presented here.

"The blessed Apostles [Peter and Paul]," Irenaeus said, "having founded and built up the church [in Rome], committed into the hands of Linus the office of the episcopate. . . . To him succeeded Anacletus, and after him in the third place, Clement was allotted

---

[14] *The Fathers of the Early Church*, vol. 3, 184.
[15] Ibid.
[16] Neuner and Dupuis, *The Christian Faith*, 154.

THE GREAT APOSTASY

the bishopric. . . . In this order and by this succession the ecclesiastical tradition from the Apostles and the preaching of the truth has come down to us."[17]

Eusebius wrote, "Paul testifies that Crescens was sent to Gaul [2 Tim. 4:10], but Linus, whom he mentions in the Second Epistle to Timothy [2 Tim. 4:21] as his companion at Rome, was Peter's successor in the episcopate of the church there, as has already been shown. Clement also, who was appointed third bishop of the church at Rome, was, as Paul testifies, his co-laborer and fellow-soldier [Phil. 4:3]."[18]

And Augustine wrote, "For if the lineal succession of bishops is to be taken into account, with how much more certainty and benefit to the Church do we reckon back till we reach Peter himself, to whom, as bearing in a figure the whole Church, the Lord said: 'Upon this rock will I build my Church, and the gates of hell shall not prevail against it!' The successor of Peter was Linus, and his successors in unbroken continuity were these: Clement, Anacletus. . . ."[19]

An old proverb states, "You cannot give what you do not have." Peter, having the primacy, could and did give it to his successors in the episcopate. For it was precisely in his office as Bishop of Rome that he exercised universal jurisdiction and enjoyed preeminence of honor. Peter did not stand apart from or outside the list of bishops of Rome. All those who succeed him assume his primacy and jurisdiction. What was given first by Christ to Peter is now given to each of Peter's successors.

---

[17] Irenaeus, *Against Heresies* 3,3,3 [A.D. 180]. Some have tried to argue that since Peter and Paul are referred to as building the Church of Rome in this passage, this somehow argues against the Catholic position. But it does not. The Catholic Church has always proudly noted that both men labored in Rome, Peter serving as its bishop during the final period of his life, and Paul serving as a brilliant theologian and evangelist. When the time of their martyrdoms in the Neronian persecution drew near, the two of them entrusted the care of the Church of Rome to Peter's successor as bishop, Linus.

[18] Eusebius, *Church History* 3:4:9-10 [A.D. 312].

[19] Augustine, *Ad Generosum* 53, 1, 2.

Apostolic Succession and the Perpetuity of the Church

The history and tradition of the Catholic Church have taught, from its institution, the handing on of the apostles' authority and power through the line of bishops. Mormons dispute this, claiming that the twelve apostles held a unique role that, because it was not replicated in their successors, was lost to the primitive Church. This absence of apostolic "keys" is a sign of the great apostasy.

The problem with the Mormon understanding of the twelve is that it doesn't go far enough. The twelve *did* have a unique position—one *so unique* that it was held only by them. The requirements for being a member of the twelve was having been a witness of Jesus' entire earthly ministry, as clearly stated in Acts 1:21–22. This requirement was taken so seriously that not even Paul and Barnabas, when they became apostles, were admitted to the twelve because they had not been witnesses to Christ's earthly ministry. The twelve served a special role in the first century as the link between Jesus' earthly ministry and the subsequent development of Christianity. Not even other apostles, who had been commissioned by the risen Christ only after his ministry, could do that.

But while the twelve were a special body unique to the first generation of Christians, the apostles in general—both those in the twelve and others like Paul and Barnabas—*did* pass on their apostolic authority to the bishops of the Church, as is amply indicated in the writings of the early Church Fathers, such as Clement I of Rome, who wrote, "They [apostles] appointed their earliest converts, testing them by the spirit, to be the bishops and deacons of future believers. . . . They appointed those who have already been mentioned, and afterwards added the further provision that, if they should die, other approved men should succeed to their ministry."[20]

---

[20] Clement I of Rome, *Epistle to the Corinthians*, A.D. 80.

Ignatius of Antioch noted that, "Indeed, when you submit to the bishop as you would to Jesus Christ, it is clear to me that you are living not in the manner of men but as Jesus Christ, who died for us.... It is necessary, therefore—and such is your practice—that you do nothing without the bishop, and that you be subject also to the presbytery, as to the Apostles of Jesus Christ our hope, on whom we shall be found, if we live in Him."[21]

He added, "In like manner let everyone respect the deacons as they would respect Jesus Christ, and just as they respect the bishop as a type of the Father, and the presbyters as the council of God and college of Apostles. Without these, it cannot be called a Church."[22]

In yet another letter, Ignatius of Antioch wrote,

> You must all follow the bishop as Jesus Christ follows the Father, and the presbytery as you would the Apostles. Reverence the deacons as you would the command of God. Let no one do anything of concern to the Church without the bishop. Let that be considered a valid Eucharist which is celebrated by the bishop, or by one whom he appoints. Wherever the bishop appears, let the people be there; just as wherever Jesus Christ is, there is the Catholic Church. Nor is it permitted without the bishop either to baptize or to celebrate the agape; but whatever he approve, this too is pleasing to God, so that whatever is done will be secure and valid [Ignatius of Antioch, *Letter to the Smyrnaeans*, A.D. 110].

Irenaeus said,

> It is possible, then, for everyone in every Church, who may wish to know the truth, to contemplate the tradition of the Apostles which has been made known throughout the whole world. And we are in a position to enumerate those who were instituted bishops by the Apostles, and their successors to our own times: men who neither knew nor taught anything like these heretics rave about. For if the Apostles had known hidden mysteries which they taught to the

---

[21] Ignatius of Antioch [disciple of St. John the Evangelist], *Letter to the Trallians*, A.D. 110.
[22] Ibid.

elite secretly and apart from the rest, they would have handed them down especially to those very ones to whom they were committing the self-same Churches. For surely they wished all those and their successors to be perfect and without reproach, to whom they handed on their authority [Irenaeus, *Against Heresies*, A.D. 180].

It is necessary to obey those who are the presbyters in the Church, those who, as we have shown, have succession from the Apostles; those who have received, with the succession of the episcopate, the sure charism of truth according to the good pleasure of the Father. But the rest, who have no part in the primitive succession and assemble wheresoever they will, must be held in suspicion [ibid.].

The true knowledge is the doctrine of the Apostles, and the ancient organization of the Church throughout the whole world, and the manifestation of the body of Christ according to the successions of bishops, by which successions the bishops have handed down the Church which is found everywhere; and the very complete tradition of the Scriptures, which have come down to us by being guarded against falsification, and which are received without addition or deletion; and reading without falsification, and a legitimate and diligent exposition according to the Scriptures, without danger and without blasphemy; and the pre-eminent gift of love, which is more precious than knowledge, more glorious than prophecy, and more honored than all the other charismatic gifts [ibid.].

"The path of those . . . who belong to the Church, goes around the whole world;" Irenaeus concluded, "for it has the firm tradition of the Apostles, enabling us to see that the faith of all is one and the same."[23]

Firmilian of Caesarea wrote, "Therefore, the power of forgiving sins was given to the Apostles and then to the Churches which these men, sent by Christ, established; and to the bishops who succeeded them by being ordained in their place."[24]

And in the *Apostolic Constitutions*' "Invocation in the Ordination of Bishops," we read, "Grant to him, almighty Master, through

---

[23] Irenaeus, *Against Heresies*, A.D. 180.
[24] Firmilian of Caesarea, *Letter to Cyprian*, A.D. 255.

Your Christ, possession of the Holy Spirit, so that he may have, according to Your mandate, the power to remit sins, to confer orders according to Your precept, and to dissolve every bond, according to the power which You gave to Your Apostles."[25]

Finally, Cyprian of Carthage wrote, "Cornelius was made bishop [of Rome] by the decision of God and of his Christ . . . by the college of venerable priests and good men, at a time when no one had been made before him—when the place of Fabian, which is the place of Peter, the dignity of the sacerdotal chair, was vacant."[26]

The succession in the Roman Church was but one manifestation of the apostles' understanding that the Church was to continue beyond their deaths. In similar manner, each of the twelve, along with Paul, ordained men to the ministry of overseer or bishop. These pastors were charged with teaching and defending the Catholic faith (2 Tim. 1:6, 13, 4:1-2).

Jesus' words and deeds indicated his intentions. During the Last Supper, after he had bestowed upon them the incomparable gift of the Eucharist, the Lord further assured the apostles of his abiding presence. In the High Priestly Prayer of Christ, a verbal "last testament" before his death, he promised:

> I will not leave you comfortless (I will not leave you orphans. [NAB]): I will come to you [John 14:18]. And I will pray the Father, and he shall give you another Comforter, that he may abide with you for ever [John 14:16]. Nevertheless I tell you the truth; It is expedient for you that I go away: for if I go not away, the Comforter will not come unto you; but if I depart, I will send him unto you [John 16:7]. But when the Comforter is come, whom I will send unto you from the Father, even the Spirit of truth, which proceedeth from the Father, he shall testify of me [John 15:26]. The Comforter, which is the Holy Ghost, whom the Father will send in my name, he shall teach you all things, and bring all things to your remembrance, whatsoever I have said unto you [John 14:26].

---

[25] *Apostolic Constitutions*, A.D. 400.
[26] Cyprian of Carthage, *Letter to Antonianus*, A.D. 251.

He made this promise just before his crucifixion. At the end of his earthly ministry, just before his return to the Father, he guarantees the twelve, "Lo, I am with you alway, [sic] even unto the end of the world" (Matt. 28:20).

This pledge of fidelity empowered the apostles to fulfill Christ's final command to them:

"Go ye therefore, and teach all nations, baptizing them in the name of the Father, and of the Son, and of the Holy Ghost: Teaching them to observe all things whatsoever I have commanded you" (Matt. 28:19-20).

The recipients of this promise would not live forever. The span of the globe and the stretch of centuries would prohibit their personal preaching to all mankind. So Paul, teaching about the Church's divine organization, writes, "You are no more strangers and foreigners, but you are fellow-citizens with the saints and the household of God, built upon the foundation of the apostles and prophets, Jesus Christ Himself being the chief cornerstone" (Eph. 2:19-20).

A foundation presupposes a structure will be built upon it. A house needs but one foundation. This foundation has been established once for all in the Church: the Lord Jesus Christ and his apostles. Because their faith was confirmed by the Spirit of God at Pentecost, the twelve's ministry as foundation stones lasts forever. The structure built upon Peter the rock and his brethren lasts forever.

God wants "all men to be saved, and to come unto the knowledge of the truth" (1 Tim. 2:4). For the truth to be known, it must be available to all people and they must be able to find it. This presupposes an ever-present, authoritative teacher defining and proclaiming the good news of salvation. None but the Catholic Church maintains the signs of unity and universality in both time and space. None but the Catholic Church bears in its body the marks of apostolic vigor and communal holiness. The Catholic Church *is* Christ's one, true, and original Church.

16. A Not Quite Total Apostasy?

Mormons commonly state that all true followers of Jesus Christ, individually and collectively, eventually died or apostatized shortly after the establishment of the Church. So, as the original twelve died, they left no successors to their apostleship. Likewise, according to the Book of Mormon, Jesus Christ visited the American continent soon after his ascension and established his Church in the Western Hemisphere, choosing twelve "disciples" and endowing them with all necessary authority to carry on his work (3 Nephi 12). They, too, eventually died, and the Nephite Christian church lapsed into apostasy within a few centuries of the Savior's visit. Jesus Christ was thus a two-time loser.

But if one digs deeply enough, one discovers that Mormons do not quite mean what they say when they speak of all believers dying or apostatizing. They actually claim that four individuals —the apostle John plus three Nephites from Jesus' New World church—did not apostatize *or* die!

According to Doctrine and Covenants 7, Jesus promised John that he would be allowed to "tarry" until the Second Coming and "prophesy before nations, kindreds, tongues and people." In 1829, Smith and Oliver Cowdery inquired by the Urim and Thummim (two stones set in bows like eyeglass frames) as to whether John had died. The revelation that came was a translation of a parchment written and "hidden up" by John that stated,

> And the Lord said unto me: John, my beloved, what desirest thou? For if you shall ask what you will, it shall be granted unto you.
>
> And I said unto them: Lord, give unto me power over death, that I may live and bring souls unto thee.
>
> And the Lord said unto me: Verily, verily, I say unto thee, because thou desirest this thou shalt tarry until I come in my glory and shalt prophesy before nations, kindreds, tongues, and people.

And for this cause the Lord said unto Peter: If I will that he tarry till I come, what is that to thee? For he desired of me that he might bring souls unto me, but thou desiredst that thou speedily come unto me in my kingdom.... And I will make thee to minister for him and for thy brother James; and unto you three will I give this power and the keys of this ministry until I come [D&C 7:1-4, 8].

Mormon doctrine maintains that one of the original twelve apostles (from Palestine) has never died, has in fact held a ministry of prophecy akin to that of the current "prophets, seers, and revelators" of the LDS church. Indeed, Christ gave John the Revelator the "keys" to minister until the Lord comes. Here, then, is at least one true Christian, bearing full priesthood authority, who did not die or apostatize. To non-Mormons, this claim sounds ludicrous. One reason, of course, is John's seeming absence from Church history. Another is the records of his death found in the writings of the early Church Fathers. Why would they write about his death (and point out his tomb) if he was still alive? Why did he go into hiding if his mission was to preach before nations? Surely the presence of an immortal, unkillable man who is guaranteed life until the Second Coming would be an enormous witness to Christians and non-Christians. If John is alive now, why doesn't he come forward and announce himself before the world?

More fundamentally, the claim made on John's behalf is directly contrary to Scripture and the words of John himself. In the first century, Jesus *did* make a remark to Peter concerning John tarrying till the Second Coming, and consequently a rumor began that John would not die, but at the end of his Gospel, John specifically states that Jesus' remark did *not* mean that he would remain alive during all of the Christian age:

[Jesus said to Peter:] Verily, verily, I say unto thee, When thou wast young, thou girdedst thyself, and walkedst whither thou wouldest: but when thou shalt be old, thou shalt stretch forth thy hands, and another shall gird thee, and carry *thee* whither thou wouldest not. This spake he, signifying by what death he should glorify God. And when he had spoken this, he saith unto him, Follow me.

Then Peter, turning about, seeth the disciple whom Jesus loved following; which also leaned on his breast at supper, and said, Lord, which is he that betrayeth thee? Peter seeing him saith to Jesus, Lord, and what shall this man do? Jesus saith unto him, If I will that he tarry till I come, what is that to thee? follow thou me. Then went this saying abroad among the brethren, that that disciple should not die: yet Jesus said not unto him, He shall not die; but, If I will that he tarry till I come, what is that to thee? This is the disciple which testifieth of these things, and wrote these things: and we know that his testimony is true [John 21:18–24].

John specifically states that Jesus "said not unto him, He shall not die" but only "*If* I will that he tarry till I come." It was a rhetorical question to Peter saying, in essence, "It is none of your concern what kind of death John has, or even if he dies at all; focus on the task I am giving *you*."

Smith and Cowdery, however, chose not only to revive the ancient rumor that John would not die and not only asserted his immortality as a fact but turned Jesus' remark about John into the very promise of immortality that John denied was a promise of immortality!

According to the Book of Mormon, there are also three Nephites who have lived for centuries: "And he [Jesus] said unto them [three of the twelve Nephites chosen to direct the newly established Church in the Americas]: Behold, I know your thoughts, and ye have desired the thing which John, my beloved, who was with me in my ministry, before that I was lifted up by the Jews, desired of me. Therefore, more blessed are ye, for ye shall never taste of death; but ye shall live to behold all the doings of the Father unto the children of men, even until all things shall be fulfilled according to the will of the Father, when I shall come in my glory with the powers of heaven" (3 Nephi 28:18).

It would appear that we have here three more apostolic witnesses to Christ, men who neither fell away nor died. They were promised that they would remain to see all the works of the Father among mankind throughout the centuries of time. However, the fate of these three Nephites is unclear. The Book of Mormon suggests at one point that the three, known as the "beloved disciples," were taken from the earth: "But wickedness did prevail upon the face of the whole land, insomuch that the Lord did take away his beloved disciples, and the work of miracles and of healing did cease because of the iniquity of the people. . . . The beloved disciples were taken away out of the land" (Mormon 1:13, 16).

Nevertheless, Mormons popularly claim that the three are still around. McConkie writes that these three Nephites are continuing their assigned ministry at this time, and there have been occasions when they have appeared to members of the church in this final dispensation.[1]

Needless to say, Christians find the idea of the three immortal Nephites even less plausible than that of an immortal apostle John. The Nephite people never existed, meaning none of them were immortal, and the statement about their being "taken away" looks like an attempt to explain away their absence from the earth in Smith's day.

Nevertheless, let us suppose the three exist and that they, together with the apostle John, are immortal and on the earth. That makes a total of four outstanding Christian witnesses who allegedly survived the great collapse of Christianity. Why was not the Church preserved through them? Mormons do not know. Though all four men possessed "the keys," given by Jesus himself, and clearly had his authority to minister on his behalf, though all four possessed the high priesthood authority that Mormons deem essential to the church, for some inexplicable reason, God did not preserve either the Old World church or the New World church through them. Instead, Mormons claim, he took his Church back to heaven, though leaving the four (or at least John) on earth, but not as officers of his Church.

Mormons, therefore, do not point to the four as a remnant preserving the Church on earth between the Great Apostasy and the re-establishment of the church by Smith. The theological reason why Mormons do not say the Church was preserved by the

---

[1] *Mormon Doctrine*, 793.

four immortals is that this would undercut the basis of the current Mormon church. If Christ's Church had been preserved on earth through the four immortals, it would have been impossible for Smith to re-establish it on earth. The most that could have happened would be for Smith to play a key role in its re-flowering, but this contradicts Smith's claims concerning his role and the Mormon church's teaching concerning his role.

PART FOUR

The Mormon Gods

17. Polytheism, Mormon Style

Although Mormons believe there are innumerable gods, they are expected to worship only the God of this world, the one they call "Heavenly Father." Because of the social stigma attached to the term "polytheism," Mormons wish to avoid it, though it is the correct description of their teaching, according to Mormon apologist Van Hale.

"[S]ince polytheism refers to a belief in the existence of more than one god—clearly a Mormon doctrine—why have Latter-day Saints refused to use this common term to define their doctrine of God?" Hale wrote. "The answer is that while the term is appropriate, the technical definition is not the only consideration in this instance. Through the centuries, polytheism has been used to refer to ancient systems of gods totally foreign, if not repugnant, to contemporary Mormonism. As a result, tradition has imbued it with a negative connotation. Today, only Mormonism's opponents apply the term "polytheism" to Mormon beliefs. A more acceptable term to Mormons is "plurality of gods." This phrase conveys the doctrine of many gods without polytheism's negative connotations."[1]

Mormons avoid the term "polytheism" to put a more positive "spin" on Mormon teaching, but whether it is called polytheism or plurality of gods, the beliefs are the same. First, God the Father is a separate and distinct personage and God. Jesus Christ and the Holy Ghost constitute two other separate and distinct personages and subordinate gods. These three make up one godhead by virtue of their common purpose: Each wants the same thing. Second, while those three gods rule this world and receive honor and obedience from earthly creatures, there are other worlds, each with

---

[1] Van Hale, "Defining the Contemporary Mormon Concept of God," *Line Upon Line*, 10.

its own god or gods, who are as supreme in their spheres as our three gods are in ours.[2]

Biblical References

To support the idea that there are multiple gods, Mormons use a number of biblical passages.

Genesis 1:26a: "And God said, Let us make man in our image."

The Hebrew word for God here is *Elohim*, which is a plural form. Correct grammar requires that the pronouns "us" and "our" also be plural. The rest of verses twenty-six and twenty-seven is in the singular: "So God created man in his own image, in the image of God created he him, male and female created he them." What then are we to make of the plural Elohim?

Several possibilities are reasonable. First, Elohim is a plural of majesty. The sacred writer places into the Lord's mouth words of grandeur and awe, similar to the practice of earthly monarchs who refer to themselves as "we." Second, God is addressing his heavenly courts, the angels, who had also been made in his image, having life, knowledge, virtue and power. Third, the Father was addressing the Son and Holy Spirit. After all, the Three Persons exist, dynamic and creative, from all eternity.

Regardless of which of these is the literal interpretation of the text, it is clear that Genesis alludes to God using a plural noun form—"Elohim"—but singular verb and pronoun forms. The Trinity explains these many/one references, for in one sense God is three persons, while in another sense he is one being.

Psalm 82:1: "God standeth in the congregation of the mighty; he judgeth among the gods."

Mormons argue that the reference to "gods" here proves their claim that there are multiple divine beings. This betrays a lack

---

[2] The belief in many gods, while worshiping and obeying only one of them, is called "henotheism" or "monolatry."

of knowledge of the Hebrew language, in which this psalm was written. The Hebrew term used here is *elohim*, the same name used in Genesis 1:26. But there is more than one meaning for this term. It can mean the one, supreme God. It can refer to idols or other false gods. It can also mean "judges," those whose earthly power reflects that of the Divine Judge.

This is no different than the English term "Lord," which sometimes can refer to God the Father, sometimes to Jesus Christ, sometimes to members of parliament and sometimes to judges and other magistrates. When a barrister in a British court refers to the judge as "My Lord," there is no hint that he might be referring to the judge as a god. The parallel between the Hebrew use of the term *elohim* and the British use of the term *Lord* is so close that Psalm 82 could be re-cast as: "The Lord standeth in the congregation of the mighty; he judgeth among the lords. How long will ye judge unjustly, and accept the persons of the wicked? Selah. Defend the poor and fatherless: do justice to the afflicted and needy. Deliver the poor and needy: rid them out of the hand of the wicked. They know not, neither will they understand; they walk on in darkness: all the foundations of the earth are out of course. I have said, Ye are lords; and all of you are children of the most High. But ye shall die like men, and fall like one of the princes. Arise, O Lord, judge the earth: for thou shalt inherit all nations."

It is *elohim's* judicial aspect that is present in Psalm 82, as illustrated by the declarations that the Lord "judgeth," that he condemns the humans who "judge unjustly," exhorting them to "do justice to the afflicted and needy." Note also the closing petition for God to "Arise . . . [and] judge the earth." This judicial/magisterial interpretation is constant in Jewish literature and by far the most likely sense in Psalm 82.[3]

---

[3] Some Christian commentators do, however, allow for a different interpretation. Some say the passage is a satirical jibe at the false gods of the heathens. The one true God demonstrates to his people how their neighbors' gods are useless in providing help. See Reginald C. Fuller et al., *A New Catholic Commentary on Holy Scriptures*, 472.

It is far more likely, certainly, than the Mormon hypothesis of multiple divine beings—especially since Mormons claim that there are only three such beings attached to our earth (prominently mentioned in the psalm), all of whom are just judges requiring no chastisement.

Matthew 3:16-17 (and its parallels): "Jesus, when he was baptized, went up straightway out of the water: and, lo, the heavens opened unto him, and he saw the Spirit of God descending like a dove, and lighting upon him: And lo a voice from heaven, saying, This is my beloved Son, in whom I am well pleased."

James E. Talmage presented the usual Mormon interpretation of this scene, saying, "The Trinity—Three personages composing the great presiding council of the universe have revealed themselves to man: (1) God the Eternal Father; (2) his Son, Jesus Christ; and (3) the Holy Ghost. That these three are separate individuals, physically distinct from each other, is demonstrated by the accepted records of divine dealings with man. On the occasion of the Savior's baptism, John recognized the sign of the Holy Ghost; he saw before him in a tabernacle of flesh the Christ, unto whom he had administered the holy ordinance; and he heard the voice of the Father. The three personages of the Godhead were present, manifesting themselves each in a different way, and each distinct from the others."[4]

Mormons argue that all three persons of the "Trinity" (note their misappropriation of the term—again, an attempt to "sound Christian" even though it means taking a Christian term and giving it a foreign meaning) were manifested at the Lord's baptism. Catholics agree. The mistake is made in assuming that "distinct" means "separate," and physically separate at that. The Blessed Trinity of Catholic definition is one God, one divine nature, in three divine and distinct persons. Catholics are not modalists, though confused Mormons sometimes consider them to be. Modalism is the heresy that states there is one God who manifests himself in

---

[4] *Articles of Faith*, 39-40.

different modes or expressions, sometimes as Father or as Son or as Spirit. One nature, one divine person. According to modalism, in heaven, God is the Father; while incarnate upon the earth he was the Son; in his enduring influence throughout time he is the Holy Spirit.[5] This is not the doctrine of the Trinity, but an avoidance of its true nature. Though Mormon scholars shouldn't be required to grasp its depths any more surely than do their Catholic counterparts, it's not unreasonable to expect them to do a minimal amount of research and discover at least the Christian understanding of the Trinity.

If modalism were the most apt way of describing the Trinity, the Mormon critique would be justified. We acknowledge the laughable scenario of a one-personed God having to take on three separate roles in the baptism account. The same applies to the Mormons' derision of what they take to be the Trinity in those cases when Jesus prays to the Father. They chide: "So, in Gethsemane he was praying to himself, since you Christians claim there is only one God?" No, Jesus Christ was praying to his Father, a distinct person but not a separate God. Whenever a Mormon reveals his confusion over how three can be one and one can be three, he can be helped to see a distinction within the one divine nature (one God) possessed by three co-equal, co-eternal divine persons.

Consider the following parallel: A being, by definition, is anything which exists, anything to which the verb "to be" can be applied. Consequently, a snowflake is a being, a book is a being, a human is a being, an angel is a being and God is a being. But not all beings are personal. Snowflakes and books are impersonal beings. Humans and angels, however, are personal beings. This shows that the concept of person and the concept of a being represent two separate categories. As a result, if there are some beings that are less than one person (a snowflake, a book), and some beings that are exactly one person (a human, an angel), then there is no reason that there cannot exist beings that are more than one person (God).

---

[5] Leonard George, *Crimes of Perception*, 209–211.

If Mormons have trouble grasping this point, it is due to a defective grasp of either the meaning of words (being, person) or the concept of separate categories. From a logical point of view, there is no problem discussing a multi-personal being. Person and being are two categories that do not match up to each other in a one-to-one manner. And far from reducing God to an impersonal abstraction, the concept shows that God is even *more personal* than we are, since he is three divine persons.

Acts 7:55–56: "He [St. Stephen, the first martyr], being full of the Holy Ghost, looked up steadfastly into heaven, and saw the glory of God, and Jesus standing on the right hand of God, And said, Behold, I see the heavens opened, and the Son of man standing on the right hand of God."

Here, too, Mormons tell us, are seen three separate gods. For extra measure, this passage also reasserts the belief in God the Father's physical body, otherwise, he would not have a right hand on which Jesus could stand. The analysis of Matthew 3:16–17 applies here. Additionally, Stephen does not say he sees God's body, but rather his glory. This is simply a poetic rendering of the awe and majesty Stephen experienced in seeing open before him the sure way to martyrdom and reunion with Christ. "The right hand of God" is an equally poetic expression similar to our saying that "so-and-so is my right-hand man." Further, Scripture makes several references to the "right" being the place of honor, power and privilege.

John 10:34: "Jesus answered them, Is it not written in your law, I said, Ye are gods?"

The reference is to Psalm 82:6. As we saw there, the term *elohim* was not used as a reference to divinities but according to one of its other Hebrew usages, as a reference to human judges. Consequently, if Psalm 82 did not establish the existence of multiple divinities, neither will this passage, which is based upon it.

Just previously in the chapter, in John 10:30, Jesus had solemnly declared, "I and my Father are one." The Pharisees took up rocks to stone him for making himself God (v. 33).[6] In responding, Jesus quoted the passage from Psalm 82, drawing a contrast between the two applications of the term "God." First, Christ said, God called "gods" those corrupt judges whom he would soon punish. Then, because Christ alluded to his own divinity, his hearers were ready to lynch him. If patently evil men can retain the designation of "gods," how is it the Pharisees are so outraged when Christ, an obviously good and holy man, may also use the title? The Lord's question is a rhetorical one, since he knew that the Pharisees understood the distinction between "gods" as applied to mere human judges and "God" applied by Jesus Christ to himself. The Jewish leaders interpreted Christ's comments correctly; they just did not accept them.

The Mormon interpretation will not work in any case, however, since as the background in Psalm 82 makes clear, the humans spoken of as "gods" were evil and unjust, requiring rebuke from the true God. But on the Mormon thesis, only the good and righteous can become gods, and none become gods during this life. The situation thus does not fit the Mormon hypothesis.

1 Corinthians 8:5: "For though there be [those] that are called gods, whether in heaven or in earth, (as there be gods many, and lords many)."

The context of this verse is the eighth chapter of 1 Corinthians, which deals with the obligation of Christians not to give scandal

---

[6] B. H. Roberts, a Mormon Church general authority, wonders why Jesus did not take the opportunity here to explain to his opponents the intricacies of three persons in one God. Roberts contends that since Christ was silent here regarding the Trinity, the plurality of gods is "proved" by default (*The Mormon Doctrine of Deity*, 31–32). Roberts commits a classic example of the logical fallacy known as the argument from silence. There are many reasons Jesus would not go into the details of the doctrine of the Trinity at this point. For one, he was facing a crowd of people on the verge of stoning him—people who were enraged at him for implying his own divinity and who were in no mood for a lecture about the precise nature and internal relationships of the Godhead.

to their weaker brothers in the faith.[7] In the course of the chapter, Paul mentions the divinities believed by pagans to exist in heaven or earth. The Christians of Corinth, most of whom had converted from paganism, were faced with a practical dilemma. Most of the meat sold in the marketplace came from animals sacrificed to the pagan gods or idols. Paul was asked if a Christian could buy and eat this meat, knowing that it had pagan connections. In theory, yes, he answered, since we know that other gods do not exist; they are "nothing in the world." Besides, "there is none other God but one" (v. 4). Thus, meat sacrificed to idols is nothing special, since there are no other gods to whom it could be offered. However, he advised Christians to consider the tender faith and scrupulous consciences of their weaker members. If these saw the stronger Christians buying meat offered to gods, would their faith be offended? If so, it would be better not to buy the meat, even though the mature Christian knows that, though there are many entities that are merely called gods and lords, there is only one God.

Paul is not asserting the existence of pagan divinities, but merely alluding to the popular belief of Gentiles at the time. When he says that "for us" there is only one God, he is referring to us Christians, who know the truth concerning the divine.

Mormons claim Paul is endorsing the Mormon position of henotheism. Although there are many gods, "to us there is but one God, the Father" (v. 6).[8] This will not work. Here is the full context:

> (4) As concerning therefore the eating of those things that are offered in sacrifice unto idols, we know that an idol is nothing in the world, and that there is none other God but one. (5) For though there be that are called gods, whether in heaven or in earth (as there

---

[7] Curiously, the chapter summary for 1 Corinthians 8 in the Mormon Bible makes no mention of the topic addressed. Instead, it reads: "There are gods many and lords many—To us there is one God (the Father) and one Lord, who is Christ."

[8] Thus *Mormon Doctrine*, 577.

be gods many, and lords many,) ⁽⁶⁾But to us there is but one God, the Father, of whom are all things, and we in him; and one Lord Jesus Christ, by whom are all things, and we by him [1 Cor. 8:4-6].

Verse 5, allegedly teaching a plurality of gods, fits between the statements in verse 4 declaring "there is none other God but one" and verse 6, "there is but one God." Is it likely that Paul would break off his exhortation on the one Lord and his proper worship to interject that, by the way, plurality of gods is a required dogma? The Mormon interpretation of "to us there is but one God the Father" suggests that, while there are innumerable gods, each with his own world and children to govern, as far as our own particular experience goes, we are governed by and therefore answerable to only one of those gods.

Notice also the sudden, interplanetary context that Mormons are forced to give the passage. No longer are we talking about idol meat offered to pagan gods by idol worshippers here on earth. The reader must leap to a science fiction context that envisions other inhabited planets with other gods and other races worshipping them. This is not credible. The context in which Paul speaks is "we Christians" compared to Gentile idolaters, right here on this earth, not we earthlings compared to extraterrestrials worshipping their own planetary gods.

Christians know that men have created and will continue to raise up other gods and lords, displacing the one true God. Such gods may be subtle religious and philosophical systems masquerading as sources of light. It is not that we limit our adoration and service to just one of millions of gods; it is that we know no other God but him who made all things (1 Cor. 8:4b).

Non-biblical References

As we have noted, the doctrine of multiple gods is not found in the Book of Mormon, which was written before Smith had invented it. Later Mormon scriptures do, however, record the doctrine.

Abraham 4:26–27: "And the Gods took counsel among themselves and said: Let us go down and form man in our image, after our likeness. . . . So the Gods went down to organize man in their own image."

The Book of Abraham is a translation Smith made from some papyrus rolls he bought in 1835 from a traveling salesman of Egyptian artifacts. By miraculous methods, Smith discovered that the hieroglyphics were written by Abraham and were a history of his encounters with the Lord and with hostile pagans during his sojourn in Egypt. Chapter 4 of this short work treats the gods' plan for creation.

Smith had learned a few facts about the Hebrew language and concluded that the plural ending "-im" on *elohim* pointed to a plurality of gods. But one can no more conclude that all Hebrew words ending in *-im* are plural than one can conclude all English words ending in *-s* or *-es* are plural. Nevertheless, Smith canonized his notion in the Book of Abraham. Abraham 4:26–27 repeats much of Genesis 1:26–27, except that here, unlike the Hebrew text, the pronoun references have been changed to plural. Abraham 4:27 reads that the gods made "man in *their* own image," while Genesis 1:27 says that God created "man in *his* own image."

Doctrine and Covenants 121:26, 28, 32: "God shall give unto you knowledge by his Holy Spirit, yea, by the unspeakable gift of the Holy Ghost, that has not been revealed since the world was until now. . . . A time to come in the which nothing shall be withheld, whether there be one God or many gods, they shall be manifest. . . . According to that which was ordained in the midst of the Council of the Eternal God of all other gods before this world was, that should be reserved unto the end thereof, when every man shall enter into his eternal presence and into his eternal rest."

Smith wrote this to his followers while he was jailed in Liberty, Missouri, in 1839. He spoke of a time when all will know, by the Holy Spirit's power, the true number of the gods. The prophet foretold the answer at the end of the passage—at the end of this world. Catholics agree that at the end of the world it will be manifest to all how many gods there are, though polytheists will be disappointed.

Mormon Theological Writings

The biblical record and latter-day revelation provide Mormons with only a brief glimpse of the "glorious"[9] doctrine of polytheism. It is left to Mormonism's official teachers to expound this central belief for the faithful's edification. In doing so, Smith stretched his knowledge of Hebrew to the breaking point and beyond.

"In the very beginning the Bible shows there is a plurality of Gods beyond the power of refutation," according to Smith. "It is a great subject I am dwelling on. The word Eloheim [sic] ought to be in the plural all the way through—Gods. The heads of the Gods appointed one God for us; and when you take [that] view of the subject, it sets one free to see all the beauty, holiness and perfection of the Gods. All I want is to get the simple, naked truth, and the whole truth."[10]

Smith's successor was no less direct. Brigham Young is called by some Mormons the "American Moses" because he led the Mormons to their "promised land" in Utah after Smith's death. This plain-spoken second prophet left no doubt in the minds of his listeners as to the tenets of their faith.

"How many Gods there are, I do not know," Young said. "But there never was a time when there were not Gods and worlds, and when men were not passing through the same ordeals that we are now passing through. That course has been from all eternity, and it is and will be to all eternity."[11]

---

[9] *Mormon Doctrine*, 577.
[10] *Teachings of the Prophet Joseph Smith*, 372.
[11] *Discourses of Brigham Young*, 22.

While Young confessed ignorance as to the exact number of gods, Orson Pratt, perhaps the first Mormon systematic theologian and an apostle under Smith, Young, and John Taylor, fine-tuned the plurality of gods doctrine somewhat, stating, "If we should take a million of worlds like this and number their particles, we should find that there are more Gods than there are particles of matter in those worlds. . . . One world has a personal God or Father, and the inhabitants thereof worship the attributes of that God, another world has another, and they worship his attributes, and besides Him there is no other; and when they worship Him they are at the same time worshiping the same attributes that dwell in all the personal Gods who fill immensity."[12]

Taylor contrasted the "true and living" gods of the Mormons with the "dead" God of orthodox Christianity.

"It will . . . be necessary to treat the subject of the 'Living God,'" Taylor said, "in contra-distinction to a dead God, or, one that has, 'no body, parts, or passions,' and perhaps it may be well enough to say at the outset that Mormonism embraces a plurality of Gods—as the Apostle Paul said, there were 'gods many, and lords many,' (1 Cor. 8:5) in doing which, we shall not deny the Scriptures that has been set apart for this world, and allows one God; even Jesus Christ, the very eternal Father of this earth; and if Paul tells the truth—'by whom also he made the worlds'" (Heb. 1:2).[13]

Taylor not only misrepresents the Catholic belief in a living, personal God, he also displays a frequent Mormon confusion about the person of Christ, calling him the "eternal Father" of this earth. Taylor also combines polytheism and henotheism (Scripture "allows one God" for this world).

Contemporary Mormon apostles do not shrink from proclaiming a plurality of gods, though virtually all make some attempt

---

[12] *Journal of Discourses* 2:345–346. Note the mélange of polytheism and henotheism.

[13] *The Gospel Kingdom*, 27.

to limit their reference to the three gods they call Heavenly Father, Jesus Christ and the Holy Ghost. Some apologists actually use the term "trinity" to refer to these three separate personages, further obscuring the nature of their beliefs.[14] All, however, will insist that the Mormon Godhead is the only God (or three gods) whom the Mormons worship and obey.

McConkie forces Mormonism's belief in three separate gods into the traditional monotheistic frame. In the article entitled "Monotheism" in his encyclopedic *Mormon Doctrine*, he wrote, "Monotheism is the doctrine or belief that there is but one God. If this is properly interpreted to mean that the Father, Son, and Holy Ghost—each of whom is a separate and distinct godly personage—are one God, meaning one Godhead, then true saints are monotheists. Professing Christians consider themselves monotheists as distinguished from polytheists, those pagan peoples who believe in a host of gods whose powers are exercised only in their own fields" (410).

Further, under "Polytheism," he proclaimed, "The saints are not polytheists," since polytheists, according to McConkie, believe in and worship more than one god. Mormons, he suggests, do believe in the existence of many gods and lords, but have nothing to do with any but the "one Godhead," composed of three separate gods who are united in their purpose and work (579).

This is just word games. McConkie is making up his own definitions for words that already have established meanings. He misleads Mormons in this attempt at redefining the meanings of monotheism and polytheism. Monotheism teaches there is one Supreme Being without equal. There never was and never will be

---

[14] For instance, Mark E. Petersen, *Isaiah for Today*, 125: "Those who say that there was no evidence of the Trinity in the Godhead in Old Testament times simply do not have all the facts. The Father, Son, and Holy Ghost have labored with and for this earth from its beginning and will do so until the end." See also James E. Talmage, *A Study of the Articles of Faith*, 40–42 and B. H. Roberts, *The Mormon Doctrine of Deity*, 193.

a different or an additional God. "One Godhead containing three gods" is not the same as "one God," regardless of Mormonism's packaging. If the term "polytheists" so offends Mormons because it can be taken to mean those who worship a multitude of gods (which Mormons do not[15]), they are not entitled to violate the common meaning of "monotheists" by extending it to include just a couple more gods.[16]

It would be well for Mormon apologists engaged in such mutilation of the dictionary to recall Isaiah's warning, "Woe unto them that call evil good, and good evil; that put darkness for light, and light for darkness; that put bitter for sweet, and sweet for bitter!" (Is. 5:20).

---

[15] McConkie is insistent that Latter-day Saints worship only the Father, to the exclusion of the Son and Holy Spirit; see "Our Relationship with the Lord," BYU Devotional, March 2, 1982, though this flies in the face of other Mormon statements.

[16] Daniel C. Peterson and Stephen D. Ricks, in *Offenders for a Word*, argue that Mormonism "must surely be described as monotheistic," while "traditional Christianity itself is not straightforwardly monotheistic" (71). As proof, they cite Muslim condemnation of Christians as "polytheists" and Thomas Jefferson's depiction of Catholic theology as a "mere relapse into polytheism, differing from paganism only by being more unintelligible" (ibid.). The authors teach at BYU.

18. Mormon God Number One —A Glorified Man

The Mormon church has officially accepted the later version of the First Vision which reports that both God the Father and Jesus Christ appeared in bodily form to the young Smith. The believer's testimony of this version sustains his belief in two fundamental teachings on the Godhead: God the Father has a physical body, and there exist a plurality of gods. Mormons try to support these two radical positions by appealing to Scripture and other works.

God the Father's Body

BIBLE PASSAGES

When arguing that God the Father has a body, Mormons commonly appeal to passages speaking of man as being created in the image of God (Gen. 1:26-27, 9:6) and passages mentioning a particular body part in connection with God—face (Ex. 33:11), arms and hands (Deut. 4:34; Ps. 98:1; Is. 30:30), eyes (2 Sam. 22:25; Ps. 33:18; Lam. 2:18), mouth (Num. 12:6-8, 30:2; Josh. 9:14; 2 Thess. 2:8), feet (Nahum 1:3), ears (Num. 11:18; 1 Sam. 8:21).

The passages referring to man as being made in God's image do not refer to a bodily similarity but a spiritual one. Humans, like angels, are rational creatures, and this places them in a category entirely distinct from everything else in creation. It is in their rational faculties that they are most like God, and so this constitutes the basis on which they can be said to be in his image. As Jews and Christians have always recognized, and as Scripture clearly teaches, God is a spirit and so has no physical form, and so the only image of him that *could* exist in man would be a spiritual one.

A couple of the "body part" passages Mormons cite are ones that speak of God appearing to Moses:

> Exodus 33:11: "And the Lord spake unto Moses face to face, as a man speaketh unto his friend."

> Numbers 12:6-8: "If there be a prophet among you, I the Lord will make myself known unto him in a vision, and will speak unto him in a dream. My servant Moses is not so, who is faithful in all mine house. With him will I speak mouth to mouth, even apparently, and not in dark speeches; and the similitude of the Lord shall he behold."

But there are grave problems with taking these verses to mean that God had a physical body that Moses could view. That interpretation is directly contradicted by other Bible passages. For example, later in the same chapter as the Exodus 33:11 quotation, we read, "Thou [Moses] canst not see my face: for there shall be no man see me, and live" (Ex. 33:20).

God specifically tells Moses that he *cannot* see his face, implying that he *has not* seen his face. The earlier reference to Moses speaking "face to face" with God must therefore either be a metaphor referring to God's clear and direct manner of communicating with Moses—as opposed to other prophets, who received revelation only "in dark speeches" (other translations: "in riddles")—or it must be a reference to a theophany or a vision.

A theophany is a time when God generated an artificial appearance for himself. Theophanies occur, for example, when God manifested himself in the burning bush or when the Holy Spirit descended at Jesus' baptism in the form of a dove. These instances did not display God's *real* form (for he has no real, physical form). They were artificial appearances that God temporarily assumed to make it possible for humans to interact with him in a special way. Of course, it is easiest for humans to interact with God if he appears as another human, and so we occasionally find theophanies in which God appears in human form, for example, when he visits Abraham to announce the birth of Isaac.

Much more frequent are visions in which a person receives a *mental* impression of God. In visions, God appears in a variety of ways, among them human. However, since these are mental images, they also do not depict an actual, physical form for God, but only a mental impression that he chooses to bestow on the visionary to facilitate interaction.

In Exodus 33:11 Moses *must not* have seen God's face. This had to be either a figure of speech, a theophany or a vision, none of which implied that God has an actually existing, physical body that Moses saw. This applies equally to the parallel passage in Numbers 12:6-8, where God was said to speak to Moses "mouth to mouth"—a synonym for "face to face."

We can just as easily deal with Mormon interpretation of the other "body part" passages, for they are clear examples of what is linguistically known as "anthropomorphic language." This occurs whenever something other than a human is described in human terms, speaking as if it had a human form or human attributes. In literature, anthropomorphic language is frequently encountered when discussing animals (as in Aesop's Fables), concepts (as with Psalm 85:10: "Mercy and Truth are met together; Righteousness and Peace have kissed each other") and deities. In fact, almost any time we talk about something non-human, we eventually use human terms to describe it.

This is certainly the case in the biblical literature, in which the infinite, transcendent Lord is made more understandable by being spoken of, analogously, in human terms. Hebrew speech, which has a particular delight for powerful, poetic expressions, loves to picture God's attributes in human terms. Descriptions of God's all-seeing eyes, all-hearing ears and powerful arm are references to his omnipotence. When we read of his outstretched hands, it is a reference to his willingness to help man.[1]

Many of the passages draw out the implications of the anthro-

---

[1] See John L. McKenzie, "Aspects of Old Testament Thought," *The New Jerome Biblical Commentary*, 1288.

pomorphic metaphors they use. Thus, Psalm 98:1 reads, "O sing unto the Lord a new song; for he hath done marvellous things: his right hand, and his holy arm, hath gotten him the victory."

Even Mormons would acknowledge that God did not use his supposed physical arm to fight a battle for Israel.

The passages using anthropomorphic language to describe God as if he had human body parts are a subset of a larger group of verses in which other metaphors are used, not all of them human. By considering some of the elements of this larger set, we can see the problem with interpreting the anthropomorphic passages literally. Among the other verses are the following:

> Deuteronomy 4:24: "For the Lord thy God is a consuming fire, even a jealous God."
>
> Deuteronomy 32:4: "He is the Rock, his work is perfect: for all his ways are judgment: a God of truth and without iniquity, just and right is he."
>
> Psalm 91:4: "He shall cover thee with his feathers, and under his wings shalt thou trust."

As we will see in the section on the Mormon view of man, the LDS church refers to additional biblical passages to support its notion of God the Father having a corporeal body. For now, the Mormon proselytizer has offered the Catholic a few well-chosen references from the Bible, expecting that these will be sufficient to loosen the latter's hold on the spiritual character of God. An informed Catholic, however, could disarm this weak attack on the orthodox understanding of the divine nature by referring to passages avoided by the Mormon exposition. Consider the following:

> Numbers 23:19: "God is not a man that he should lie; neither the son of man, that he should repent."
>
> Hosea 11:9: "I am God, and not man."

These are problematic for Mormons because they do indeed believe that God is a perfected, exalted man. Here, the Lord makes it clear that he is no kind of a man at all.

John 4:24: "God is a Spirit: and they that worship him must worship him in spirit and in truth."

Jesus is addressing the Samaritan woman at the well. She declares that the Lord of Israel is to be worshiped on Mt. Gerizim, after the custom of the Samaritans, and not on Mt. Zion, in Jerusalem, as was the practice of the Jews. Some Mormon apologists focus on the second part of the verse: "and they that worship him must worship him in spirit and in truth."

"See," they argue, "man is expected to worship God the Spirit in spirit. Man is not merely spirit, nor can he divest himself of his corporeality in order to offer proper worship to the Lord. Therefore, and by extension, God is not merely spirit; he possesses a spirit, but he also possesses a body."[2]

Christ responds by explaining that, because he is spirit, the Father cannot be limited to one place. He is all-present. This would not be possible if he had a physical body, as Mormons believe.

Elsewhere, Christ explains the nature of a spirit, saying, "A spirit hath not flesh and bones, as ye see me have" (Luke 24:39).

While Jesus has a body because of his incarnation, he is quite clear in stating that spirits do not.

Mormon theology holds that God the Father is a resurrected man who once lived on an earth similar to this one. He learned obedience to the (Mormon) gospel, faithfully fulfilled all the commandments, eventually died and was raised by his own God and Father to exaltation or godhood. This, Latter-day Saints teach, served as the pattern for Jesus Christ's own life, death and resurrection to glory;[3] therefore, the bodily substance Jesus possessed after his resurrection mirrors that which was first held by his Father.

It is a doctrine of Catholic faith that Jesus Christ possesses

---

[2] See, for instance, *A Sure Foundation*, 97 (by an anonymous Mormon author).

[3] Lorenzo Snow, fifth Mormon prophet: "Through a continual course of progression, our heavenly Father has received exaltation and glory, and he points us out the same path." Quoted in *Doctrines of the Gospel*, 92.

forever his glorified body. He ascended bodily into everlasting glory, taking his place at the right hand of the Father. (Mormons would, of course, consider this to be a spatial arrangement.)[4] In fact, Catholics are not at all hesitant to proclaim the goodness and eternal destiny of the human body: Mary is the first in what will be a great procession of creatures returning body and soul to God. Jesus makes a clear distinction between his risen body and beings who have only spiritual natures, such as his Father, making it possible for him to be described in John 4 simply as "a Spirit."

Other New Testament verses also reveal problems with the Mormon view.

> Colossians 1:15: "[Jesus Christ] is the image of the invisible God, the first-born of every creature."
>
> 1 Timothy 1:17: "Now unto the King eternal, immortal, invisible, the only wise God, be honor and glory for ever and ever. Amen."

Mormons say God the Father is invisible only because he is, in his bodily state, millions of miles from earth. By his incarnation and life among us, Jesus bridged those light years. The problem with this is that the Father, on the Mormon supposition, would be equally capable of traversing the distance and appearing to people on earth. Indeed, he supposedly did so for Smith. Furthermore, since Paul was writing after Christ's ascension, when Christ was with God in heaven—presumably light years away—Christ was *just as invisible* as the Father. These problems are solved when you accept the fact that Paul was comparing Jesus, who, because of his human nature is *not* invisible, to the Father, who, because of his purely spiritual nature, *is* invisible. Through the incarnation, Christ provides us with a visible demonstration of the character of the intrinsically invisible God.

---

[4] In contrast, Augustine explains the Catholic view: "[Christ] is in bliss, and it is from the bliss that is called 'the right hand of the Father' that the name of this bliss is derived.... To be at the right hand means the same as to be in the highest bliss.... When we speak of God's 'sitting,' this does not denote a bodily position but the judicial authority that is never lacking to his Lordship." Augustine, *Faith and the Creed* 7:14.

Nevertheless, McConkie argued in *Doctrinal New Testament Commentary*,

> Christ is the image of the Father physically and spiritually, in person and in personality. Physically the Resurrected Lord—who ate and drank with his disciples after he attained immortality, and whose body of flesh and bones they felt and handled—is in "the express image of his [Father's] person." (Heb. 1:3.) They look alike; in appearance one could pass for the other. Spiritually our Lord is "in the form of God" (Phil. 2:6); he has acquired all of the attributes of godliness in their perfection; as it is with the Father, so it is with him; he is the embodiment of justice, mercy and truth, of faith, hope and charity, of wisdom, virtue and knowledge, and of every good thing; thus he is in the likeness of and a projection of the personality of the Father [Vol. 3, 25].

Aside from the amusing observation that "in appearance one could pass for the other" (Mormon iconography of the First Vision shows two identical figures, complete with flowing white hair, beards, and robes), McConkie appears to have stumbled unaware upon the correct meaning of the Hebrews and Philippians references. True, the Son is the "express image" and "in the form" of God. But it is Christ who embodies or fleshes out justice, mercy and all the other virtues. His Father is these virtues. McConkie said it, but did not really see it. This is all the more clear in his neglect of the rest of Philippians 2:6–7, which reads, "Who, being in the form of God, thought it not robbery to be equal with God: But made himself of no reputation, and took upon him the form of a servant, and was made in the likeness of men."

The Son of God, being in the very form of God, emptied himself and took on the form of a man. If, as Mormons believe, God and man share the same form and nature, then the Son's incarnation would have required no change or abandonment of one form for another. But Paul taught that a radical condescension had to be made: The omnipotent Master took upon himself the altogether foreign form of a slave.

The above are some of the biblical passages Catholics could use in responding to the Mormon belief that God the Father has a body of flesh and bones. However, Mormons will not be content to confine their discussion to what Scripture (or the Church Fathers, for that matter) teach about the incorporeality of God. They can't do that, because Scripture (and the Fathers) are set against them. It is, therefore, of vital importance for Mormon apologetics to introduce non-biblical material, including the Joseph Smith Translation ("Inspired Version") of the Bible; Mormon scriptures (Book of Mormon, Doctrine and Covenants, Pearl of Great Price); Mormon theological works, especially those by prophets, apostles, and other general authorities; and personal "testimony."

1. *The Joseph Smith Translation (Inspired Version)*

When he began his work in 1830, Joseph Smith did not have a knowledge of biblical languages. His translation [of the Bible] was not done in the usual manner of a scholar, but was a revelatory experience using only an English text. He did not leave a description of the translating process, but it appears that he would read from the KJV [King James Version] and dictate revisions to a scribe.[5]

In other words, the "translation" was a matter of removing from the sacred text whatever parts Smith decided had been falsely added and adding new parts to supply what he said had been maliciously removed. His guiding principle in this process seems to have been a need to find in the Bible adequate basis for his ever-changing beliefs. His method was a mixture of intuition and invention.

For example, knowing that Exodus 33:20 would put the lie to his First Vision and his notion of a corporeal God, Smith amended the text to read (added portions in italics[6]): "And he [God] said unto Moses, Thou canst not see my face *at this time, lest mine anger*

---

[5] "Joseph Smith Translation of the Bible," *Encyclopedia of Mormonism*, vol. 2.

[6] In the two following passages, also, text that Smith added or altered will be placed in italics.

be kindled against thee also, and I destroy thee, and thy people; for there shall no man among them see me at this time, and live, for they are exceeding sinful. And no sinful man hath at any time, neither shall there be any sinful man at any time, that shall see my face and live."

Likewise, with John 1:18 (which is verse 19 in Smith's version): *"And no man hath seen God at any time, except he hath borne record of the Son; for except it is through him no man can be saved."*

The same is true for his mishandling of John 4:24. In place of "God is a Spirit," Smith wrote: *"For unto such has God promised his Spirit."*

Smith also added to the original text in 1 John 4:12: "No man hath seen God at any time, *except them who believe."*

Mormons think it possible for a mortal to see God, providing he be free of sin and have the requisite faith. Only the Mormon version of the Bible teaches this.[7]

2. Mormon Scriptures: The Doctrine and Covenants

Most of the one hundred thirty-eight sections (chapters) of the Doctrine and Covenants purport to be revelations from the Lord Jesus to or through Smith. A few are revelations to other church leaders. Others do not claim to be revelations at all, but matters of business or history. The following passage is among the most outspoken: "The Father has a body of flesh and bones as tangible as man's. . . ." (D&C 130:22).

This instruction, given by Smith a little over a year before he died, summarized a teaching he had been testing for some time. We see it take on a fuller form in his "non-scriptural" works.

---

[7] More will be discussed later on the Mormon scriptures. It should be noted, though, that the Latter-day Saints use the King James Version, referring to the Inspired Version only in footnotes.

3. Mormon Theological Works

Smith was a prolific writer and speaker. Besides writing the Book of Mormon, the Doctrine and Covenants, the Pearl of Great Price and the Inspired Version of the Bible, he composed diaries, histories, letters and lectures. Young and other Mormon prophets and apostles have left volumes of their own religious speculations. From these we can cull a greater understanding of the Mormon doctrine of deity.

It would not be an exaggeration to say that many active Mormons have never heard the full teaching of their church on the nature of the Godhead. Though the complete teachings are available in various publications, many members do not investigate their beliefs beyond the basics, something that is true in most churches.

Consider the "King Follett Discourse," given by Smith less than three months before his death, in 1844:

> I will prove that the world is wrong by showing what God is. I am going to enquire after God; for I want you all to know him, and to be familiar with him; and if I am bringing you to a knowledge of him, all persecutions against me ought to cease. You will then know that I am his servant; for I speak as one having authority. I will go back to the beginning before the world was, to show what kind of being God is. What sort of a being was God in the beginning? Open your ears and hear, all ye ends of the earth, for I am going to prove it to you by the Bible, and to tell you the designs of God in relation to the human race, and why he interferes with the affairs of man.
>
> God himself was once as we are now, and is an exalted man, and sits enthroned in yonder heavens! That is the great secret. If the veil were rent today, and the great God who holds this world in its orbit, and who upholds all worlds and all things by his power, was to make himself visible—I say, if you were to see him today, you would see him like a man in form—like yourselves in all the person, image, and very form as a man; for Adam was created in the very fashion, image and likeness of God, and received instructions from, and walked, talked and conversed with him, as one man talks

and communes with another [*Teachings of the Prophet Joseph Smith*, 344–345].

Except for the detail, there is not much difference between this quotation and those cited earlier in the chapter. Mormons interpret the selected Bible passages and D&C section as indicating that God is in very form a man. The significance here, however, is the origin of the reference. This is not some citation taken from a Bible believed to have been corrupted by the Catholic Church. For the faithful Mormon, these words from Smith's lips are distilled, pure truth, revealed to him directly by God in the latter days and taught by him for the edification and salvation of his followers. For the believer, the teachings of the prophet are the ultimate conduit of all truth.[8]

In the question of the Father's physicality, Young wrote,

> Some would have us believe that God is present everywhere. It is not so. He is no more every where present in person than the Father and Son are one in person. [Note Young's misunderstanding of the Trinity of thinking the Father and the Son are one Person rather than two Persons in one Being.] God is considered to be everywhere present at the same moment; and the psalmist says, "Whither shall I flee from thy presence?" He is present with all his creations through his influence, through his government, spirit and power, but he himself is a personage of tabernacle [material], and we are made after his likeness [*Discourses of Brigham Young*, 24].

Because he possesses a human body, even though glorified, God is present to his creation only by influence, Young said, much like the sun, fixed at a vast distance, warms and gives light to the earth.

McConkie is similarly direct in his exposition of God's nature. "[M]ost of those professing belief in God consider him to be an

---

[8] See Ezra Taft Benson, "Fourteen Fundamentals in Following the Prophets," BYU Devotional Assembly, February 26, 1980. Benson's first point reads: "The prophet is the only man who speaks for the Lord in everything." His second point is: "The living prophet is more vital to us than the standard works [the Bible and Mormon scriptures]."

indefinable force, essence, or power of an incomprehensible nature," he said. "According to revelation, however, he is a personal Being, a holy and exalted Man, a glorified, resurrected Personage having a tangible body of flesh and bones, an anthropomorphic Entity, the personal Father of the spirits of all men."[9]

The Mormon apostle makes several errors. The first is an error of fact. Assuming he is attacking, as was his habit, the orthodox Catholic understanding of God the Father, he is mistaken in saying that most Christians who profess belief in God consider him some vague, amorphous entity. This is certainly not true. God is a personal being greater than all others, possessing all virtues, not a vague, nebulous force. The second error is one of logic: McConkie equates "personal being" with a tangible body. Yet later in the same book, McConkie defines the Mormon Holy Ghost, saying, "The Holy Ghost is the third member of the Godhead. He is a Personage of Spirit, a Spirit Person, a Spirit Man, a Spirit Entity" (358).

We will study the Mormon understanding of the Holy Spirit later. For now, notice that, for McConkie, the Holy Ghost is one personal being who does not possess a tangible body.

4. Personal "Testimony"

A final non-biblical source to which Mormons may appeal in support of the corporeality of the Father—or any other Mormon teaching—is personal testimony. After having presented all the evidence he can gather from the Bible, Mormon scriptures and Mormon writers, the proselytizer solemnly bears witness that "these things are true." He knows it, he says, because the Holy Spirit of God has revealed it to his heart. He has prayed about God and his nature and the Lord has told him, clearly and unmistakably, that God the Father has a body of flesh and bone. The Mormon church's teaching in this matter is true. He knows it, he testifies to it, in the name of Jesus Christ. Amen.

A simple and altogether proper retort would be for the Cath-

---

[9] *Mormon Doctrine*, 250.

olic to bear his own testimony: "I know that God the Father is a being of pure spirit, immortal and invisible, yet our personal and loving Father nonetheless. I know that his Son founded the Catholic Church, which remains faithful to its Lord in all things. I testify that the pope is Christ's Vicar on earth. I say this in the name of Jesus Christ. Amen."

The folly and uselessness of basing one's faith on "gut feelings" should be apparent. It is impossible to prove or disprove a testimony. Yet Mormon leaders urge every member to gain and maintain strong testimonies on each Mormon doctrine. They will serve, they say, as the paramount "proof" of the individual's faith and the truthfulness of the "restored" gospel. As the member associates only with staunch Mormons, reads only approved literature, listens only to acceptable speakers, and follows all the directives of the Mormon church, he will find that he becomes more and more convinced of the rightness of his religion and his participation in it. His testimony is strengthened on a level deeper than the rational, enabling him to remain unbending even in the face of uncongenial fact.[10]

---

[10] Regarding my own case, some may wonder how, knowing that any being we call God must be infinite, timeless and unchanging in all those qualities we call attributes, could I have accepted that there could be three and more such supreme beings? It defies both logic and common sense. But I did acquiesce. Unlike most converts, I knew very well what the Mormon doctrine of deity was when I accepted baptism. My clearest understanding, in hindsight, is that this was simply one more of those doctrines which, though I could not fully understand at the time, I assumed would become clearer and more acceptable as I "grew in my testimony" of the restored gospel. *Mea culpa*. Having allowed myself to be guided by emotion and intuition, which to some Mormons is often translated as "the Holy Ghost," I guess I just crossed my fingers and hoped my thinking would eventually catch up with my feeling. In speaking to Mormon groups, I genuinely endorsed all the doctrines of the LDS church because I did, on some level, accept them, or presumed that I would eventually grow stronger in my testimony of them. I yearned to be a faithful and obedient member of the Mormon church and to share my new faith with others. If at times I had to "talk myself" into an enthusiasm that had not yet penetrated my mind, I was nonetheless sincere in wanting to believe all the teachings of the Mormon church.

19. Mormon God Number Two —Our Elder Brother

As with many other LDS beliefs, the teachings on Christ are a maze of misunderstanding, misdefinition and misapplication. Mormon scriptures are contradictory, and their prophets deny, redefine or ignore one another's teachings. In previous chapters, we have presented first the Mormon explanation of their beliefs, followed by a Catholic critique. This chapter will be different; before we plunge into the tangled jungle of Mormon "Christology," we will first get our bearings and remind ourselves of the true doctrine of Christ as taught in the Bible, in Sacred Tradition and by the magisterium.

Jesus Christ: One Divine Person with Two Natures (The "Hypostatic Union")

Anticipating our look at the Trinity in chapter 21, we affirm that the second person of the Trinity became a man to redeem mankind from sin and open the gates to life eternal. It is Catholic dogma that the second person of the Trinity, the divine Logos, took on human nature at the time of the incarnation. When Jesus Christ was conceived in the Virgin's womb, he became fully man, with a one hundred percent human nature, human will and human intellect. Moreover, as the Son of the Everlasting Father begotten from all eternity, he retained the fullness of his divine nature, divine will and divine intellect. The divine person who lived among us and died at our hands was fully man and fully God. Christ was not two persons, but only one. A "person" is the subject who acts, the agent; a "nature" is that which, among other things, determines what a person can do. A person with a human nature thinks and acts as a man. A person with a divine nature thinks and acts as God.

When the Word (the second person of the Trinity) became flesh (a man), the omnipotent Lord took on a human nature without relinquishing the divine nature he possessed from all eternity. If we keep this in mind, we will be able to untangle the confusion Mormons experience when they cite various passages from the Bible that appear to indicate Christ's inferiority to the Father.

Frank Sheed[1] gives us the useful term "double stream" to refer to the modes of Christ's words and actions. At times Jesus speaks or acts simply as a man. He is tired, hungry, or sad. He prays to God the Father. He feels anguish in Gethsemane and on Calvary. Christ, in his human nature, was a man like us in all things but sin (Heb. 4:15).

At other times, however, he says and does things that go far beyond the words and actions of a mere man. He demands his followers love him above all others, even family. No one who comes to him will be confounded. All must learn of him, for he is the way, the truth, and the life. He sealed his words with divine signs: giving sight to the blind and life to the dead. Because he possessed a divine nature as well as a human one, Jesus accepted without hesitation the adoration of his followers.

The Gospels are replete with accounts of the apostles' stumbling attempts to understand their master. While at times he evinced "merely" human compassion for a hungry crowd or a widowed mother, he responded in a manner truly divine: He fed the crowd and raised the dead son. He gently reproved the mother of James and John, saying it was not his but his Father's decision to grant a place of privilege in the kingdom (Matt. 20:20–23). Soon after, however, the Lord claimed authority to judge all men, to separate them and to usher **them** to seats of glory or places of torment (Matt. 25).

This double stream is braided not only through the words and actions of the Lord Jesus but also through the meditation and

---

[1] *Theology for Beginners*, 87–88.

reflection of his apostles and evangelists. Thus, Paul can affirm that Christ emptied himself of glory, took on the form of a servant and humbled himself (Phil. 2:6–8), while also proclaiming that in Christ "dwelleth all the fullness of the Godhead bodily" (Col. 2:9).

With this as our anchor to the apostolic faith, let's look at the widely divergent beliefs of the Mormons.

Elohim and Jehovah—Two Separate Gods

Simply put, Mormons say that the biblical name "Jehovah" (or, in some Bible translations, Yahweh) refers always and only to Jesus Christ in his pre-mortal existence, while the biblical name "Elohim" refers always and only to God the Father.

"Among the spirit children of Elohim, the first-born was and is Jehovah or Jesus Christ, to whom all others are juniors."[2]

As such, Christ was the God of Israel, the one through whom all revelations and prophecies were made. The King James Version of the Bible, along with many others, avoids using the actual term Jehovah (or Yahweh), supplying in its place the names of LORD or GOD in small capitals.

Mormons also, at least on some occasions, acknowledge that "Elohim" is used as a personal name for God the Father.[3] So Elohim is the Eternal Father and Jehovah is his Son, Jesus Christ, before his incarnation. Therefore, according to Mormons, whenever the term LORD or GOD appears in Scriptures, it refers to Jehovah, or Jesus Christ. Just as, according to LDS thought, the Father and the Son are two separate Gods, then Elohim and Jehovah are the names of two separate Gods. Elohim is not Jehovah; Jehovah is not Elohim. The First Presidency insisted on this distinction.[4]

---

[2] Joseph F. Smith, *Gospel Doctrine*, 70.

[3] *Mormon Doctrine*, 224.

[4] See Talmage, *Articles of Faith*, 466–473. This distinction is especially emphasized in the Mormon temple rituals.

But Genesis 2:4 states, "These are the generations of the heavens and of the earth when they were created, in the day that the Lord God made the earth and the heavens."

The same expression is used ten more times in that chapter alone.[5] The word Lord translates Jehovah; God translates Elohim. The reference is to but one God, "Jehovah-Elohim." But Mormons retort that just as Jesus is *a* god, Jehovah is *one of* the elohim (gods). That this is not a credible explanation is seen by examining several other verses.

Isaiah 9:6 states, "Unto us a child is born, unto us a son is given: and the government shall be upon his shoulder: and his name shall be called Wonderful, Counselor, The mighty God, The everlasting Father, The Prince of Peace." The prophecy incontestably refers to Christ, but "the mighty God" actually translates the original Hebrew "Elohim."

Deuteronomy 10:17 presents the altogether unparalleled majesty of Jehovah, "For the LORD your God is God of gods, and Lord of lords." That is, Jehovah is the supreme God.[6]

Consider Psalm 45:6–7: "Thy throne, O God, is for ever and ever. . . . Therefore God, thy God, hath anointed thee with the oil of gladness. . . ." Here, God the Father is speaking to his Son, calling him God. These verses are cited in Hebrews 1:8–9.

It should be clear that Jehovah is called Elohim throughout the Old Testament: "Hear, O Israel: The LORD our God is one LORD" (Deuteronomy 6:4: "Jehovah our Elohim is one Jehovah"). Their Greek equivalents, "Kyrie" and "Theos," are also used interchangeably in the New Testament. Recall Thomas' exclamation, "My Lord and my God" (John 20:28).

Though Mormons try to resolve the difficulty of the identification of Jehovah with Elohim by saying that Jehovah, Jesus, is

---

[5] Additional occurrences include Genesis 27:20, Exodus 3:6–7, Isaiah 40:3 and Jeremiah 32:18. The combination "Jehovah Elohim" occurs over five hundred times in the Old Testament.

[6] Supreme in the sense that he is the only real God, all other deities being phantasms, figments of man's imagination.

a god, such sleight of hand proves even more worthless in those places where God the Father is actually called Jehovah.

Look at Psalm 110:1: "The LORD said unto my Lord, Sit thou at my right hand." The heading in the Mormon Bible for this psalm states: "A Messianic Psalm of David—Christ shall sit on the Lord's right hand. . . ." The first LORD is Jehovah; the second Lord is Adonai. Elohim is not even mentioned. Christ (here, Adonai) shall sit at the Lord's (here, Jehovah's) right. This Lord or Jehovah is the Father.

In Matthew's account of the Lord's temptation, Jesus rebuked Satan: "It is written, Thou shalt not tempt the Lord thy God." Further, when the Devil asked Jesus to worship him, Jesus replied: "Get thee hence, Satan: for it is written, Thou shalt worship the Lord thy God, and him only shalt thou serve" (Matt. 4:7, 10). Christ was referring to Deuteronomy 6:16, "Ye shall not tempt the LORD your God," and Deuteronomy 10:20, "Thou shalt fear the LORD thy God; him shalt thou serve, and to him shalt thou cleave, and swear by his name." Christ, in referring here to the LORD, or Jehovah, was pointing to the Father, not to himself.

Catholics agree that Jehovah, or LORD or GOD, refers at times to Jesus Christ. There are passages where that is the case, fully in accord with the doctrine of the Trinity. But because it also designates the Eternal Father, Jehovah is one being who is manifest in three persons. Mormons' attempted distinction between Elohim and Jehovah has been maintained almost from the beginning of their religion.[7] But such straightforward, though incorrect, presentations of belief are the exception. Most of the Mormon doctrines of Christ are couched in familiar "Christian" vocabulary, as if to minimize their offensiveness and deflect justifiable indignation. Christ's pre-existence, virgin birth and atonement are three elements of belief common to Catholics and Mormons. The similarities, however, begin and end with the mere vocabulary.

---

[7] Some of the earlier accounts of the First Vision did not allow for this division. The Book of Mormon also resists this plural-god system.

The Pre-existence of Christ

The three persons of the Holy Trinity are co-equal and co-eternal. There was never a point at which one or the other of the persons did not exist as almighty God. What is predicated of the essence of one of the persons is true of the others as well. This is the constant teaching of the Catholic Church and other Christian bodies.

Mormon theology, too, speaks of the "pre-existence" of Christ, or his "pre-mortal" life. While the terms are similar to those used in orthodox Christian discussion, the connotation differs. According to Mormons, Jesus is their elder brother, since he was the firstborn in the spirit world. God the Father and one of his heavenly wives begot Christ's spirit at some point in the eternity before earthly creation. This was made possible because the Father had finally attained exaltation for himself. As part of the blessings of godhood, he was given an eternal wife or wives with whom to procreate spirit children. The *Encyclopedia of Mormonism* quotes a 1909 statement of the First Presidency of the Church, which reads, "Jesus, however, is the firstborn among all the sons of God—the first begotten in the spirit, and the only begotten in the flesh. He is our elder brother, and we, like him, are in the image of God. All men and women are in the similitude of the universal Father and Mother, and are literally the sons and daughters of Deity" (MFP 4:203).[8]

Some literature critical of Mormonism focuses on this idea of a Heavenly Father and Heavenly Mother continually procreating billions of spirit children. Current Mormon teaching, knowing how sensitive the issue is and how quickly it can lead to the Mormon church being embarrassed and accused of blasphemy, tries to avoid speculating on the procedure of begetting new spirit babies, and most members give it little thought.[9] It is sufficient to say that

---

[8] Vol. 2, "Firstborn in the Spirit."

[9] More attention is recently being paid to the nature and number of the Heavenly Mother(s), though little besides her (their) existence has been

Jesus was the first spirit baby to issue from this process, which Mormons argue based on several Scripture passages.

Psalm 89:27 states, "Also I will make him my firstborn, higher than the kings of the earth." This psalm is a song of praise to King David, the Lord's anointed, through whom God established his kingdom. Jesus, the Son of David, fulfilled the prophecy.

The problem for the Mormon apologist is that it applies in its first and literal sense to King David and not to the future Messiah. Since King David was *not* God's literal firstborn, and since one cannot choose to make any person one's firstborn biologically, it is clear that when the psalm speaks of God making King David his firstborn, higher than the (other) kings of earth, it is speaking of him designating David as his firstborn legally or relationally.

The concept of the firstborn was very important in Hebrew society and went beyond being the first biological child. The firstborn held a place of honor and of responsibility in the family, with attendant rights and duties. Thus the firstborn inherited an extra share of the family property (Deut. 21:15-17) and he had the duty of looking after the other family members, who did not so inherit, if they fell on hard times.

It was through the line of the firstborn that the family as a social institution was normally maintained, though in exceptional cases a firstborn could forfeit his place to one of the younger children. This happened, for example, in Jacob's family. His biological firstborn—Reuben—slept with one of his fathers wives (not his mother) and for the crime lost his position (Gen. 49:4). His next two oldest brothers—Simeon and Levi—got the family in severe trouble when they massacred a town of Canaanites, and for their act, Jacob denied them also the role of leading the family after

---

revealed. The attitude among faithful Mormons is, "When Heavenly Father wants to tell us more about Heavenly Mother, he will reveal it through his prophets. Until then, it is useless to speculate." Some do speculate, however, and write and speak about this divine female parent, for which a few have been excommunicated. Since this book deals with what is—or has been—taught as Mormon doctrine, we will not treat further of this contentious subject.

he was gone (Gen. 49:5-7). Jacob eventually decided to give the birthright to the sons of Joseph (1 Chron. 5:1), and specifically to Ephraim (Jer. 31:9), who had been born last and whom Jacob had adopted (Gen. 48:5).

The concept of firstborn could be used metaphorically, as well. Thus, when God describes the entire nation of Israel as his firstborn (Ex. 4:22), it is not biologically true. God does not biologically beget nations, nor was Israel the first nation in existence. When the term "firstborn" is applied to it, then, it signifies the place of favor and prestige (as well as responsibility and duty) that Israel has with God. The same is true when David is referred to as God's firstborn. While all the kings of the earth held their authority from God (Rom. 13:1), David had a special place of favor (and responsibility) before God as his social or legal "firstborn" among kings.

This is the sense in which Psalm 89 speaks of David as God's firstborn, and since the spiritual sense that applies to Christ is built upon the literal sense, you cannot use the passage to prove any other kind of firstborn relationship between Jesus and God the Father. Jesus, as the Messiah, the King of kings and Lord of lords, is God's *new* firstborn among kings, higher than all the rest. That is all the verse can be shown to mean.

Another passage to which Mormons appeal is Romans 8:29, which reads, "For whom he [God the Father] did foreknow, he also did predestinate to be conformed to the image of his Son, that he [Christ] might be the firstborn among many brethren."

The Greek "he might be" refers to a process to be completed only in the future. That is, the many brethren of whom Jesus is the firstborn are those who will follow him into resurrected glory. Christ, considered in his human incarnation, is the author and finisher of our faith (Heb. 12:2) and the first to inherit the glories of the Christian dispensation. He is the firstborn into the glories of the Christian destiny. All other, later souls to enter them may be described as fellow children, but Christ will always be the firstborn because it was he who won and opened these glories to us.

It should also be mentioned that Christ is "the firstborn from the dead" (Col. 1:18) by virtue of his glorious resurrection—yet another non-biological use of "firstborn," further demonstrating Mormon inability to use the term to argue that Christ was the first spirit baby produced by God the Father.

Mormons also use Colossians 1:15-17, which reads in context, "[The Son] is the image of the invisible God, the firstborn of every creature: For by him were all things created, that are in heaven, and that are in earth, visible and invisible, whether they be thrones, or dominions, or principalities, or powers: all things were created by him, and for him: And he is before all things, and by him all things consist."

The phrase "firstborn of every creature" has tempted Mormons and other groups, like the Jehovah's Witnesses, to argue that the Son is a created being. This is because of a misunderstanding of the Greek involved in the passage and the overall context. The Greek phrase translated "firstborn of every creature" can equally be translated—in fact, better translated—"the firstborn over all creation." Here again, the term "firstborn" is used in a non-biological sense. It symbolizes his position and status relative to the Father and over all created things.

Because he is over all created things, he himself is not a created thing, as they are. This is part of why he is over them, for as the passage points out, "For by him were all things created." The connective "for" immediately follows the statement that he is the firstborn over all creation and explains why he has that status. He is over everything because everything was created through him. The passage says the same thing four different ways: (1) "all things were created by him;" (2) "all things were created . . . for him;" (3) "he is before all things;" and (4) "by him all things consist." In all of these ways, Christ is the firstborn over all creation, and in none of them is he hinted to be the biologically firstborn spirit baby of the Father.

Mormons also hold that Christ had to grow into godhood. Mormon doctrine states that Jehovah, the first spirit son of Elohim and his wife, "advanced and progressed" through the eons and ages of premortality until, "as Abraham described, he stood as one 'like unto God' (Abraham 3:24)."[10] Thus, Jesus had already developed to the stage of deity before he took on mortal flesh in this world. This in itself is a Mormon anomaly, since the LDS church contends one must have a physical body before he can progress to godhood (Abraham 3:26). Somehow, Jesus obtained godhood and served as Jehovah, God of the Jews in the Old Testament, without getting a body first.

Spirits Are Made of Matter?

A further departure from traditional Christian doctrine is the declaration that everything is matter. That which we would call spirit or soul is simply matter in a more refined form, Smith taught.

"There is no such thing as immaterial matter," he said. "All spirit is matter, but it is more fine or pure, and can only be discerned by purer eyes; We cannot see it; but when our bodies are purified we shall see that it is all matter" (Doctrine and Covenants 131:7-8).

This spirit element is co-eternal with God.

"There never was a time," Smith said, "when there were not spirits; for they are co-equal [co-eternal] with our Father in heaven."[11]

Moreover, the earthly elements, that which we more readily call matter, also are eternal (D&C 93:3).

This concept is convenient for Mormons in asserting the "eternity" of Christ. The intelligence or spirit matter used in forming the Son's "spirit body" was uncreated, eternal. At some point in the ages of time before our earth was "organized,"[12] the divine Father and Mother gave birth to Christ's spirit body: that is, they organized, in an unknown way—at least analogous to earthly

---

[10] First Presidency message, quoted in the current Mormon manual, *The Life and Teachings of Jesus and His Apostles*, 15.

[11] *Teachings of the Prophet Joseph Smith*, 353.

[12] Because they say spirit and matter are eternal, Mormons deny that God could bring forth creation from nothing. Rather, he merely organized and gave direction to the elements that were already available to him.

procreation[13]—pre-existing spirit matter and fashioned a body for Jehovah in the exact shape and form of a human man. Mormons say that the spirit body of a person has the very appearance of the person's future physical body (D&C 77:2). All plants and animals were similarly formed first with their spirit bodies (Moses 3:5).

Jehovah is, according to Mormonism, the firstborn because his was the first spirit body formed by his heavenly parents. There then followed the spirit bodies of all other rational beings. In this, Christ is not only our elder brother, but also a brother to Lucifer and all the fallen spirits who refused the Father's plan of salvation. The Mormon church says the "ingredients" eventually used to form Christ's spirit body existed forever. Yet Colossians 1:16-17 clearly states that the Son created all things and is himself uncreated.

We do well to remember the distinction presented earlier between Christ's divine and human natures. As the second person of the Trinity, the Son exists eternally. There never was a time when he was not. Because God is perfect and therefore changeless (change implying a movement either toward or away from some ideal or perfection), the Son did not undergo a "reformation" of component elements, bringing him into self-awareness or personhood. Jesus possessed both a divine and a human nature from the moment of his conception. He did not grow into divinity while living a mortal life among men. Mormons admit that Christ became God before he took on a mortal estate. Sometimes, though, their terminology is reminiscent of Greek or Roman mythology, as the following passage illustrates:

> [Mary], heavy with child, traveled all that distance on mule-back, guarded and protected as one about to give birth to a half-Deity. No other man in the history of this world of ours has ever had such an ancestry—God the Father on the one hand and Mary the Virgin on the other. . . . [Jesus] lived in a lowly home, the only man born to this earth half-Divine and half-mortal.[14]

---

[13] Otherwise there would be no basis for calling them Father and Mother, but only builders or organizers.

[14] *The Life and Teachings of Jesus and His Apostles*, 10.

Of course, Catholics recognize that Jesus Christ is fully divine (Col. 2:9) and fully human (Heb. 4:15), not a hybrid—half one and half the other. Just how pagan the above account sounds is brought out when one recognizes what Mormons mean when they speak of God the Father and Mary as Jesus' parents. It could perhaps be interpreted in a manner similar to Greco-Roman myths about Zeus, who departed from his heavenly spouse, Hera, to impregnate human females, such as Alcmene, Danae, and Semele, who then gave birth to half-human, half-divine demigods, like Heracles, Perseus, and Dionysius.[15]

Mormons and the Virgin Birth

Catholic understanding of the Virgin Birth of our Lord is simply stated: Mary was a virgin at the time of the annunciation, when Jesus was conceived in her by the power of the Holy Spirit; she remained a virgin throughout her pregnancy and the birth of Christ;[16] in fact, she remained a virgin forever. The support of Scripture is weighty:

> Isaiah 7:14: "Behold, a virgin shall conceive, and bear a son, and shall call his name Immanuel."
>
> Luke 1:34-35: "Then Mary said unto the angel, How shall this be, seeing I know not a man? And the angel answered and said unto her, The Holy Ghost shall come upon thee, and the power of the Highest shall overshadow thee: therefore also that holy thing which shall be born of thee shall be called the Son of God."
>
> Matthew 1:18: "Now the birth of Jesus Christ was on this wise: When as his mother Mary was espoused to Joseph, before they came together, she was found with child of the Holy Ghost."

---

[15] This is not to disrespect Mormon teaching. Nevertheless, LDS commentators open their church to such criticism by their imprudent and thoughtless characterizations.

[16] While the Fathers of the Church vouch for the miraculous character of Christ's birth, the Church makes no proclamation on the physiology by which the Lord was born to a Virgin Mother. See Ludwig Ott, *Fundamentals of Catholic Dogma*, 205.

Matthew 1:22-23: "Now all this was done, that it might be fulfilled which was spoken of the Lord by the prophet, saying, Behold, a virgin shall be with child, and shall bring forth a son, and they shall call his name Emmanuel, which being interpreted is, God with us."

The early creeds—Apostles' and Nicene—also give witness to this truth. Mormons, however, believe that Mary was a virgin only before conceiving her divine Son. They do not believe that she was a virgin when he was conceived or afterward because they believe conception occurred in the ordinary, natural way. Jesus, in the Mormon view, was no more born of a virgin than any child whose mother preserved her virginity until he was conceived.

When Mormons speak of Jesus Christ as the "only begotten Son" of the Father, they mean only that he was the only son whose physical body (as opposed to spirit body) the Father *physically* begot. Taylor wrote, "He, in the nearness of his relationship to the Father, seems to occupy a position that no other person occupies. He is spoken of as his well beloved Son, as the only begotten of the Father—does not this mean the only begotten after the flesh?"[17]

Heber J. Grant, seventh Mormon prophet, reiterated the belief. "We believe absolutely that Jesus Christ is the Son of God," Heber said, "begotten of God, the first-born in the spirit and the only begotten in the flesh; that he is the Son of God just as much as you and I are the sons of our fathers."[18]

Smith wrote, "Jesus Christ is the heir of this Kingdom—the only begotten of the Father according to the flesh."[19]

And Joseph Fielding Smith, tenth Mormon prophet, wrote, "Our Father in heaven is the Father of Jesus Christ, both in the spirit and in the flesh. Our Savior is the Firstborn in the spirit, the Only Begotten in the flesh."[20]

Active Mormons claim that God the Father and "Heavenly

---

[17] *The Gospel Kingdom*, 115.
[18] *Millennial Star*, January 1922, 2.
[19] *History of the Church* 5:556.
[20] *Doctrines of Salvation* 1:18.

Mother" not only brought forth the spirit of Christ in the pre-existence, they believe the Father also directly participated in the Lord's earthly conception. This inventive doctrine, understandably, raises the ire of many devout Christians, particularly as it has found expression in the theological discourses of some Mormon prophets and apostles. For example, Young said, "The man Joseph, the husband of Mary, did not, that we know of, have more than one wife, but Mary the wife of Joseph had another husband. [The babe in] the manger was begotten, not by Joseph, the husband of Mary, but by another Being. Do you inquire by whom? He was begotten by God our heavenly Father."[21]

Fielding Smith's father, Mormon prophet Joseph F. Smith, speaking to young children, said, "You all know that your fathers are indeed your fathers and that your mothers are indeed your mothers.... You cannot deny it. Now, we are told in Scriptures that Jesus Christ is the only begotten Son of God in the flesh. Well, for the benefit of the older ones, how are children begotten? I answer just as Jesus Christ was begotten of his father."[22]

McConkie taught that "Christ is . . . the Only Begotten Son . . . of the Father. . . . Each of the words is to be understood literally. Only means only. Begotten means begotten; and Son means son. Christ was begotten by an immortal Father in the same way that mortal men are begotten by mortal fathers."[23]

"God the Father is a perfected, glorified, holy Man, an immortal Personage. And Christ was born into the world as the literal Son of this Holy Being; he was born in the same personal, real, and literal sense that any mortal son is born to a mortal father. There is nothing figurative about his paternity; he was begotten, conceived and born in the normal and natural course of events, for he is the son of God, and that designation means what it says."[24]

Pratt said, "[T]he fleshly body of Jesus required a Mother as well

---

[21] *Journal of Discourses* 2:268.
[22] *Family Home Evening*, 1972, 125.
[23] *Mormon Doctrine*, 546–547.
[24] Ibid., 742.

as a Father. Therefore, the Father and Mother of Jesus, according to the flesh, must have been associated together in the capacity of Husband and Wife: hence the Virgin Mary must have been, for the time being, the lawful wife of God the Father."[25] Mary thus had two husbands, the Father and Joseph. She was perhaps the only woman lawfully permitted to engage in polyandry.[26] In the "meridian of time," as Mormons call it, God the Father looked with favor upon his handmaid, Mary of Nazareth. He visited her and, by the natural, literal process of sexual intercourse described above by Mormon authorities, left her pregnant with his Son. In trying to describe how Mary, in the process of natural intercourse with her glorified Father and God, could remain a virgin, McConkie resorted to redefining the term: A virgin is a woman who has not had sexual intercourse with a mortal man. The Heavenly Father is a resurrected, immortal man. Therefore, Mary did not lose her virginity.[27]

The Resurrection

Catholics can see how difficult, even dangerous, it is to discuss fundamental beliefs with those who repackage and re-label doctrines. Terms that appear to be familiar references to orthodox Christian teaching can not be taken at face value. Conversely, Mormons sometimes are unable to perceive what Christians are saying, even in those cases when Mormons happen to agree. Like the boy who cried wolf, after a certain number of iterations the process of communication becomes unreliable, even when the message is true.

A case in point is the doctrine of Christ's resurrection. On this subject, Mormons happen to correctly recognize that Jesus was physically raised from the dead. But because of the layers of mis-

---

[25] *The Seer*, 158–159.

[26] Her situation is unusual also in that the "Heavenly Father" was turning aside from the "Heavenly Mother."

[27] See *The Mortal Messiah*, vol. 1, 314.

communication and re-definition their leaders have built up between them and Christians, many Mormons fail to realize that Christians also believe Jesus to be bodily raised from the dead. This is a misperception that is even suggested to them by their leaders.

"And virtually all the millions of apostate Christendom have abased themselves before the mythical throne of a mythical Christ," according to McConkie, "whom they vainly suppose to be a spirit essence who is incorporeal,[28] uncreated, immaterial, and three-in-one with the Father and the Holy Spirit."[29]

You have to wonder if leaders capable of making statements like this are only deficient in their understanding of the Catholic faith or if, knowing the falsity of their assertions, they make them anyway. Catholics know that the entire sacramental structure of the Church, its very life, depends upon the abiding, transfigured humanity of Jesus Christ, now raised to the highest bliss. According to Pope Leo the Great, "Human nature has taken its place high above all the creatures of heaven . . . in order to sit on the throne of the eternal Father and to share on this throne the glory of him [God the Father] with whose being it was linked through the Son."[30]

Jesus Christ—A Subordinate God

Catholics adore God alone. We give full worship and obedience to the Father, the Son and the Holy Spirit. The three are co-eternal, all-holy persons. We pray to and adore each member of the Trinity, seeking to cultivate a relationship of love and reverence with

---

[28] By virtue of his incarnation, resurrection and ascension, the glorified Lord is not incorporeal or immaterial. His divine nature is eternal; his human nature, once created, endures forever.

[29] *Mormon Doctrine*, 269. In this same article, "False Christs," the Mormon apostle groups together "desert monasteries . . . mountain hermitages . . . Jesuit retreats, and . . . meeting places of secret cults" to which "hosts of misguided souls have trekked" in pursuit of Christ.

[30] Sermon 73:4. See also Christoph Schönborn, *From Death to Life*, 22, 34.

each person. This cannot be said for Mormons. Jesus Christ is a second god. There was a time in which he did not exist, but had to await the organization of his spirit by his Father. Thereafter, he was obedient to Heavenly Father in all things and progressed to eventual godhood,[31] working out his own exaltation—somehow, even though he did not have a body, as Mormon theology requires. Now, he has achieved a fullness of divinity and is spoken of as fully God, equal with his Father. But he was not always so.[32]

Not only does Mormon theology teach Christ's former inferiority, its spirituality insists he be excluded from the honor accorded the Father, the supreme God of this universe. Therefore, all prayers, whether personal or public, are to be addressed to the Father only. No one is to pray to the Son or the Holy Ghost. Though his picture adorns most Mormon homes and chapels; though he is referred to on almost every page of the Book of Mormon (including 2 Nephi 25:26: "And we talk of Christ, we rejoice in Christ, we preach of Christ, we prophesy of Christ. . . ."); though every prayer and testimony is concluded "in the name of Jesus Christ," yet are Mormons forbidden to pray to Christ.

One of the most difficult adjustments I had to make in converting to Mormonism was ceasing to pray to Jesus. In trying to live a life faithful to Mormon requirements, I understood that I should not offer prayer to Christ, including even short aspirations

---

[31] *Mormon Doctrine*, 129.

[32] Mormon writers cite Luke 2:52: "And Jesus increased in wisdom and stature, and in favour with God and man." The Mormon application of this verse is erroneous. Jesus grew in wisdom and age and grace in regards to his human, acquired nature; not in regard to his divine, essential nature. His human nature was susceptible to learning through experience and education. He developed as a human child through boyhood to manhood. His soul was free from all sin; he could not sin; his human nature was anointed and sanctified by the Trinity, making him the Christ. Nevertheless, we may speak of him growing in grace insofar as by his holy life he accumulated righteous deeds and grew in the admiration of men. The divine Son possessed the fullness of all things from all eternity, and needed no training period in pre-mortality nor opportunities during his earthly life to achieve divine perfection and completion.

or "arrow" prayers sent heavenward throughout the day: "Jesus, I love you." "My Jesus, mercy." "Thank you, Lord."

Perhaps other Catholics were accustomed to praying mainly to the Father. I wasn't. Jesus Christ, especially under his title of the Sacred Heart, was my usual focus both in meditation and in practicing the presence of God during the day. It was difficult to give him up as a center of daily worship.

This subordination of the Son to the Father is at times perceived as so vital a part of Mormon doctrine that McConkie turned his sights on a Brigham Young University professor who had written a book encouraging members to cultivate a personal relationship with and devotion to the Lord Jesus. Seeking to undo the harm this pernicious aberration could cause the young, ignorant Mormons, McConkie conducted a "devotional" or assembly at the university in Provo, Utah, on March 2, 1982. While naming neither the professor (who continues as a BYU instructor and an author) nor the book, the apostle made it clear that he was about the business of correcting the writer and rescuing "spiritually immature" student-readers from "inordinate" desires for excellence in a personal relationship with Jesus Christ (p. 19).[33]

McConkie claimed his words were more than his own opinion. "I shall express the views of the Brethren, of the prophets and apostles of old, and of all those who understand and are in tune with the Holy Spirit. . . . Everyone who is sound spiritually and who has the guidance of the Holy Spirit will believe my words and follow my counsel" (p. 1).

As to the origin of the idea that one needs a personal relationship with Christ, McConkie has no doubt: It is the devil (p. 2). Proof of Satan's enormous influence is found in the creeds of Christendom, which codify "lies about God." The lies are, rather, the falsehoods McConkie preaches about the Christian teaching

---

[33] The page references are to the typed copy of the talk, "Our Relationship with the Lord," provided by McConkie and made available through Utah Lighthouse Ministry. Punctuation and capitalization are as in the original. His edict was repeated several years later in *Ensign* magazine (June 1988, 59).

on God. Christians say God "is an immaterial, incorporeal nothingness. They say he is one-god-in-three, and three-gods-in one who neither hears, nor sees, nor speaks. Some even say he is dead, which he might as well be if their descriptions identify his being" (p. 3).[34]

Despite McConkie's vehemence in discouraging personal relationships with Christ, other Mormon authorities taught differently.

"Jesus Christ is to be worshiped by men and angels; and worship is an honor to be paid only to true Deity," said B. H. Roberts nearly eighty years before McConkie declared what he said was the eternal practice of refusing divine worship to the Savior.[35]

Scripture is full of references to people worshipping Jesus in the New Testament[36] and, in the Old Testament, to the worship of Jehovah—with whom Mormons identify Jesus. Nevertheless, McConkie remained adamant.

"We worship the Father and him only and no one else," he said. "We do not worship the Son and we do not worship the Holy Ghost. I know perfectly well what the Scriptures say about worshiping Christ and Jehovah, but they are speaking in an entirely different sense—the sense of standing in awe and being reverentially grateful to him who has redeemed us. Worship in the true and saving sense is reserved for God the first, the Creator" (5).

He may know "perfectly well" what Scripture says, but his interpretation is deficient. In the New Testament, Jesus unmistakably accepts worship as God, as when Thomas falls at the feet of his risen Lord: "And Thomas answered and said unto him, My Lord and my God" (John 20:28).[37] Regarding the Old Testament references to the worship of Jehovah, it is incredible that one could

---

[34] Citing some of McConkie's many libelous statements about the Catholic faith would be a good antidote to the Mormons' allegations that *they* are a misunderstood and persecuted church.

[35] See his *Mormon Doctrine of Deity*, 190. Compare with Hebrews 1:5–6.

[36] Matt. 2:11, 8:2, 9:18, 15:25, 28:9, 28:17, John 9:38.

[37] See also Kenneth Baker, S.J., *Fundamentals of Catholicism*, vol. 2, 234–237.

claim that they do not represent true worship. Jehovah set up a priesthood specifically for his worship, the psalms enthusiastically exhort the reader to worship Jehovah (Ps. 29:2, 45:11, 96:9, 99:5, 99:9); we are specifically told to worship Jehovah as our Creator (the very thing McConkie said we must not do).

"O come, let us worship and bow down: let us kneel before the LORD our maker" (Ps. 95:6).

The tangle of Mormon error is further exposed when one notices that we are specifically instructed to worship Jehovah and not any other God whatsoever, which would preclude worshipping Elohim.

"For thou shalt worship no other god: for the LORD, whose name is Jealous, is a jealous God" (Ex. 34:14).

McConkie's directive, "Don't worship Jehovah, worship his Father," contradicts the Ten Commandments, which read in part, "I am the LORD thy God, which have brought thee out of the land of Egypt, out of the house of bondage. Thou shalt have no other gods before me" (Ex. 20:2–3).

The testimony of the early Church Fathers is equally clear that Jesus Christ, as God, is to be worshipped and honored as God.

"We worship [Christ] as the Son of God."[38]

"Inasmuch as the powers in heaven, the Angels and Archangels, were ever worshipping him, and do even now worship the Lord in the person of Jesus, the fact that the Son of God is still worshipped when he became man is for us a grace and an extraordinary exaltation."[39]

"We worship the Lord of creation, the Incarnate Word of God. . . . Knowing that the Word was made flesh, we recognize him as God even after he has come in the flesh."[40]

"Let us worship Christ as God, and believe that he also was become man."[41]

---

[38] *The Martyrdom of Saint Polycarp*, A.D. 155.
[39] Athanasius, *Discourses against the Arians* 1, 42, A.D. 358.
[40] Athanasius, *Letter to Adelphus* 3, A.D. 370.
[41] Cyril of Jerusalem, *Catechetical Lectures* 12, 1, A.D. 350.

McConkie was also adamant in denying that the prayers of the faithful are presented by Christ to the Father.

"This is plain sectarian [i.e., Christian] nonsense," he said. "Our prayers are addressed to the Father, and to him only. They do not go through Christ, or the Blessed Virgin, or St. Genevieve or along the beads of a rosary" (20).

In addition, McConkie said, "[Y]ou have never heard one of them [prophets or apostles of the LDS church] advocate this excessive zeal that calls for gaining a so-called special and personal relationship with Christ" (21).

Nevertheless, in *Gospel Principles*, copyrighted and published by the Mormon church and used in the training of new members, we read, "We need to have a personal relationship with him [Christ]" (61).

The date of printing of this text is 1992. Its first copyright notice is given as 1978, and research into that edition yields a similar statement: "Each of us needs to study the life of the Savior and strive to keep his commandments throughout our lives in order to develop a personal relationship with him" (53).

It is assumed the First Presidency of the Mormon church gives final approval on teaching materials used to foster the faith and spirituality of the members. That would mean this admonition was promulgated for at least three years before McConkie asserted no such statement existed.

Jesus Christ: Husband and Father

When people think of the Mormon teaching regarding polygamy, they think of it in a nineteenth-century context. But for Mormons the teaching has implications for earlier and later stages of history. For example, Mormon leaders have asserted that Christ taught his apostles polygamy and that this was one of the key factors leading to his crucifixion. President Jedediah M. Grant, member of the First Presidency with Brigham Young, taught the ultimate cause of the Lord's crucifixion.

"The grand reason," Grant said, "of the burst of public sentiment in anathemas upon Christ and his disciples, causing his crucifixion, was evidently based upon polygamy, according to the testimony of the philosophers who rose in that age. A belief in the doctrine of a plurality of wives caused the persecution of Jesus and his followers. We might almost think they were 'Mormons.'"[42]

Mormons believe polygamy was a divine mandate at earlier stages of history. It also is a divine mandate in future stages, such as our life in heaven. Given these claims, it is natural for Mormons to think that Jesus, as the model Son of the Father, is one who follows the polygamy mandate. Though currently the Mormon church does not have an official position on the subject, Mormon leadership has not always been so tentative. Orson Hyde, apostle under Smith and Young, declared Christ was not only married, but was a polygamist who also fathered children. According to Hyde,

> It will be borne in mind that once on a time there was a marriage in Cana of Galilee; and on a careful reading of that transaction, it will be discovered that no less a person than Jesus Christ was married on that occasion. If he was never married, his intimacy with Mary and Martha, and the other Mary also whom Jesus loved, must have been highly unbecoming and improper to say the best of it.
>
> What did the old Prophet mean when he said (speaking of Christ), "He shall see his seed, prolong his days, &c." Did Jesus consider it necessary to fulfil every righteous command or requirement of his Father? He most certainly did. This he witnessed by submitting to baptism under the hands of John. "Thus it becometh us to fulfil all righteousness," said he. Was it God's commandment to man, in the beginning, to multiply and replenish the earth? None can deny this, neither that it was a righteous command; for upon an obedience to this, depended the perpetuity of our race. Did Christ come to destroy the law or the Prophets, or to fulfil them? He came to fulfil. Did he multiply, and did he see his seed? Did he honour his Father's law by complying with it, or did he not? Others may do as they like, but I will not charge our Saviour with neglect or

---

[42] *Journal of Discourses* 1:346.

transgression in this or any other duty [*Journal of Discourses* 4:259–260].[43]

Many are familiar with Mormon preaching on the great benefits of family. Jesus, many members think, must have shared fully in those blessings. Although this notion of Jesus as polygamist and father is believed by large numbers of Mormons, it is not currently among those positions to which the Mormon church is willing to officially and publicly commit itself. Of course, it's not discussed much, if at all, with outsiders.

---

[43] See also Orson Hyde, *Journal of Discourses* 2:210: "I discover that some of the Eastern papers represent me as a great blasphemer, because I said, in my lecture on Marriage, at our last Conference, that Jesus Christ was married at Cana of Galilee, that Mary, Martha, and others were his wives, and that he begat children. All that I have to say in reply to that charge is this—they worship a Savior that is too pure and holy to fulfil the commands of his Father. I worship one that is just pure and holy enough 'to fulfil all righteousness;' not only the righteous law of baptism, but the still more righteous and important law 'to multiply and replenish the earth.' Startle not at this! for even the Father himself honored that law by coming down to Mary, without a natural body, and begetting a son; and if Jesus begat children, he only 'did that which he had seen his Father do.'"

20. Mormon God Number Three —Another Son

The Mormon View

"The Holy Ghost," said Fielding Smith, "is the third member of the Godhead. He is a Spirit, in the form of a man. . . . As a spirit personage the Holy Ghost has size and dimensions. He does not fill the immensity of space, and cannot be everywhere present in person at the same time."[1]

He taught that, unlike the first two members of the Mormon Godhead, the Holy Ghost has a spirit body only. In this, he is subject to the Father and the Son, to whom his task is to bear witness. Though often employing the neuter pronoun "it" in referring to this third god, Mormons claim, "[T]he Holy Ghost is a male personage. Note how often Jesus refers to the Holy Ghost as 'he' and 'him'. . . . He is a male personage of spirit as was Jesus before he was born of the Virgin Mary."[2]

In other words, the Holy Ghost possesses arms, legs, a head and torso. These features are as yet, however, only in spirit form, such as Christ was before the Father and Mary provided him with a body at his conception in Nazareth. The Holy Ghost cannot be "physically" present in more than one place at a time. In this, he is like the other two gods. Mormons imagine that, like the sun, the gods' influences can radiate throughout creation while they remain fixed at some galactic distance.[3]

Apparently in response to some unusual speculation among the members, Fielding Smith also warned that "the Holy Ghost is not

---

[1] *Doctrines of Salvation* 1:38.
[2] *A Marvelous Work and a Wonder*, 115.
[3] According to the Book of Abraham, chapter three, God the Father lives somewhere near a planet or heavenly body named Kolob.

a woman, as some have declared, and therefore is not the mother of Jesus Christ."[4] Little else is now taught as to the person, origin or destiny of the Holy Ghost. But earlier prophets and apostles, employing their gifts of inspiration and revelation, have made forays into the theological thicket of Pneumatology, or the doctrine of the Holy Spirit, and have emerged with curious finds.

Pratt's quest, though backed by his claim to apostolic revelation, apparently ran aground in a quagmire of confusion. In 1855 he stated, "I will tell you what I believe in regard to the Holy Ghost's being a person: but I know of no revelation that states that this is the fact, neither is there any that informs us that it is not the fact, so we are left to form our own conclusions upon the subject, and hence some have concluded that they were right, and that others were not. It is in fact a matter of doubt with many, and of uncertainty, I believe, with all, whether there be a personal Holy Spirit, or not.

"I am inclined to think, from some things in the revelations, that there is such a being as a personal Holy Ghost, but it is not set forth as a positive fact, and the Lord has never given me any revelation upon the subject, and consequently I cannot fully make up my mind one way or the other."[5]

Pratt then cited several biblical passages that could be used to support the idea that the Holy Ghost is a person, followed by verses he thought could indicate that the Holy Ghost is not a person. His belief, however, rested on his opinion and not on divine revelation. This was an odd predicament for Pratt, who just a few sentences before had proclaimed the sufficiency of heavenly inspiration to understand even the deepest of "mysteries."

"For my own part," he wrote, "I see no mystery about it [doctrine of the Godhead]; the subject is plain and simple to those who enjoy the gift of the Holy Ghost."[6]

---

[4] *Doctrines of Salvation* 1:39.
[5] *Journal of Discourses* 2:338.
[6] Pratt is reported to have entertained the notion that the Holy Ghost exists also as a "diffused fluid substance," "full of wisdom and knowledge," whose powers vibrate throughout nature.

While Elder Pratt's conclusions were inconclusive, Smith's message was lightning sharp. But, like the proverbial lightning, his teachings rarely hit the same point twice. Many of Smith's doctrinal musings are found in the Lectures on Faith, a series of teachings given to the early Latter-day Saints. They were prepared by Smith and his counselor, Sidney Rigdon. The teachings, McConkie wrote, "[W]ere not themselves classed as revelations, but in them is to be found some of the best lesson material ever prepared on the Godhead; on the character, perfections, and attributes of God."[7]

In lecture five we read,

> There are two personages who constitute the great, matchless, governing, and supreme power over all things, by whom all things were created and made.... They are the Father and the Son—the Father being a personage of spirit, glory, and power, possessing all perfection and fullness, the Son, who was in the bosom of the Father, a personage of tabernacle [i.e., having flesh], made or fashioned like unto man, or being in the form and likeness of man, or rather man was formed after His likeness and in His image....
> And He being the Only Begotten of the Father, full of grace and truth, and having overcome, received a fullness of the glory of the Father, possessing the same mind with the Father, which mind is the Holy Spirit, that bears record of the Father and the Son, and these three are one; or, in other words, these three constitute the great, matchless, governing, and supreme power over all things [48-49].

Found in this one passage are the roots of peculiarly Mormon ideas, some of which have since been abandoned, redefined or explained away. First, note that we are told that there are "two personages" possessing "matchless" and "supreme power" over all else. Then, that the Father is a "personage of spirit," with no

---

[7] *Mormon Doctrine*, 439. Included with the Doctrine and Covenants from 1835, the Lectures on Faith were quietly dropped by the Mormon church from that volume of scripture in 1921. See Thomas G. Alexander, "The Reconstruction of Mormon Doctrine: From Joseph Smith to Progressive Theology," in *Sunstone*, July-August 1980, 24-33. Alexander, a BYU history professor, describes the process the Mormon hierarchy used in its deliberate alteration of previous doctrinal formulations.

comment on his alleged physicality. As if to further emphasize the purely spiritual nature of God the Father, his Son is referred to as a "personage of tabernacle," or flesh, in whose likeness man was made. Man here is said to be in the image of the Son; nothing is said about man's creation in the image of a physical Father. The "mind" of the Father and the Son is one and is the Holy Ghost. A "mind" is not a "personage," so Smith in the first sentence refers to just two personages as constituting the great creators and rulers of the world. We begin with two and end with three; not three "personages," however, just "three," though it appears that Smith raised a quality (mind) to a level commensurate with personhood. To term this process of thought regarding the Godhead, its character and nature, as clear and useful was perhaps a great act of faith on the part of Elder McConkie. Though Mormon writers mock Catholics for the mystical mathematics that asserted "one is three is one," Mormon theology fares no better with this "two is three" Godhead.

But perhaps this is glib. After all, there has been continuous revelation for the Mormons, who now testify that the Holy Ghost is indeed a personage. Apostle Pratt may have waffled on this; Smith may have declared the Holy Ghost to be merely the "mind" of God. The contemporary Mormon knows better because, about eight years after the lectures were composed, Smith gave contradictory instructions to Mormon church members. In Doctrine and Covenants 130:22, questions raised by the fifth lecture on faith were resolved by prophetic fiat:

"The Father has a body of flesh and bones as tangible as man's [and is not simply spirit]; the Son also; but the Holy Ghost has not a body of flesh and bones, but is a personage of Spirit. Were it not so, the Holy Ghost could not dwell in us."

Keep in mind that the Holy Ghost, because he has a spirit body, is bound by time and space. He can be in only one place at a time. What, then, does Smith mean when he says that in order to dwell in us the Holy Ghost must be a personage of spirit only, not of flesh and bones? If the Spirit is limited to a single place, even as a spirit, how can he dwell in us? Mormons say that he dwells in us by his influence, which permeates the universe. But they say this of the Father and the Son, too, and these two are said to have fleshly bodies.

Mormons consider the Holy Ghost to be subordinate to both the Father and the Son. President Heber C. Kimball, Young's first counselor, taught that "the Holy Ghost is a man; he is one of the sons of our Father and our God; and he is that man that stood next to Jesus Christ, just as I stand by brother Brigham."[8]

Thus, the Holy Ghost is a spirit brother to Jesus, Lucifer and us. He seemingly received spirit birth after Christ, the firstborn, and is subordinate to both him and the Father. He is, by virtue of his assigned mission, the messenger of the Father, revealing and testifying to the truth.[9] In fulfilling his role, the Holy Ghost is seen as very powerful. Fielding Smith wrote, "When a man has the manifestation from the Holy Ghost, it leaves an indelible impression on his soul, one that is not easily erased."[10]

Moreover, the Holy Ghost, in his spirit body, is to be a comforter to believers, strengthening their faith. A common expression for being convinced of the correctness of a teaching or the divine pedigree of a church talk is "I felt the Spirit." Mormons say they "feel of the Spirit" on many occasions. A moving talk at a Sunday meeting, a pious piece of music or a touching video may bring a Mormon to tears. Such emotions are usually taken as proof that the Holy Ghost has once again ratified the faith of the presenters and audience.

During my eighteen months in the Mormon church, I gave several talks, each dealing with my "conversion experience." Most of the meetings were with groups of fewer than two hundred people; occasionally I spoke to home study groups of a dozen or so members and a few times the audiences were estimated at fifteen hundred and more. In every case, at the conclusion of my remarks, people would testify that they knew I was called by God

---

[8] *Journal of Discourses* 5:180.
[9] *Gospel Principles*, 37.
[10] *Answers to Gospel Questions* 2:151.

into the Mormon church because the Spirit had told them; they felt deeply the authenticity of my Mormon faith, which in turn ratified and strengthened their own.[11]

I sat through many Sunday meetings, especially "fast and testimony" meetings,[12] watching as women and men openly wept when speaking of their love for God, Christ, their parents, spouse, children or friends. No doubt these members were sincere, loving, and honest in their faith and the expression of it. But unlike many, I did not consider such displays of emotion proof of the Holy Ghost's movement.

St. Teresa of Jesus and St. John of the Cross, two of the Catholic Church's greatest mystics, reported the gift of supernatural raptures and ecstasies. Yet they continually warned against misinterpreting feelings for faith. When confronted by Mormons bearing fervent testimony to the truth of some doctrine or another, Catholics must not mistake the intensity or even sincerity of the feeling for actual truth. After all, a Catholic who has apprehended the great truths of God "by study and also by faith" is even more justified in testifying to them with head and heart.

We have already seen that Christ and the Holy Ghost, because they possess bodies (the one of flesh and bones, the other of spirit only), are limited spatially. Where that specific location is, Mormon theology does not reveal. It is possible, however, for any one of the three gods in the Mormon Godhead to visit the earth from time to time "in person."[13] A righteous Mormon may sincerely

---

[11] During this time, I never gave a talk grudgingly or from a sense of duty, though I could not speak as often as invited. Had I accepted every request to speak, I would have been overwhelmed with commitments. So I tried to keep my schedule to about one talk a month. But by mid-April 1995, I had concluded that the problems I saw with Mormonism were too large to sidestep, and I refused all further invitations to speak or otherwise publicize my conversion.

[12] Mormon worship is described in later chapters.

[13] Victor L. Ludlow, in *Principles and Practices of the Restored Gospel*, 57, claims that the Holy Ghost, "as a spirit person, can actually enter into the body of a human being." How frequently this is done, or if it can be done to more than one person simultaneously, is not stated. Another interesting twist: Apostle

hope for and expect such a divine meeting. There certainly is no lack of anecdotal literature reporting the visitation of divine or other supernatural personages.

The gift of the Holy Ghost, along with his spiritual gifts, is conferred only by the laying on of hands by one possessing the proper priesthood authority. This "confirmation" ordinance is generally imparted immediately after baptism. Such action bestows on the member the right to receive guidance and inspiration from the Holy Ghost, who, previous to Mormon baptism, could only occasionally guide the non-member. Though a person has received the laying on of hands, there is no assurance that he has received the Holy Ghost. The blessing of the Spirit's company is given only to the person who is faithful and desires his assistance.[14] According to the manual *Gospel Principles*, "To be worthy to have the help of the Holy Ghost, we must seek earnestly to obey the commandments of God. We must keep our thoughts and actions pure" (139).

This Pelagian philosophy is typical of Mormonism's emphasis on the individual's obligation to perfect himself. Spencer W. Kimball, twelfth Mormon prophet, proclaimed, "Man is a god in embryo and has in him the seeds of godhood, and he can, if he will, rise to great heights. He can lift himself by his own bootstraps as no other creature can do. He was created not to fail and degenerate but to rise to perfection like his Lord Jesus Christ."[15]

It seems, then, that in order to enjoy the right of the Spirit's aid,

---

LeGrand Richards interpreted the words of Christ in John 16:7 ("It is expedient for you that I go away: for if I go not away, the Comforter will not come unto you. . . .") to mean that both Jesus and the Holy Ghost cannot remain on the earth and serve together. Unhappily, Richards concedes, Jesus has not explained why both he and the Holy Ghost have not been allowed to occupy space on this planet at the same time. See *A Marvelous Work and a Wonder*, 115–116.

[14] *Mormon Doctrine*, 313.

[15] *Teachings of Spencer W. Kimball*, 28. However, Kimball noted, the "Lamanites" (Native Americans) are not able to lift themselves by their own bootstraps. (See 604, 612, 614.)

the Mormon must have progressed to a sanctified state in which he has relatively little need for the Holy Ghost's help. McConkie ended further speculation about the Holy Ghost, his nature or mission by declaring, "In this dispensation at least, nothing has been revealed as to his [Holy Ghost's] origin or destiny; expressions on these matters are both speculative and fruitless."[16]

The Catholic Belief

We believe in the Holy Spirit, the Lord and giver of life, who, with the Father and the Son, is worshiped and glorified. He is an eternal person, the third of the Trinity. He is one in being with the Father and the Son. He exists from all eternity and is immutable in his perfection and glory. To him be all praise and adoration. It is the Holy Spirit who dwells personally in all souls alive by grace. As such, he is the paraclete and advocate, the consoler and testifier to all truth. The Spirit, together with the Father and the Son, is the creator, redeemer and sanctifier of the world. In the Church, we encounter the Holy Spirit in Scripture he inspired; in sacred Tradition, which he preserves; in the Church's teaching authority, which he directs; in the sacraments, by which he brings us to Christ; in prayer, which he fortifies; in ministries, which edify the Church; and in the lives of holy members, who witness to God's holiness.[17]

Further discussion on the person and nature of the Holy Spirit is presented in the following section dealing with the Holy Trinity.

---

[16] *Mormon Doctrine*, 359. Nevertheless, some Mormon thinkers believe that the Holy Ghost must, at some future point, receive a physical body, as is the pattern for all other gods and would-be gods.

[17] See *Catechism of the Catholic Church*, no. 688.

21. The True Godhead —The Blessed Trinity

Mormons will insist, especially in discussion with Catholics and other Christians, that they believe in only one God. They manage this by stating that the three gods are fully united in will, purpose and plan. We examined briefly the term "henotheism" (worship of one God among many gods) as it applies to Mormon belief. There appear to be two levels on which this theistic scheme operates. First, Mormons believe that, though there are many gods existing outside the Mormon Godhead, these gods are remote and oblivious to the affairs of our universe. They are busy directing the worlds and creatures they have themselves formed. But Mormons claim to worship and obey only the "one" God for this world, who shares the same nature and attributes possessed by other gods in other places and times.

A second level of henotheism prevails within the Mormon Godhead. That is, the Father is the supreme God; only he is to be adored and prayed to. He begat, in some prior eternity, both the Son and the Holy Ghost as spirit babies, as he did for all our "spirit bodies" as well.[1] God, according to Mormonism, is not the creator of time. He is in and limited by time. Nor is he the creator of matter. Matter is eternal, and he is composed of matter. In the next chapter we will consider the implications of these beliefs,

---

[1] Van Hale, a Mormon apologist, admits that "a precise theological term for the Mormon doctrine of deity is still not readily available." He proposes as a working definition a "homoiousion, tritheistic henotheism." That is, three gods, among many, who are similar, though not the same, in nature. See "Defining the Contemporary Mormon Concept of God," in *Line Upon Line*. Compare this with the God revealed in Scripture and taught by the Catholic Church: One only God in three persons who possess the same divine nature.

particularly as they influence the Mormon doctrine of man. For now, these assertions demonstrate the Mormon god to be finite, limited, bounded by realities not of his own making.

Nevertheless, Mormon theology also speaks of his omnipotence, omnipresence and omniscience.[2] McConkie, ever ready to dress up distinctive Mormon doctrines in more appealing Christian clothing, defined a God more absolute than the one preached by earlier Mormon prophets and apostles.

"This great God, the Lord Almighty, . . . is omnipotent, omniscient, and omnipresent," McConkie wrote. "He has all power, knows all things, and by the power of his Spirit, is in and through all things."[3]

Yet Mormon standard works, prophets and theologians reveal that, despite McConkie's revisionist attempts, the Mormon god is merely a perfected man who can know and do more than any other being (Robson, 70). He is different from his sons and daughters only in degree and not in kind, in chronology but not in essence.[4]

Mormon authorities contradict each other on this topic, too. Smith, Pratt and Roberts revealed that God exists in time and space. But McConkie, contemporary apostle Neal A. Maxwell and others, testify to a divine omniscience that would require extra-temporality of its possessor.[5]

---

[2] A good summary of the differing Mormon positions is in Kent E. Robson, "Omnipotence, Omnipresence, and Omniscience in Mormon Theology," in *Line Upon Line*, 67–75.

[3] Cited in Robson, 69.

[4] Sterling M. McMurrin, in *The Theological Foundations of the Mormon Religion*, 2–3, states: "It is typical of Mormon writers to insist that even God is natural rather than supernatural. . . . It is perhaps not entirely inaccurate to describe Mormonism as a kind of naturalistic, humanistic theism."

[5] See references in Robson, 70–71.

The Biblical Basis for the Trinity

"I say to the whole world," Young said, "receive the truth, no matter who presents it to you. Take up the Bible, compare the religion of the Latter-day Saints with it, and see if it will stand the test."[6]

Together with other Mormon leaders, Young challenged the Christian world to measure Mormon beliefs by the standard of the Holy Bible. But the Mormon Godhead receives no scriptural support. Rather, the orthodox Catholic teaching on the Trinity is threaded through the pages of both testaments.

I often was asked by Mormons, "Aren't you glad now to have a correct understanding of the Godhead? Isn't it a relief to have given up the impossible dogma of the Trinity for a God who is personal, approachable and understandable?" I had never found it a strain to accept the belief in one God in three persons. It wasn't until I questioned my Mormon beliefs in other areas that I began to see that the Mormon Godhead was rationally implausible.

"On more than one occasion the Christ has made known that a knowledge and acquaintance with God is basic to exaltation [salvation]."[7] But, as we've seen, Mormons have disagreed from the beginning on the nature and person of God. Moreover, they say that theirs is a God of revelation and that man's purpose in life is to learn his nature.[8] But Mormons do not know God's origin, though they believe he had one. They cannot account for their God sharing his infinity[9] with other gods, a contradiction of terms.

The Mormon Godhead is no antidote to the difficult truth of

---

[6] *Journal of Discourses* 16:46.
[7] Spencer W. Kimball, *Conference Reports*, April 1964, 93.
[8] *Mormon Doctrine*, 318.
[9] Mormons have long spoken of the "infinity" of their principal God. See, for example, James E. Talmage, *The Articles of Faith*, 39–40.

the Trinity. The Mormon God seeks to satisfy reason, but ends up confounding it. The Mormon God seems more like a man who has achieved more than others, perhaps, and deserves greater respect—but that's all.

The doctrine of the Trinity holds that there is one God and in him subsist three distinct persons who are all equally divine. This provides a useful template for organizing the biblical material.[10]

There Is One God

The Book of Mormon contains a number of passages (Alma 18:5, 27-28. 22:8-11; Mosiah 15:3-5) that indicate Mormons at an early stage also believed in only one God. In this, they were following the teaching of true, Christian Scripture.

> Deuteronomy 6:4: "Hear, O Israel: The LORD our God is one LORD."

> Deuteronomy 32:39: "See now that I, even I, am he, and there is no god with me."

> 2 Samuel 7:22: "Wherefore thou are great, O LORD God: for there is none like thee, neither is there any God beside thee."

> Isaiah 42:8: "I am the LORD: that is my name: and my glory will I not give to another."

> Isaiah 43:10-11: "I am he: before me there was no God formed, neither shall there be after me. I, even I, am the LORD; and beside me there is no saviour."

> Isaiah 44:6, 8: ". . . I am the first, and I am the last; and beside me there is no God. . . . Is there a God beside me? yea, there is no God; I know not any."

---

[10] It is beyond the scope of this work to offer more than a cursory treatment of this foundational Christian doctrine. Most introductory works on Catholic apologetics supply useful approaches to this mystery of faith. See in particular *Theology and Sanity*, 47-123.

Observe particularly that in Isaiah 43:10-11, God says that no God was formed before him, neither will there be any formed after him. This is a direct contradiction to the Mormon doctrine of eternal progression, since our God could not have come from an infinite line of gods who worked out their own godhood, neither can we progress to godhood and become gods in the future.

Mormons claim that Jesus, in his pre-mortal state as Jehovah, is the reference point of all the texts above. According to this idea, then, Christ is the only God; there were no gods formed before him nor shall any develop in the future. We have the Lord's word for this: If anyone were to know the number and condition of any other gods, it would be he. Yet he tells us he is the only God and he knows of none other. Should Mormons retort that the entire Godhead is here referred to, they still don't avoid the dilemma. God the Father would surely remember the obedience he was obligated to offer his own Father-god in order to progress to deity. This is a god who reportedly preceded in time the Mormon Elohim and exceeds him forever in glory and honor. See also Isaiah 44:5, 14, 21-22, 45:5, 6, 14, 18, 21, 22, 46:9.

> Isaiah 44:24: "For thus says the LORD, your Redeemer, who formed you from the womb: 'I am the LORD, who made all things, who stretched out the heavens alone, who spread out the earth—Who was with me?'" (RSV).

Mormonism teaches Christ was creator of this world. If so, he was acting with the authority of Elohim. How, then, would Mormons answer the Lord's question in verse twenty-four?

> John 17:3: "And this is life eternal, that they might know thee the only true God, and Jesus Christ, whom thou hast sent."
>
> 1 Corinthians 8:4: ". . . there is none other God but one."
>
> Galatians 3:20: ". . . God is one."
>
> Ephesians 4:6: "[There is] one God and Father of all, who is above all, and through all, and in you all."

This is impossible if God the Father achieved godhood only by adhering either to his own divine Father's commands or to eternal laws not of his own making.

> 1 Timothy 1:17: "Now unto the King eternal, immortal, invisible, the only wise God, be honour and glory for ever and ever. Amen."
>
> 1 Timothy 2:5: "For there is one God, and one mediator between God and men, the man Christ Jesus."
>
> Jude 25: "To the only wise God our Saviour, be glory and majesty, dominion and power, both now and ever. Amen."

THERE ARE THREE PERSONS IN THE ONE GOD

Besides the accounts of Christ's baptism (Matt. 3:16–17; Mark 1:9–11; Luke 3:21–22; John 1:31–34), where all three persons of the Trinity are manifest (the Son in the flesh, the Spirit under the form of a dove and the Father as a voice from heaven), other New Testament passages attest to the existence of three divine persons in one God.

> Matthew 28:19: "Go ye therefore, and teach all nations, baptizing them in the name of the Father, and of the Son, and of the Holy Ghost."

Notice that Christ directs his apostles to perform baptism in the singular name (not names) of the Trinity. There are also passages addressing the divine personhood of the Son and the Spirit.

> John 20:28: "And Thomas answered and said unto him, My Lord and my God."
>
> Acts 5:3–4: "But Peter said, Ananias, why hath Satan filled thine heart to lie to the Holy Ghost . . . ? Thou hast not lied unto men, but unto God."
>
> Hebrews 1:8: "Unto the Son he [God the Father] saith, Thy throne, O God, is for ever and ever."

In these passages, Christ and the Holy Spirit are called God. Mormons do not dispute this. But when these references (and those that follow) are combined with belief in only one God, orthodox Catholics conclude there is a Trinity of divine persons in the one God. Mormons say there are three gods in one Godhead. The unity within that Godhead is only moral or intentional. That is, the three gods so closely agree on all things that they could be said to be "one" in a metaphorical sense. But this is not what is indicated in the passages, and Catholics do not bifurcate the divine will from the divine being. Hence, there is an essential, and not just accidental, oneness of persons.

As we have seen, Mormons preach a subordinated Godhead. This is also contrary to the clear meaning of Scripture. In the following passages, which are only representative (not exhaustive), we will submit several "attributes" of God and show how each of the three persons possesses them in their fullness.

The Three Persons Are God the Creator

[Father] Genesis 2:7: "And the LORD God formed man of the dust of the ground, and breathed into his nostrils the breath of life."[11]

[Son] John 1:3: "All things were made by him; and without him was not any thing made that was made."[12]

[Holy Spirit] Job 33:4: "The Spirit of God hath made me, and the breath of the Almighty hath given me life."[13]

The Three Persons Are the Lord

[Father] Romans 10:12: ". . . the same Lord over all is rich unto all that call upon him."

[Son] Luke 2:11: "For unto you is born this day in the city of David a Saviour, which is Christ the Lord."[14]

[Holy Spirit] 2 Corinthians 3:17: "Now the Lord is that Spirit. . . ."

---

[11] See also Psalm 102:25.
[12] See also Colossians 1:16.
[13] See also John 1:2 and Psalm 104:30.
[14] See also John 20:28.

The Three Persons Are Eternal

[Father] Psalm 90:2: "Before the mountains were brought forth, or ever thou hast formed the earth and the world, even from everlasting to everlasting, thou art God."

This passage says there was an intelligence that exists from all eternity and this person is God from all eternity; hence, God did not develop and grow into godhood. From all eternity, he was God.

[Son] Revelation 1:8: "I am the Alpha and Omega, the beginning and the ending, saith the Lord, which is, and which was, and which is to come, the Almighty."

[Holy Spirit] Hebrews 9:14: "How much more shall the blood of Christ, who through the eternal Spirit offered himself without spot to God, purge your conscience from dead works to serve the living God?"

The Three Persons Are True

[Father] John 7:28: "Then cried Jesus in the temple as he taught, saying, Ye both know me, and ye know whence I am; and I am not come of myself, but he that sent me is true."[15]

[Son] Revelation 3:7: ". . . These things saith he that is holy, he that is true, he that hath the key of David."

[Holy Spirit] 1 John 5:6: ". . . it is the Spirit that beareth witness, because the Spirit is truth.

The Three Persons Are Holy

[Father] Revelation 15:4: "Who shall not fear thee, O Lord, and glorify thy name? For thou only art holy."

---

[15] See also John 14:6.

[Son] John 6:69: "We believe and know that you are the Holy One of God" [NIV].[16]

[Holy Spirit] Psalm 51:11: "Cast me not away from thy presence; and take not thy Holy Spirit from me."

The Three Persons Are All-present

[Father] Jeremiah 23:23–24: "Am I a God at hand, saith the LORD, and not a God afar off? Can any hide himself in secret places that I shall not see him? saith the LORD. Do I not fill heaven and earth? saith the LORD."

[Son] Matthew 18:20: "For where two or three are gathered together in my name, there am I in the midst of them."[17]

[Holy Spirit] Psalm 139:7: "Whither shall I go from thy spirit? or whither shall I flee from thy presence?"[18]

The Three Persons Are All-knowing

[Father] 1 Kings 8:39: "Then hear thou in heaven thy dwelling place, and forgive, and do, and give to every man according to his ways, whose heart thou knowest; (for thou, even thou only, knowest the hearts of all the children of men)."

[Son] Colossians 2:2–3: "That their hearts might be comforted, being knit together in love, and unto all riches of the full assurance of understanding, to the acknowledgment of the mystery of God, and of the Father, and of Christ; In whom are hid all the treasures of wisdom and knowledge."

[Holy Spirit] John 14:26: "But the Comforter, which is the Holy Ghost, whom the Father will send in my name, he shall teach you all things, and bring all things to your remembrance, whatsoever I have said unto you."[19]

---

[16] See also Hebrews 4:15.
[17] See also Ephesians 1:22.
[18] See also Ephesians 2:18–22.
[19] See also 1 Corinthians 2:10–11.

The Three Persons Are All-powerful

[Father] Job 42:2: "I know that thou canst do every thing, and that no thought can be withheld from thee."[20]

[Son] Colossians 2:9–10: "For in him dwelleth all the fulness of the Godhead bodily. And ye are complete in him, which is the head of all principality and power."[21]

[Holy Spirit] 1 Corinthians 12:7, 11: "Now to each one the manifestation of the Spirit is given for the common good. . . . All these are the work of one and the same Spirit, and he gives them to each one, just as he determines" [NIV].

Various ways of coming to belief in God have been proposed by Catholic thinkers including Thomas Aquinas, Anselm, Blaise Pascal, and Jacques Maritain.[22] While useful in defending against atheism and agnosticism, these arguments, if used alone, often produce a "thin" God, one still lacking in the personhood of the Christian Lord. Divine revelation and the supernatural faith that assents to it are necessary for the fullness of faith. Doctrines central to Catholic belief—the Trinity, incarnation, and resurrection—are truths that can be known by God's word. Philosophical and theological systems aid in explaining more precisely those things that have been handed down to us from Christ and the apostles.

---

[20] See also Luke 1:37.
[21] See also Matthew 28:18.
[22] Peter Kreeft and Ronald K. Tacelli, *Handbook of Christian Apologetics*, 48–86.

PART FIVE

God in Embryo:
The Mormon Doctrine of Man

22. Pre-Existence of Man

Mormons are optimistic about man. By denying the doctrine of original sin and all the spiritual, social, and psychological limitations implied by it, and by asserting the absolute freedom of man to act as he chooses, they paint a triptych of "pre-mortal," mortal, and post-mortal humanity. Man is co-eternal with God and able to become perfect to the same degree and in the same manner as he is now perfect.

The future progress of individual men and women is made possible only by the eons of time each individual person spent in the company of the Heavenly Father and Mother in what Mormons call the pre-existence. Catholics are familiar with the concept of pre-existence from the teaching on the eternal nature of the Son and the Holy Spirit, persons co-eternal and co-equal with God the Father. But the Mormon church claims that all matter is co-eternal with God. Even that which we would term "spiritual" or immaterial is considered just a more refined or purer matter by Mormons. God can neither make nor annihilate anything or anyone. His act of creation, according to current Mormon doctrine, is merely the organizing of eternal elements into some recognizable or functional form.[1]

---

[1] From his superficial study of Hebrew, Smith erroneously concluded that *bara*, the Hebrew verb translated as "created" in the opening verses of Genesis, could mean only "organize." Thus, God organized the heavens and the earth from matter already in existence. He likens this to the actions of any artisan who takes available raw material and fashions it according to his liking. But *bara* is distinct from the Hebrew words used to refer to making or organizing things. *Bara* is used *only* in reference to God's actions. No one else in Scripture "creates" in the same sense. Creation from nothing is meant. Moreover, the Hebraic expression "the heavens and the earth" is a "merism," a way of expressing totality by using two opposite terms. By making the heavens and the earth, God made everything, including the matter and spirit Mormons suppose to have had no beginning.

Human Pre-existence

Separate and conscious individual men and women have not existed from all eternity, but the components of their bodies and their spirits have, Mormons say. Smith claimed that Christ revealed to him that "man was also in the beginning with God. Intelligence, or the light of truth, was not created or made, neither can it be" (Doctrine and Covenants 93:29).

Thus, some aspect of individual, conscious existence was uncreated.[2] At some point, God the Father, together with his heavenly wife or wives, "organized" pre-existent intelligence and other spiritual elements and formed the "spirit body." This process is called "spirit birth."[3] As regards these spiritual entities, McConkie stated, "These spirit beings, the offspring of exalted parents, were men and women, appearing in all respects as mortal persons do, excepting only that their spirit bodies were made of a more pure and refined substance than the elements from which mortal bodies are made."[4]

Our spirit bodies had minds with intellect, free will, emotions, and memory. They also had arms and legs, all composed of matter, albeit extraordinarily fine and intangible. (Note the similarity to the composition of Mormonism's Holy Ghost.)

As spirit children of our Heavenly Father and Mother, we possessed unique talents, abilities and personalities that we cultivated during our pre-mortal lives and then brought to earth. We are on a continuum, then, learning and doing again here what we once learned and did before. In their "heavenly family," spirit children of God and his wife grew as brothers and sisters, with Jesus, the

---

[2] But the Mormon publication, the *Evening and the Morning Star*, contradicted Smith's views: "The Creator, who having created our souls at first by an act of his will, can either eternally preserve them or absolutely annihilate them" (October 1832, 77).

[3] The actual method whereby billions of human beings were first given spirit birth has never been officially defined by Mormonism.

[4] *Mormon Doctrine*, 589.

firstborn of these spirits, as their elder brother. Men and women have the potential to become gods and goddesses, and the Mormon handbook *Gospel Principles* teaches, "If we choose to do so, we can become perfect, just as they are" (11).

During the long period of pre-mortal preparation, some were chosen and trained to assume positions of leadership, according to the Book of Abraham.

"Now the Lord had shown unto me, Abraham, the intelligences that were organized before the world was; and among all these there were many of the noble and great ones" (Abraham 3:22).

Adam, Abraham, Jesus, and Smith belonged to this elect group. But it was not to the great ones alone that earthly tasks were assigned and training provided. Each person has been sent to earth to live under conditions merited by the level of his or her obedience in the pre-existence. Mormons even claim to provide the individual member with insight into his pre-mortal behavior through a patriarchal blessing. Those who did not perform well in the pre-existence receive inferior status in this life. Thus the Mormon church still has "on the books" the teaching that blacks inherited dark skin and other racial characteristics in this life because of poor performance in the pre-existence. This teaching is now profoundly embarrassing to the Mormon church, whose current prophet has downplayed and dismissed it when interviewed. Nonetheless, it remains part of Mormon teaching—at least until Mormon leaders find a way to reinterpret it out of existence or otherwise summon the will to repudiate it.

The Mormon church says a physical body is required for all people to return to their Heavenly Father and to progress to their own godhood. Therefore, it is necessary that each of the Lord's spirit children be born of earthly parents. Man's mortal existence is one of probation: He will be tested to see if he will obey the divine will and thus merit exaltation or fullness of life. Thus, according to God's merciful plan, each of his spirit children is sent into the world at the proper time, equipped with the abilities and talents he or she developed in the mansions of the Lord before earthly birth.

Contemporary Mormons advance several biblical passages to

support their notion of the pre-existence of human spirits. But Mormonism's earliest teachings did not depart significantly from orthodox Christianity, according to some Mormon theologians.[5]

Before examining the passages cited by Mormons, we need to note a distinction between "ideal" existence and "real" existence. Ideal existence describes the existence, in the mind of God, of all things before they were ever brought into being. Real existence designates existence apart from or outside God's mind. For instance, God has an idea of your great-great-great grandson. The boy thus exists "ideally" in the mind of God. But the child has no "real" existence, and will not until he is conceived. Neither the boy's body nor his soul will "really" exist until his conception.

A simple analogy is seen in the process of planning versus making a painting or piece of furniture. The artist first considers his project in his mind. At that point, the object has an "ideal" existence. When the thought is transformed into a tangible, sensible thing, the object "really" exists, outside the maker's mind. The analogy limps, of course, in that God creates from nothing and need expend neither time nor energy to actualize his thought. God also is outside time and so there is a sense in which all things in history are contemporaneous with God's idea of them. However, God's idea of a thing is still independent of the created reality, since he would have had the ideas of everything in the world even if he had chosen not to create it.

Had Mormons adverted to this simple distinction between ideal and real existence, they would not have advanced most of the following passages to support their un-Christian notion of pre-existence.

BIBLICAL REFERENCES

Jeremiah 1:5: *"Before I formed thee in the belly I knew thee; and before thou camest forth out of the womb I sanctified thee, and I ordained thee a prophet unto the nations."*

---

[5] See Blake T. Ostler, "The Idea of Preexistence in Mormon Thought," in *Line Upon Line*, 127–144.

Mormons see in this verse both the pre-existence of the human soul before its insertion into a human body and the pre-mortal selection and training of a great prophet. "Jeremiah could not have been so called and ordained before he was born if he did not exist."[6] Apostle LeGrand Richards presumes too little of the passage. He limits God to immediate knowledge of that which already and really exists. But the all-knowing and all-present God has certain knowledge of all things, and he "foreknows" his creation. The Lord's ideal knowledge of Jeremiah precedes the prophet's real coming into existence at his conception. A parallel is seen at Romans 4:17. There, Paul explains that the Lord could call Abraham the father of many nations even before the old man had borne even one son, since God "calls into existence the things that do not exist" (RSV).

Job 1:6: "*Now there was a day when the sons of God came to present themselves before the* LORD, *and Satan came also among them.*"

Mormons say these "sons of God" were human beings in their pre-mortal, spirit bodies. This interpretation fails to appreciate metaphor in the Bible. The term "son" is a key metaphor in patriarchal societies, such as ancient Israel. A person associated with something can be described as the "son" of that thing. As the *New Bible Dictionary* explains, "'Son' (Heb. *ben*, Aram. *bar*) is commonly used in Semitic languages to denote membership of a class, as 'son of Israel' for 'Israelite', 'son of might' for 'valorous.'"[7]

Similarly, in Scripture we read of the "sons of the South" (referring to natives of the Southern kingdom of Judah), the "sons of thunder" (referring to the fiery character of James and John, the sons of Zebedee), and so forth. In the case of "sons of God," the term indicates a person who has a godly character or a special

---

[6] *A Marvelous Work and a Wonder,* 39.
[7] *The New Bible Dictionary,* (Wheaton, Illinois: Tyndale House Publishers, Inc.) 1962.

association with the Lord. It can be applied metaphorically to righteous men and to angels, as it is here in Job.

Job 38:4, 7: "*Where wast thou. . . . When the morning stars sang together, and all the sons of God shouted for joy?*"

See the comment above. In fact, verses four through six read: "Where wast thou [Job] when I laid the foundations of the earth? declare, if thou hast understanding? Who hath laid the measures thereof, if thou knowest? or who hath stretched the line upon it? Whereupon are the foundations thereof fastened? or who laid the corner stone thereof?"

In response to Job's questioning of the Lord's providence and plan, God asks, rhetorically, "Where were you when I created this world and provided for its steady course?" God—and Job—knew the answer. After two more chapters of divine interrogation, Job finally replies, with humility and then silence. "I am vile; what shall I answer thee? I will lay mine hand upon my mouth" (40:4). The only place Job existed when the Creator was laying out the universe was in the mind of God.

Ecclesiastes 12:7: "*Then shall the dust return to the earth as it was: and the spirit shall return unto God who gave it.*"

The "dust" referred to is the human body at the point of death. Mormons reckon that the spirit, because it returns directly to God, must have existed prior to its joining with a human body. The passage simply affirms that God gave the spirit to the human form without implying anything about the pre-existence of the spirit. The union the spirit may achieve with God when the body dies may be spoken of in poetic terms as a return to its Creator, but nothing beyond this can be established from the language of one of the Bible's poetic books.

Acts 17:29: "*Forasmuch then as we are the offspring of God, we ought not to think that the Godhead is like unto gold, or silver, or stone, graven by art and man's device.*"

In this verse Mormons find support for two of their distinctive claims: the pre-existence of man's spirit and the possibility of progressing to the perfection enjoyed by the Father. We will address the second point in chapter 24. For now, we only have to note that "offspring" of God may be correctly interpreted in two ways. We are God's offspring insofar as we are created by him in his image (rational, volitional beings). Further, as we accept his rule and confess his Son, we become his children by adoption. We will never be his natural children, for we possess forever but a human nature.[8] Though he will not become what the Father is, yet by grace and perseverance, man is heir to all the Father has.

Mormons insist upon a literal, generative "fatherhood" for God and miss the obvious connection between "fatherhood" and creation. Malachi 2:10 makes this point clear: "Have we not all one father? hath not one God created us?" God is our Father because he created us.

Hebrews 12:9: "*[S]hall we not much rather be in subjection unto the Father of spirits, and live?*"

The distinction between "ideal" and "real" pre-existence is necessary here. Also, the writer emphasizes the immediacy of the soul's creation. Whereas man's body is formed by a cooperative act between God and the human parents, man's soul is created by God alone. In this sense it is fitting to call him the "Father of spirits."

1 Corinthians 15:44: "*It [the dead] is sown a natural body; it is raised a spiritual body. There is a natural body, and there is a spiritual body.*"

Mormons grasp at this text to prove the existence of "spirit bodies," but chapter fifteen deals with the resurrection, first of Christ, then of his faithful. Those who die find their corruptible bodies

---

[8] Mormons believe men, angels, and gods are all of the same "race." There is no qualitative difference. Angels are simply God's messengers, humans in either a pre-mortal or post-mortal state. (Fallen angels, or devils, however, will never receive physical bodies and are thus damned forever.)

buried. At the resurrection, Christ will give to his elect a "spiritual" (supernatural) body, perfect and immortal. As Augustine commented, "This is called a spiritual body not because it has become a spirit but because it is in such a way subject to the spirit, to fit it for its heavenly abode, that every kind of earthly weakness and imperfection is changed into a heavenly permanence."[9]

Two verses later Paul expressly repudiates the Mormon contention that things exist first spiritually and only later physically or "naturally."

"It is not the spiritual which was first," he writes, "but the physical, and then the spiritual" (15:46, RSV).

If Mormons insist on interpreting the former verse's "spiritual" as reference to a literal, pre-existent spirit body, then they must be consistent and accept that Paul denies their theology in the latter verse. We must first share in the mortal nature of the first Adam before we are permitted to share in the immortal nature of the Second Adam.[10]

The root cause of the Mormon misunderstanding of 1 Corinthians 15:44-46 is a failure to grasp the meaning of the Greek term here translated "spiritual." The term—*pneumatikos*—is not synonymous with "spiritual" but carries the thought of *supernatural*. This is the case, for example, just a few chapters earlier, when Paul explains to the Corinthians, "Moreover, brethren, I would not that ye should be ignorant, how that all our fathers were under the cloud, and all passed through the sea; And were all baptized unto Moses in the cloud and in the sea; And did all eat the same spiritual meat [that is, food; the KJV term "meat" does not indicate flesh in particular]; And did all drink the same spiritual drink: for they drank of that spiritual Rock that followed them: and that Rock was Christ. But with many of them God was not well pleased: for they were overthrown in the wilderness" (1 Cor. 10:1-5).

---

[9] *Faith and the Creed*, VI.
[10] See *A New Catholic Commentary on Holy Scriptures*, p. 1159.

GOD IN EMBRYO: THE MORMON DOCTRINE OF MAN

Paul refers to the Israelites' spiritual food and drink during the Exodus, meaning the physical foods of manna, quail, and water that God provided in a *supernatural* manner. This was not food made out of some kind of spirit substance. The parallel Paul draws is to the supernatural food and drink that is miraculously provided in the Eucharist—Christ's own body and blood. We must not think our participation in the Eucharist will guarantee salvation, Paul argues, because the Israelites had food miraculously provided for them, just as we do, and yet many of them were struck down by God's justice.

∽

Several verses Mormons use to support the pre-existence of all things actually refer only to Christ (Col. 1:15). Catholics accept fully the pre-existence of the Son and the Holy Spirit. What's more, unlike Mormonism, the Catholic Church teaches that the three are co-eternal. One did not exist as God at any time "before" the other persons "developed" into Gods. One example of a verse applying solely to Christ but twisted by Mormonism to include all men in a pre-existent life with God is John 17:5: "And now, O Father, glorify thou me with thine own self with the glory which I had with thee before the world was."

Other verses Mormons use do more harm than good to their cause. We agree that both the following verses refer to the pre-existence of the Son of God. Psalm 2:7 reads: "I will declare the decree: the Lord hath said unto me, Thou art my Son: this day have I begotten thee." Paul proclaimed to the people of Antioch that Christ's resurrection was the literal fulfillment of this passage (Acts 13:33). But the term "Lord" is the equivalent of Jehovah. According to Mormons, then, Jehovah (Christ) was speaking to himself, calling himself his Son. We suspect Paul did not get snared by this impossible interpretation.

In citing passages that speak of God in a fatherly sense with respect to us, or that refer to us in a filial sense with respect to God, Mormons never address what they would have to in order to show that such passages imply biological (or a heavenly equivalent) reproduction. Nobody denies the presence of such language in Scripture, but the question is: How is the language to be interpreted? Literally or metaphorically? One cannot declare that the language must be taken literally, as if literal language was superior. Hebrew speech is full of metaphors. It can be shown that passages with the paternal/filial language in question are metaphorical. If Mormons want to assert that some are literal, they will have to do some work to show this. And since they are *not* backed up by apostolic Tradition as expressed in the early Church Fathers' writings, they will have to show divine procreation from the biblical text itself. Not surprisingly, Mormons don't grapple with this.

Non-biblical References

Because the Bible doesn't prove man's pre-existence, Mormon scriptures must provide passages supporting teachings unknown to the Bible's inspired authors.[11]

Mormon Scriptures

Doctrine and Covenants 76:24: "That by him, and through him, and of him, the worlds are and were created, and the inhabitants thereof are begotten sons and daughters unto God."

Though this is a cardinal text for Mormon claims of a pre-existent race of humans begotten by a Heavenly Father, the context of this passage makes it clear that the "sons and daughters unto God" referred to are those who, through their faith in Christ, have received life everlasting. Ironically, contemporary Mormons misapply this passage, just as they misapply Bible texts using the metaphor of sonship for the righteous.

---

[11] That is not to say that Mormon writings or leaders have agreed on the nature of pre-existent man. See Van Hale, "The Origin of the Human Spirit in Early Mormon Thought," in *Line Upon Line*, 115–126.

GOD IN EMBRYO: THE MORMON DOCTRINE OF MAN

Doctrine and Covenants 138:53, 56: "*The Prophet Joseph Smith, and my father, Hyrum Smith, Brigham Young, John Taylor, Wilford Woodruff, and other choice spirits who were reserved to come forth in the fulness of times to take part in laying the foundations of the great latter-day work. . . . Even before they were born, they, with many others, received their first lessons in the world of the spirits and were prepared to come forth in the due time of the Lord to labor in his vineyard for the salvation of the souls of men.*"

This section, the last numbered portion of the Doctrine and Covenants, is an account of a vision by sixth president Joseph F. Smith. Though including his father and the first four presidents of the Mormon church among the "choice souls" of the heavenly council, he modestly stops short of canonizing his immediate predecessor and himself.

Moses 3:5: "*And every plant of the field before it was in the earth, and every herb. . . . For I, the Lord God, created all things, of which I have spoken, spiritually, before they were naturally upon the face of the earth. . . . And I, the Lord God, had created all the children of men; and not yet a man to till the ground; for in heaven created I them. . . .*"

Moses 6:51: "*And he called upon our father Adam by his own voice, saying: I am God; I made the world, and men before they were in the flesh.*"

∼

In Revelation 12:7 we read the account of Michael's battle with Satan and his fellow rebels.[12] The war involved angelic spirits, one-third of whom resisted God and were banished from heaven. But Mormons believe this passage refers to a war among pre-existent human spirits. The defeated third did not keep their "first estate" (Jude 6) and were thus deprived of future mortal birth and

---

[12] Current Mormon doctrine teaches that Michael is actually the pre-existent Adam. The temple ceremonies make it clear that Michael joined with Elohim and Jehovah in creating this earth.

eventual godhood. These are the tempting, evil spirits at loose in the world. The other two-thirds chose to follow Christ's plan for salvation and fought against Satan and his band. Some fought more valiantly than others. The less valiant are sent to earth hobbled by poverty, illness, ignorance, and moral and spiritual indifference. The others, diligent and obedient all during their pre-mortal life, are the special ones sent to earth during the "latter-days," or the Mormon era. According to Mormon prophets, they are born white; the very best are probably born into Mormon families: "According to Mormon teaching, there is a reason why one man is born black and with other 'disadvantages,' while another is born white with great advantages. The reason is that we once had an estate before we came here, and were obedient, more or less, to the laws that were given us there. Those who were faithful in all things there received greater blessings here, and those who were not faithful received less."[13]

Orson Pratt taught that "among the Saints is the most likely place for these [choice] spirits to take their tabernacles, through a just and righteous parentage. They are to be sent to that people that are the most righteous of any other people upon the earth; there to be trained up properly, according to their nobility and intelligence, and according to the laws which the Lord ordained before they were born. This is the reason why the Lord is sending them here. . . . The Lord has not kept them in store for five or six thousand years past, and kept them waiting for their bodies all this time to send them among the Hottentots, the African negroes, the idolatrous Hindoos, or any other of the fallen nations that dwell upon the face of this earth. They are not kept in reserve in order to come forth to receive such a degraded parentage upon the earth; no, the Lord is not such a being; His justice, goodness, and mercy will be magnified towards those who were chosen before they were born."[14]

A consequence of labeling oneself or one's group "choice" and

---

[13] *Doctrines of Salvation* 1:61.

[14] Orson Pratt, *Journal of Discourses* 1:62–63.

"elect" is the denigration of all who do not meet the arbitrary criteria. Joseph Fielding Smith has labeled blacks and other persons of color as an "inferior race."[15] Some Mormon thinkers, however, are distancing themselves from this teaching.[16]

We do not remember our pre-earth life, Mormons say, because that would be unfair to God's plan. We are here to prove ourselves worthy of godhood, and any "help" from memory regression could affect our free agency. How this could be so was never clear to me. Nevertheless, each pre-mortal spirit is covered by a veil of forgetfulness when entering an earthly body. While no one can know for certain his pre-mortal status, much might be deduced from his current situation.[17]

Several times Mormons proposed to me the possibility that God had chosen me in the pre-existence to do exactly as I had done: convert to Mormonism and become its advocate. They imagined that this was God's way of rewarding, however tardily, some good deed I had done with him in heaven. A flattering thought, of course, and similar to that enjoyed by most Mormons who see their birth into (or conversion to) the Mormon church as a seal of God's special favor, perhaps even as reward for pre-mortal valor.

Some Mormons only half-jokingly exchange "reminiscences" with each other, supposing that a *déjà-vu* experience, or a certain affinity, indicate former acquaintance in the pre-existence. Persons look familiar, comments sound familiar, statements resonate because, in fact, they were encountered before, in the eternity before mortal life.

---

[15] Joseph Fielding Smith, *The Way to Perfection*, 101. The prophet said, "Millions of souls have come into this world cursed with a black skin."

[16] See, for example, Truman G. Madsen, *Eternal Man*, 55–61.

[17] Mormon teenagers and adult converts are given a "patriarchal blessing," an individualized, prophetic statement meant, in part, to give a general comment on the member's situation in the pre-existence and future expectations as a member of the Mormon church. See Appendix IV for a copy of my patriarchal blessing.

23. Fall Forward? Mormonism on Original Sin

Mormons deny the existence of original sin. Those pre-mortal spirits who retained their "first estate" (did not rebel with Satan) received training and preparation in the heavenly mansions adequate to equip them to learn and follow the Mormon gospel in their "second estate," or mortality.[1]

The second Article of Faith states, "We believe that men will be punished for their own sins, and not for Adam's transgression." Mormons call Adam's disobedience of God's law a transgression, the deliberate breaking of one law in order to obey a higher law. As the Book of Mormon claims, "Adam fell that men might be; and men are, that they might have joy" (2 Nephi 2:25).

Though Mormons continue to use the term "fall," they interpret it to be a "fall forward," or a "fall upward." The *Gospel Principles* manual states, "[The] fall was a necessary step in the plan of life and a great blessing to all of us. Owing to the Fall, we are blessed with physical bodies, the right to choose between good and evil, and the opportunity to gain eternal life. None of these privileges would have been ours had Adam and Eve remained in the garden" (33-34; see Moses 5:11).

There is no biblical basis for such an idea. Mormons suppose that Adam and Eve, brought forth by a direct act of God, did not possess a fullness of joy. The implication further is that they did not possess physical bodies until after their transgression (a debatable point among Mormon scholars). They were unable to choose between right and wrong. In their original state they would not enjoy eternal life.

---

[1] Actually, the "second estate" extends from the beginning of earthly life through death and up to the point of personal resurrection.

Where does Genesis say any of this? Where in the biblical record do we read that Adam and Eve would be unable to "be fruitful and multiply" as long as they remained in the garden, free from transgression? From what passage do we infer that they were deficient of any happiness? And does not God's command to them clearly imply they had the ability to choose to obey or not? In what way, then, could Adam's sin have helped the human race?

Mormons find support only in the Book of Moses, Smith's rewriting of the first chapters of Genesis, and in the temple endowment presentation. In this latter work, Adam's dilemma is heightened by Eve's partaking of the fruit. Initially rebuffed in his temptation of Adam, Satan turns to Eve and convinces her to eat. She then reports her action to Adam, with the sentiment that, since she has sinned, she will be banished from the garden and Adam. How, then, could they fulfill God's command to have children?

Adam accepted this reasoning and partook. He manfully did his duty; as a consequence he and his wife entered mortality, with all its pleasures and pains, triumphs and defeats. Only by this could he and his progeny hope to exercise their free agency and return to God some day and progress to godhood. Thus, the Mormon church says, Adam's action was noble and heroic, not sinful. Since there was no original sin in the garden, there can be no original sin passed to each of Adam's descendants.

Part of Mormonism's denial of original sin stems from their misunderstanding of the Catholic teaching. Often Mormon thinkers do not make necessary distinctions between doctrines held by Catholics and those held by Protestants. Frequently, Mormonism treats as universal Christian doctrine beliefs held by only Protestants or only fundamentalist Protestants.[2] For example, under the heading "Original Sin Theory," McConkie wrongly concluded,

---

[2] Sterling McMurrin goes so far as to proclaim: "The central dogma of traditional Christian orthodoxy is the doctrine of original sin." *The Theological Foundations of Mormonism*, 57.

"In contrast to the doctrines of free agency and personal accountability for sin, modern Christendom has the false doctrine of original sin."[3]

McConkie either does not know or does not give the Catholic understanding of original sin. Certainly, original sin does not nullify man's free will or exempt him from personal responsibility for his choices. The *Catechism of the Catholic Church* summarizes the doctrine, "Man, tempted by the devil, let his trust in his Creator die in his heart and, abusing his freedom, disobeyed God's command. This is what man's first sin consisted of. All subsequent sin would be disobedience toward God and lack of trust in his goodness" (CCC 397).

Adam had a real choice. Every human being may choose to obey or not obey the will of the Lord. Adam's fall was not an improvement for the human race. It was not merely a mild "transgression;" it was "sin." Paul explains, "Wherefore, as by one man sin entered into the world, and death by sin; and so death passed upon all men, for that all have sinned" (Rom. 5:12).

The one man, Adam, stood as representative of the entire human race. That race had, at the first, been endowed by its Creator with the unmerited gift of sanctifying grace, the supernatural life of a son or daughter of God. Being in God's image, Adam was formed with intellect and will, with holiness and all virtue. In Genesis 2:17, God warns Adam that, should he disobey him and eat of the fruit of the tree of the knowledge of good and evil, he would die "in the day that thou eatest thereof." Satan, the father of lies, later chides Adam and Eve, "Ye shall not surely die" (3:4).

With their disobedience, Adam and Eve did not experience immediate temporal death. But on that very day they did indeed die. They killed the life of grace in their souls; they lost their original holiness; they became fearful of God. Though the worst consequences of the original sin, these were not the only ones. Adam and Eve were now subject to frustration, pain and physical death.

---

[3] *Mormon Doctrine*, 550.

They were alienated from themselves, each other, and all nature. Original harmony among all creation became brutal discord.[4]

The progression—or rather, regression—of sin is unmistakable in the first eleven chapters of Genesis. Our first parents' sin alienated them not only from God but from their very selves. For the first time they experienced shame in their nakedness and wished to hide from each other. Nature itself rebelled against the ones who introduced sin. It would no longer yield its goods easily. Man must toil and sweat to earn his daily bread; woman must labor to bring forth children. There then followed, in the account of Cain and Abel, the sins of envy and murder, isolating man from man. Sin abounded, and the earth had to be flooded clean of sinful humanity by an act of nature. Man and beast were imbued with a fear of each other.

This downward spiral of alienation continued: man against himself, against God, against others, against nature. The final scene, in Genesis 11, depicts the ultimate fragmentation of nation from nation, setting the scene for an enduring history of battle and strife, torment and death.

Does this sound like a fall forward?

The "fall," Mormons claim, refers only to the changes that came upon Adam and Eve (and hence all mankind) after their transgression: They were given mortality and the power to have children. They were to experience pain and physical death so that they might also know their opposites. Beyond this, "Adam and Eve also suffered spiritual death. This meant they and their children could not walk and talk face to face with God."[5] These two "valiant spirits" among the Father's noblest children in the pre-existence were taken from his presence and placed into the world we now know, there to make their way through mortality back to God's presence and eventual godhood.

Compare this with what was truly lost by Adam and his descendants: the presence of grace in the soul; the right to eternal

---

[4] Cf. *Catechism of the Catholic Church*, 398–400.
[5] *Gospel Principles*, 33.

life; the friendship of God; the preternatural gifts of immortality and bodily wholeness. Scripture teaches, and the Catholic Church affirms, that Adam and Eve were not the only ones to suffer the consequences of their first sin. By the sin in the garden, all men inherit death. Romans 5 states, "Death passed upon all men" (v. 12); "through the offence of one many be dead" (v. 15)[6]; "by one man's offence death reigned" (v. 17); "sin hath reigned unto death" (v. 21).

Adam introduced into the perfect world "another law" which now wars against the inherently good nature of man as it was first created. (See Romans 7:23 and Galatians 5:17.)

Man is not just a passive "victim" of the disharmony introduced by Adam's fall. All men are, by Adam's sin, themselves sinners. As Paul states, "Death reigned from Adam to Moses, even over them that had not sinned after the similitude of Adam's transgression" (Rom. 5:14).[7] And "by the offence of one judgment came upon all men to condemnation" (Rom. 5:18). Finally, "as by one man's disobedience many were made sinners" (Rom. 5:19).

Biblical prophets support the Catholic Church's understanding of original sin. Thus, David can say, "Behold, I was shapen in iniquity; and in sin did my mother conceive me" (Ps. 51:5). Likewise Solomon, "Who can say, I have made my heart clean, I am pure from my sin?" (Prov. 20:9). And Jeremiah, "The heart is deceitful above all things, and desperately wicked: who can know it?" (Jer. 17:9).

Pope Paul VI, in the *Credo of the People of God*, explains how every person shares in Adam's sin:

> We believe that in Adam all have sinned. From this it follows that, on account of the original offense committed by him, human nature, which is common to all men, is reduced to that condition in which it must suffer the consequences of that fall.... Consequently, fallen human nature is deprived of the economy of grace

---

[6] Here and elsewhere, "many" is properly translated "all."

[7] In other words, death, as a consequence of Adam's sin, was assigned to all people, including those who did not commit such sins as had Adam.

which it formerly enjoyed. It is wounded in its natural powers and subjected to the dominion of death which is transmitted to all men. It is in this sense that every man is born in sin. We hold, therefore, in accordance with the Council of Trent, that original sin is transmitted along with human nature, not by imitation but by propagation, and is, therefore, incurred by each person individually [§6].

Human nature has been "wounded" in its natural abilities and has been "deprived" of that supernatural grace with which it was first endowed. This doctrine differs greatly from the "total depravity" preached by many Protestant groups (and misunderstood by Mormons to be the belief of all Christians). Human nature did not become wholly evil. It did become inclined to evil. Anger, concupiscence, and other passions were no longer perfectly subjected to man's reason. The flesh rebelled against the spirit (Rom. 7:23). With his intellect clouded by disordered passion, man wandered from God and fell into repeated sin. Man relinquished and God withdrew the supernatural gifts, including original justice, which at creation had been bestowed as an additional blessing on man's human nature. Thus, men and women today continue to inherit their human nature, even though weakened, from Adam and his descendants. But supernatural life, as an undeserved gift granted to the first man, was lost by him and consequently not available to his descendants. Thomas Aquinas provides an apt analogy.

"A king may reward a soldier with the grant of an estate which is to be handed on by him to his heirs," Aquinas taught. "If the soldier then commits a crime against the king, and must forfeit the estate, it cannot afterwards pass to his heirs. In this case the sons are justly dispossessed in consequence of their father's crime."[8]

Mormonism's confusion stems in part from its belief in premortal existence. If each human spirit is generated and tutored by divine parents, it would be blasphemous to think these spirits would come into mortal life with encumbrances other than those of their own pre-mortal making. Therefore, until a person can

---

[8] *Light of Faith*, 223–224.

choose for himself (Mormons say this begins at the age of eight, "the age of accountability"), he is free of sin.

Catholics recognize that God does not punish individuals for sins they have not committed and that children below a certain age do not have sufficient use of reason to know the moral status of their actions. However, no realistic appraisal of children's behavior could suppose that they are innocent moral paragons. If they were, then there would be no need to "put away childish things," as Paul says (1 Cor. 13:11).

The foundation for sin is temptation, which consists of disordered desire—too much desire for one thing, too little for another. Children are often exemplars of disordered desire. The child who wails and declares that you do not love him or that he will hate you if you do not buy him a particular toy obviously desires it too much. A child who wants to eat candy all the time desires other kinds of food too little. While children only become accountable for acting on their disordered desires as they gain control of them and get a more rational perspective regarding them, it cannot be denied that children, like adults, are marred by the fallen nature which is prone to disordered desire or "concupiscence," to use its technical name.

This concupiscence is not sinful (temptation is not a sin, only giving in to temptation is sinful), but it is something we inherit from our first parents, Adam and Eve. The situation is analogous to that of a couple who worked in a nuclear or chemical plant and foolishly exposed themselves to an agent that would damage their genetic codes. Once this was done, their descendants would pay the price for their parents' folly. It is not the descendants' fault if they are born with damaged genetic codes, but the parents who exposed themselves to a gene-damaging agent. In the same way, it is not our fault that we are born with a damaged human nature, prone to disordered desires and the temptations that follow, but it nevertheless is something we inherit from our first parents.

The two things that Mormons perceive to be problematic in the doctrine of original sin—the idea that we are personally guilty on account of Adam's sin and that we are consequently punished

—are not part of the Catholic teaching on original sin. What *is* problematic, however, is the Mormon account of the fall. It is true that, as a result of the fall and our consequent redemption by Christ, we will be elevated to a higher estate than we otherwise would have held. The fall was *not* a good thing, even if God used it to bring about something even better for us. God may enter into all things to work good for those who love him (Rom. 8:28), but that does not mean that God regards all things as good. He certainly does not so regard the transgression of Adam.

The Mormon account of the fall (aside from the details of how it misrepresents the biblical text) portrays God as an abusive parent who puts his children in double-bind situations where they cannot obey, because they are given conflicting instructions and will suffer no matter which set they follow. Further, by implying that Adam *should* have broken God's law, the Mormon fall account teaches a lesson of spiritual disobedience and repeats the lie of Satan—that it was a good thing to transgress God's commandment. As a result, the Mormon creation account cannot be described, on a spiritual level, as anything other than non-biblical and un-Christian.

24. Eternal Progression

The doctrine of pre-existence deals with man in his life before coming to earth. Man's mortal life begins in a state of freedom from all sin. By adherence to Mormon belief and practice, a person's mortal probation then opens into a future glorious with the promise of eventual godhood. This process is termed "eternal progression." Mormons believe that each person was set on the path to eventual deity during the eternities he spent with his divine parents in heaven before his mortal birth. As a literal son of God in spirit form, his destiny is to grow into godhood as surely as an acorn is to become an oak. Only lack of obedience and perseverance can thwart this plan of salvation.

Man's destiny is to become like his Heavenly Father: a glorious, omnipotent god. As such, he will have the fullness of what Mormons call "exaltation," and will grow in splendor and honor throughout the eternities to come. As God before him, each deified man (with his wife or wives) will be given lordship of his own domain.

"Each one of you has it within the realm of his possibility to develop a kingdom over which you will preside as its king and God," said Spencer W. Kimball. "You will need to develop yourself and grow in ability and power and worthiness, to govern such a world with all of its people."[1]

The differences between man and God are merely those of chronology and quantity. Mormons claim that over a vast expanse of time, Heavenly Father progressed or developed into God by following the pattern of his own Father-God. Besides having achieved deity, majesty, and glory, Heavenly Father was permitted (along with his wife or wives) to organize pre-existent spirit

---

[1] Spencer W. Kimball, in an address to Institute of Religion students; cited in *Doctrines of the Gospel Student Manual*, 29.

material, or intelligences, into "spirit children." These he trained and tutored before sending them to earth in fleshly bodies. Those who become faithful Mormons and fulfill all the commandments of God and their church will attain likeness to God the Father and become gods themselves. The process is then repeated in some other world of the "new" god's making.

With respect to a "quantitative" difference among the gods, inspired Mormon prophets contradict one another. For example, does God the Father continue to grow in knowledge and power? Mormons are taught that "if there was a point where man in his progression could not proceed any further, the very idea would throw a gloom over every intelligent and reflecting mind. God himself is increasing and progressing in knowledge, power, and dominion, and will do so, worlds without end. It is just so with us."[2]

Just as a righteous man may progress eternally in knowledge of and dominion over some creation, God himself continues to grow, deepening his understanding of his own creation and extending his power over it, stated President Wilford Woodruff, colleague of Smith and Young.

Smith's great-nephew and the tenth Mormon prophet, Joseph Fielding Smith, repudiated his predecessor.

"It seems very strange to me," Fielding Smith said, "that members of the Mormon church will hold to the doctrine, 'God increases in knowledge as time goes on. . . .' I think this kind of doctrine is very dangerous. I don't know where the Lord has ever declared such a thing."[3]

But in one area Mormons do tend to agree. God the Father progresses in glory and honor as his children reach their own godhood. By working out their own "eternal life," God's sons and daughters give him a boost in his own status. A rough idea of this "progress" might be seen in the following example. Two men are climbing a mountain. One man is about twenty feet below the

---

[2] *Journal of Discourses* 6:120.
[3] *Doctrines of Salvation* 1:7-8.

other in the ascent. They are attached to each other by a rigid pole. As the lower creeps up the face of the cliff, the man in the upper position is automatically pushed higher. Because there is a fixed distance maintained between the two men, the lower man will never reach "parity" with the upper man, though he will reach the level where the upper man had once been.

That's the Mormon understanding of man's eternal progression. Though a person will, through his careful and successful efforts, eventually achieve godhood and become as God the Father is *now*, he will never "catch up" with God, since his own progress contributes to the process whereby the Heavenly Father grows in glory. By implication, this process extends eternally in both directions. That is, the Father and God of God the Father increases in majesty as his son, Elohim, is elevated by, in turn, his own elite Mormon offspring. Correspondingly, the newly crowned kings and gods produce their own children in the worlds to come and, by their children's obedience, will be propelled to greater godly heights.

The following analogy illustrates the situation well. Godhood is like a "pyramid" sales machine. Each participant generates new participants, who raise his own status. As his status in the structure rises, so does that of those above him. The key difference is that, with the Mormon idea of godhood, there is no "top" to the pyramid structure, since the process has allegedly been going on infinitely far back into the past. Because there is no original starting point for the process, the normal logical problems associated with an infinite temporal regression ensue.

How different this self-promoting view of man is from the simple summary of true Christian spirituality offered by John the Baptist: "He must increase, but I must decrease" (John 3:30). Nevertheless, Mormons use several verses from the Bible to justify their theory of man's eternal progression. Most of these verses have been dealt with in the chapters on the Mormon Godhead. They include: Psalms 82:6; John 10:34–36; Acts 17:28–29; and 1 Corinthians 8:5–6. However, several other passages are adduced:

Matthew 5:48: "Be ye therefore perfect, even as your Father which is in heaven is perfect."

Mormons ask, "Would the Lord give us a commandment if he knew we could not keep it?" They conclude that "we, in this life, should try to perform every duty and keep every law and thus endeavor to be perfect in our sphere as the Father is in his."[4] Mormon authorities teach contradictory messages on this striving for perfection. The kinder, gentler tone of current Mormon conference talks seeks to allay some Mormons' perfectionist tendencies and the depression of inevitable failure. Man is not, members are now advised, expected to become totally perfect in everything in this life. There will be time beyond the grave for continued progress in virtue. Godhood is bestowed only in the next life anyway.

To understand Matthew 5:48, we must consider the context. Jesus is delivering the Sermon on the Mount. All verses leading to this one speak of the moral goodness his followers must develop. They must resist temptations; they must not divorce and remarry; they must not swear idly; they must bear no lust or anger in their hearts; they must love even their enemies. In a word, they are to be perfect models of the Lord's own loving kindness.

The parallel in Luke's account of the Sermon on the Mount makes the point even more clear: "But love ye your enemies, and do good, and lend, hoping for nothing again; and your reward shall be great, and ye shall be the children of the Highest: for he is kind unto the unthankful and *to* the evil. Be ye therefore merciful, as your Father also is merciful" (Luke 6:35–36).

The kind of perfection Jesus is urging is perfection in showing mercy—that is, showing it to all people, even our enemies. In both Matthew and Luke's version the exhortation to be like the Father immediately follows a discussion of how we should be kind even to our enemies, just as God gives blessings to the righteous and the wicked.

---

[4] Joseph Fielding Smith, *The Way to Perfection*, 7.

God is from all eternity "perfect" and "complete." In no sense does Matthew 5:48 imply that a man who abides by Christ's law of love will become a perfect god. He becomes, rather, a perfect man. The teaching of the Second Vatican Council makes this clear:

> The Lord Jesus, divine teacher and model of all perfection, preached holiness of life (of which he is the author and maker) to each and every one of his disciples without distinction: "You, therefore, must be perfect, as your heavenly Father is perfect" (Mt. 5:48). . . . The followers of Christ, called by God not in virtue of their works but by his design and grace, and justified by the Lord Jesus, have been made sons of God in the baptism of faith and partakers of the divine nature, and so are truly sanctified. . . . But since we all offend in many ways (cf. Jas. 3:2), we constantly need God's mercy and must pray every day: "And forgive us our debts" (Mt. 5:12) [*Lumen Gentium*, 40].

We are to become perfect, by God's grace, by growing into the moral image of God and his Son. This is what the process of sanctification involves. We can grow to share in God's communicable, moral attributes, but nothing here suggests that we can take on God's incommunicable, ontological attributes and so become gods ourselves. We are to be *like* God in our moral, behavioral character, not *the same as* God in our essence.

Revelation 3:21: "To him that overcometh will I grant to sit with me in my throne, even as I also overcame, and am set down with my Father in his throne."

We might suppose that Jesus could literally sit upon a heavenly throne, for he has forever a glorified body. It is also possible that each of those who are with him may sit physically on the throne, for they too will possess resurrected bodies forever. God the Father, of course, sits on no throne, for he has no physical body. The throne is a symbol of authority. Because the book of Revelation is symbolic, the details of its symbols cannot be read in a literalistic manner. The city of New Jerusalem is not really going to be a giant cube, sitting on the earth, with sides twelve thousand stadia (fifteen hundred miles) long (Rev. 21:10). Neither will New

Jerusalem literally have gates made out of giant pearls or streets made of pure, transparent gold (Rev. 21:21). All of this is meant to symbolize the spiritual grandeur of the city and the size of the population (the redeemed of all ages) that belongs to it. In the same way, Jesus is not really a wounded lamb with seven eyes (Rev. 5:6); rather, this symbolizes the fact that he was sacrificed on our behalf and the fact that he is all-knowing.

All that can be safely established from passages like Revelation 3:21 is that Christ will share his authority with believers in the next life. Nor can men assert that there is a physical throne they will occupy, or that this is one step in an eternal progression. Saying we will be given a share of Christ's authority is not the same thing as saying we will continue to increase even further in authority, or that Christ himself is increasing in authority through time.

Revelation 21:7: "He that overcometh shall inherit all things; and I will be his God, and he shall be my son."

In its anthropocentrism, the Mormon church reads into this promise of the Lord Jesus more than the text can support. By making man the measure of all things, the Mormon church "finds" in passages such as this the assurance that its faithful members will not only receive the fullness of God's gifts, but will receive the fullness of his divine nature as well. Only those who deny the biblical doctrine of the oneness of God could make so serious an error.

Moreover, the verse states that the relationship will remain that of God and son, or God and creature. Some Mormons agree that, even after becoming a god himself, a man will remain in a subordinate position to his Heavenly Father. But what, really, does that mean? The deified man, with his wife (or wives) and family will occupy themselves with the making and populating of their own world. The new god will devise his own plan of salvation for his spirit children. He will receive the prayer and adoration of his children, just as he, while on this earth, worshiped his Heavenly Father. To what extent, then, will he be subjected to the god before him? In what way is the current Heavenly Father ancillary to *his* god? Mormon doctrine does not resolve this.

The most fundamental problem with the Mormon interpretation of this passage, however, is that it fails to note the way sonship is used. It is an *adoptive* sonship, not a biological sonship. God *promises* that those who overcome will become his sons. The Greek tense of the verb is future, which means the same thing as the future tense does in English. It denotes something that hasn't happened yet. Since we have not yet overcome, we are not yet sons in the sense this verse is talking about. This means that the kind of sonship being discussed is one that not only is an acquired sonship but one that we have not yet acquired. This is *not* the same as the sonship envisioned by Mormons, in which we are *already* God's biological (or heavenly biological) sons.

The passage promises that if we overcome the spiritual obstacles we encounter in this life, if we remain faithful to God, we will be granted the adoptive status of sons and have intimate, spiritual union with our God in the afterlife.

~

Some Mormon writers seek support for their belief in the potential godhood of man in writings of early Church Fathers, particularly those of the East.[5]

Athanasius, for instance, stated, "God made himself a man in order that man might be able to become God."[6] Basil the Great called the deification process "that which is best of all."[7]

Mormon writers interpret the early Fathers' use of the term "deification" as synonymous with the Mormon teaching that men can become gods, growing in power and majesty into the stature that God the Father now wields. This is but one more example of the Mormons' redefining of traditional Christian terms.[8]

---

[5] See *Offenders for a Word*, 75–92.
[6] *On the Incarnation* 54, 3.
[7] *The Holy Spirit* 9, 23.
[8] There is a bitter irony here. Mormons accuse the Catholic Church of hav-

Cardinal Christoph Schönborn, a principal editor of the *Catechism of the Catholic Church*, included a chapter entitled "Is Man to Become God?" in his *From Death to Life*. In it, he presents the true understanding of deification. Because the second person of the Blessed Trinity became human in Jesus Christ, humanity may be "deified" in and through him. The saving work of Christ began with his incarnation. What he assumed he ultimately redeemed. Man's deification is based on this. There is no such thing as "self-deification." It is a gift effected only through grace and consists in man's being made into the closest possible configuration to God.

St. Maximus the Confessor, a seventh-century Byzantine theologian, provides us with the definition of this human mirror of deity: "The one deified through grace receives for himself *everything* that God possesses, apart from the identity of substance."[9] Man receives all God *has*; he does not become all God *is*.

The last qualifier is important, and it runs throughout the early Church Fathers. Whenever deification is spoken of, it is always with the proviso that we do not become gods in the sense the Father is a God. We never take on the incommunicable, ontological attributes of the Godhead. We only, by grace, receive the communicable attributes of holiness, justice, mercifulness, and so forth. Catholics recognize that man is created to be a son of God, an heir of the kingdom, a partaker in the divine nature. That is what it means to have been created in the "image and likeness of God" and to be redeemed and given union with God. The Catholic Church goes so far as to say that "deification" is nothing other than true "humanization."[10] Christ's grace leads man

---

ing imported many Greek and other pagan philosophies, incorporating them into a sorry substitute for the true gospel of Christ. Yet several contemporary Christian authors dismiss the entire notion of deification as itself a hellenizing of the original Christian message. See Cardinal Christoph Schönborn, *From Death to Life*, 42.

[9] Schönborn, 48.

[10] Christ "reveals man to man.... [H]e does not take away our humanity, but on the contrary he *humanizes us*, giving our personal and social life full meaning," said Pope John Paul II in an Angelus address, February 23, 1997.

back to his original condition, his original dignity, before the fall. Fallen nature is redeemed and restored.

Mormons emphasize good works, faithful obedience, performance of ordinances, and "pulling oneself up by one's bootstraps" —to use Kimball's phrase—as the means of achieving eventual deification. Members are continually urged to become perfect and thus merit godhood. Many good members sincerely participate in their church in hopes that they, too, will one day be equal with God. How different this seems from the self-emptying of Christ, who for our sake became a servant of all, not minding the lowliness.

Though a chief tenet of Mormon belief, members do not often discuss eternal progression. Perhaps this is because much of the teaching is new and, understandably, offensive to Christians. Perhaps, too, it's because the theme is a central concern of the temple ceremony, which must be kept hidden from the unworthy. Or perhaps it's because discussing one's ambitions to godhood is not a fit topic for polite conversation. I do recall a talk given in an elders' quorum meeting, however, which serves as an example of the Mormon's emphasis on his own worthiness. One of the officers of this group was speaking to the men as we were preparing to attend the dedication of the Bountiful, Utah, temple. His words were something like this: "By the time of the dedication in a few weeks, I hope to be spiritually ready that I might see the Lord Jesus in the temple. We know that he appears to his people in the temples and I think I can be worthy for this blessing." All who listened seemed to take this at face value. Nothing in the leader's statement was seen as exaggeration or self-praise.

It's not so long a step from hoping to *see* God here to hoping to *be* a god hereafter.

25. Waiting for the End: The Intermediate State

"If we don't convince you now, we'll always have another chance after you die!"

That could be the motto of the Mormon missionary or member intent on presenting his "gospel" to a non-member. A person's opportunities do not end with death. Rather, he is merely transferred from the material world to the spiritual world, with all his abilities and deficiencies, virtues and vices, plans and desires intact. In the spirit world, these qualities will continue to develop along the path set during earthly life—unless a "spirit missionary" can convince the disembodied soul to convert and accept Mormonism.

Two Salvations: One a Gift, One a Wage

In the Mormon view, Jesus Christ, by his suffering in Gethsemane and on Calvary, assured immortality for all mankind. Just as death entered the world through Adam's "transgression," life forever was restored by the Lord's obedience and atoning sacrifice. This is the "universal salvation" spoken of by Mormonism. When Mormons speak of the "gift" of unending life, they refer to the fact that the human soul is immortal and will be rejoined to the body at the resurrection on the last day. This is the result of the Lord's own death and resurrection. Mormons assert their belief in salvation "by grace alone." But salvation in this sense refers only to immortality of soul and resurrected body.

Personal salvation, *eternal life*, and *exaltation* are terms Mormons use to describe the fullness of salvation, life with God, life as a god. McConkie clearly presents this second level.

"Immortality is one thing," he said, "eternal life another. Immortality is to live forever in a resurrected state; it is to have a tangible body of flesh and bones. After the judgment, immortal beings are assigned their places in the celestial, terrestrial, and telestial kingdoms. Eternal life is the name of the kind of life possessed by the Eternal One, by the Eternal Father. It is reserved for those immortal beings who gain an inheritance in the highest heaven of the celestial realm."[1]

So in Mormon vocabulary there are two meanings to the term "salvation." The general salvation of all men means every person will be resurrected; the immortal body and spirit (together, these are called the "soul" by Mormons) of each person continues into eternity. Individual salvation is reserved to the faithful Mormon. By his obedience to the Mormon church, he merits life everlasting with God the Father, progressing over time into a god himself.

The Spirit World

Death, as we've seen, is not a period to a person's life of faith and obedience. For the Mormons, it is at most a semi-colon; so much more can be accomplished after passing "beyond the veil." Mormons believe that when a person dies he takes with him all his knowledge, habits, and limitations acquired while in his earthly state. These either help or hinder further development in the spirit world.

Spirit beings have the same bodily form as mortals except that the spirit body is in perfect form. All spirits are in adult form. They were adults before their mortal existence, and they are in adult form after death, even if they die as infants or children.[2]

Death of the body leads to what Mormons call a "partial" judgment.[3] The eternal destinies of most men and women are not

---

[1] *A New Witness for the Articles of Faith*, 152.
[2] *Gospel Principles*, 290.
[3] Joseph F. Smith, *Gospel Doctrine*, 448.

GOD IN EMBRYO: THE MORMON DOCTRINE OF MAN 355

fixed at death. Rather, the spirits of all the dead enter the "spirit world," which is composed of two main divisions, paradise and spirit prison.

The Book of Mormon notes, "[T]he spirits of those who are righteous are received into a state of happiness, which is called paradise, a state of rest, a state of peace, where they shall rest from all their troubles and from all care, and sorrow . . . until the time of their resurrection" (Alma 40:12, 14).

These spirits include those who on earth lived faithful Mormon lives and endured in their faith to the end. Here also are the spirits of those who were taught and accepted the Mormon religion after their deaths.[4] But paradise isn't heaven. It's the temporary dwelling of the righteous in the spirit world.[5] The spirits there are free from sorrows and trials. They are organized and governed by the Mormon church as it exists in the realm of the spirits. Woodruff taught, "The same Priesthood exists on the other side of the veil. . . . When a man dies and his body is laid in the tomb, he does not lose his position. . . . Every Apostle, every Seventy, every Elder, etc., who has died in the faith, as soon as he passes to the other side of the veil, enters into the work of the ministry."[6]

Because there are so many more dead non-members than living,

---

[4] But only if a living Mormon has undergone temple baptism and other rituals on their behalf.

[5] In fact, Smith maintained that "paradise" doesn't always mean "paradise." Referring to the Lord's words to the repentant thief on the cross, Smith explained, "There is nothing in the original word in Greek from which this was taken that signifies paradise; but it was—'This day shalt thou be with me in the world of spirits: then I will teach you all about it and answer your inquiries.'" (*Teachings of the Prophet Joseph Smith*, 309.) President Kimball also asserted, "Another mistaken idea is that the thief on the cross was forgiven of his sins when the dying Christ answered: 'Today shalt thou be with me in paradise.' (Luke 23:43.) These men on the cross were thieves. How could the Lord forgive a malefactor?" (*The Miracle of Forgiveness*, 166.) With this eccentric application, paradise can mean, for the Mormon, the whole spirit world, composed of both the "saved" and the "damned."

[6] *Journal of Discourses* 22:333–334.

the activity of the Mormon church beyond the grave is believed to be correspondingly more intense. Young, describing Smith as the triumphant ruler and director of that spirit world, said, "He reigns there as supreme a being in his sphere, capacity, and calling, as God does in heaven."[7]

In the Mormon view, the righteous and the wicked are separated in the spirit world. Those spirits undeserving of paradise are sent to spirit prison. The Book of Mormon, describing these damned beings, says, "[T]hey have no part nor portion of the Spirit of the Lord; for behold, they chose evil works rather than good; therefore the spirit of the devil did enter into them . . . and these shall be cast out into outer darkness; there shall be weeping, and wailing, and gnashing of teeth. . . . [T]hey remain in this state . . . until the time of their resurrection" (Alma 40:12–14).

Imprisoned here are the souls of all those who have not yet accepted the Mormon faith. Because opportunity and free choice remain open to them, they may still progress, even to the point of being able to leave their prison and enter paradise, there to await a more joyful resurrection. Also in this "hell" are found those who rejected the Mormon gospel after it was preached to them either on earth or in spirit prison. They have had and lost their chance to escape the maximum penalty and must remain in spirit prison until the resurrection of their bodies. All those in spirit prison are subject to continual temptations and devilish enticements. Mormons believe that it is foolish and dangerous for a person to procrastinate the time of repentance, thinking that he can always make up for his negligence in the spirit world. Even if he were there given a clear-cut opportunity for conversion, his evil earthly tendencies follow him beyond the grave and are exacerbated by frustrated material desires and increased torment by the Tempter.

---

[7] *Journal of Discourses* 7:289.

GOD IN EMBRYO: THE MORMON DOCTRINE OF MAN 357

Missionaries in the Spirit World

All who die go first to one or the other of these divisions in the spirit world. The spirits of children who have not reached the age of accountability go directly to paradise.[8] All others are judged according to their faith and deeds performed during mortality. They'll be measured by the various records kept on them, not only in the "book of life" but also in church and temple registers. Those confined to spirit prison may achieve release if they accept the Mormon gospel. This necessitates a system of missionary work undertaken by the righteous spirits in paradise who are sent to convert the unrighteous in spirit prison. This mission work is thought to eclipse in size the proselytizing efforts of the Mormon church on earth.[9]

According to Joseph F. Smith, this vast undertaking may include the leadership of the original twelve apostles, along with that of Joseph and Hyrum Smith, Young, Taylor and all the other latter-day prophets. The gospel they lived and preached here they continue to preach in the hereafter: "The gospel must be preached to them. We are not perfect without them—they cannot be perfect without us."[10]

With so dedicated a corps of missionaries, Mormon leaders are optimistic about results. The fifth prophet, Lorenzo Snow, believed that "when the Gospel is preached to the spirits in prison, the success attending that preaching will be far greater than that attending the preaching of our Elders in this life. . . . The circumstances there will be a thousand times more favorable."[11]

An imprisoned spirit who hears and believes in the Mormon gospel becomes an aspirant for release from spirit prison. He may join the Mormon church as it is organized in the spirit world.

---

[8] The spirits of the dead retain human form.
[9] Brigham Young, *Journal of Discourses* 2:137.
[10] Quoted in *We Believe*, 168.
[11] *Collected Discourses* 3, October 6, 1893.

As a member, he is freed from hell[12] and brought into paradise. The same requirements incumbent upon living candidates apply to the dead convert: faith, repentance, baptism, and the laying on of hands. While the disembodied human spirit can take the first and second steps in response to the preaching of missionary spirits, the third and fourth steps are ordinances that can be performed only on a whole human person. With no body, the converted spirit cannot be immersed in baptismal waters, nor does he have a head on which those having the proper authority may place their hands. This conundrum serves as a basis for the vast genealogy efforts of the members, together with the entire structure of proxy temple work.

Supposed Scriptural Basis for Missionary Work among the Dead

Mormon scholars cite two passages from the First Epistle of Peter as the basis for their belief that suitable deceased Mormons are able to preach to deceased non-members, giving the latter the opportunity to change their eternal destinies.

1 Peter 3:18–20: "For Christ also hath once suffered for sins, the just for the unjust, that he might bring us to God, being put to death in the flesh, but quickened by the Spirit: By which also he went and preached unto the spirits in prison; Which sometime [once] were disobedient, when once the long-suffering of God waited in the days of Noah, while the ark was a preparing, wherein few, that is, eight souls were saved by water."

1 Peter 4:5–6: "[The unrighteous Gentiles] shall give account to him that is ready to judge the quick and the dead. For this cause was the gospel preached also to them that are dead, that they might be judged according to men in the flesh, but live according to God in the spirit."

---

[12] "Hell" has many meanings for Mormons. Spirit prison is one of many.

But Hebrews 9:27 is unambiguous: "[I]t is appointed unto men once to die, but after this the judgment." Moreover, Jesus' parable of the rich man and Lazarus (Luke 16:19–31) illustrates the status of men after their deaths. The righteous attain everlasting peace; the wicked are consigned to a torment that no further divine action can soften. ("If they hear not Moses and the prophets, neither will they be persuaded, though one rose from the dead.") The possibility of passing from hell into a more blissful abode is ruled out. ("There is a great gulf fixed.") The place and time to work out our salvation is here and now (2 Cor. 6:2).

There are a number of ways these citations from 1 Peter can be interpreted. For the sake of argument, let us look at the interpretation that is closest to the Mormon view, but still within the bounds of what Scripture allows. It can be granted, at least for the sake of argument, that the group of spirits in prison from 1 Peter 3:18 are the same as the group of "the dead" mentioned in 1 Peter 4:6.[13] It may further be granted that this group died because of their sins during Noah's age, that they had the gospel preached to them by Christ during the three days he lay in the tomb, and that they are saved.

None of this requires that they were given a "second chance" after death. The Bible passages cited above specifically rule this out. This life is the time of trial, and a person's eternal destiny is fixed at the time of his death. Accordingly, the dead in this passage would consist of those who disobeyed during Noah's time, for whose sins the flood came. However, the group was not worthy of damnation, either because they repented as the floodwaters rose or because they sinned grievously enough to warrant the severe

---

[13] The spirits mentioned may be angelic rather than human spirits, depending on the interpretation of Genesis 6:1–2. Cf. W. J. Dalton, S.J., *Christ's Proclamation to the Spirits* (Rome: 1965). Similarly, "the dead" may be a reference to Christians who were alive at the time they heard the gospel but who have now died. Nevertheless, for the sake of argument, we will assume that both of these groups are the same and that they are human spirits.

temporal punishment of death but not grievously enough to warrant the even more severe, eternal punishment of damnation. In any event, their behavior was not enough to grant them safety in the ark, but not enough to put them in hell.

They consequently waited in the place of the dead until the coming of Christ, who opened heaven to them, that they might "live according to God in the spirit" (1 Peter 4:6). The preaching of the gospel in this case was what it was to ancient Israel —the announcement of the good news that the expected Messiah had come. It is important to remember (though many in the present world do not) that the gospel was not simply a message given to encourage people to repent and seek eternal life. It was an announcement of good news to the righteous in Israel who had been waiting for it and for the unrighteous who needed to repent. These righteous in Israel were already leading devout and holy lives and were already in God's good graces. For them, the coming of the Messiah was a joyous event ushering in the blessings of the Messianic age. For the unrighteous, it was a call to repent.

The righteous dead received the good news in the same way as the righteous in Israel: It was a time of joy signaling the blessings of the Messianic age, which for them meant getting to go to heaven. Some of them may have led bad lives and even brought on their own deaths through sin, but they still repented and ended life in God's grace, and now the time for their entrance to heaven had arrived. Messiah had come and opened the way. It was only fitting that this good news should be announced to them.

This interpretation is fully in accord with the text of 1 Peter 3:18–4:6 and it is fully in accord with Scripture's other declarations, cited above, that this life is the time of trial and that after this life no repentance is possible. Mormons are able to get the passage to fit their agenda only by ignoring the remainder of what Scripture has to say.

The Millennium—a Digression

Together with Jehovah's Witnesses and some fundamentalist Protestant groups, Mormons believe in a literal one-thousand-year reign of Christ and his faithful followers upon this earth. This millennium, as it is called, will follow Christ's triumphant Second Coming, heralding the world's end.[14] Mormons teach that the New Jerusalem, established by the Lord when he returns to the earth, "will be built upon the American continent," near Independence, Missouri.[15]

As Mormons see it, when Christ returns, he will reign on earth for one thousand years. He will preside over the Mormon church and world governments. His staff and all others in leadership positions will be righteous Mormons, some of whom will have been alive at the Second Coming, others of whom will be resurrected from paradise.

The chief spiritual work of the millennium will be the redemption of the dead. Until then, as active Mormons painfully acknowledge, the present system of proxy temple ordinances must suffice. Yet even with the Mormon church's immense resources, it is simply impossible to uncover the millions of names of unbelievers who died leaving no record.[16]

---

[14] Millenarianism arose from an incorrect interpretation of Revelation 20:1-4. Rather than falling into a too literalistic interpretation of this passage, the Catholic Church (and some other Christians) teach that the "binding of Satan" and the "thousand-year reign" are symbolic terms indicating, respectively, the thorough victory of Christ over sin and death, and the age of grace in which faithful Christians live, whether on earth or already in heaven. Therefore, the "millennium" began early in the Church age and continues until the final unleashing of the forces of evil, just before the Second Coming and the end of the world.

[15] See *Encyclopedia of Mormonism*, "Independence, Missouri."

[16] The church occasionally changes the "minimum information" requirements. A first and last name may be necessary, along with birth and death dates, parents' names, spouse's name, marriage date and so forth. Other times, only some of the data may be required for a valid proxy ordinance.

Mormons are faced with the conceptual dilemma: The missionary work in spirit prison could prove immensely successful, yet the names of the newly converted dead humans are unavailable to those on earth. The resulting converts must languish in hell until the "work" has been done for them in a Mormon temple. The millennial reign is supposed to correct this injustice, according to Joseph F. Smith.

"That this work [delivering the spirits of new converts from spirit prison] may be hastened so that all who believe, in the spirit world, may receive the benefit of deliverance," he said, "it is revealed that the great work of the Millennium shall be the work in the temples for the redemption of the dead; and then we hope to enjoy the benefits of revelation through the Urim and Thummim, or by such means as the Lord may reveal concerning those for whom the work shall be done, so that we may not work by chance, or by faith alone, without knowledge, but with the actual knowledge revealed unto us."[17]

The names of the unknown dead will be revealed during the millennium in different ways. Righteous Mormons who have been resurrected to rule with Christ will have become acquainted with many of the post-mortal converts and will supply their names to the temples.[18] (Mormons believe that their temples must survive to and through the millennium, and are constructed accordingly.) Also, the Urim and Thummim may be consulted. It is hoped that they, or some other divine device, will once again be available for consultation in learning about the dead for whom proxy work is expected to be done.

---

[17] *Doctrine of the Gospel Student Manual*, 104.
[18] *Doctrines of Salvation* 2:251–252.

26. Mormon Heavens

Three Degrees of Glory?

All this effort on behalf of the dead has a dual purpose: To offer the deceased soul the opportunity for improved eternal status and to assure for oneself the heavenly glory promised to those who faithfully carry out their temple duties. While Mormons strive to attain for themselves and those they have represented in the temple the "celestial" kingdom, the "terrestrial" and "telestial" kingdoms are left to the "also-rans."

Three heavens or kingdoms? Where is that in the Bible?

Mormons find a basis for their belief in three kingdoms in 1 Corinthians 15:40–42: "There are also celestial bodies, and bodies terrestrial: but the glory of the celestial is one, and the glory of the terrestrial is another. There is one glory of the sun, and another glory of the moon, and another glory of the stars: for one star differeth from another star in glory. So also is the resurrection of the dead. It is sown in corruption; it is raised in incorruption."

Smith's reworking of this epistle added "bodies telestial," creating a term used exclusively to refer to the lowest of the three Mormon heavens. Is this the plain sense of the verses? Did Paul teach a graded system of heavens? Will some men and women become gods and goddesses and receive from their children the same adoration we now offer to God the Father? Will even murderers, adulterers and idolaters be given a heaven so beautiful it surpasses description? The Mormon church answers yes. But the context says no. Recall that chapter fifteen of 1 Corinthians is Paul's glorious teaching on the redemption of mankind and our ultimate victory in Christ's resurrection. He answers the questions: "How are the dead raised up? and with what body do they come?" (1 Cor. 15:35) in the verses immediately following.

"You fool!" Paul writes. "What you sow is not brought to life unless it dies. And what you sow is not the body that is to be but a bare kernel of wheat, perhaps, or of some other kind; but God gives it a body as he chooses, and to each of the seeds its own body.... There are both heavenly bodies and earthly bodies, but the brightness of the heavenly is one kind and that of the earthly another.... So also is the resurrection of the dead. It is sown corruptible; it is raised incorruptible. It is sown dishonorable; it is raised glorious. It is sown weak; it is raised powerful. It is sown a natural body; it is raised a spiritual body" (verses 36–38, 42–44; NAB).

Paul, in his distinction between "celestial" and "terrestrial," is not comparing different kingdoms of heaven but different human bodies. "Kingdoms" are not even mentioned. The terrestrial body, rather, is the mortal, fleshly, natural man; the celestial body is that of the immortal, spiritual, supernatural man raised to eternal life.

In verses forty-seven through forty-nine, Paul hammers home the distinction by contrasting the "earthy" man, Adam, with the "heavenly" man, the Second Adam. We have all borne the image of the first, earthy man. By God's grace believers will also bear the likeness of Christ.

There surely will be different degrees of glory in heaven, possessed by individuals according to how they lived their lives. This is Paul's point in mentioning the different degrees of glory (brightness) among the celestial bodies—the sun, the moon, the stars with their different levels of brightness. Our souls in like manner will shine with different degrees of heavenly glory, according to our rewards from God. The passage certainly teaches that, but it does not teach that there will be three different kingdoms for us to occupy according to our level of glory. It compares our non-glorious earthly forms to the glorious, resurrected forms we will have later. To make this comparison, it contrasts the objects we encounter on this earth, which are non-glorious, to the objects we see in the physical heavens and which have a spectrum of different degrees of brightness.

It's clear the context does not permit Mormons to derive three heavenly kingdoms from a treatment of two kinds of bodies. Thus, they offer a second verse to bolster the belief in three levels of eternal heavens.

GOD IN EMBRYO: THE MORMON DOCTRINE OF MAN

"I knew a man in Christ above fourteen years ago, (whether in the body, I cannot tell; or whether out of the body, I cannot tell: God knoweth;) such an one caught up to the third heaven" (2 Cor. 12:2).

In commenting on this verse, Mormon apostle LeGrand Richards explained, "It is obvious that there could not be a third heaven unless there is also a first and a second heaven. We therefore have three heavens...."[1]

Well, yes and no. A thorough reading of Scripture discloses the term "heaven" or "heavens" referring to three distinct realities. First, there is what may be called the atmospheric heaven, consisting of the air or sky (Deut. 11:11; Job 35:5; Is. 45:8). It is where "the birds of heaven" fly. Second, there is what may be called the celestial heaven, consisting of the physical, stellar region beyond the atmosphere (Gen. 2:1; Jer. 4:23; Joel 2:10). It is where we see "the stars of heaven." Third, there is what may be called the spiritual heaven, which consists of the good, non-physical realm beyond this universe (Ps. 103:19; Luke 12:33; Matt. 6:9). It is where "the angels of heaven" are.

Paul's reference to being caught up to the third heaven need mean no more than that he was caught up to the heaven where God and the angels are. It does not require us to assert that there are two lower, spiritual heavens, since Scripture demonstrably uses the term "heaven" to refer to two lower, physical heavens—the physical atmosphere and the physical cosmos.

This is not to say that there *cannot* be different heavenly regions. Some have even spoken of there being seven heavens. God can make as many heavens as he wants. The point is that the Mormon doctrine cannot be substantiated from Scripture. Mormons cannot even advert to the Book of Mormon to find a basis for this view. It is spelled out only in revelations received by Smith and, years later, by his nephew, Joseph F. Smith, and recorded in the Doctrine and Covenants, especially sections 76 and 138. From those writings we learn the following.[2]

---

[1] *A Marvelous Work and a Wonder*, 254.
[2] Apostle Melvin J. Ballard delivered a discourse on the subject in 1922,

1. The Celestial Kingdom

This highest heaven is reserved for "[t]hose who keep the full law and obey all the commandments of God. . . . These receive a fulness of the blessings, power, and glory of the Father."[3] Only Mormons who have been faithful to the Mormon gospel to the end of their mortal lives or those who accepted the Mormon faith in the netherworld[4] can enter this heaven.

Celestial people "are they into whose hands the Father has given all things" (D&C 76:55), including "thrones, kingdoms, principalities, and powers" (D&C 132:19). What the Father has already received in the course of his own spiritual quest he now confers upon the most faithful of his children, those who have entered into the highest level of the celestial kingdom.[5]

Although a small minority actually live in such a way as to be worthy to attend a Mormon temple (an absolute for being saved in the highest heaven), it is not through lack of encouragement and direction by their priesthood leaders. The same may be said for Mormon efforts in proselytizing. From the time he first hears the message of the "restored gospel," the convert is exhorted to live righteously so as to be ready to receive all the ordinances necessary for final exaltation. Though it is hoped for all, in the end only a few will become gods of their own worlds.[6]

---

taking D&C 76 as his basic text. The speech is available under the title *Three Degrees of Glory*. Ballard praises this portion of Mormon scripture as the "greatest revelation the Lord, Jesus Christ, has ever given to man, so far as record is made" (3).

[3] *Doctrines of Salvation* 2:21.

[4] See *Doctrines of Salvation* 2:134–135.

[5] Mormons believe that the celestial kingdom is itself divided into three levels. Only those Mormons who reach the highest level in the highest kingdom qualify for the fullness of salvation, or godhood. Mormons in the lower levels of the celestial kingdom will have no increase (spirit children) and will be servants into the eternities. See D&C 131:1–5.

[6] "[F]ew men will become what God is. And yet, all men may become what he is if they will pay the price." *Three Degrees of Glory*, 9.

Those saved in the celestial kingdom will enjoy the government of God the Father, assisted by the Son and Holy Ghost. They will be priests and kings (and priestesses and queens) and ministering angels. As for the actual location of this heaven, we may take a hint from the tenth Article of Faith, which asserts, "We believe in the literal gathering of Israel and in the restoration of the Ten Tribes; that Zion (the New Jerusalem) will be built upon the American continent; that Christ will reign personally upon the earth; and, that the earth will be renewed and receive its paradisiacal glory."[7]

Perhaps the most notable of all gifts given to those in the highest heaven is that of "eternal life," often referred to by Mormons as "eternal increase." Only Mormon couples who have been "sealed" to each other for all eternity within a Mormon temple have the chance to become gods and goddesses and enjoy eternal increase. It works as follows. Upon being resurrected, the husband and wife[8] who have led worthy Mormon lives and are admitted into the celestial kingdom are granted the opportunity of eternal progression. That is, by a gradual unfolding of "advancement and experience," they gain a fullness of truth and become one with the Father. Ultimately, they assume a place, in another world, similar to that held by God in our own world. They shall have a "continuation of the seeds forever and ever" (D&C 132:19). Thus Young proclaimed that there would be "no end to the increase of the faithful."[9]

What all this means, simply, is that the exalted Mormon and his celestial wife or wives will bear children ("seed") after the resurrection. These spirit children will be reared, in their own

---

[7] The Mormon church will build this New Jerusalem in Jackson County, Missouri, according to revelations given in the Doctrine and Covenants. (See 42:9, 62, 67; 45:66; 57:2; 84:2, 4 and the chapter heading).

[8] Or wives. A man may be sealed as an eternal husband to more than one woman. Because the practice of polygamy was officially suspended by the Mormon church in 1890, no plural unions are recognized on earth at this time. Christ is supposed to restore the practice at his Second Coming.

[9] *Journal of Discourses* 10:5.

"pre-existence," in much the same way our own God and Father reared his children before sending them into mortality.

Though not a great deal is taught about the plans of salvation for the offspring of this earth's Mormons who will become gods, it's generally considered that they, like us, will have to take on mortal flesh, live on their respective earths, and learn obedience to the commands of their particular god (one of us).[10] Young taught, "Sin is upon every earth that ever was created, and if it was not so, I would like some philosophers to let us know how people can be exalted to become sons of God, and enjoy a fulness of glory with the Redeemer. Consequently every earth has its redeemer, and every earth has its tempter; and every earth, and the people thereof, in their turn and time, receive all that we receive, and pass through all the ordeals that we are passing through."[11]

Does this mean that every Mormon couple who has achieved godhood must some day endure the rebellion and banishment of countless spirit children, along with the shameful death of their "firstborn" in atonement for the rest? This doesn't sound much like the heaven described in Revelation 21:4, where God shall wipe away all tears, and there shall be no more sorrow, pain or death.

If you confront a Mormon with the statement, "You believe men can become as great as God," he may answer, "No, we don't." The reply is deceptive. It is a tenet of Mormonism that man may become as God is now, no matter how long and tortuous the path. Over the great flow of time, a faithful Mormon may attain the same lofty majesty and power now manifested by God the Father. In that sense, he will become then as God is now. But since God himself continually progresses in glory and "dominions" (*Mormon Doctrine*, 239), a celestial couple who have set off on the path of divinity will never catch up with him.

---

[10] Orson Pratt, *The Seer*, 37.
[11] *Journal of Discourses* 14:171–172.

Families in Heaven—The Catholic Teaching

Elder McConkie once decreed that one of the "most important things that any member of The Church of Jesus Christ of Latter-day Saints ever does in this world [is to] marry the right person, in the right place, by the right authority. . . ."[12] What this means, simply, is to marry a fellow Mormon in a Mormon temple. No other marital arrangement is recognized as part of the "new and eternal covenant," and no other can bind the spouses to each other and both to their children for all eternity. Mormons assume that Catholic (and all other) marriages are meant to last "until death" but not beyond. Therefore, Mormons conclude, spouses separated by death will remain eternally separated. Only the Mormon church provides the antidote to this everlasting loneliness by "sealing" forever in heaven that which has been bound for time here on earth. This leads to a common Mormon evangelization tactic. What follows is an example of a common Mormon missionary strategy following the death of a non-Mormon's loved one:

Bill and Marian were married for thirty-two years when Bill died of cancer. A few weeks after Marian returned to work, one of her co-workers approached her with a sympathetic smile and asked to talk.

"I know, Marian, how hard it is to lose someone close to you. My husband died two years ago, and there's not a day goes by that I don't think about him and talk to him. I'm so grateful for my faith, because I know that I will rejoin Jim after I die. We will be together forever. And it's only my church that can give this kind of assurance."

"What church is that?"

"The Church of Jesus Christ of Latter-day Saints. Sometimes people call us the Mormons. You see, when most people get married, the priest or minister uses words such as 'till death do you part,' or 'as long as you both shall live.' It's not that way with us.

---

[12] *Mormon Doctrine*, 118.

We are married not only for time but for all eternity. So, even though I ache from the loss of Jim, I know that we'll be partners again. And we'll have our children with us, too. I'd love to talk to you more about this, and help you see how you and Bill can continue as a family unit forever."

The Mormon paints the Catholic position as hurtful and untenable. No matter how deep the love and total the commitment, at a spouse's death, the relationship is dissolved. Should both spouses eventually go to heaven, they will be, at best, separate individuals whose only common ground is the adoration of some ethereal Essence.

But this is not the Catholic teaching. Heaven does not lessen the love, affection and intimacy we will have with others. It will heighten it. Marriage and sex will not be part of our future lives, as Jesus made absolutely clear (Matt. 22:30), but that does not mean we will love our former spouses or other loved ones any less. We will love them more! More than we ever did in this life, and we will feel this same love reflected back to us from them.

Further, we know that the Trinity, the touchstone of Christian orthodoxy, is the paradigm of all relationships. It's in the light of these divine relationships that we see and appreciate our earthly bonds with family and friends. Rather than being annulled at death, these ties are transfigured and glorified in heaven.[13] We await this glorious resurrection, not only of our bodies but also of our loves. The precise expression of our transformed earthly relationships is for now unknown, for "eye hath not seen, nor ear heard, neither have entered into the heart of man, the things which God hath prepared for them that love him" (1 Cor. 2:9). What we do know is that it will far surpass anything we have experienced thus far (2 Cor. 4:17).

In that blessed state we shall forever celebrate the union with our Lord and with our brothers and sisters. We shall know and love our family and friends in heaven. From that love, we shall

---

[13] See Peter Kreeft, *Everything You Ever Wanted to Know about Heaven*, 117ff.

reach out to the vast throng of the saved, that we may know and love, just as we are known and loved.[14]

Finally, it should be noted that the Mormon slogan "Families are Forever" comes with a great deal of small print. Families can be together forever only if each member attains the highest degree of the highest heaven. Parents of mediocre children must leave them behind in a "lower heaven,"[15] knowing that their offspring will never achieve the godhood they have. A mother may end up as an eternal, non-divine servant to her more active Mormon daughter-goddess. Or, a husband who doesn't live valiantly on earth may have to watch as his pious, resurrected wife is sealed forever to a more faithful Mormon man with whom she brings forth the other man's "spirit children."

Catholics responding to such misleading Mormon propaganda should remind the Mormon that, even if the "restored" teaching on eternal families were true, very few indeed are the Mormons who would continue on forever in intact familial groups because "few men will become what God is."[16]

---

[14] Consider Matthew 22:30: "For in the resurrection they neither marry, nor are given in marriage, but are as the angels of God in heaven." A Mormon may aim this verse at a bereaved Catholic and add the idea that "There will be no marrying, neither giving in marriage among those who reject the truth of the everlasting gospel. That privilege is confined to those who keep the commandments of the Lord in their fulness and who are obedient to the laws of God" (Joseph Fielding Smith, *Doctrines of Salvation* 2:73). The implication is that the Lord's injunction doesn't apply to faithful Mormons. To get the real sense of Christ's description, make some simple substitutions. "In the resurrection, they neither baptize nor are baptized . . . neither ordain nor are ordained. . . ." That is, the action of the earthly sacraments is ended. The effect endures forever.

[15] Occupants of a higher realm are permitted to visit from time to time those in a lower; the reverse is not true, however.

[16] *Three Degrees of Glory*, 9.

2. The Terrestrial Kingdom

Should Margaret Mary, Mother Teresa, or Pope John Paul II encounter and reject Mormon missionaries in the afterlife, the best they can hope for is a second-place heaven Mormons call the terrestrial kingdom. Little has been "revealed" about this middle heaven. Mormonism presumes to address, rather, those whose intentions and efforts are directed instead to the highest place, or eventual godhood.

Those ultimately consigned to this secondary heaven are "they who are not valiant in the testimony of Jesus" (D&C 76:79), those who died without law, the "honorable men of the earth, who were blinded by the craftiness of men. These are they who receive of the presence of the Son, but not of the fulness of the Father" (D&C 76:72, 75–76). They therefore will have to make do with living in the presence of the subordinate Mormon deity, Jesus.

Two main groups of people are included here. First are Mormons who failed to live up to all the requirements of the Mormon gospel. They'll have no eternal family and their path to godhood is ended. Mormon theologians believe it possible to advance in degree within the terrestrial kingdom, but those who reach its "summit" cannot then make a jump into the lower categories of the celestial kingdom.

The second category comprises "all those who have lived clean lives, but were not willing to receive the gospel . . . and those who refused to receive the gospel when they lived on the earth, but in the spirit world accepted the testimony of Jesus."[17] Some terrestrial occupants, then, will be the morally righteous people of every faith and walk of life who, though they had the Mormon message made plain to them, refused to accept it and convert. They failed

---

[17] Joseph Fielding Smith, *Answers to Gospel Questions* 2:208–210.

to accept Mormonism because they were "blinded by tradition and love of the world."[18] Nevertheless, their sincerity and good works merit them a place with Jesus Christ. Additionally, those who rejected the Mormon faith when it was first (and adequately) presented to them, but who accept it after death, in spirit prison, are entitled only to this lower heaven.[19]

Though refused godhood, terrestrial occupants enjoy the company of other, like-minded, decent people. And, just as their celestial betters have a hand in ruling them, they in turn exert a measure of authority over those in the lowest heaven. It should be noted that the name Smith gave to this second, intermediate kingdom, is indefensible. It's as if Smith did not know that the word "terrestrial" means "earthly."

It appears that Smith wished to appropriate the term "terrestrial" because it is used in 1 Corinthians 15 as an alternative to "celestial." He wanted to call the highest heaven the "celestial" kingdom, and so he used the other term mentioned in the passage—"terrestrial"—to refer to the next highest heaven. Anyone who knows the meaning of these English terms will not be taken in by their misuse.

3. *The Telestial Kingdom*

Further confirmation for the thesis advanced above is found in the fact that, when Smith wanted a word to describe the lowest heaven, he was forced to make one up. He took the two terms mentioned in 1 Corinthians 15—"terrestrial" and "celestial"—and ran them together to get "telestial."

According to Mormons, the glory of this lowest heaven "surpasses all understanding" (D&C 76:89). To it are assigned "liars, sorcerers, whoremongers, and adulterers" (D&C 76:103). Neither the Father nor the Son enter this kingdom of glory, so its

---

[18] Joseph Fielding Smith, in *Doctrines of the Gospel Student Manual*, 92.
[19] Victor L. Ludlow, *Principles and Practices of the Restored Gospel*, 241.

inhabitants have to make do with yet another lower Mormon god, the Holy Ghost.[20]

These are "the filthy who suffer the wrath of God on the earth, who are thrust down to hell where they will be required to pay the uttermost farthing before their redemption comes"[21]—i.e., after they have experienced a particularly nasty form of purgatory. (The "hell" referred to here is merely spirit prison.) Murderers and the like will be confined to it until the Lord's plan has been fulfilled, at which time they will be resurrected and sent to this realm of indescribable beauty and joy.[22]

The population of the telestial kingdom will be vast: "Most of the adult people who have lived from the day of Adam to the present time will go to the telestial kingdom. . . . [T]hey will be 'as innumerable as the stars in the firmament of heaven, or as the sand upon the seashore.'"[23] After having been purged of their gross failings in spirit prison and tutored in the art of cooperative living, the world's wicked will be raised and glorified in a place so wonderful as to defy description.

As this shows, Mormons are virtual universalists. That is, they believe in the eventual salvation of just about everyone. Though the three kingdoms differ greatly in the opportunities available for future progress, each provides its occupants with pleasure and happiness never attainable on earth. The "eternal" damnation experienced by murderers, adulterers, thieves, and others will at some

---

[20] *Doctrines of Salvation* 2:5.

[21] Ibid., 22.

[22] Mormonism occasionally speaks of "eternal" or "everlasting" damnation. As with many other terms, this also is redefined to suit peculiar Mormon theology. McConkie cited three levels of meaning: first, eternal damnation is the opposite of eternal life or exaltation in the highest level of the celestial kingdom; second, it may specify those destined to inherit the telestial kingdom or even the realm of Satan and his angels; third, it refers to the type, kind, and quality—but not duration—of torment suffered by all those in spirit prison, a punishment that will cease when the sinner comes forth in the final resurrection. See *Mormon Doctrine*, 235–236.

[23] *Mormon Doctrine*, 778.

point end and these sinners will find themselves in a comfortable and companionable eternal bliss.

4. The Sons of Perdition

A fourth destiny is posited for Satan, his angel followers and the few mortals who are found undeserving of any degree of glory. Those who commit the unpardonable sin, who sin against the Holy Ghost, who are incorrigibly wicked, will suffer the fullness of torment and frustration forever (in the usual sense of the word). Lucifer and Cain are among those who "willfully and utterly pervert principles of righteousness and truth with which they were once endowed."[24]

Apostates from the Mormon religion may be included among the reprobate, according to McConkie.

"Apostates exhibit varying degrees of indifference and of rebellion," he said, "and their punishment, in time and in eternity, is based on the type and degree of apostasy which is involved. Those who become indifferent to the Church, who simply drift from the course of righteousness to the way of the world, are not in the same category with traitors who fight the truth, and with those whose open rebellion destines them to eternal damnation as sons of perdition."[25]

Mormons complain that there are some among them who "leave the Mormon church, but don't leave it alone." These "apostates," once believing and active Mormons, not only repudiate their former faith but openly speak against it. They may be candidates for utter perdition.[26]

---

[24] *Encyclopedia of Mormonism*, vol. 3.
[25] McConkie, *Doctrinal New Testament Commentary* 3:76.
[26] The qualifier is added because, as some Mormon thinkers explain, it all depends on how enlightened their testimony was. Those who had received a definitive conviction on the truthfulness of the Mormon church and then reject it are, indeed, forever lost.

The Catholic Response—Rewards

Mormons find their belief in varying degrees of reward to be consistent with a just and fair deity. Thinking that men should receive the glory to which they are entitled, and no more, they propose not only the three degrees of glory or heavens, but also gradations within each kingdom. By misunderstanding or misrepresenting the Christian teaching on heaven, Mormon leaders have presented yet another straw man to be wrestled down by their more sensible truths.

James E. Talmage taught, "The false assumption, based upon sectarian dogma, that in the hereafter there shall be but two places, states, or conditions for the souls of mankind—heaven and hell, with the same glory in all parts of the one and the same terrors throughout the other—is untenable in the light of divine revelation."[27]

On the contrary, this has never been Catholic teaching. In the Father's house there are many mansions (John 14:2). All those who are saved will live forever in the presence of Almighty God —Father, Son, and Holy Spirit—in heaven. We shall all enjoy the Beatific Vision, union with the Lord. There shall be no wanting; there'll be no "progression" to a higher level of happiness or enjoyment, since we shall have received the fullness of redemption, and it will be more than we can possibly imagine.

Mormons are correct when they accept the Catholic teaching that earthly lives of faithfulness and righteousness affect our eternal status. The enjoyment of the saved (or torment of the damned) will not be uniform or generic. We have Christ's clear teaching in Matthew 13, the parable of the sower, and Matthew 25, the parable of the talents. Paul also weighs in on the subject repeatedly (Rom. 2:5; Gal. 6:6-10). Those who heard God's word or who received his blessings exhibited different levels of faith and were rewarded accordingly.

---

[27] *Articles of Faith*, 91.

In other words, sanctifying grace is offered freely to each of us. Our responsibility is continually to open our lives to the Lord's influence, to "stretch" our spiritual capacities to receive from him the fullest possible share in the divine gifts and to respond with lives of devotion and service. Consider a thimble, a gallon jug, and a bathtub. Each can be full and yet contain different amounts. So it will be with us in heaven. Each of us will have cultivated his spiritual life to the point that he can receive varying amounts of joy and beatitude, varying degrees to which he can take in the blessedness of the Beatific Vision. Even the smallest apprehension of the Beatific Vision is more beatitude than can be conceived in this life.

"For I reckon," says Paul, "that the sufferings of this present time are not worthy to be compared with the glory which shall be revealed in us" (Rom. 8:18).

PART SIX

Mormon Revelations and Scriptures

27. Mormon Revelations, Mormon Scriptures

The Mormon church is centered on divine revelations and scriptures that are alien to historic Christianity. These revelations and scriptures take many forms, but they are all regarded as having divine authority and as being obligatory to the Mormon faith. On the day of my Mormon baptism, Elders Whitesides and Sadler, the two young missionaries who had prepared me for membership, presented me with a leather-bound "quad." This tome contains the four "standard works" that Mormons accept as scripture. First, there's the King James version of the Protestant Bible. Then follow the specifically Mormon writings: the Book of Mormon, the Doctrine and Covenants and the Pearl of Great Price.

Though in theory Latter-day Saints accord divine inspiration to each of these books, common practice indicates differently. Mormon leaders have been less than consistent in their treatment and teachings of the texts, most notably the Bible and the Book of Mormon. Smith gave these special prominence in the Mormon Articles of Faith, stating, "We believe the Bible to be the word of God as far as it is translated correctly; we also believe the Book of Mormon to be the word of God" (Eighth Article of Faith).

Though the Bible and the Book of Mormon have a special place, there are other sources of the word of God. The Doctrine and Covenants is primarily a record of the "divine revelations" made to Smith; the Pearl of Great Price contains his rewriting of the first several chapters of Genesis and also a "translation" he made of some ancient Egyptian papyri supposedly written by the patriarch Abraham. Ironically—though not surprisingly since the Bible rejects Mormon teaching—Mormons express doubt about the reliability of the Bible, though the other works are accepted as faithful records or translations of divine teaching.

This section will respond to a number of key Mormon assertions: 1) The Bible is incomplete; books belonging to it have been lost or deliberately removed by the Catholic Church; 2) The Lord did not speak a full and final Word in the life and death, works and teachings of his divine Son; rather, he continues to reveal new truths; 3) The Book of Abraham in the Pearl of Great Price was miraculously translated by Smith from papyri he bought from a roving purveyor of ancient curiosities; 4) The Book of Mormon is the "most complete" of any book, accurately recording the social and religious history of pre-Columbian American tribes; that it was divinely preserved for centuries and then miraculously translated by an uneducated farm boy.

Catholics acknowledge the full word of God is not confined to the pages of the Old and New Testaments. Unlike Mormons, however, we recognize that the fullness of God's revelation came once for all in Christ. As the New Testament states, "The faith . . . was once delivered unto the saints" (Jude 3). No new, supplementary revelations are needed.

Christ's divine teachings that have been handed down in written form we call the Bible. Knowledge and instruction handed on by word of mouth from the apostles to their successors—that is, by oral teaching—is faithfully preserved and taught as apostolic tradition. These are the two modes through which the word of God is passed down to us. Fallen human intellect, especially under pressure of dark forces, is likely to misunderstand or misapply God's word. Consequently, Christ did not leave us a book and a set of audio tapes, but a living teaching authority—called the magisterium, which is composed of bishops, successors of the apostles—to make sure that his word is faithfully preached and interpreted to the end of time.

This living teaching authority is indicated in Jesus Christ's command to his apostles: "Go and teach all nations" (Matt. 28:19). The one who is to learn must know who the teacher is and must trust him. That the Church teaches with the authority of Christ is clear from his assertion, "He that heareth you heareth me; and he that despiseth you despiseth me" (Luke 10:16). To hear and heed the Church is to attend to Christ and his plan for our salvation. The eternal Word, with the Father from the beginning, became flesh and showed us not only his glory but his will. While nothing can be added to this wondrous revelation, it is the Church's mission to meditate upon it through all generations, to preserve and protect it, to explain and defend it. Thus, Scripture and Tradition blend in a harmony of truth spoken with finality by the Son and echoed in all ages by his Church, preserved and perpetuated by the teaching authority Christ established. Thus Paul speaks truly when he declares "the Church of the living God" to be "the pillar and ground of the truth" (1 Tim. 3:15).

28. Visions and Versions

Smith's First Vision is the foundation stone of Mormon belief. If he did not have some initial divine revelation, then he could not have had subsequent ones. Moreover, if his account of his first divine revelation cannot be trusted, then neither can his accounts of later ones. His account of his First Vision is therefore of crucial significance.

Mormons understand the importance of the First Vision for their belief system. LDS apostle John A. Widtsoe wrote that "the First Vision of 1820 is of first importance in the history of Joseph Smith. Upon its reality rest the truth and value of his subsequent work."[1]

Mormons cannot deny the historicity of the First Vision and remain in good standing with their church. LDS author and church historian James B. Allen writes, "Belief in the vision is one of the fundamentals to which faithful members give assent. . . . The story is an essential part of the first lesson given by Mormon missionaries to prospective converts, and its acceptance is necessary before baptism."[2]

The Mormon church holds this vision as proof of two things: All Christian churches are irreparably lost, and *only* the church organized by Smith may presume to offer salvation to mankind. Without these two principles, Mormonism would be a false church teaching a false gospel.

LDS members are high in their praise of the First Vision and its significance. Joseph F. Smith stated, "The greatest event that has ever occurred in the world, since the resurrection of the Son of God from the tomb and his ascension on high, was the coming

---

[1] Widtsoe, *Joseph Smith—Seeker After Truth*, 19.
[2] James B. Allen, "The Significance of Joseph Smith's 'First Vision' in Mormon History," *The New Mormon History*, 37.

of the Father and of the Son to that boy Joseph Smith, to prepare the way for the laying of the foundation of his kingdom—not the kingdom of man—never more to cease nor to be overturned. Having accepted this truth, I find it easy to accept of every other truth that he enunciated and declared during his mission of fourteen years in the world. He never taught a doctrine that was not true. He never practiced a doctrine that he was not commanded to practice. He never advocated error. He was not deceived. He saw; he heard; he did as he was commanded to do; and, therefore, God is responsible for the work accomplished by Joseph Smith—not Joseph Smith. The Lord is responsible for it, and not man."[3]

These sentiments are echoed by his successor, Spencer W. Kimball, who said, "Joseph Smith's First Vision restored knowledge of God. Of all the great events of the century, none compared with the First Vision of Joseph Smith."[4]

Despite such praise, what is supposed to have happened during the First Vision is unclear. It appears that at one time there was no First Vision account and that what is now known as the First Vision was a later invention. In order to see this, we need to examine the chronology of Smith's claimed contacts with the supernatural.

The Book of Mormon was published in 1830. For anyone to take it seriously, Smith had to have some explanation of where the book came from and why it should be regarded as authoritative. Even while the work was in preparation, Smith would have needed a justification for asking his friends to take dictation as he "translated" it. The justification offered was that the Book of Mormon was a book of scripture, written on golden plates, that God was miraculously allowing Smith to translate. Anyone hearing this explanation would naturally have questions, such as how he found the plates and how he knew all this. Even if Smith had accidentally stumbled across the plates, he obviously would have needed contact with the supernatural to understand what they

---

[3] Joseph F. Smith, *Gospel Doctrine*, 495.
[4] Spencer W. Kimball, *The Teachings of Spencer W. Kimball*, 428.

were and what he was to do with them. To answer these kinds of questions, Smith stated that he had been visited by an angel who showed him where the plates were and explained what to do. After a time, however, Smith began to report that this encounter with an angel (actually one of several) was not his first contact with the supernatural. He claimed that prior to his angelic encounters he had experienced an event, now called the First Vision, in which God the Father and God the Son appeared to him. This paved the way for the later angelic encounters and the finding of the golden plates.

Over the years, Smith recounted the story of the First Vision many times. Some of these recitals have been preserved, either because Smith wrote or dictated them or because they were written by those who heard Smith giving an oral recounting of the event. Almost certainly there were other oral accounts that no one recorded. Here we will focus only on those accounts that Smith played a role in preserving. Accounts written by others based on what they heard Smith say on a particular occasion are useful to historians in developing as full a picture as possible of how the First Vision story changed over time. However, because these were not superintended by Smith, they may contain omissions and errors regarding what Smith claimed if, for example, a person misheard what was said.

Because of discrepancies in the accounts that Smith was involved in preserving, the Mormon church has been reluctant to see these accounts distributed, and for many years attempted to suppress more than one early account of the First Vision story. Despite these efforts, several different accounts are now available. Others may be discovered in the future. For our purposes, we will look at the following group of accounts:

1. *The 1832 Ledger Version.* This is the only known account that was written (partly) in Smith's own hand. It was a six-page account written on three leaves in a ledger book. The beginning and end were penned (at Smith's dictation) by Frederick G. Williams, but the middle portion, including the details of the vision, was

written in Smith's own handwriting. This account was for many years suppressed by the Mormon church and held in its archives, though word of it emerged from time to time. Its text was revealed to the public when BYU student Paul R. Cheesman gained access to it and, apparently not realizing its significance, reprinted it in an appendix to his 1965 master's thesis. Following this, *Brigham Young University Studies* published a photographic reproduction of the original document in spring 1969.

2. *The 1835 Diary Version.* Though we normally think of diaries as being written by the person whose name the work bears, this diary was dictated by Smith. The scribe who took down the account of the First Vision recorded in Smith's diary in 1835 was Warren Parrish. This version was also not published until spring 1971, when it appeared in *Dialogue: A Journal of Mormon Thought* in an article by Dean C. Jessee of the church historical department.

3. *The 1838 Official Version.* This account serves as the basis for the current official Mormon version of the First Vision. It was dictated to James Mulholland in 1838 but was not printed until 1842, when it was published in the Mormon publication *Times and Seasons* with minor editorial changes. It now appears in the Mormon scripture known as the Pearl of Great Price, where it is part of the Joseph Smith—History section.

For the relevant text from these accounts, see appendix II, "Joseph Smith's Vision Accounts."

The gist of the current, official account, as it was transcribed in 1838, is as follows: In 1820 there was a set of great revivals in the Christian churches in the area of Palmyra, New York, and much local discussion concerning which church was right. This led Smith, then fourteen years old ("in my fifteenth year," 1:7, cf. 1:22–23), to ponder which church to join. One day in the spring of 1820, Smith retired to the woods to pray about his concerns. As he did so, he was attacked by a powerful force that rendered him unable to speak and made him think he was doomed to destruction. However, he cried out to God and was delivered. A pillar of light descended on him and he saw two identical, glorious persons. The first—God the Father—identified the second as God the Son. When Smith asked which sect he should join, the Son told him that he should join no church, that they were all wrong, that all their creeds were abominations.

However, other versions Smith gave of the event contradict this account in several respects. The different accounts of the First Vision do not harmonize either among themselves or with the externally verifiable facts of history. Here we will consider several issues that reveal the First Vision's lack of credibility, such as its alleged timing and the persons who allegedly appeared in it.

In the 1838 official account of the First Vision, Smith reports that an atmosphere of intense revivalism conducted by various Protestant sects had served as the impetus to his prayer for guidance in 1820. Correspondingly intense criticism supposedly followed his announcement of the vision (Joseph Smith—History 1:21-26).

Thanks to historical research done primarily by Rev. Wesley P. Walters, we have an independently verified picture of the religious climate in the Palmyra area during this period.[5] This information appears to undermine the account canonized in the Pearl of Great Price, and hence, the official position of the Mormon church. Specifically, during the years 1819-1823, no revivals in the whole Palmyra area were recorded by the Presbyterian, Methodist, or Baptist churches. Also, there were no gains in membership recorded for Presbyterians in 1820, only six members were added to the Baptists and the Methodists lost sixty-nine during the years 1819-1821. This contradicts Smith's assertions in the 1838 official account that "great multitudes" aligned themselves with these churches in 1820 (Joseph Smith—History 1:5).

---

[5] Wesley P. Walters, *New Light on Mormon Origins from the Palmyra (N.Y.) Revival*, 1967, 4-18. Expanded treatment of Smith's Palmyra years is also found in Walters' and H. Michael Marquardt's *Inventing Mormonism*, 1994, especially 15-41.

Walters found, however, that in late 1824 and early 1825 a great deal of revivalist activity occurred, with many conversions to local sects. Methodists recorded over one hundred fifty new members, while Baptists and Presbyterians each gained about one hundred additional members.

In the Mormon newspaper *Messenger and Advocate*, in an account of early Mormon history composed with Smith's cooperation, Oliver Cowdery admitted that the "religious excitement" that led Smith to pray to God for guidance occurred in 1823. This is of special significance because Cowdery specifically makes a correction on this point. Earlier he had stated that Smith was fifteen at the time. Apparently, someone pointed out the chronological problem and now Cowdery pointedly states that this was a typesetting error—that Smith was seventeen at the time of the religious revivalism and that the year was 1823. This is important to keep in mind, he said, in order to understand other elements of the chronology. The **definiteness** with which he says this strongly suggests that he checked this key point with Smith, with whose help he was writing the history of the Mormon church in the publication.

Since Smith claims that his vision took place in the spring (1:14), this could only mean the spring of 1825. Thus, based on two pieces of information that would make it easy to remember when the vision occurred—the time of year and the fact that the prayer which led to it had been prompted by large revivals in the local churches—the independently verifiable facts of the period would place the First Vision no earlier than 1825. This new time schedule plays havoc with Smith's assertions. No longer an innocent boy of fourteen, Smith would have been a young man of nineteen according to this re-dating, and almost anyone should be able to remember if events of this significance occurred when one was fourteen or when one was nineteen.

That chink in the official account plays havoc with other key Mormon dates. If the First Vision did not take place until 1825, then Smith could not have had his vision of the angel Moroni, as he claimed, on September 21, 1823 (Joseph Smith—History 1:27). In this vision, the angel told him that he would find the golden plates on which the book of Mormon was written (ibid. 1:34-35, 42), but he would not obtain possession of them for another four years (ibid. 1:53, 59). This would mean that Smith did not obtain the plates until September of 1829. But we know that Smith's "translation" of the book of Mormon was already completed by June of 1829 and was in preparation for printing, which occurred in March of 1830, just a month before the founding of the Mormon church.

The conclusion that must be drawn is that Smith's First Vision was not associated with the only revival to have occurred in Palmyra. That revival took place too late to fit the rest of his chronology, and his account of events in canonized Mormon scripture would have to be wrong in one or more respects: The First Vision did not occur in 1820 or it was not associated with a revival or Smith was not promised the plates in 1823 or he did not wait four years to receive them. Or better still, the vision simply never happened at all.

The problems are even greater with the personages Smith was supposed to have seen during the event. Here, not only is independently verifiable evidence against Smith's claims, but his assertions themselves are at odds with each other. In the current official version, Smith declared that the "two Personages" who appeared to him were God the Father and Jesus Christ (ibid. 1:17). This is clear from the fact that one of the personages pointed to the other and said, "This is My Beloved Son. Hear Him!"—an unmistakable allusion to the declaration given by God the Father at the baptism of Christ (Matt. 3:17) and especially at his transfiguration (Matt. 17:5).

But the other accounts do not agree. According to the 1832 diary account, Smith reported only one person was manifested to him. This person identified himself by saying, "I am the Lord of glory I was crucifyed [sic] for the world"—a clear reference to God the Son.[6] The 1835 diary account also disagrees with the

---

[6] Smith also does not say that he saw the Son, merely that the Son spoke to him while a pillar of light rested on him (Smith). This account also states that the event took place in "the 16th year of my [Smith's] age"—i.e., 1821.

1838 official account. In the diary account, Smith claimed that two unnamed persons appeared to him. In this account also, the second person is recorded as doing most of the talking, and Smith notes that he "testified also unto me that Jesus Christ is the son of God"—which would suggest the second person was not himself the Son. Smith also stated, "I saw many angels in this vision."

Further complications arise when one considers the statements of Smith's successors as Mormon prophets, Brigham Young and John Taylor. According to them, Smith had been visited by an angel, from whom he asked advice as to which church to join.[7] If there had been a single, consistent account of how the Mormon religion was started, how could these men *not* have known it?

So, whom did Smith encounter, as he put it in the official account, on that "morning of a beautiful, clear day, early in the spring of eighteen hundred and twenty"? God the Father and Jesus Christ, as the official version has it? Or only Christ, as Smith wrote in 1832? Or two unnamed personages with angels, as he wrote in 1835? Or one or more angels, as Smith's inspired successors maintained? Surely a heavenly visitation with such eternal consequences would engage a person's complete attention and memory.

Mormonism uses the First Vision and its consequences to emphasize that their church was "persecuted" from the beginning. The official First Vision account is useful for this purpose because Smith asserted that shortly after the vision he experienced "persecution" on account of it:

> Some few days after I had this vision, I happened to be in company with one of the Methodist preachers, who was very active in the before mentioned religious excitement; and, conversing with him on the subject of religion, I took occasion to give him an account of the vision which I had had. I was greatly surprised at his behavior; he treated my communication not only lightly, but with great contempt, saying it was all of the devil, that there were no such things as visions or revelations in these days; that all such things had ceased with the apostles, and that there would never be any more of them.

---

[7] See *Journal of Discourses* 2:171, 13:78, 18:329, 20:167.

> I soon found, however, that my telling the story had excited a great deal of prejudice against me among professors of religion, and was the cause of great persecution, which continued to increase; and though I was an obscure boy, only between fourteen and fifteen years of age, and my circumstances in life such as to make a boy of no consequence in the world, yet men of high standing would take notice sufficient to excite the public mind against me, and create a bitter persecution; and this was common among all the sects—all united to persecute me [Joseph Smith—History 1:21-22].

Now, it is true that Smith and his co-religionists experienced derision and criticism in the years following organization of the Mormon church. Local newspapers reveled in making sport of the Mormons and their preposterous claims. The news of another novel doctrine or practice would provoke denunciation from the press. But as Smith biographer Fawn Brodie recorded, "The Palmyra newspapers . . . took no notice of Joseph's vision at the time it was supposed to have occurred."[8]

Some Mormons claim that Smith, knowing the vision's grave nature and the shock it would cause to traditional Christian systems, deliberately withheld information on this revelation until a later time. But this is inconsistent with Smith's report that his story caused "a great deal of prejudice" and "great persecution, which continued to increase" to the point that "all the sects—all united to persecute me."

There is no evidence that any of this occurred, and given the already established problems with the First Vision's official version, no historical credence can be given to this alleged opposition on account of the vision.

Further evidence that the First Vision was not publicly revealed and not a source of "persecution" is found in an 1835 newspaper account of Smith's early visions. This account, prepared by Cowdery and Smith, appeared in the February 1835 *Messenger and Advocate* and mentions angelic encounters Smith had in his bedroom in 1823. It conspicuously *does not* mention the First Vision

---

[8] Fawn M. Brodie, *No Man Knows My History*, 23.

account. This is not because Smith had not yet invented the idea of the First Vision. He had, for it was recorded in the 1832 ledger account. Either Smith had forgotten the ledger story when the newspaper article came out, or he was deliberately misleading his flock. More and more the evidence shows that the First Vision story was a late creation worked into Mormon chronology, likely because Smith was unable to remember the stories he had told about his early supernatural encounters.

Those who point out the discrepancies in the stories are accused by Mormon authorities as lacking a spirit of fidelity and submission to authority. Mormon apostle Neal A. Maxwell wrote, "In our own time, Joseph Smith, the First Vision, and the Book of Mormon constitute stumbling blocks for many—around or over which they cannot get—unless they are meek enough to examine all the evidence at hand, not being exclusionary as a result of accumulated attitudes in a secular society. Humbleness of mind is the initiator of expansiveness of mind."[9]

How curious that this Mormon apostle applauds a thoroughgoing examination of all the data available on a subject, yet would draw the line when such research proves unable to support the official versions. Some Mormon apologists find the only way to explain the contradictions is to deny they exist. For instance, James B. Allen, former Mormon church historian, observed, "The variations in these and other accounts suggest that in relating his story to various individuals at various times, Joseph Smith emphasized different aspects of it and that his listeners were each impressed with different details. This, of course, is to be expected, for the same thing happens in retelling any story."[10]

---

[9] Neal A. Maxwell, *Meek and Lowly*, 76.

[10] Allen, 48-49. The same thought is echoed by former mission president Richard I. Winwood in *Be Not Deceived*: "[T]he basic truths disclosed in each account are in complete harmony. The differences that do exist are simple grammatical changes or observations that show different facets of the same event" (40). Winwood contends these "differences in details" were a result of Smith's having an "enormously significant message" couched in "complex and

It's difficult to imagine a more disingenuous statement from a Mormon defender. The case at point is not merely a conflict over how many angels may have appeared, or how many "personages" even. The discrepancy involves what President Ezra Taft Benson termed the "bedrock theology" of the LDS church.[11] Is it, therefore, likely that Smith would forget that the Father and the Son appeared to him? Is it likely, as some Mormon apologists propose, that the version which mentions only one personage (the Son) does not thereby rule out the presence in bodily form of the Father? Is it likely that the version that mentions two undefined personages, one of whom mentions Jesus Christ in the third person, could actually refer to both the Father and the Son? And is it likely that the version described by later Mormon prophets as comprised of angels only could really intend to refer to Christ as an angel?

Non-Mormon and even some Mormon scholars deny the authenticity of the First Vision and view Smith's account of it as an imaginative projection back into his young adolescence for ratification of the doctrines he taught later. The persecution he allegedly experienced at the hands of the clergy in 1820 not only served to awaken in his mind a favorable comparison with the apostle Paul, but was a precursor to conflicts that centered on Smith during his later adult life.

Why is the dating of the First Vision so important, and what are we to make of the Mormon church's insistence on the earlier date? One possible explanation involves Smith's attempt to authenticate his own mission along with his changing theology. A vision displaying Father and Son in bodily form would ratify the radical changes he had made in the doctrine of God. Further,

---

astounding events" (41). Others argue it was not an unlettered and innocent farm boy who was understandably overwhelmed, but a religious leader whose determination to provide "evidence" for his peculiar theology nevertheless succumbed to his own forgetfulness. He simply couldn't keep track of the various versions he'd spun.

[11] Benson, 101.

an earlier vision, to an ingenuous youngster, might serve to bypass the critics' complaints of a more mature manipulation of the so-called "founding event" of Mormonism.

Besides, the date of 1820 or so would be needed, given that Smith had reported subsequent visitations by angels from heaven each year from 1823 to 1827, when he was finally permitted to receive the golden plates of the Book of Mormon. After all, how many within his group would have remembered or even been familiar with the dating of the Palmyra revival that allegedly sent Smith to the grove in prayer?

We do not argue that the vision actually occurred during the 1824–1825 revival; rather, we believe it never happened at all. In trying to justify himself before his followers, Smith made up the story of a divine visitation and commission. His major logistical blunder was misdating the precipitating revival.

29. The Book of Mormon

We've all seen the commercials. A lovely young woman looks out upon a noisy sea. In the background, a lighthouse rises. The woman shares her faith in Jesus Christ and his Father's plan for man. This faith, she affirms, is bolstered by her belief in the Book of Mormon, "another testament of Jesus Christ."[1] We, too, may find consolation by calling a toll-free number and asking for a copy.

One could get the impression that, aside from the writings in the Book of Mormon, no other source is available to provide the basis and purpose of Christian faith. It comes with a string of bona fides. Smith stated that it is "the most correct of any book on earth, and the keystone of our religion, and a man would get nearer to God by abiding by its precepts than by any other book."[2]

Upon forming his new church in the same year, Smith further asserted that he had been given "power from on high, by the means which were before prepared, to translate the Book of Mormon; which is a record of a fallen people, and the fulness of the gospel of Jesus Christ" (D&C 20:8–9).

And Jesus Christ, in a revelation given to Smith the year after its first printing, is said to have proclaimed that in the Book of Mormon "is the fulness of the gospel" (D&C 42:12). But what is this fullness? What saving truths, omitted in the "traditional" Word of God as understood by Catholics (or, for that matter, by Protestants), are found in the Book of Mormon? Why should

---

[1] Only within the last twenty years has the Mormon church officially titled the Book of Mormon as being an additional witness to Christ. This fits with the general pattern of "Christianizing" its public persona. The same is true of its recently redesigned logo, which features the name "Jesus Christ" in letters to stand out from the rest of the church's name.

[2] *History of the Church* 4:461.

Catholics and other Christians even consider the possibility of further scripture? We will examine the arguments Mormons make for their namesake book—and why these arguments fail—in the next two chapters. First, however, we will take a look at the book itself and its history, real and imagined.

The Mormon church presents the Book of Mormon as a companion volume of scripture. With over five hundred pages written in language reminiscent of the King James Version and formatted to look like a standard Bible, the text looks "scriptural." The work is comprised of fifteen books, each written by an ancient American prophet and carefully preserved and handed down to succeeding generations.[3] As the book came forth from the pen of Smith's scribes, it had no chapter or verse divisions. These were added after Smith's death. As he dictated the work to his scribes, Smith assumed a form of English intended to sound similar to that found in the seventeenth-century King James Version of the Bible. He used "thou," "thee," "ye" and verb endings of "-eth" and "-est." But not consistently. It is only *imitation* Jacobean English. (See, for example, Mosiah 2:19, 3:19, 3:34, 4:22 and 4:24.). The 1981 version contains chapter headings recently written by church authorities. The Book of Mormon has been constructed to "look" and "sound" scriptural. Technical apparatus such as footnotes, cross-references and an index have been added in recent years, further enhancing its outward similarity to popular Bible editions.

The book professes to be a religious and secular history of Hebrews who fled Jerusalem and certain persecution in 600 B.C. Lehi, a prophet and contemporary of Jeremiah, led his wife, children and their spouses through the Arabian wilderness to the shores of "the large waters." After much hardship and contention, the righteous son Nephi built a ship and they sailed to a new "promised land," but not before having obtained a collection of brass plates on which was recorded the Pentateuch (or first five

---

[3] Actually, Smith claimed the book was a translation of an abridgment of writings a hundred times greater in volume.

books of the Old Testament) and a record of the Jews, from the beginning to that day. All the while, Nephi had been making metal plates of his own and engraving on them a record of his family's labors. Upon arriving in the western hemisphere, and after the death of Lehi, Nephi's brothers Laman and Lemuel rebelled against him, forcing him and his followers to separate from them. Because of their unbelief, the Lamanites were cursed with a "skin of blackness" (meaning a darker, American Indian skin tone) and became a source of persecution to the Nephites. At Nephi's death in the mid-sixth century,[4] his younger brother Jacob took up the story and the plates. Several other prophets followed Jacob, maintaining written records of the Nephites or "American Hebrews."

During these years, the settlers were promised a Messiah, named Jesus Christ, who would be born of Mary, a virgin, in the land of Jerusalem! Even the exact year of his birth was announced! The Nephites, then, were favored with prophets more enlightened than their counterparts in Palestine, who were those most associated with the coming of Christ.

Throughout these centuries, and reflecting the same theme sketched for Israel by Old Testament authors, the Nephites enjoyed periods of material prosperity when they followed the Lord's voice and languished in misery when they didn't. Much of the book gives vivid descriptions of the punishing battles waged between Nephites and Lamanites, a fact which has led some to wonder why so much time and space was used in the dull, repetitive recording of bloody slaughter.[5]

Evil kings, corrupt judges, "secret combinations" (or "gangs" of robbers), persecution of the righteous, their subsequent apostasy and restoration, massive genocide—this is the stuff of the Book of Mormon. There are occasional discourses on religion, most of which remind the reader of the words of Old Testament

---

[4] The present version of the Book of Mormon supplies dates on each page.

[5] Especially since the gold plates were said to have contained only a hundredth part of the records available. See Words of Mormon 5. Also, 1 Nephi 19:6 and Mormon 9:32–33.

prophets, the Sermon on the Mount or the teachings of Paul, despite the chronological problems this poses. Toward the end of the Nephite-Lamanite record we find inserted, out of chronological sequence, the "Book of Ether." These fifteen chapters are said to be the record of yet another group of Hebrew émigrés, dispersed at the Tower of Babel. Following the "brother of Jared," who had had a vision of the "spirit body" of Jesus Christ, these righteous ones built barges and sailed for the promised land of America. The "Jaredites" soon split into factions, warring with one another throughout a succession of kings, prophets, murder, and intrigue. Some of their prophets predicted the coming forth of the Book of Mormon and the establishing, in America, of the New Jerusalem. Predictably, the forces of good and evil ultimately arrayed themselves in a final battle. Millions are killed; indeed, every single Jaredite but one is slain. The prophet Ether recorded the devastation on twenty-four metal plates, which were then later discovered by Nephites and appended to their own writings.

Without doubt, the high point of the Book of Mormon is recorded in Third Nephi. This book covers the period from A.D. 1-35. Raids, murders, government upheavals, tempests, earthquakes, and fires preceded Jesus' appearance on the American continent. According to Mormonism, Jesus Christ showed himself to the people of America in the year 34. He ministered to them, selected twelve disciples, preached a second Sermon on the Mount, healed the sick, instituted "the sacrament" (bread and wine) and established a second church, paralleling the one in the Old World.[6] After informing the American Nephites that they were the "other sheep" of John 10:16, Jesus departed to visit yet more "other sheep," presumably the ten lost tribes of Israel.

The Book of Mormon story ends early in the fifth century. By the fourth century, war and carnage had consumed the faithful Nephites and reprobate Lamanites. After gathering hundreds

---

[6] Just as the Church established on Peter in Palestine was beginning to apostatize, so too this American Church would fall into total corruption within a couple of centuries.

of thousands of warriors to the Hill Cumorah (located in New York state), the Nephites were massacred by the sword by an even greater army of "dark and filthy" Lamanites,[7] who themselves lost thousands of men.

Only Moroni, the son of the Nephite prophet Mormon,[8] survived. To him his father had entrusted the centuries-old records of God's American prophets, to which Moroni added a few concluding chapters.[9] Before dying in 421, Moroni placed the gold plates in a stone and cement box and buried it in a hillside near present-day Palmyra, east of Rochester, New York.

The "Coming Forth" of the Book of Mormon

On April 6, 1830, more than fifty people, mostly members of the Smith and Whitmer families, gathered at the Whitmer[10] home in Fayette, New York. Smith was elected and ordained the first elder, a seer, prophet, translator, and apostle of the "Church of Christ." This was seen as only right, since he alone discovered, translated, and interpreted the fledgling church's founding text. Just ten years before, according to the *current* official Mormon accounts, the boy Smith had seen the Father and the Son in bodily form. Three years later, in 1823, Smith said an angel appeared

---

[7] Mormon 5:15. Mormons frequently identify contemporary Native Americans as descendants of these Lamanites. See *The Teachings of Spencer W. Kimball*, especially chapters 21–22.

[8] The Book of Mormon takes its name from this prophet, who had abridged the thousands of records kept by his predecessors. His son Moroni's image adorns the spires of many LDS temples.

[9] In Smith's day, several burning theological issues occupied the attention of scholar and layman alike. Such topics included the nature of religious authority and priesthood; the necessity of baptism; the validity of infant baptism; the administration of the Flesh and Blood of Christ. The thirteen pages of the book of Moroni neatly resolved all these disputes, which just happened to be the contemporary concerns of Smith's day.

[10] David Whitmer and his family were associates of Smith; David was one of the three witnesses to the Book of Mormon.

to him in his bedroom.[11] While praying, the seventeen-year-old Smith beheld a vision of Moroni, who appeared in brilliant light, wearing a white robe and hovering above the bed. This Moroni was the resurrected Nephite warrior and last custodian of the gold plates. He revealed that God had chosen Smith to discover and translate the record of America's ancient inhabitants. After quoting several chapters from the Bible, Moroni ascended to heaven. A short while later, Moroni returned and repeated his words exactly, "without the least variation." After leaving a second time, Moroni returned for a third visit that same night, again charging Smith with the same words. The following day, exhausted from his angelic visitations, Smith was returning home from work in the fields when he fell helpless to the ground. For a fourth time, Moroni appeared to him with the same message, this time adding that he should inform his father of the vision.

Joseph Smith, Sr., is said to have believed his son and told him to obey the angel's voice. After having heard four times the description of the plates' resting place, Smith had no trouble locating the hill and burial spot. He described seeing a large stone partially submerged in the dirt. After lifting the rock with a lever, he discovered a stone and cement box, in which lay the gold plates, a breastplate and the Urim and Thummim.[12] When Smith tried to remove the plates, Moroni appeared and stopped him, saying he could retrieve them only after another four years. In the meantime, Smith was to return to the same spot on the same day each year to receive further heavenly "instruction and intelligence."[13]

---

[11] According to the Mormon periodical, *Times and Seasons*, the angel's name was Nephi (vol. 3, 753). This was later changed to Moroni in the *History of the Church* 1:11. Both accounts are said to have been written by Smith.

[12] The Urim and Thummim are mentioned five times in the Old Testament. These were small objects, kept in a breast piece worn by the high priest and drawn out in the manner of lots to discern God's will and instruction (Ex. 28:30). For Smith, however, they were supposed to be an apparatus similar to reading glasses, only with stone lenses. This makes no sense when compared to the Old Testament texts mentioning them (1 Sam. 14:41-42).

[13] See Joseph Smith—History 1:27-54.

The religious revivals in the Palmyra area did not occur until 1824–1825, not in 1820 as Smith claimed. Since Smith linked his vision of the Father and the Son to the confusion he felt over competing preachers, "three years later" would be 1827 at the earliest for the first visitation of Moroni. Add to that the four years' waiting period before Smith could obtain the plates and the additional time for translating and publishing; 1832 would be the earliest the Book of Mormon could have come off the presses, two years too late for the 1830 edition that actually came out.

The 1824–1825 revival and the 1830 printing of the Book of Mormon are objective, documented facts. Smith's multiple visions and visits to the Hill Cumorah are not. But we do have verifiable information on the activities of the young man in the years between his visions and the publication of his book. On March 20, 1826, the twenty-year-old Smith was arrested and brought before Justice Albert Neely in Bainbridge, New York. He was found guilty of "glass looking" and fined. This date falls *after* his visions. From the First Vision and subsequent meetings with the angel, Smith learned that he had been chosen to restore the only true church to the earth; he was to preach repentance to all nations; he was to rely on the Lord for all things; he was to live worthily that he might obtain the golden scriptures. He was, in fact, to be the founding prophet of the final dispensation. Yet he had persisted as a "glass looker," trying to use occult powers to find things. Using seer stones, divining rods and other devices to locate supposed buried treasure was common for the time. Smith's father and older brothers also engaged in occult treasure hunting. Smith himself is reported to have used a witch hazel forked rod, though his medium of choice was an egg-shaped, chocolate-brown stone in which he claimed to see the locations of buried gold and silver. Such activities were illegal, and prosecution was more likely when the digging turned up nothing. Such was the case in Smith's 1826 trial. He had been hired to find a lost Spanish silver mine in northern Pennsylvania. Smith claimed to have located the spot with the help of his seer-stone and encouraged the diggers in their work. As the work progressed, however, and no treasure had been unearthed, Smith claimed a "powerful enchantment" had settled on the place to prevent the discovery.[14] Litigation ensued. In later years, when asked about this period in his life, Smith answered that he had indeed been a money digger, but that it was "not a very profitable job," for he "only got fourteen dollars a month for it."[15]

Some wonder that a man blessed with heavenly visits and instruction could persist in activities condemned in Scripture.[16] The Mormon response is benign. Smith said, "I am a rough stone. The sound of the hammer and chisel was never heard on me until the Lord took me in hand."[17] He was foolish; he was young; boys will be boys; everybody used peep stones in his day. But nobody else had conversed with God and Christ, had sat at the feet of heavenly messengers for spiritual tutorials. Nobody else had been chosen to bear the burden of restoring Christ's church after centuries of error and superstition. What else would constitute the Lord's refining hammer and chisel if not those years of instruction and formation? Smith did not undergo the life-changing experience of Paul upon his encounter with the Lord, which changed him instantly from a great persecutor to one of the greatest saints (Acts 9). The "boys will be boys" defense rings as hollow as Smith's money-digging abilities.

Smith's involvement with the occult is not the only puzzling behavior during the years between the First Vision and the printing of the Book of Mormon. Recall that Christ told the boy Smith to join no church, for they were all corrupt, all their creeds an abomination. Not one taught the truth. Yet there is evidence that Smith did in fact enter a probationary period with the Methodist church

---

[14] See *Inventing Mormonism*, 65ff.

[15] *Teachings of the Prophet Joseph Smith*, 120. Smith offers his own version of the Spanish mine failure in Joseph Smith—History 1:56.

[16] Deuteronomy 18:10–11: "There shall not be found among you any . . . that useth divination, or an observer of times, or an enchanter, or a witch, Or a charmer, or a consulter with familiar spirits, or a wizard, or a necromancer."

[17] *History of the Church* 5:423.

in 1828. His first-born son had just died; perhaps the bereaved father had looked to his wife's church for some comfort. Notice that this time comes after the official dating of 1827 for Smith's receipt of the gold plates: he would have been dallying with Methodism at the same time he was harboring and translating the ancient document. Furthermore, why was his wife Emma still a Methodist? They had married in January 1827, a few months before Smith took possession of the plates. If all churches were wrong, why wasn't Emma convinced enough to leave hers?[18] More confusing still is the religious affiliation of Smith's mother and brothers during most of the 1820s. Records of the Palmyra Presbyterian Church show that Lucy Mack Smith and her sons Hyrum and Samuel began to neglect "public worship and the sacrament of the Lord's supper" about September 1828. Still Presbyterians eight years after the official dating of the First Vision? Had Smith been unable to convince even his own family?[19]

As with Mormon theology, so with Mormon history: Multiple versions are ignored or explained away and earlier documents are edited or rewritten to "correct" teachings and incidents no longer considered to be "faith-promoting." Getting a straight story on Mormon doctrine and history proves as slippery to obtain as the elusive gold of "glass lookers."

The "Translation" of the Book of Mormon

After obtaining the gold plates, Smith related, he was beset on all sides by greedy and envious men. But by the grace of God and his own "extraordinary strength," Smith managed to retrieve the plates from their hiding place and carry them three miles to his home, all the while fighting off three separate attacks from armed men. The legend is made even more impressive since, by Mor-

---

[18] She did accept Mormon baptism three months after the Mormon church was organized. See references in *Mormonism—Shadow or Reality?* 162ff.

[19] See *No Man Knows My History*, 410-411.

mon reckoning, the plates weighed about sixty pounds.[20] Smith recorded that local persecution threatened his abilities to translate the "reformed Egyptian" of the plates. He and Emma were forced to move from Manchester, New York, to her father's home in Susquehanna county, Pennsylvania.[21] Once there, Smith employed his benefactor, Martin Harris, as his first scribe. One hundred and sixteen pages were translated, and Smith reluctantly[22] permitted Harris to bring the translation home to show his wife and others. This text was lost. (Some claim Mrs. Harris destroyed the pages to prevent her husband from further folly and financial loss.) The Lord, aggrieved by this callous disregard for his sacred work, sent an angel to take back the plates and the Urim and Thummim, leaving Smith to a short period of torment and regret. When the sacred objects were returned, Smith used his wife Emma as scribe, though her household chores gave her little time for the task. In answer to Smith's prayers, the Lord sent Cowdery, a distant relative and schoolteacher. Cowdery served as scribe for the bulk of the work that, according to Mormon history, took merely seventy-five working days.[23]

Descriptions of the method by which Smith "translated" the gold plates are as changeable and confusing as the rest of Mormon theology and history. Francis W. Kirkham, an authority on the Book of Mormon, said, "The conclusion is that no one knows the procedure or exact method of the translation. All that is known is contained in these words, 'It was translated by the gift and power of God, with the aid of the Urim and Thummim' (vol. 1, 196).

According to the *Encyclopedia of Mormonism*, Smith said that "it

---

[20] See Daniel H. Ludlow, *A Companion to Your Study of the Book of Mormon*, 18–21. Ludlow quotes from *History of Joseph Smith by His Mother, Lucy Mack Smith*.

[21] Joseph Smith—History 1:61.

[22] Smith had inquired of the Lord, who twice forbade him to surrender the pages. After Martin's persistent whining, however, Almighty God gave in. See D&C 3:12–15; B. H. Roberts, *Outlines of Ecclesiastical History*, 310; Ludlow, 23–24.

[23] See Francis W. Kirkham, *A New Witness for Christ in America*, vol. 1, 81.

was not intended to tell the world all the particulars of the coming forth of the Book of Mormon; and . . . it was not expedient for him to relate these things."[24]

However, Smith's wife Emma, David Whitmer, and Harris claimed Smith used his occult seer-stone or stones in the process of translating. Whitmer stated,

> I will now give you a description of the manner in which the Book of Mormon was translated. Joseph Smith would put the seer stone into a hat, and put his face in the hat, drawing it closely around his face to exclude the light; and in the darkness the spiritual light would shine. A piece of something resembling parchment would appear, and on that appeared writing. One character at a time would appear, and under it was the interpretation in English. Brother Joseph would read off the English to Oliver Cowdery, who was his principal scribe, and when it was written down and repeated to Brother Joseph to see if it was correct, then it would disappear, and another character with the interpretation would follow. Thus the Book of Mormon was translated by the gift and power of God, and not by any power of man [*An Address of All Believers in Christ*, 12].

Emma Smith said she "frequently wrote day after day, after sitting by the table close by him, he sitting with his face buried in his hat, with the stone in it, and dictating hour after hour with nothing between us."[25]

According to this version of the process, the plates were neither necessary nor even present during the translation process. Mormons make it clear that Smith knew no foreign language, including the so-called reformed Egyptian of the plates.[26] All the more

---

[24] "Book of Mormon Translation by Joseph Smith," *Encyclopedia of Mormonism*, vol. 1.

[25] *The Saints' Herald*, May 19, 1888, 310, quoted in Tanner, 41.

[26] It's puzzling that Lehi and his sons, all Palestinian Hebrews, would write in the language of their enemies, for at the time they left Palestine, Egypt was a threatening military power that warred across Judah. Even more strange is the fact that all the succeeding American Nephite prophets would have known and used, for a thousand years, a language totally unsupported by historical evidence. We *have* records written in Egyptian in this period, as well as long

remarkable, they say, that this unlettered youngster could have produced such a work. Only the power of God could do it.[27]

We find here a trait common to the book and translation process. In all things, the Book of Mormon must outdo the Bible. The wars are more fierce, the victories more glorious.[28] While in Palestine, three hours of darkness accompanied Christ's death; in America, it was three days. In the Bible, Thomas is invited to touch the resurrected Lord. In the Book of Mormon, a multitude approached him, one by one, for a tangible witness. And in the translation of these books, we are assured that, though the Bible has been subjected to the errors of mistranslation and even outright treachery, the Book of Mormon was translated under divine inspiration. Jesus Christ himself imparted divine approbation to Smith's work as a translator.[29]

According to the rote dictation account by Emma Smith, Whitmer and Harris, there could be little room for doubting the validity of the English translation, on the *assumption* that Smith's claims were true. A word or phrase appeared on the seer stone, Smith read it aloud to the scribe, who then repeated it. If accurate, the process would continue. If not, Smith would repeat the translation. What greater case could be made for the plenary verbal inspiration of scripture? Yet we'll see that thousands of changes have been made to the Book of Mormon, some by Smith in his lifetime, others as recently as 1981.

A second version of the translation process, one with greater appeal to modern Mormon scholars, has Smith pondering a passage

---

before and after, and there is no trace of the language the Book of Mormon was written in.

[27] Most LDS scholars conclude that Smith employed the Urim and Thummim, the name frequently given to his seer stone. They also agree that Smith brought no other books or papers to his translation sessions.

[28] In Alma 56–58, we read of two thousand righteous boys sent into battle against the Lamanites. Though the enemy suffered severe casualties, not one of the young men was slain.

[29] See D&C 1:29 and 20:8.

or message, then rendering it into the idiom of the day according to his best, divinely aided efforts. That he was neither a linguist nor grammarian is of no account. The account is true, though individual words may betray poor diction or spelling. Rather than acting as an impassive conduit through which the correct translation flowed, Smith is said to have studied it out in his mind, finally asking for divine approval of his work (D&C 9:8). In this way, Mormon apologists avoid difficult questions of anachronism and plagiarism.[30]

Smith remained vague on the subject of translation, though according to eyewitness accounts, he used a seer stone. These accounts are finessed by current church spokesmen.[31] What we don't have are the plates themselves. (Moroni took them back for good after the translation was made.) We don't have a single record of "reformed Egyptian," on this or any other continent. So we have no means of independently verifying Smith's work. This is completely unlike our ability to authenticate the text of the Old and New Testaments. Though we have no original monographs, we have translations of biblical books much closer in age to the originals than any other document of antiquity. We have also the means of comparing the text and its translation with other writings in ancient Hebrew, Aramaic, and Greek. We have tangible, ac-

---

[30] Stephen D. Ricks, of BYU, argues for a combination of methods. See "Translation of the Book of Mormon: Interpreting the Evidence," in *Journal of Book of Mormon Studies*, Fall 1993, 201–206.

[31] Apostle Neal A. Maxwell summed up the conflicting descriptions: "Perhaps the details of translation are withheld also because we are intended to immerse ourselves in the substance of the book rather than becoming unduly concerned with the process by which we received it" ("By the Gift and Power of God," *Ensign*, January 1997, 41). The text is accompanied by an illustration showing Smith seated before the gold plates, with Cowdery taking dictation less than two feet away. Smith does not appear to be using the Urim and Thummim and the plates are not hidden from Cowdery. This does not match the descriptions of the process given by Smith's scribes.

cessible manuscripts written in known, translatable languages[32]—not the airy, vanishing, "golden plate" manuscript behind Smith's "translation."

Who Wrote the Book of Mormon?

There are several theories. Some progressive Mormons believe the Book of Mormon to be inspired writing, though not historical. They say it is primarily a work of Smith (and possible collaborators), meant to be a nineteenth-century commentary on Scripture. It was subsequently blessed by God and went forth to the world as additional scripture. While not depicting actual history, it is an extended parable of God's love for all nations. By abandoning insistence on the book's ancient origin, Mormons are freed from the impossible task of defending its many archaeological, geographical, and linguistic anomalies, and can concentrate on its spiritual message.[33] Orthodox Mormons reject this liberal position with its anti-historical bias.

Over the past century and a half, various works have been advanced as possible sources of the Book of Mormon. One currently popular theory is that Smith knew of and borrowed freely from Ethan Smith's *View of the Hebrews*, published in 1823, with a second edition in 1825. B.H. Roberts noted that "it is more than likely that the Smith family possessed a copy of this book . . . that either by reading it, or hearing it read, and its contents frequently discussed, Joseph Smith became acquainted with its contents."[34]

Roberts finds that the material in *View of the Hebrews* "is of a character and quantity to make a ground plan for the Book of Mormon" (op. cit., 240). For example, both books assert the Hebrew

---

[32] See Henry G. Graham, *Where We Got the Bible*, 48ff.

[33] This approach is typified by Anthony A. Hutchinson in "The Word of God is Enough: The Book of Mormon as Nineteenth-Century Scripture," *New Approaches to the Book of Mormon*, 1–19.

[34] *Studies of the Book of Mormon*, 155.

origin of the American Indians. Both works draw heavily from the prophet Isaiah. Both discuss Jerusalem's destruction and the remnant's dispersion. The founding parties split into the civilized and good and the barbaric and evil, with prolonged war between them a dominant theme. The forces of evil ultimately defeat the righteous party in both books. Both works display anachronisms in their treatment of ancient American art, language, navigation, and metalwork. Both stories employ the use of objects similar to the Hebrew Urim and Thummim. Ethan Smith quotes a "lost book of God" that is to come forth in the future; Joseph Smith brings forth such a book (ibid., 240–242).

The Book of Mormon's earliest editions betrayed many spelling, grammar, and punctuation errors. Whether these were the fault of Smith, his scribes, or the printer is not the point. They are not the crux of the problem. Rather, was it possible that Smith could create, either by reworking others' writings or composing from scratch, the story we find in the Book of Mormon? Roberts said it was.

"[W]as Joseph Smith possessed," Roberts asked, "of a sufficiently vivid and creative imagination as to produce such a work as the Book of Mormon from such materials as have been indicated . . . from such common knowledge as was extant in the communities where he lived in his boyhood and young manhood; from the Bible, and more especially from the *View of the Hebrews*, by Ethan Smith? That such power of imagination would have to be of a high order is conceded; that Joseph Smith possessed such a gift of mind there can be no question" (ibid. 243).

The Book of Mormon's inaccuracies contradict both reason and faith. The Mormon hierarchy has given up trying to prove the geography, archaeology, and anthropology of the text, requiring, instead, a redoubling of members' wholly subjective spiritual "testimonies." The theology presented in the book ignores most Mormon doctrines, making it hard to describe it as the "fulness of the [Mormon] gospel" it was claimed to be (D&C 20:9). It also denies orthodox Christian teachings on the Godhead, the nature of the atonement, infant baptism and the Eucharist.

Mormon leaders recently added to the Book of Mormon the subtitle, "Another Testament of Jesus Christ."[35] It might more accurately be called, "A Testament to Another Christ" and to a church not his own.

---

[35] This is itself a historical anachronism. In the historical sense, a "testament" is not a set of books but a covenant. When we use the phrase "Old Testament" and "New Testament" we are using abbreviations, a verbal short-hand, for the longer designations "the Books of the Old Testament" (that is, the divine covenant made through Moses) and "the Books of the New Testament" (that is, the divine covenant made through Christ). The Book of Mormon's new subtitle, however, uses the term "testament" in an anachronistic sense that apparently ignores its historical origin and proper use.

30. Arguments Made on Behalf of the Book of Mormon

While dictating the Book of Mormon, Smith discovered there were to be three special witnesses who would know that it was true.[1] A further revelation from Christ confirmed that these three would add their testimony to Smith's (D&C 5:11).[2] The three men chosen to attest to the reality of the gold plates were Cowdery, Harris, and Whitmer. Mormon hagiography would have us believe these men were known for "truthfulness and sobriety."[3] Widtsoe wrote, "The Book of Mormon plates were seen and handled, at different times, by eleven competent men, of independent minds and spotless reputations, who published a formal statement of their experience."[4]

Two separate testimonials are printed at the front of the Book of Mormon. The first is the word of the three witnesses already mentioned; the second is the statement of eight additional men.

The Three Witnesses

Cowdery, Whitmer, and Harris said "an angel of God came down from heaven, and he brought and laid before our eyes, that we be-

---

[1] See 2 Nephi 27:12–13. Verse twelve states that "none shall behold it save it be that three witnesses shall behold it." The Lord amends himself in the next verse: "There is none other which shall view it, save it be a few according to the will of God."

[2] Three verses later the Lord says "to none else will I grant this power, to receive this same testimony among this generation."

[3] "Book of Mormon Witnesses," *Encyclopedia of Mormonism*, vol. 1.

[4] *Joseph Smith—Seeker After Truth*, 338; quoted in *Mormonism—Shadow or Reality?* 52.

held and saw the plates, and the engravings thereon." This supernatural marvel, they claimed, was shown to them "by the power of God, and not of man."[5] These three were emotionally primed for the part. Smith related how, upon learning there were to be three witnesses, they importuned him "to inquire of the Lord to know if they might not obtain of him the privilege to be these three special witnesses." Their pleas became so urgent that Smith complied. He received, in answer, a reply from the Lord. "It is by your faith that you shall obtain a view of them," Christ told the three.[6] All three men desired this renowned preferment. But when they retired to the woods with Smith, nothing happened. So they prayed longer and harder, each crying out in turn for the divine confirmation. At one point, Harris left the group, believing himself to be the obstacle to their prayers. Moments later, Smith recorded, a light descended upon him, Cowdery, and Whitmer, and an angel appeared holding the gold plates. A heavenly voice confirmed that Smith's translation was correct. Smith then went in search of Harris, who asked for Smith's assistance in prayer. Smith had the same vision, and Harris exclaimed ecstatically, "Mine eyes have beheld, mine eyes have beheld."[7]

Current Mormon doctrine argues that the Book of Mormon is a literal translation from literal gold plates; therefore, the witnesses saw physical plates with their physical eyes. But an equally literal reading of the account, written by Smith himself, could lead us to conclude this incident was, at most, a psychological or emotional movement brought about by fervent wishing and insightful coaching. If the three witnesses were to verify his work, why didn't Smith just show them the plates? He still had the plates in his possession.[8]

As for the three witnesses, the forty-six-year-old Harris was the oldest. He was religiously inconstant before his conversion

---

[5] From the testimony printed in the front of the Book of Mormon.
[6] D&C 17; see also *History of the Church* 1:51-53.
[7] *History of the Church* 1:54-55.
[8] See Ludlow, 32.

to Mormonism[9] and subsequently as well.[10] Because of his criticism of Smith's financial dealings, Smith excommunicated him in 1837, though he was rebaptized in 1842. Cut off from it yet again, Harris joined and left several splinter "Mormon" groups, as well as the Shakers.[11] According to research by the Tanners, Harris's ultimate return to the Mormon church five years before his death was motivated by deepening poverty and loneliness (his family had left him in Ohio and gone to Utah) and the prospects of a restored place of honor among Mormons.[12]

Cowdery, the Mormon church's "Second Elder," worked closely with Smith not only in the dictation of the Book of Mormon but in the defining episodes of the early Mormon movement.[13] Like Smith, his cousin, Cowdery possessed a magical mindset and was adept at using a forked divining rod before he met Smith in 1829.[14] Cowdery was excommunicated in 1838, allegedly for forgery and dishonesty, and for speaking ill of the Lord's prophet. In fact, Cowdery had accused Smith of "a dirty, nasty, filthy affair" with an orphaned teenaged girl living in the Smith home. It was a charge he never recanted.[15] The Tanners have gathered documentation indicating Cowdery joined the Methodist church after his expulsion from Mormonism. According to this material, Cowdery

---

[9] Before his conversion to Mormonism, he was a Quaker, a Baptist, a Presbyterian and believed in universalism.

[10] Along with Cowdery and Whitmer, Harris had also given support to a dancing seeress and her black seer stone. See Brodie, 205.

[11] See *Millennial Star* 8:124. This American utopian group was led by Ann B. Lee, who described herself as Jesus Christ in his second coming. The Shakers also had a divinely revealed text, *A Holy, Sacred and Divine Roll and Book: From the Lord God of Heaven, to the Inhabitants of Earth*, published in 1843, to which Harris is said to have given as much credence as he had the Book of Mormon. See *The Case Against Mormonism*, vol. 2, 50ff.

[12] *The Case Against Mormonism*, vol. 2, 30–31.

[13] See Joseph Smith—History 1:68ff.

[14] D. Michael Quinn, *Early Mormonism and the Magic World View*, 84–86.

[15] The girl, Fannie Alger, was later listed as the first of Smith's plural wives. See Brodie, 182, 458. See *History of the Church* 3:16ff.

made a "full and final renunciation" of his Mormon beliefs, and was "sorry and ashamed of his connection with Mormonism."[16] That he may further have disavowed the Book of Mormon could be inferred from the words of a poem printed in the Latter-day Saints' journal *Times and Seasons*:

> Or Book of Mormon not his [God's] word Because denied, by Oliver?[17]

Cowdery was rebaptized into the Mormon church in 1848, but he died—without having received his endowments—in 1850. Cowdery remained disaffected with the Utah church to the end, according to Whitmer,[18] who was excommunicated in 1838 for having a "dissenting spirit." He never returned to the Mormon church. Rather, he first lent support to dissident groups and later formed his own church, based on the Book of Mormon but rejecting Smith as a fallen prophet and many of the doctrines Smith promulgated in later years.[19]

Though the witnesses are portrayed as sensible and forthright men by Mormon apologists, Smith himself held a different view. He called Harris a "wicked man."[20] All three, Smith wrote, "are too mean to mention; and we had liked to have forgotten them."[21] Whitmer, apparently a spokesman for some dissenters, was called a "dumb ass" who "prays out cursings instead of blessings."[22]

Mormons make much of the fact that these three men, though excommunicated from the Mormon church, never denied their

---

[16] *The Case Against Mormonism*, vol. 2, 15–16. Also, *The Mormon Hierarchy: Origins of Power*, 545.

[17] Vol. 2, 482. The context, briefly, is that denials do not negate a truth. Though my watch is broken, that does not prove there is no time.

[18] *The Mormon Hierarchy: Origins of Power*, 545.

[19] *Encyclopedia of Mormonism*, vol. 4.

[20] Actually, it was the Lord who had so branded Harris. Smith was simply recording a revelation he had received. See D&C 3:12; 10:1, 7.

[21] *History of the Church* 3:231–232. Smith's list also included John Whitmer, one of the eight witnesses.

[22] Ibid., 228.

testimonies of the gold plates. We've seen that this may not be true in the case of Cowdery. We don't know all of the things they said in these periods. What we do know is that unlike the apostles of Christ, they did not remain true and valiant witnesses to what they had supposedly seen. Unlike the apostles, who went to their deaths proclaiming Christ, the three Mormon witnesses became disaffected and fell away. All three were highly suggestible and ripe for spiritual exploitation. We have no evidence that professional convert Harris ever denied his testimony of Shakerism, either. Cowdery's religiously excitable nature is shown in his claim to have seen the plates in a vision before he ever met Smith.[23] And if the Mormon church extols Whitmer's witness, it must also contend with his statement, made the year before his death: "If you believe my testimony to the Book of Mormon; if you believe that God spake to us three witnesses by his own voice, then I tell you that in June, 1838, God spake to me again by his own voice from the heavens, and told me to "separate myself from among the Latter Day Saints. . . . In the spring of 1838, the heads of the church and many of the members had gone deep into error and blindness."[24]

Cowdery, Whitmer, and Harris fell under the sway of Smith's charismatic enthusiasm. Their own credulous natures, combined with a hunger for novelty and favor, led them to accept uncritically what was, at best, a self-induced emotional episode.[25] This same gullible spirit and desire for position provided incentive for them not to repudiate their Book of Mormon testimonies.[26]

---

[23] Dean Jessee, *The Papers of Joseph Smith*, vol. 1, 10.

[24] *An Address to All Believers in Christ*, 27.

[25] I don't, however, wish to make light of Whitmer's testimony, in particular. He produced several conflicting statements. See, for example, Daniel C. Peterson's review of *Mormonism*, by Kurt Van Gorden, in *FARMS Review of Books*, Volume 8, Number 1, 1996, 99ff.

[26] David Whitmer became president of his own church, one which accepted the truth of the Book of Mormon but rejected Joseph Smith and most of his later revelations, including polygamy. Martin Harris eventually returned to a church eager to honor him and claim him again as its own.

The Eight Witnesses

For some reason, Smith found it expedient to add eight more testimonies to those of the original three witnesses, though Christ had told Smith, "And to none else [but the three witnesses] will I grant this power, to receive this same testimony among this generation" (D&C 5:14).

This time the witnesses included Joseph Smith, Sr., Joseph's brothers Hyrum and Samuel, and Hiram Page (married to David Whitmer's sister), who comprised one group. The other four were David's brothers: Christian, Jacob, Peter, Jr., and John.[27] Another Whitmer sister was married to Cowdery. Thus, all the witnesses, except financial benefactor Martin Harris, were closely related.

Mormon missionaries tell you these eight men both saw and handled the plates. In fact, according to another Smith brother, William, his father and brothers and the others "hefted" only something covered with a sack. John Whitmer seems to be the only one to give an independent statement that he handled the plates uncovered. Yet he, too, stated that they were shown to him "by a supernatural power."[28] If the plates were physical objects in Smith's possession, what need is there for heavenly assistance in seeing them?

As for the character of the eight witnesses, Page produced his own seer stone and made prophecies, leading Whitmer and Cowdery also astray. Though they did not deny their testimonies, Jacob Whitmer and Page apostatized from the Mormon church; John Whitmer was excommunicated. By 1847, all eleven witnesses were either dead or had joined competing sects.[29]

---

[27] Mormon iconography presents these eight men as one group, gathered around a tree stump on which sits the stack of gold plates. According to John Whitmer, however, the plates were "seen" by two separate groups of four men.

[28] *History of the Church* 3:307.

[29] See *The Mormon Hierarchy*, 188.

A statement by Mormonism's second prophet may add additional perspective. Though the Mormon church presents the witnesses' testimony as firm and constant, Young noted, "Some of the witnesses of the Book of Mormon, who handled the plates and conversed with angels of God, were afterwards left to doubt and to disbelieve that they had ever seen an angel. One of the Quorum of twelve[30]—a young man full of faith and good works, prayed, and the vision of his mind was opened, and the angel of God came and laid the plates before him, and he saw and handled them, and saw the angel, and conversed with him as he would with one of his friends; but after all this, he was left to doubt, and plunged into apostasy, and has continue [sic] to contend against this work. There are hundreds in a similar condition."[31]

Who "some of the witnesses" were is not specified, though the Mormon church proclaims only eleven official witnesses. Yet Young claims some (hundreds?) of those who actually spoke with angels and handled the plates later doubted and disbelieved this experience. It's not any more difficult to talk yourself *into* believing in something as *out of* believing in it once the former is done.

Biblical Support for the Book of Mormon?

Mormons try to conscript several Bible passages that they believe prove the Bible spoke of another inspired work which was to be brought forth in the "latter days."

Ezekiel 37:15–17: "*The word of the* LORD *came again unto me, saying, Moreover, thou son of man, take thee one stick, and write upon it, For Judah, and for the children of Israel his companions: then take another stick, and write upon it, For Joseph, the stick of Ephraim, and for all the*

---

[30] None of the eleven witnesses served in the Quorum of the Twelve Apostles.
[31] *Journal of Discourses* 7:164.

house of Israel his companions: And join them one to another into one stick; and they shall become one in thine hand."

Mormons rely greatly on this as a proof text to demonstrate not only the possibility of divine scripture aside from the Bible, but also the Book of Mormon's doctrinal equality with it. They assume that the "stick of Judah" is the Bible, while the "stick of Joseph" is the Book of Mormon. In these, the latter days, the two have been joined together, forming the bulk of Mormon scripture.

Mormonism's professed literal interpretation of Scripture does not extend to hundreds of passages it rejects as corrupted or that it skews to suit its own purposes. In the case of Ezekiel 37, Mormons not only neglect the plain sense of the words but also ignore their true interpretation, given by God, in the very same chapter.[32]

First, the Hebrew term translated as "stick" (*aits*) is never used anywhere in the Old Testament to mean "book," "scroll," "writing" or anything similar. It is variously translated as "wood" or "branch," "timber" or "tree."[33]

Second, Ezekiel 37:16 refers to the prophet's writing on a second stick "For Joseph." It is Ezekiel, not Smith or any imputed Book of Mormon author, who is to do the writing.[34] Even granting the Mormon attempt to use "stick" to refer to scrolls, the Book of Mormon is said to have been engraved on metal plates, not wrapped around "sticks."

Third, the correct interpretation of this symbolic action of the prophet is given just a few verses later. Ezekiel is to take the two sticks, put them end to end and hold the joined ends in his hand. He thus displays to the people a "single" stick, once again united.

---

[32] In fact, LeGrand Richards speaks of how "simple" and "direct" this Old Testament passage is in its foretelling of the Book of Mormon. See *A Marvelous Work and a Wonder*, 67–68.

[33] See 1 Kings 17:12; 2 Kings 6:1–7. Mormons may counter that parchment was written on and then wound around sticks, producing scrolls, but the Hebrew term for this is always *sepher*, never *aits*.

[34] Moreover, if "For Judah" refers to the Bible, we cannot grant that Ezekiel is its sole author—or Judah, who wrote none of it.

That is to say, the scattered remnants of the Southern ("Judah") and Northern ("Joseph") kingdoms of Israel will be returned from exile, restored to their land, and made one nation again: "They shall be no more two nations, neither shall they be divided into two kingdoms any more at all" (Ezek. 37:22).

With divine impetus, Ezekiel first spoke this parable of redemption then enacted it. Only Mormonism can manage to mistake "timber" for "scrolls" and "nations" for "metal plates."[35]

Take a look at the entire passage, and in a more modern translation: "The word of the LORD came to me: 'Son of man, take a stick and write on it, "For Judah, and the children of Israel associated with him;" then take another stick and write upon it, "For Joseph (the stick of Ephraim) and all the house of Israel associated with him;" and join them together into one stick, that they may become one in your hand. And when your people say to you, "Will you not show us what you mean by these?" say to them, Thus says the Lord GOD: Behold, I am about to take the stick of Joseph (which is in the hand of Ephraim) and the tribes of Israel associated with him; and I will join with it the stick of Judah, and make them one stick, that they may be one in my hand. When the sticks on which you write are in your hand before their eyes, then say to them, Thus says the Lord GOD: Behold, I will take the people of Israel from the nations among which they have gone, and will gather them from all sides, and bring them to their own land; and I will make them one nation in the land, upon the mountains of Israel; and one king shall be king over them all; and they shall be no longer two nations, and no longer divided into two kingdoms. They shall not defile themselves any more with their idols and their detestable things, or with any of their transgressions; but I will save them from all the backslidings in which they have sinned, and will cleanse them; and they shall be my people, and I will be their God" (Ezek. 37:15–23, RSV).

---

[35] Recall Christ's treatment of the parable of the Sower and the Seed: He later explained clearly to his followers the meaning of his lesson. We see the exact process at work in this passage from Ezekiel: divine message, followed by divine explanation. No other rendering is permitted.

As the text makes clear, this is a prophecy of national reunification, not about the appearance of hidden scriptures.

Isaiah 29:4: "And thou shalt be brought down, and shalt speak out of the ground, and thy speech shall be low out of the dust, and thy voice shall be, as of one that hath a familiar spirit, out of the ground, and thy speech shall whisper out of the dust."

Latter-day Saints say Smith, as a teenager in upstate New York, was chosen by God to bring back to earth the true church, long lost in apostasy and error. Part of this restoration was to include the bringing forth of additional scriptures. The first of these, Smith was told, would be found buried in a hill near his farm. On gold plates he would find ancient writings by prophets who lived on the American continent between 600 B.C. and A.D. 421.

Apostle LeGrand Richards noted the "obvious" interpretation of Isaiah: "[T]he only way a dead people could speak 'out of the ground' or 'low out of the dust' would be by the written word, and this people did through the Book of Mormon. Truly it has a familiar spirit for it contains the words of the prophets of the God of Israel."[36]

There are a number of problems with this, not the least of which is the fact that Richards, along with most other Mormon apologists, apparently did not know the meaning of the term "familiar spirit," leading to his misapplication of it. A familiar spirit—a term especially common in King James-era English—is a supernatural spirit or demon that attends a person, such as a witch or medium, often in the form of an animal. Thus cats used to be regarded as common forms for the familiar spirits of witches to take.

Nevertheless, for Mormons, the passage means that ancient inhabitants of the Americas (who were, according to Mormon theology, fully Christian) speak to us today from the pages of writings they wrote and preserved. These were then discovered, translated and published by Smith. Their message is "familiar" to all those who have already had the Bible preached to them.

---

[36] *A Marvelous Work and a Wonder*, 68.

Let's look to the context. The "thou" first referred to in verse four is spoken to "Ariel, the city where David dwelt" (v. 1)—as such, it is the city of Jerusalem. The Lord, through Isaiah, warns this once-noble city (Jerusalem) that it will be besieged and brought to a bitter end. The city in which sacrifices were burnt on the altar of the temple will itself become an altar, its inhabitants the unwilling holocaust. It will become the altar hearth of God.[37] God's unfaithful people, brought down to the ground, will "whisper" to all who will hear: "This is the punishment for our sins." The term "whisper" was often used of speech racked by direst fear and shock. In the same way, it applied to the shrill voice used to communicate with the spirit world. Thus the reference to a "familiar spirit," which Richards completely misunderstands. The Hebrew term involved—*owb*—appears in the Old Testament over a dozen times, each in a context of spiritism, mediums, or sorcery[38]—indicating either the necromancer who has the familiar spirit or the familiar spirit itself. The message in this case: Just as it is vain to practice necromancy, in vain will the punished people of Jerusalem cry out for relief. Their collective voice will mimic the impotent murmuring of a necromancer channeling his familiar.

The passage is thus a prophecy of the siege of Jerusalem, not of the reappearance of hidden scriptures.

Isaiah 29:11–12: "*And the vision of all is become unto you as the words of a book that is sealed, which men deliver to one that is learned, saying, Read this, I pray thee: and he saith, I cannot; for it is sealed: And the book is delivered to him that is not learned, saying, Read this, I pray thee: and he saith, I am not learned.*"

In the course of "translating" the Book of Mormon, Smith copied onto paper some characters he said were on the gold plates. He

---

[37] One meaning for "Ariel" is altar hearth/hearth of God. Cf. *A New Catholic Commentary on Holy Scripture*, 586.

[38] See, for instance, Deuteronomy 18:9–12; 1 Chronicles 10:13; 2 Chronicles 33:6; Isaiah 8:19.

gave this sample to Harris and asked him to bring it to New York City, to a Columbia professor named Charles Anthon. Mormons claim Anthon read the original characters (written, Smith said, in reformed Egyptian—an imaginary language never known to any linguist nor discovered by any archaeologist), comparing them with Smith's translation. Supposedly, he pronounced it correct. When he asked Harris to see the rest of the original, Harris informed him that he could not, since the plates were sealed and revealed only to Smith. Anthon is then quoted as saying, "I cannot read a sealed book" (Joseph Smith—History 1:65). "Professor Anthon did not realize that he was literally fulfilling the prophecy of Isaiah," Richards wrote.[39]

Not surprisingly, Professor Anthon's version is different. Roberts, in his *Comprehensive History of the Church*, cites a letter written by Anthon to anti-Mormon writer E. D. Howe a few years after the incident. In it the professor stated, "Upon examining the paper in question, I soon came to the conclusion that it was all a trick—perhaps a hoax.... The paper contained anything else but Egyptian hieroglyphics" (vol. 1, 101, 103).

Not only is Professor Anthon being misused in the service of Mormon apologetics, so is the text of Isaiah. Not only is the verse pulled from its context, but not one of its elements corresponds to Mormon eisegesis.[40] Isaiah was addressing the hard-hearted who refused to listen to a prophet's warning. What he called "sealed" was not a book but the ears and eyes of those who rejected the Lord. Further, according to Harris, Anthon read the translation and pronounced it correct. According to Isaiah, the learned man *cannot* read the text. Finally, according to Mormonism, the book went first to Smith, the unlearned man who translates it, and only later did a small portion of it go to the professor. In Isaiah, the learned man first receives the book and fails; only then is it delivered to the unlearned—who also fails. Nothing is said of a translation. Look at the passage in a more recent translation: "And the

---

[39] *A Marvelous Work and a Wonder*, 50.

[40] Eisegesis, reading something that is not there into a text due to the influence of an agenda.

vision of all this [the siege and deliverance of Jerusalem] has become to you like the words of a book that is sealed. When men give it to one who can read, saying, 'Read this,' he says, 'I cannot, for it is sealed.' And when they give the book to one who cannot read, saying, 'Read this,' he says, 'I cannot read'" (Is. 29:11–12, RSV).

We're at a loss, then, to understand in what "literal" sense this passage is fulfilled by the events reported at the time of the Book of Mormon's creation. Read plainly and in context the verses are simple to understand. The people of Jerusalem have refused to listen to the prophecy announced to them of their own deliverance from the coming siege of Jerusalem, which occurred in 701 B.C., when the Assyrians came and seemed about to conquer Jerusalem, yet suddenly, mysteriously were unable to finish the siege. This was the "marvellous work and a wonder" (Is. 29:14) that God performed for Judah—providing deliverance at the last minute, confounding the wisdom of the wise, who all expected the city to fall.

Mormons and others who misuse Scripture take a variety of approaches. One is to read selectively, picking and choosing among those passages which appear to conform to their predetermined theology. A second, more subtle distortion of Scripture orchestrates the present to make it appear to conform to the biblical record. Calling Mormon church offices the same names as those used in the early Church is one example. Some scholars, including active Mormons, have doubts about the accuracy of the official version of the Anthon meeting.[41]

2 Corinthians 13:1: "This is the third time I am coming to you. In the mouth of two or three witnesses shall every word be established."

The footnote to this verse in the Mormon Bible cites Deuteronomy 19:15 and refers to the Book of Mormon. To Mormons, the Bible stands as one (flawed and incomplete) witness to Jesus

---

[41] See Sidney B. Sperry, *The Problems of the Book of Mormon*, 55–56. Also, Jerald and Sandra Tanner, *Mormonism—Shadow or Reality?* 105–106.

Christ, while the Book of Mormon is an additional, "most correct" testimony. Again, Mormonism and its reputed literalism miss the literal and fuller meanings. Paul is admonishing the Corinthians: He has spoken to them twice, and intends to return for a third visit, confirming them once again in the gospel he first preached. There is no talk of books at all.

More importantly, Latter-day Saints overlook the fact that the Bible already presents the testimony of not two or three, but dozens of witnesses to God's saving actions in Christ. From Moses through the apostles, the sacred authors recorded in prophecy, in vision and in eyewitness accounts the life, ministry, death and resurrection of Christ. Most of these men sealed their testimonies with martyrs' deaths. No stronger confirmation could be made for the divinity of Jesus Christ than that of Matthew, John, and Paul. There's no need for extra-biblical reports.[42] Jude, an Apostle and eyewitness to Christ, makes it clear that the "common salvation"—that which is available to all people—"was once for all delivered to the saints" (Jude 3, RSV). The testimony of these holy men was enough to convince them that Jesus was the Son of God and Savior. Christians didn't need the Book of Mormon then to affirm their faith in the Lord. They didn't need it throughout centuries of persecution; they didn't need it to establish vast missionary and humanitarian services; they didn't need it to achieve lofty and even miraculous heights of sanctity. And they don't need it now.

John 10:16: "And other sheep I have, which are not of this fold: them also I must bring, and they shall hear my voice; and there shall be one fold, and one shepherd."

Mormon footnotes teach that these words of Christ were fulfilled when, after his death and resurrection, he visited the Americas to establish a church among the Nephites who had migrated there

---

[42] Though substantial information from contemporary Jewish and pagan sources supports biblical accounts, including those of the Lord's life and death, no such support exists for any Book of Mormon event.

centuries before.⁴³ These lost sheep were supposedly the descendants of Hebrews who had fled Jerusalem and journeyed to America at the time of Jeremiah. The Book of Mormon purports to be the religious and historical records of these ancient "Christians" (as they called themselves, even before the coming of Jesus), written and preserved by American counterparts of Hebrew prophets.

Under the rubric, "God is no respecter of persons" (Acts 10:34), the Mormon church finds its rationale for the above interpretation and argues that God deals fairly with all his children. Since Christ was sent to Palestine to teach and establish a church among the Jews there, it was only right that he come also to the Americas and establish a church there as well. As so often is the case with Mormon arguments, if they prove anything, they prove too much. The "God is no respecter of persons" principle, both in Acts 10 and elsewhere (Rom. 2:11), is applied in a specifically Jewish-Gentile context, showing that God treats all groups fairly. Thus a Mormon could not limit the "no respecter of persons" principle to just those who are members of the house of Israel (Old World or New World Israel). It includes all men, everywhere. If, because of this principle, he had to come to North America and start a church to be fair to the people there, then he would have to visit every continent, and all the peoples on those continents, and start new, independent churches everywhere, in order to show that he is no respecter of persons.⁴⁴

The logical alternative is to say that God shows his grace by starting a single, unified church—somewhere—that is to receive all men, Jew and Gentile. By having a single church, when it ex-

---

⁴³ See 3 Nephi, beginning at 10:18.

⁴⁴ Some Mormons hint that there may be a third locale that has yet to be discovered. Maxwell stated, "How many folds there are we know not." See *Not My Will, But Thine*, 52. Maxwell even asserts that yet another corpus of scripture will come forth from these other folds, adding a third voice of testimony to that of the Bible and the Book of Mormon. See *Plain and Precious Things*, 12. However, even Mormons do not claim that Jesus directly founded a church for each geographically separated people in the first century, which would be the logical conclusion of their take on the "no respecter of persons" principle.

pands, men will have no doubt about which one they are to join. Until the time that this church reaches them, they will be judged based on whatever knowledge of God they have—however much or little that may be—and their willingness to follow his truth if they had known what it was. The "other sheep" Jesus mentions are the righteous Gentiles, who did not belong to the "fold" of God's chosen people, Israel, but who would respond to the gospel when preached to them. While Christ's earthly ministry served the Jewish people almost exclusively, his great commission to the apostles before his ascension sent them into all the world to preach, baptize and thus unite his believers in one fold (Matt. 27:19). Because "he that heareth you heareth me" (Luke 10:16), to hear the gospel from the lips of his disciples is to hear Jesus himself.

The understanding of the "other sheep" as the Gentiles who would come to believe in Christ is the natural understanding of the passage. Mormons sometimes ask Christians, "If the 'other sheep' weren't in the New World, then who were they?" In response, a Christian often will be perplexed at the fact the question was asked and say, "Well, they're the Gentile Christians, of course. How could anyone think the text suggests otherwise?" The New Testament has a running theme of how salvation comes from the Jews to the Gentiles. It appears across multiple books, in all of the Gospels and most of the epistles. Jesus' statement about gathering other sheep in the future is simply one more instance of the gospels dealing with this theme.

The fact that Mormons sometimes do not spot the obvious, face-value interpretation of the text reveals how little Mormons have been exposed to the historic understanding of the passage and how little they have been encouraged to think through its rationale. They have not tried to understand the New Testament as a whole, integrating and understanding its individual passages with other passages and with the general historical backdrop. Instead, they have had the interpretations of certain alleged proof texts force-fed to them in a way that keeps them from knowing of the existence of other, more plausible interpretations.

Personal Subjectivism: Moroni 10:3-4

Eager Mormon missionaries present people with copies of the Book of Mormon and ask them to read selected passages. A favorite portion presents the prophet Moroni exhorting the readers of the book, "Behold, I would exhort you that when ye shall read these things, if it be wisdom in God that ye should read them, that ye would remember how merciful the Lord hath been unto the children of men, from the creation of Adam even down unto the time that ye shall receive these things, and ponder it in your hearts. And when ye shall receive these things, I would exhort you that ye would ask God, the Eternal Father, in the name of Christ, if these things are not true; and if ye shall ask with a sincere heart, with real intent, having faith in Christ, he will manifest the truth of it unto you, by the power of the Holy Ghost" (10:3-4).

In other words, an investigator should prayerfully read the selected passages, ponder them and ask God if they—in fact, the book itself—are true. The Holy Ghost will then give to the sincere seeker a sign of confirmation. (Mormons describe this as a "burning in the bosom," warm and pleasant feelings, a clear insight, a certain conviction.) Notice, however, that the cards are stacked. Only the honest inquirer will be favored with a confirmation. If you receive no sign, you were not sincere or did not pray hard enough. Conversely, if you pray and find the truth, there's no room for doubt! If God tells you the Book of Mormon is true, there's no need for further debate. Contradictory evidence is to be disregarded as not "faith promoting;" hold, rather, to your subjective, internal testimony and ignore objective, external evidence that is brought against it.

Nowhere in the Bible nor in Catholic doctrine do we find God commanding a person to pray to find out if the teachings are true. Jesus spoke God's word to his followers, but never counseled them to pray for an internal verification of his ministry. Rather, he provided *external* verification through the miracles he performed. The fact no such pray-for-internal-guidance passage is in the Bible is why Moroni 10:3-4 is in the Book of Mormon. Smith knew he needed a way to turn the whole conversion process into a subjective exercise for his potential followers, a way to cut the cords to objective evidence and rational discussion. If people are asked to pray for guidance, and they ignore the way God normally provides it—through external evidence—then they will rely on feelings. Some may even be intrigued enough by new, secret revelations that the appeal of mystery itself will cause them to believe the revelations. This attitude of hopeful expectancy could lead someone to generate feelings of confirmation that he is told to interpret as divine revelation, which, of course, he does not wish to disobey.

As a biblical supplement to Moroni 10:3-4, Mormons use James 1:5: "If any of you lack wisdom, let him ask of God, that giveth to all men liberally, and upbraideth not; and it shall be given him."

This is a promise of guidance in response to a prayer for wisdom, not a promise that guidance will come as an internal, personal revelation giving rise to a feeling. The young Smith reported he adverted to James 1:5 in his attempt to find which church was true. This is pointed out to potential converts, and then Moroni 10:3-4 is brought out when they are asked to pray concerning whether the Book of Mormon is true. But Mormons misuse James 1:5 as a "biblical hook," something to grab the attention of unwary investigators. James 1:5 promises wisdom, not knowledge. We don't pray to God to have something revealed to us by direct, divine revelation. We study, research, and depend upon the assistance of others. For example, I don't pray that I can know calculus or French. I study them. I may pray for the wisdom to apply my knowledge in a way that pleases the Lord, but I don't ask him to directly reveal the knowledge of those subjects to me without study and research. Nor do I ask God to tell me if shoplifting and cheating are wrong. I may, rather, pray for the grace to abide by his will.

In his letter, James exhorted his readers to pray for the wisdom to understand the hand of God in their present temptations (1:2-4). The Bereans (Acts 17:11) understood this, and verified Paul's teachings, "searching the scriptures daily" to see if they were true, if they accorded with God's word. Paul likewise told the Thessalonians to "stand fast, and hold the traditions which ye have been taught, whether by word, or our epistle" (2 Thess. 2:15). In like manner, all men are called upon to test their beliefs against the dual rule of Scripture and Tradition. Those who prefer to rely on their inner "testimony" rely on the temptations of the heart, which "is deceitful above all things, and desperately wicked: who can know it?" (Jer. 17:9; see also Matt. 15:19.)

When asked to pray whether the Book of Mormon is true, Catholics should say "no," lest they invite grave spiritual danger by ignoring the objective evidence God has already given concerning the truth of the Catholic faith and the falsity of the Mormon faith. That abundant evidence is easily available. Organizations such as Catholic Answers, which published this book, exist principally to provide people with such evidence.

To reject this evidence in favor of one's own, subjective emotions is a sin—the sin of ingratitude for the wealth of evidence God has already given us. To reject it and further ask for a special, personal revelation is, further, the sin of presumption. When presented with a fervent, and often sincere, testimony of the Book of Mormon by a Latter-day Saint, the Catholic may offer his own testimony. He might also offer the Mormon a copy of the *Catechism of the Catholic Church*, or of a papal encyclical or life of a saint, and ask the Mormon to read and pray if it be true. If accepted, set up an appointment to discuss the material with the Mormon —but be ready to share with him what he is not willing to share with you: the objective, external evidence for what is being discussed. If rejected, ask why. Does the Mormon already "know" it's not true? If so, how? In the same way, you as a Catholic know the Book of Mormon (and all other Mormon writings) are not the Lord's truth. Then discuss with the Mormon missionary the problems of praying for subjective guidance in such cases—the danger of interpreting one's own feelings as the voice of God, or the fact one is ignoring evidence God has already given. See if he can admit that it is dangerous to ignore the evidence he has concerning something and pray for a subjective feeling that it is true. You have to be prepared for the occasional missionary who will fail to see the point, however. A young missionary elder in Phoenix, Arizona, once told me he would accept an invitation to read the *Koran* and ask the Lord if it were true. When I pressed him, he said he'd do the same for a Louis L'Amour western. Ah, the breadth of "ongoing revelation."

31. Problems with the Book of Mormon

Those who believe in any but the true gospel are accursed, Paul proclaims. If he, or "an angel from heaven," preach anything other than the pure faith delivered once by Christ to his apostles, they are under condemnation.[1] Neither Scripture nor Tradition makes provision for "another testament" of Jesus Christ, much less one containing a gospel at odds with the one contained in the New Testament. If its dubious coming forth, its implausible translation and its unreliable witnesses are not enough to expose it as fraudulent, its contents certainly are.

Geography and Archaeology

Most Bibles contain maps based upon archaeological findings in the regions where Bible history unfolded. Ruins of several biblical cities have been located. In fact, fifty-five percent of the places mentioned in the Bible have been located. Scholars have also mapped Paul's missionary route and Palestine at Jesus' time. Even the Mormon edition of the Bible has these maps, as well as those of ancient Palestine, the exodus from Egypt and the kingdoms of Israel and Judah, together with maps of their neighboring enemies.

The Book of Mormon, however, has no maps. Smith and other early collaborators taught that Lehi's party landed somewhere on the west coast of Central or South America. From there, the competing factions of Nephites and Lamanites spread southward and northward.[2] According to the standard account, the last great battle

---

[1] See Galatians 1:8.
[2] In *History of the Church* 2:79, Smith relates his discovery of the skeleton of

between Nephites and Lamanites took place in central New York State. There, hundreds of thousands of men, women, and children were slaughtered, their bodies left to the ravages of weather and beasts. But neither Mormon nor non-Mormon archaeologists have been able to point to a single artifact to support the notion that the "Hill Cumorah" region in New York was the battleground of any fierce, final war. (Mormons also claim that the entire Jaredite nation was killed in the same spot, a thousand years before the Nephite-Lamanite battle; see Ether 15.)

Recent efforts by LDS apologists have focused on shifting the scene from the implausible "two continent" theory—that is, the belief that the American Hebrews inhabited both Central/South America and North America—to one localized solely in Meso-America. Restricting the geographical scope of the book is attractive because of the difficulties in reconciling the two-continent theory with what we now know about New World archaeology and American Indians' racial origins.[3]

John L. Sorenson, BYU professor emeritus of archaeology, asserted the Book of Mormon story took place in southern Mexico and Central America, though he was not the first scholar to

---

a "white [converted] Lamanite" in a burial mound in Spring Hill, Missouri. (Note that Smith was able to do more with a hoe and shovel in "discovering" Nephite remains than any Mormon research team launched since.) God revealed to Smith that the warrior's name was "Zelph." He had been slain by an arrow in the last great battles between Lamanites and Nephites, early in the fifth century. Current Mormon apologists argue that Smith had not had the opportunity to "edit" this portion of his multi-volume history of the Mormon church before his death, so it may be dismissed as irrelevant. See David A. Palmer, "The Land of the Nephites" (book review), in *Review of Books on the Book of Mormon*, vol. 2, 1990, 69. Yet previous editions of the Book of Mormon included footnotes that depicted the book's events as having taken place in far-ranging locales across the Americas.

[3] According to some holding the restricted geography hypothesis, the Book of Mormon's Hebrew-descended characters populated only certain parts of the New World. This allows the American Indians found in other regions to continue to have the Asian ethnic origin suggested by modern anthropology.

do so.[4] Mormon missionaries often (erroneously) claim that evidence pours in daily from Central American digs confirming the Book of Mormon's historicity. Similarly, a rumor had long been circulating among Mormons that the Smithsonian Institute had used the Book of Mormon as a scientific guide in its archaeological studies. After hearing this from Mormon missionaries, many people have queried the Smithsonian, which has prepared a standard reply: "The Smithsonian Institution has never used the Book of Mormon in any way as a scientific guide. Smithsonian archaeologists see no direct connection between the archaeology of the New World and the subject matter of the book."

A similar statement from the National Geographic Society—also beleaguered by inquiries about the supposed archaeological value of the Book of Mormon—points out: "Neither the [National Geographic] Society nor any other institution of equal prestige has ever used the Book of Mormon in locating archaeological sites. Although many Mormon sources claim that the Book of Mormon has been substantiated by archaeological findings, this claim has not been scientifically substantiated. However, several locations in the Bible have."

It is not surprising that these two groups distance themselves from the Book of Mormon as an archaeological source, for even Sorenson's Central American hypothesis has grave problems, particularly concerning geography and archaeology.[5]

Sorenson maintained that the vast spread of territory from South to North America makes it unlikely that the Nephite and Lamanite nations populated both so he looked for a more limited area in which to place the Book of Mormon scenes. His conclusion was that the "narrow neck of land" separating north and south was not, as previously believed, the Isthmus of Panama, but rather the Isthmus of Tehuantepec in southern Mexico (20-30), a mere

---

[4] See Sidney B. Sperry, "Were There Two Cumorahs?" FARMS (Foundation for Ancient Research and Mormon Studies) monograph, 1964.

[5] His most popular work is *An Ancient American Setting for the Book of Mormon*, 1985.

600 miles by 200 miles (49). Sorenson admitted to concentrating only on the points of "successful correlation," while omitting treatment of those areas that didn't fit his hypothesis (31).

The problem is that not even the areas mentioned in Sorenson's book fit the Book of Mormon text. The Book of Mormon geography is that of an hourglass. There is a land northward and a land southward, with a narrow neck between the two. The book mentions only one river, Sidon. Sorenson stated, "[T]he river Sidon flowed northward from Zarahemla."[6] Further, he added, "Its [the river Sidon's] origin was deep in the wilderness above the highest Nephite city on the river, Manti (Alma 16:6). Zarahemla was downstream."[7]

This view makes it possible to correlate the river of Sidon with the Grijalva River, which originates in the highlands of Guatemala near the border with Mexico, on the Pacific side, and flows through southern Mexico before emptying into the sea on the Caribbean side.

However, Sorenson's view of this river is contradicted by passages like Alma 56:25, 51:26 and 43:22, which place the river's origin somewhere east of Manti, rather than south, as Sorenson claimed. Furthermore, the direction of the river is more likely not that of his model. Sorenson's map of the land of Zarahemla, or the land of Nephi, does not match the Book of Mormon, either, and contradicts his placement of the cities of Melek, Ammonihah, Aaron, Nephihah, Moroni, Antionum and Minon. He also identified Lehi-Nephi with the city of Nephi, but the Book of Mormon suggests that they are distinct places, at a considerable distance from each other. Sorenson also had a problem identifying four seas that the Book of Mormon mentions, which are placed north, south, east and west (Helaman 3:8). Sorenson used the Gulf of Mexico and the Gulf of Tehuantepec respectively as the east and west seas, but where are the north and south seas?

Though Sorenson's view is popular among many Mormons, it

---

[6] Sorenson, *An Ancient American Setting for the Book of Mormon*, 10.
[7] Ibid., 23.

has not found universal acceptance, and its problems have been pointed out even by other Mormons. A critique of Sorenson's work is given by Deanne G. Matheny, archaeologist and BYU faculty member, in "Does the Shoe Fit?: A Critique of the Limited Tehuantepec Geography," in *New Approaches to the Book of Mormon*, 269ff.

Sorenson admitted that many of the "correlations" between the Book of Mormon text and his proposed geographical setting are tentative. Though limiting their search to this more confined territory, contemporary Mormon researchers have uncovered no Book of Mormon city, structure or other remains. No evidence has been unearthed to testify to the six hundred thousand Nephites who lost their lives in one day of battle in the area of the Tuxtla mountains, the revisionists' new Hill Cumorah.[8]

One of the missionaries preparing me to enter the Mormon church helped me clear up a puzzle. I couldn't understand why no bones, weapons or other identifying artifacts had been found at the Hill Cumorah near Rochester, New York. The young elder replied, "There were two Hill Cumorahs!" The battles had taken place in Mexico, though the gold plates were buried by Moroni in New York. I suppose this satisfied me at the time. I didn't know the results of digging in Mexico were the same as those in central New York. Nor did I know, contrary to Sorenson's statement (4-5), that the two-hill theory had been condemned by Mormon church leaders.

"In the face of this evidence coming from the Prophet Joseph Smith, Oliver Cowdery, and David Whitmer," said Joseph Fielding Smith, "we cannot say that the Nephites and Lamanites did not possess the territory of the United States and that the Hill Cumorah is in Central America. Neither can we say that the great struggle which resulted in the destruction of the Nephites took place in Central America."[9]

When attempting to settle the geography question, the Mor-

---

[8] Sorenson, 347-350.
[9] President Joseph Fielding Smith, *Doctrines of Salvation* 3:239.

mon church today reacts in predictable fashion: "Never mind the details—just have faith that the Book of Mormon is true."

According to a report in the Mormon church-owned *Deseret News*, "Efforts to pinpoint certain places from what is written in the book [of Mormon] are fruitless because the record does not give evidence of such locations in terms of our modern geography.... To raise doubts in people's minds about the location of the Hill Cumorah, and thus challenge the words of the prophets ... is most certainly harmful.... Why not leave hidden the things that the Lord has hidden? If He wants the geography of the Book of Mormon revealed, He will do so through His prophet, and not through some writer who wishes to enlighten the world despite his utter lack of inspiration on the point."[10]

While we agree that it's useless to debate Book of Mormon geography, it's incorrect to state that the book gives no clue as to its purported geography. Even Smith, the book's imputed translator, believed he was writing about events that took place in Central and North America. It's reasonable to assume that this divinely inspired prophet knew of what he was writing. After all, had there been confusion as to the territory, he could easily have clarified the issue in one of his many editings of this "most correct" book. Yet no area in the Western Hemisphere has yielded support for its claims.[11] Sorenson and other Mormons often claim that Book of Mormon archaeology is like biblical archaeology in its infancy and use this as an explanation for the lack of evidence. New World archaeology is not in its infancy. Thousands of archaeological studies have been conducted in the New World, yet results supporting Book of Mormon geography have not been forthcoming.

This contrasts with the biblical text, which refers to real peoples

---

[10] Church Section, *Deseret News*, July 29, 1978, 16; quoted in *Mormonism—Shadow or Reality?* 125J.

[11] One additional point: Consider the precision of the New Testament's geography, its attention to detail and its independent verification by archaeologists. To its powerful and indisputable witness, what can the fuzzy, disjointed, disproved "testimony" of the Book of Mormon add?

and places that have never needed proving. Though some groups and locations have been and still are disputed, we have always known who the Jews, the Egyptians, the Babylonians, the Romans and the Greek are. We have always known where Jerusalem, the Sea of Galilee, Rome and other biblical sites are located. The existence of several biblical persons has also been substantiated by sources outside the Bible.

The attempts of Sorenson and other Mormon scholars notwithstanding, the truth is still this: No one had ever heard of Zarahemla, Nephi, Manti or any other Book of Mormon site before 1830, and today, none of them can be positively identified. Nor had people heard of the Book of Mormon's Lamanites and Nephites, and today, no remains of tribes calling themselves such have been discovered. Nor has any person mentioned in the book been identified from other sources. The evidence presented is indirect, hypothetical and does not warrant belief in the Book of Mormon as anything other than the product of an imaginative, nineteenth-century mind.

Anachronisms in the Book of Mormon are a further indication that it's not the ancient text Mormons need it to be. Following are a few of the many Mormon assertions archaeology has proven untenable.

The Book of Mormon mentions silk in passages like 1 Nephi 13:7-8, Alma 1:29 and 4:6 and Ether 9:17 and 10:24. Linen is mentioned in those passages and in 2 Nephi 13:23, Mosiah 10:5 and Helaman 6:13. Yet neither silk nor linen was known in the New World before the coming of Europeans. Silk is made from the spinnings of the oriental silk worm, while linen is made from flax —a plant brought to the New World in 1617. Trying to account for these anachronisms, Mormon scholar John Welch proposed several substitutes, such as agave fibers and fig bark for linen, and ceiba fibers, pineapple fibers, and rabbit hair for silk.

"Mesoamerica," Welch said in *Reexploring the Book of Mormon*, "evidently exhibits almost an embarrassment of riches for the 'silk' and 'linen' of Alma 1:29. All but the most trivializing critics should be satisfied with the parallels."

While Welch believed this should silence critics, the fact remains that silk and rabbit hair are not even remotely similar, and if words can be redefined to mean anything a person wants, then they can mean anything at all, and no claim can be said to be true or false.

Another problem: In Mosiah 13:18, the Book of Mormon says the Nephites followed a seven-day week. Archaeology has shown that the ancient Native Americans used a number of calendars, but none used a seven-day week.

As for metal weapons and artifacts, scimitars (spelled *cimeters* in the Book of Mormon), a kind of sword with a long, curved, metal blade, are mentioned in Mosiah 9:16 and other verses. None, however, exist in the Meso-American archaeological record. Sorenson proposed the New World *maccuahuitl*—a club with obsidian blades—as a substitute,[12] no matter how implausible this seems.

The Book of Mormon mentions a variety of metal artifacts that were unknown in the ancient Americas. Both Jaredite and Nephite histories frequently mention the smelting and refining of ores. The book of Ether is replete with references to steel swords (7:9). Jaredite breastplates "of brass and of copper" were discovered by a Book of Mormon character (Mosiah 8:10; brass is an alloy of copper and zinc). The Nephites found and worked with "all manner of wood, and of iron, and of copper, and of brass, and of steel, and of gold, and of silver, and of precious ores, which were in great abundance" (2 Nephi 5:15). Wealth was measured in terms of metals; Nephite swords were specifically made of metals; ornaments and idols were composed of gold and silver, and a monetary system was based on these two precious metals.[13]

The Book of Mormon presents a wide variety of metal artifacts available to God's "chosen": "And we multiplied exceedingly, and spread upon the face of the land, and became exceedingly rich in gold, and in silver, and in precious things, and in fine workmanship of wood, in buildings, and in machinery, and also in iron

---

[12] *An Ancient American Setting for the Book of Mormon*, 262.

[13] See Helaman 6:31 and Alma 11.

and copper, and brass and steel, making all manner of tools of every kind to till the ground, and weapons of war—yea, the sharp pointed arrow, and the quiver, and the dart, and the javelin, and all preparations for war" (Jarom 1:8).

There are several problems with this picture. First, scholars generally agree that metallurgy was probably introduced into Meso-America around the year 900, five hundred years after the close of Book of Mormon events. Second, while there is evidence of gold, silver, and other precious ores in Latin America, little has been found in the area proposed by Sorenson and others as the scene for the Book of Mormon story. Third, Meso-Americans of the Early Classic period lacked the technology required for smelting ore.[14] Consequently, there are no artifacts of the required nature to be found in the archaeological record of the period, nor are they shown in artwork from the period.

The Book of Mormon also mentions the chariot, the Old World war vehicle. Alma 18:9 states, "And they said unto him: Behold, he is feeding thy horses. Now the king had commanded his servants, previous to the time of the watering of their flocks, that they should prepare his horses and chariots, and conduct him forth to the land of Nephi; for there had been a great feast appointed at the land of Nephi, by the father of Lamoni, who was king over all the land."

There is no evidence that wheeled vehicles were ever used in the Americas in the Book of Mormon period. To overcome this problem, some Mormons have suggested that the "chariots" mentioned did not have wheels but were like sleds. The problem with this, other than the fact that English already has a word for sled, is that sleds are not useful in battle. The long blades they run on contact the ground over a longer area than wheels, so they lack maneuverability. A chariot can make a sharp, fast turn without risk of flipping over far more easily than a horse-drawn sled can.

Another failure is the Book of Mormon's treatment of Central American flora and fauna. When Smith brought forth this text in

---

[14] Matheny, 283–297.

the early nineteenth century, there was little available to his audience dealing with the ancient archaeology of Book of Mormon lands. Smith would take his cues from the two worlds he knew best, his own and that of the Bible. Melding these, he produced not only impossible scenarios of metallurgy, but also of botany and zoology.

The Book of Mormon frequently refers to Old World animals such as asses, cows, elephants, the domesticated goat, horses, oxen, pigs and domesticated sheep. Yet the horse was extinct in the Western Hemisphere from about 7000 B.C. until the Spaniards reintroduced it in the sixteenth century, and cattle and other domestic animals were unknown in pre-Columbian America.[15] In response, Sorenson argued that these names were used by Book of Mormon authors when describing native animals with which they were unfamiliar.[16] Thus, horses were actually deer or tapirs.[17] By cattle or cows, the original writers supposedly meant bison or even deer. Elephants were either mastodons or mammoths, neither of which were alive in Central America at the time. How likely is it that the ancient American prophets, supposedly products of a Hebrew culture that knew and properly named these creatures, could call deer both "horses" and "cows"?[18] More importantly, how could Smith bring forth, under divine inspiration, a translation that failed in so basic a distinction?

Sorenson and others have attempted to explain away the problems with the named animals by saying that the Nephites applied names of animals common from their own culture to the new animals they found. They point to other instances of this phenomenon as evidence that this is a likely explanation. For instance,

---

[15] Michael Coe, "Mormons and Archaeology: An Outside View," *Dialogue*, Summer 1973, 42.

[16] Sorenson, 299ff.

[17] Besides the anachronism concern, we might inquire how a man was to ride a deer or harness a chariot to a tapir (2 Nephi 12:7).

[18] Imagine the conundrums faced by the faithful American Hebrews: Was what they called a "cow" really a horse? If so, was it still kosher?

when the Greeks first encountered the hippopotamus, they called it the river-horse (which is where our word *hippopotamus* comes from) and when the Romans first encountered the elephant, they called it the Lukanian cow. The problem with this explanation is that the ancients would invariably modify the term when basing one animal name on another. This made sure that people knew the animal was similar to the familiar one, yet not the same. Smith fares no better in his treatment of ancient American plant life. The Jaredites, dispersed at the Tower of Babel, migrated to the Western Hemisphere. According to the book of Ether, they brought with them "seeds of every kind" (2:3). Through their harvesting and processing, they were said to have had "all manner of fruit, and of grain" (9:17). The Nephites later mention corn, barley, olive trees, linen and silk.[19]

However, no remains have been found of domesticated barley, wheat, or flax (the source of linen). No other Old World plants have been identified at any archaeological sites in Meso-America dating to pre-Columbian times.[20] Smith was correct in reporting corn to be a staple of the diet, but the Book of Mormon is silent about squash and beans, the other two basic Meso-American foods.

Some Mormons have tried to find potential matches for at least a few of these. For example, Welch claimed the Book of Mormon's mention of cultivated barley is valid, based on a find of wild barley in the Phoenix, Arizona, area. However, Phoenix is not in the setting of the Book of Mormon (especially on the limited geography theory) and the barley found was not domesticated, though the barley mentioned in Book of Mormon clearly was. For instance in Alma 11:7 we are told that barley was sold at a fixed price, indicating it was an established, domestic crop with a regular price. At an August 25, 1984, Salt Lake City conference, BYU anthropology professor Dr. Raymond T. Matheny said, "There's a whole system of production of wheat and barley. . . . It's a specialized production of food. You have to know

---

[19] 1 Nephi 13:7–8; Jacob 5; Mosiah 11:15.
[20] Matheny, 300–302.

something to make flax, and especially in tropical climates. Grapes and olives . . . all these are cultures that are highly developed and amount to systems, and so the Book of Mormon is saying that these systems existed here."

Eventually people tire of hearing endless excuses and fantastic theories that are created just so they'll believe something for which no evidence exists. If someone is willing to saddle up a deer or have it pull him in a chariot, he can call it a "horse" and espouse Book of Mormon zoology. If a person can accept that verifiable American foods are ignored while nonexistent Old World food is served, he can swallow Book of Mormon botany. And if he is ready to make the Book of Mormon contradict itself to fit a preconceived, limited Tehuantepec model, he is ready to claim as factual Book of Mormon geography. For the rest of us, it is obvious that Smith's text is full of anachronisms betraying its purely human origin.[21]

Responding to the failure of archaeology in uncovering the slightest support for the Book of Mormon, LDS leaders claim study and demonstrable facts are foreign to faith. Current apostle Dallin H. Oaks recently announced, "Scholarship and physical proofs are worldly values." To focus on these, rather than faith, as a means of discovering reality is to put "the things of men" before "the things of God." Oaks concluded, "I am convinced that secular evidence can neither prove nor disprove the authenticity of the Book of Mormon."[22] Elder Boyd K. Packer, President of the Quorum of the Twelve Apostles, warns the faithful that the thirst for facts can be damaging to their faith; fidelity requires that one read "history that bolsters belief and avoids awkward or embarrassing detail."[23]

---

[21] The treatment here has of necessity been brief. Two useful sources for further study on the problems of Book of Mormon archaeology are *New Approaches to the Book of Mormon*, edited by Brent Lee Metcalfe, and *Answering Mormon Scholars*, vols. 1 and 2, by Jerald and Sandra Tanner.

[22] "The Historicity of the Book of Mormon," FARMS annual dinner, October 29, 1993.

[23] Quoted in Vern Anderson, "Mormon Publisher Willing to Shake the

Compare this dismissive attitude toward empirical evidence with Paul's presentation of the facts of Christianity. Arrested and brought before King Agrippa, Paul was called "mad" for his beliefs. He responded, "The king knoweth of these things, before whom also I speak freely: for I am persuaded that none of these things are hidden from him; for this thing was not done in a corner" (Acts 26:26).

Christian faith has a basis in discernible facts; it is the Mormon faith that does not. Elder Oaks is not alone in confusing "historicity" and "authenticity." Take, for example, the siege of Jerusalem, ordered by Sennacherib, that is mentioned in 2 Kings 19. Archaeology has confirmed the existence of this siege and that Sennacherib did not take Jerusalem. Sennacherib's own account of the siege has been found, and he boasts of having surrounded the city, but not of having taken it. That Sennacherib did this has thus been confirmed by the archaeological record. Why he failed is a matter of faith. Scripture reveals that Sennacherib's siege failed because God protected the city. "Even if archaeology cannot confirm the ultimate religious meaning of the Bible, it can clarify the historical circumstances of numerous individual texts."[24] Geographical and archaeological finds cannot, of themselves, prove the truth of Christianity. But historical and archaeological facts do demonstrate the reasonableness of faith and its human, historical underpinnings.

Language

As for the book's language, while some Mormon apologists claim that Smith did not use the Bible in composing the Book of Mormon, others say he must have, since many chapters from the Bible are repeated, almost word for word, in his book. There is a similar

---

'Sacred' Tree, *Albuquerque Journal*, July 27, 1991, E4. See also Packer's talk in *Brigham Young University Studies*, Summer 1981, 259ff, in which he stated, "In an effort to be objective, impartial, and scholarly, a writer or a teacher may unwittingly be giving equal time to the adversary. . . ."

[24] William G. Dever, "Archaeology and the Bible," *Biblical Archaeology Review*, May-June 1990, 55. See also September-October 1996, 30ff.

disagreement among scholars as to how familiar Smith was with the Bible. Orson Pratt argued that Smith "was unacquainted with the contents of the Bible."[25] Yet Smith and his mother recorded that he frequently read Scripture.[26]

In any case, let's take a brief look at the logistics. Lehi and his family fled Jerusalem in about the year 600 B.C., taking with them the "brass plates of Laban," containing the first five books of the Old Testament and the words of the prophets to the time of Jeremiah.[27] Prophetic and other writings originating in Palestine after the departure of Lehi would consequently not be available to his posterity in the Americas. Nevertheless, critics have pointed out hundreds of late-Old Testament and New Testament parallels in the Book of Mormon. Verses from Malachi, writing in the fifth century before Christ, are found in First and Second Nephi.[28] Jesus recites Malachi 3-4 in 3 Nephi 24-25, virtually verbatim from the KJV text of 1611. More than fifteen of the thirty-three chapters of Second Nephi are copied from the prophet Isaiah,[29] again using King James English.[30] Hundreds of passages from the New Testament are also repeated wholesale.[31]

Moreover, Book of Mormon stories often mimic biblical incidents while exaggerating their drama. For example, Book of Mormon prophet Ammon killed six men with a sling (Alma 17:36), while David slew only one (1 Sam. 17:50). A small group of Nephites raised their temple only twenty years after arriving in

---

[25] *Journal of Discourses* 2:288.
[26] See *Mormonism—Shadow or Reality?* 72.
[27] 1 Nephi 3:3, 20; 5:12-13; 19:10, 21; Helaman 8:19-20.
[28] Compare Malachi 4:1; with 1 Nephi 22:15 and 2 Nephi 26:4; Malachi 4:2 with 1 Nephi 22:24 and 2 Nephi 25:13, 26:9.
[29] Including chapters 50 and 51, which some scholars maintain were written after 600 B.C.
[30] Though in his work, Smith usually omitted the italicized words that its translators had added to the KJV to aid the reader in understanding the text. He was also unable to maintain consistency in his use of the archaic forms. See Mosiah 2:19, 3:19, 3:34, 4:22, 4:24.
[31] See *The Case Against Mormonism*, vol. 2, 82-100, for a comparison chart of nearly four hundred such verses.

America (2 Nephi 5), though Solomon needed 180,000 men and seven and a half years to build his (1 Kgs. 5). Christ fed the multitudes with a few loaves and fishes (Matt. 14), yet performed the same miracle using nothing in 3 Nephi 20:3–7. Both Daniel (Dan. 5) and Aminadi (Alma 10:2–3) read the writing on the wall. Like the daughter of Herodias (Matt. 14), the daughter of Jared danced for the king (Ether 8). Men lost their heads in both stories.

Just as the animal and plant life portrayed in the Book of Mormon is yanked out of time and context, so too is the book's diction. Besides archaic English and King James Version copying,[32] Smith made other linguistic lapses. Among these are his use of Greek terms, especially the use of "Christ" throughout the pre-Christian centuries. Other Greek names include Lachoneus, Timothy, and Jonas. French also made its way into the Nephite history ("*adieu*" in Jacob 7:27).[33]

Perhaps more curious are the omissions. The Nephites were a devout Hebrew people who observed the Mosaic Law, yet there is not one mention of the indispensable feast of Passover in their history. Further, though the early portions of the Book of Mormon are replete with specific and detailed "prophecies" concerning the coming of Christ (including the actual year of his birth and his mother's name), nothing new is added to our knowledge of the Savior. We are not told, for instance, about the eighteen "lost years," nor are we favored with any other information not already available in the New Testament.

Recent LDS research attempts to answer skeptics in several ways. One is to demonstrate the presence, in the Book of Mormon text, of Hebraic poetic patterns which Smith and his contemporaries

---

[32] Mormon traditionalists account for the extensive use of KJV quotations by suggesting "the Lord himself . . . chose to quote from the King James Version when it agreed with the Book of Mormon." That he would also quote its mistranslations and editorial additions baffles most other thinkers. See Brent Lee Metcalfe, "The Priority of Mosiah," *New Approaches to the Book of Mormon*, 412.

[33] Some claim Shakespeare is also represented in 2 Nephi 1:14, though Mormon apologists insist that Shakespeare and 2 Nephi were referring to Job 10:21. Compare *Hamlet*, Act 3, Scene 1.

allegedly knew nothing about. Chief among these forms is chiasmus, a kind of inverted parallelism. It works like this:

> The *Jews*
>   shall have the *words*
>   of the *Nephites*
>   and the *Nephites*
>   shall have the *words*
> of the *Jews*;
> and the *Nephites* and the *Jews*
>   shall have the *words*
>   of the lost tribes of *Israel*;
>   and the lost tribes of *Israel*
>   shall have the *words* of
> the *Nephites* and the *Jews* [2 Nephi 29:13].[34]

Several instances of chiasmus are adduced in the Book of Mormon, replicating a literary style also found in the Old and New Testaments. But the Mormon assertion that chiasmus was unknown in Smith's time, and therefore could not be duplicated, is untrue. First, the structure was perceived in the Old Testament at least eighty years before the Book of Mormon was printed.[35] Second, chiasmus is not a peculiarly Hebrew literary style; it's found in other cultures, including our own, in such things as children's nursery rhymes. For example, "Hickory, Dickory, Dock":

> *Hickory, dickory, dock*
>   The *mouse ran* up the clock
>   The clock *struck one*
>   The *mouse ran* down
> *Hickory, dickory, dock*

---

[34] See John W. Welch, "Chiasmus in the Book of Mormon," FARMS reprint, 43. See also Donald W. Parry, "Hebrew Literary Patterns in the Book of Mormon," *Ensign*, October 1989, 58ff.

[35] My thanks to the Tanners who supplied me with photocopies of letters from which this information is taken. See Christian Research Institute letter dated October 17, 1986, 1.

Third, and most significantly, it is not at all unusual that a man who sets about to create "scripture" would invoke the vocabulary, grammar and style of the only true Scripture available to him for his imitation. Even if the term chiasmus was unknown to Smith, its structure and cadence were as accessible to him as to any other reader of the Bible. That he employed it simply parallels his adoption of KJV English.

Fourth, in examining other texts that came from Smith's pen, we find examples of chiasmus in the Doctrine and Covenants. Some Mormon apologists argue that it should not be surprising to find chiasmus in the Doctrine and Covenants, a book almost completely composed of "revelations" Smith received from Jesus Christ. Chiasmus is, they say, a preferred mode of divine speech. But this ignores the presence of chiasmus even in the narrative portions of the D&C composed admittedly by Smith.[36]

Fifth and finally, chiasmus is a literary device that appears in human speech and writing even when the author does not recognize it. As a writer works, he keeps track of what has been said and what he plans to say. He makes and organizes mental lists of things to say, and of how he wants to return in the end to certain themes first sketched in the beginning. The result of this mental organization is that parallelisms, including inverted parallelisms (chiasms) can slip into the author's text.

The presence of chiasms in the Book of Mormon in no way counts as evidence of divine origin. Chiasmus is a literary device common to ancient and modern literature, used by those who are aware of it by name and imitate it deliberately (a class to which Smith may have belonged) and by those who do it unknowingly.[37]

---

[36] For example, D&C 76:28–30, 76:89–98, 107:34–38, 109:24–28, as reported in H. Clay Gorton's *The Language of the Lord*.

[37] See John Breck, *The Shape of Biblical Language* (Crestwood, New York: St. Vladimir's Seminary Press, 1994), 325–332, for the detection of a chiasmus as the organizing principle of the editorial "Medical Research Ignores Women" from the *Boston Globe*, Friday, June 22, 1990, by Ellen Goodman. At the time of writing, commentator Goodman was completely unaware of the chiastic structure she had given her editorial.

One last point in our discussion of the language of the Book of Mormon concerns all the changes made to the book's first edition, by Smith himself through the 1981 printing. Some count the four thousand changes, asking how "the most correct" of any book, translated "by the gift and power of God" would need so many corrections. Mormons are quick to argue that most of the changes involved grammar, punctuation and spelling, such as bringing subject and verb into agreement, regularizing American spelling and amending verb tense—which is true. However, it does belie the 1830 boasting that the Book of Mormon was "the most correct of any book on earth, and the keystone of our religion, and a man would get nearer to God by abiding by its precepts than by any other book."[38]

Thousands of books were in print at that time that did not require anything like that number of corrections to be made. The fact is that Smith and his scribes were modestly educated men and women who spoke what may be charitably termed a rather rustic form of colloquial American English. Matters were exacerbated by attempting to graft onto this low colloquial base a foreign diction —that of Jacobean (King James) English. The result was a potpourri of linguistic and stylistic inconsistencies, which might not be disqualifying in itself, but which certainly renders problematic any claim that the Book of Mormon is "the most correct" book ever published.

Yet not all the changes are minor and a few have serious theological implication.[39] This leads us to the third area of problems.

Theology

To investigate the vagaries of Book of Mormon theology we will note how the book's teachings are at odds with later Mormon theology. Then we will see how the book's treatment of the God-

---

[38] *History of the Church* 4:461.
[39] See the Tanners' *3,913 Changes in the Book of Mormon*, especially 5–16.

head, baptism and the Eucharist contradict traditional Christian, especially Catholic, doctrine.

THE BOOK OF MORMON—IS IT MORMON?

The Book of Mormon fails to mention many of Mormonism's distinct doctrines, such as church organization, including the First Presidency, Quorums of Seventies, high priests and the Aaronic priesthood; God as an exalted man; the plurality of gods; men becoming gods; three degrees of heavenly glory; baptism for the dead; temple work, including endowments, celestial marriage, and sealings; the Word of Wisdom; the pre-existence and eternity of all matter and spirit; and eternal progression.

Yet Smith said that the book is the "most correct" of any text on earth. It is also billed by other Mormon scriptures as containing "the fulness of the gospel of Jesus Christ" (D&C 20:8-9). The fact that the Book of Mormon *does not* contain so many things that, now, are regarded as part of the fullness of the Mormon gospel betrays the book's human origins. At the time of its writing, Smith did not anticipate adding the later, extreme doctrines he claimed were revealed to him.

But Smith's restless imagination, showmanship, and perhaps his need to control and keep the interest of his unruly, fledgling movement, led him to create even more exciting and daring doctrines. In addition to the current Mormon doctrines that were added after the Book of Mormon stage, some teachings in the Book of Mormon flatly contradict later revelations and scriptures produced by Smith and his successors. Compare the following assertions on the nature of God.

The Book of Mormon: God dwells in the hearts of men. Alma 34:36.

Doctrine and Covenants: No, that's an "old sectarian notion,[40] and is false." 130:3.

---

[40] A "sectarian notion," in this case, means the opposite of what it would in

The Book of Mormon: God created all things, in heaven and on earth. Mosiah 4:9.

The Book of Abraham: A council of Gods appointed Elohim Lord of this world. Chs. 3-4.

The Book of Mormon: There is one God. Alma 11:22-29.

History of the Church: There are many Gods. 6:475.

The Book of Mormon: God is unchanging. Moroni 8:18.

Teachings of the Prophet Joseph Smith: God progressed. 346.

The Book of Mormon: God is the "Great Spirit." Alma 22:9-11.

Doctrine and Covenants: The Father has a body of flesh and bones. 130:22.

The problems with taking the Book of Mormon as "the fulness of the gospel" are demonstrated by the existence of competing Mormon sects alongside the main Utah church, which is not the only group that regards the Book of Mormon as scripture.

The Reorganized Church of Jesus Christ of Latter Day Saints, based in Independence, Missouri, accepts the Book of Mormon but rejects such doctrines as polygamy (which the book also condemns), temple work, baptism for the dead, temple garments, eternal progression, and the plurality of gods.

On the other hand, there are numerous splinter groups, found mostly in the American West, that insist on the necessity of

---

normal English speech. Typically, a "sectarian notion" would be held by one or at most a few "sects." Here, however, it is being used to refer to a doctrine held by *all* non-Mormons. The mainstream Christian groups are unanimous in teaching that God dwells in our hearts, as Scripture proclaims. But because of the later Mormon doctrines on the corporeality of God, the doctrine must go. Consider the hubris reflected in this role-reversal—which portrays all other Christians as if they amounted to only a few, insignificant sects, outside the mainstream.

polygamy for salvation and reject a priesthood open to persons of color. Nevertheless, they testify to the historicity of the Book of Mormon and the divinity of Smith's call. A testimony of the Book of Mormon does not lead one directly into classical, Utah Mormonism, which is the largest group of Smith's many, competing offspring.[41]

The Book of Mormon—Is It Christian?

Not surprisingly, the Book of Mormon not only contradicts later Mormon beliefs but fundamental Christian beliefs as well. As a result, it cannot be embraced by anyone who wishes to avoid the anathema given by Paul in Galatians 1:8 for those who adhere to "another gospel." To make clear the doctrinal divergence of the work from Christian, and specifically Catholic, teaching, we will look at three aspects of the Book of Mormon's teaching: what it has to say about the nature of God and Christ, about original sin and baptism and about the Eucharist.

The Nature of God and Christ

The Mormon church misses no opportunity to disparage the classical Christian understanding of God as three persons in one divine being and claims it to be unbiblical. While Mormons acknowledge many gods and worship only one, this notion unfolded over time. I don't, however, think it correct to conclude, as many Protestant critics do, that the Book of Mormon affirms historical, Trinitarian monotheism. Rather, God is often presented in a modalistic fashion—that is, one God manifesting himself at different times as Father or Son. "Is the Son of God the very Eternal Father?"

---

[41] The existence of so many disagreeing "sibling" groups also belies Smith's claim to have done what Christ did not—keep a unified church together without it disintegrating into smaller, sectarian groups. See *The Encyclopedia of American Religions*, vol. 2, 187–210 for information on Mormon offshoots.

the Mormon prophet Amulek is asked in about 82 B.C. "Yea, he is the very Eternal Father of heaven and earth . . . And he shall come into the world to redeem his people" (Alma 11:38-40).[42]

In Smith's book, Jesus Christ is known and named hundreds of years before his birth. Precise predictions are made as to his time and place of birth, the name of his mother and the manner of his death. Though still observing the Mosaic Law, the ancient Nephites nevertheless belonged to Christ's church and even practiced such ordinances as Christian baptism, which had been taught, they maintained, from the time of Adam.[43]

The adequacy of Christ's redemption and grace is indirectly impugned in 2 Nephi 25:23: "We know that it is by grace that we are saved, after all we can do"—an unacceptable gospel of works, which speaks of a role for grace only after human effort, instead of speaking of grace as the indispensable source of all human efforts that are pleasing to God and as the ever-present remedy for those that are displeasing to him (i.e., sin). Moreover, Mormons deny outright the sufficiency of the Lord's atonement in its doctrine of "blood atonement."[44] Jesus Christ is presented in the New Testament as the sole and universal redeemer: "[T]he blood of Jesus Christ his Son cleanseth us from *all sin*" (1 John 1:7, emphasis added). Yet Mormons historically have held that a person's own shed blood and death are necessary for his salvation if he is guilty of apostasy or other serious sins.[45]

---

[42] See also Mosiah 3:5-8; 7:27; 15:1-5. A scholarly critique of the Mormon concepts of God, those presented in the Book of Mormon and, especially, those of Joseph Smith and later church scholars, is available in *The Mormon Concept of God: A Philosophical Analysis*, by Francis J. Beckwith and Stephen E. Parrish.

[43] See 1 Nephi 20:1; 2 Nephi 31:13-14, 17.

[44] *Doctrines of Salvation* 1:134. See also *Discourses of Brigham Young*, 467-468; James R. Clark, *Messages of the First Presidency* 3:205-206; *Mormon Doctrine*, 92.

[45] Debate continues among Mormon historians concerning the question: Did early Mormon leaders order the deaths of apostates, murderers, and the like? Non-Mormon historians have already shown that people were executed to fulfill the "blood atonement doctrine." Not coincidentally, Utah law has

The Jesus of the Book of Mormon, while not as heretical as that of later Mormon teaching, is still divergent from the Jesus of Scripture. He ends up being confused, modalistically, with his own Father, and his atonement is not sufficient to provide for his people's redemption from sin. This is not the Christ revealed in the words and lives of the New Testament saints, and any gospel focusing on this other Christ is not the gospel Paul preached. It is "another gospel" which will not save its adherents.

Original Sin and Baptism

Another area in which the Book of Mormon is deficient and heretical is its denial of original sin and prohibition of infant baptism. For Mormons, Adam's fall was a "fall forward." He transgressed one law (not to eat the fruit) in order to comply with a greater law (be fruitful and multiply). A corollary of the Mormon church's rejection of original sin is its vehement opposition to infant baptism. Responding to the sharp debate of his own day, Smith included—almost as an afterthought—several verses in Moroni, the last book in the Book of Mormon, calling the practice a "gross error" (8:6).[46] The idea is that little children are alive in Christ, guiltless, and incapable of committing sin (until about their eighth year). Thus, they need no repentance and no baptism (8:8-10). Those churches that teach otherwise are in danger of "death, hell, and an endless torment" (8:21).

The Eucharist

Yet another false doctrine expounded by the Book of Mormon is also found in Moroni chapters four and five. The elders and priests

---

long authorized death by firing squad, thus allowing condemned criminals to have their blood shed to atone for their sins. This would not be so in the case of hanging, electric chair, or lethal injection.

[46] Contemporary LDS scriptorians have added the heading, "Infant baptism is an evil abomination."

on the American continent, after reciting the required prayers, administer the sacramental bread and wine. The phrases that occasion dispute are "eat in remembrance of the body of thy Son" (Moroni 4:3) and "drink of it, that they may do it in remembrance of the blood of thy Son" (5:2). Taken at face value, the terms seem no different from the Lord's command at the Last Supper: "This do in remembrance of me" (Luke 21:19).

Mormon commentators, however, make it clear that these words preclude the historic understanding of a real change in the substance of the bread and the wine. Rather, "the sacrament" as celebrated throughout Book of Mormon times and restored in the latter days is, at best, a mere memorial of what Christ did during his final hours.

~

One may look upon the Book of Mormon as a sort of "bridge" between authentic Christianity and authentic Mormonism. Its language and themes are "familiar" enough to make it seem like a pious story about faraway Christians. Its silence concerning most central Mormon teachings misleads readers into thinking it presents the heart of Mormon dogma, a gospel that does not, at first glance, seem so different from the historical accounts of Christianity. The Book of Mormon has been called the greatest tool in converting (unsuspecting) people to Mormonism. It's widely advertised and mass-marketed. Missionaries offer free copies to anyone who will accept them. By carefully choosing plausible passages for their investigators to read, Mormon missionaries hope to convince them of the reasonableness of the Mormon message.[47] But the *real* Mormon message is not found in the Book of Mormon, but in Smith's other writings, such as the Doctrine and Covenants and The Pearl of Great Price, and in the continually changing revelations of Smith's successors.

---

[47] See Grant Von Harrison, *The Conversion Power of the Book of Mormon*, 6.

32. The Other Mormon Scriptures

The one consistent feature of LDS teaching about the Bible is that Mormon prophets and apostles contradict one another. Consider their differing attitudes toward the King James Version of the Bible.

The August 1992 issue of *Ensign* carried the "First Presidency Statement on the King James Version of the Bible." It said, in part, "In doctrinal matters latter-day revelation supports the King James Version in preference to other English translations. . . . All of the Presidents of the Church . . . have supported the King James Version by encouraging its continued use in the Church" (80).

Apostle John A. Widtsoe quoted Brigham Young as asserting, "I think it [the KJV] is translated just as correctly as the scholars could get it, although it is not correct in a great many instances. But it is no matter about that. Read it and observe it and it will not hurt any person in the world."[1]

James E. Talmage bragged, "The Church of Jesus Christ of Latter-day Saints accepts the Holy Bible as foremost of her standard works. . . . The historical and other data upon which is based the current Christian faith as to the genuineness of the Biblical record are accepted as unreservedly by the Latter-day Saints as by the members of any sect; and in literalness of interpretation this Church probably excels."[2]

The above passages illustrate one side of Mormonism's attitude toward the Bible, a position designed to establish a common bond with orthodox Christians targeted for conversion. This irenic tone is meant to lull the prospective proselyte into an unwary acceptance of the Mormons' seemingly orthodox roots.[3]

---

[1] Cited in *We Believe*, 73.
[2] *Articles of Faith*, 236–237.
[3] See *Encyclopedia of Mormonism*, vol. 1.

"Just look," the missionaries say, "we acknowledge the Bible as a vital part of our standard works. We even use the King James Version, that translation so widely known and loved by Christians. Our missionary lessons are replete with references to the Old and New Testaments. We love the Bible and testify to you that it is the word of God."

But Mormons have not always been as enthusiastic.

Apostle Orson Pratt railed, "[T]he Bible has been robbed of its plainness; many sacred books having been lost, others rejected by the Romish Church, and what few we have left, were copied and re-copied so many times, that it is admitted that almost every verse has been corrupted and mutilated to that degree that scarcely any two of them read alike."[4]

Joseph Smith himself was no less certain that "[i]gnorant translators, careless transcribers, or designing and corrupt priests have committed many errors."[5]

In fact, Smith had already canonized his position regarding the Christian Bible. In the Book of Mormon, an angel tells the prophet Nephi of the eventual fate of the Bible: "[T]hou seest the formation of that great and abominable church, which is most abominable above all other churches; for behold, they have taken away from the gospel of the Lamb many parts which are plain and most precious; and also many covenants of the Lord have they taken away. And all this have they done that they might pervert the right ways of the Lord, that they might blind the eyes and harden the hearts of the children of men" (1 Nephi 13:26-27).

We're not told by Mormons just exactly *which* verses have been mistranslated or falsely transmitted. Nor are we told the reason why the "Romish" Church would remove certain offensive verses that could subvert that Church's authority, yet leave in other verses

---

[4] *The Seer*, 213. This extreme position presents its advocates with a dilemma, since hundreds of verses of the 1611 King James Bible are quoted verbatim in the Book of Mormon, said to have been completed early in the fifth century A.D.

[5] *Teachings*, 327.

which Mormons have seized upon in an attempt to support their unique beliefs.[6]

A further puzzle: Since the LDS prophets are revered as "seers"[7] and "translators,"[8] they should be able, with divine help, to correct faulty passages and even restore those that were removed. Mormons have even talked about undertaking a project along these lines. Yet a thoroughgoing and complete "correction" and "restoration" of the Bible has not been done.[9]

The Mormon church is not content with attacking one particular Christian Bible (and, it must be said, the King James Version certainly has its flaws). They attack the corpus of Scripture generally, asserting that whole books have been deleted. Perhaps one of the most stunning Mormon attacks on Christian Scripture is found in the Book of Mormon's depiction of God mocking the Christian's belief that no other books of Scripture are needed: "Thou fool, that shall say: A Bible, we have got a Bible, and we need no more Bible. . . . Wherefore murmur ye, because that ye shall receive more of my word?" (2 Nephi 29:6, 8).

To try to prove Christian Scripture incomplete, Mormons point to passages in the Old and New Testament that mention works that are now lost. For example, Numbers 21:14 mentions "the book of the wars of the Lord." First Kings 11:41 refers to "the book of the chronicles of Solomon." First Corinthians 5:9 records

---

[6] For an account of the antiquity and accuracy of the biblical record, see *Where We Got the Bible*, Henry G. Graham, 48–67, and F. F. Bruce, *The New Testament Documents: Are They Reliable?* 7–20.

[7] The Book of Mormon defines a seer as one who "can know of things which are past. . . . By them shall all things be revealed, or, rather, shall secret things be made manifest, and hidden things come to light, and things which are not known shall be made known by them, and also things shall be made known by them which otherwise could not be known" (Mosiah 8:17).

[8] "[T]he duty of the President . . . is to be a seer, a revelator, a translator, and a prophet" (D&C 107:91–92).

[9] Though McConkie, writing almost forty years ago, promised, "There will be a not too distant day when all necessary changes shall be made in the Bible" and it will go forth to the world (*Mormon Doctrine*, 1958 ed., 352–353).

Paul's words: "I wrote unto you in an epistle. . . ." This letter would have preceded the one we now call his first to the Church in Corinth. A similar reference is made by Jude to an earlier letter of his (verse 3). It is not clear that all of the works were regarded as Scripture. Some mentioned in the Old Testament appear to have been military records and the annals of the royal court. Others might well have been, had they survived, but they didn't.

What are we to make of that? Is the Bible incomplete because such books are missing from it? Has the work of the Holy Spirit in guiding the Christian community been thwarted by the carelessness of men who "lost" some inspired teachings? Of course not. Scripture is not meant to be the collection of any and all divine revelations that have been given. Scripture itself mentions the existence of revelations whose content we know nothing about and prophets whose prophesying we know nothing about. Scripture is only a subset of the larger category of divine revelation, as Mormons admit. Scripture consists of that revelation which has been written down under the influence of divine inspiration.[10]

But particular Scriptures are meant for all people in all ages. There was a time before there had been *any* Scripture written; thus God did not intend there to be *any* Scripture for people in that age. As Scripture began to be written, piece by piece instead of all at once, God revealed his intention for people of different ages to have different pieces of Scripture available to them.

It is no surprise, then, that there might be Scriptures intended

---

[10] One could have a piece of divine revelation—a fact learned from God not capable of being known by human reason—that is written down *without* the influence of divine inspiration. Inspiration occurs when God so uses the human author, his mind and background, that God himself leads the human author to choose all and only those words that God wants used. God himself thus is the primary author of inspired texts. Many books—in fact, all good theology books—contain items of divine revelation (the Trinity, the Real Presence of Christ, the teaching of regeneration through baptism), but the authors of these books were not divinely inspired as they did their writing. They took items of revelation they knew from elsewhere and incorporated them into books written by ordinary human processes.

for a previous age but not for this one. If God allowed a particular work to pass out of existence because it was not meant for this age, that is part of God's providence. It does not mean the Church was playing fast and loose with Scripture. In fact, the books of Scripture that God did not intend for this age had already passed from the scene before the Church age began!

The odd thing is that Mormons themselves will have to admit that the canon of Scripture is not intended by God to be the set of all inspired Scriptures that have been written. Why? Because their own version of history requires the same thing to be said. When Jesus allegedly founded a church in the New World, he did not bring it the New Testament Scripture that was in existence in the Old World. Thus the canon of Scripture that the New World church was supposed to have could not be viewed as the set of all books of Scripture that had ever been written, nor as all books of Scripture then in existence. Furthermore, it is not advisable to criticize the Catholic Church for "losing books" of Scripture. First, it cannot be shown that the Catholic Church did lose any. There are certain books that are *mentioned* in Scripture that are not *contained* in Scripture. However, where is it ever said that every book Scripture mentions has to be a book of Scripture itself? Could not a Mormon prophet or apostle, when writing Scripture, mention a publication without implying that the publication was a work of divine Scripture? Even when we come to the New Testament, and the non-canonical writings mentioned in it, we need not suppose that every scrap of paper Paul wrote on or every letter he dictated after becoming an apostle was superintended by divine inspiration. Mormons would make no such claim for *their* prophets and apostles. If God chose not to have a particular Pauline missive survive, it may have been because it was not inspired or simply because it was a private revelation meant for those who received it, not a public revelation meant for all time.

The second reason Mormons should not censure the Catholic Church for losing books of Scripture is that it can be shown that the Mormon church has lost books that, according to its own account, were meant to be put in the Mormon scriptures. Yes, there are "lost books" to the Book of Mormon. Remember: When Smith was still "translating" the Book of Mormon, he loaned the manuscript to Martin Harris, his benefactor and scribe. The work, which then consisted of one hundred and sixteen pages, was lost. (Reportedly, Mrs. Harris burned them to keep her husband from folly and financial loss.) Smith never re-translated the plates to restore the missing books of Scripture; he only created a summary of them.

Ostensibly, this was because God would not *let* Smith re-translate those plates after having shown such callous disregard for the word of God. The real reason, of course, was that Smith *could not* re-translate the plates because there were no plates to translate. Smith was making it up as he went along and could not remember everything he had said. He could never duplicate what he had dictated in the original manuscript, and if the real manuscript turned up later (maybe it was only being hidden), he and his "translations" would be exposed as frauds. So Smith didn't *attempt* to restore the lost books of the Book of Mormon. Instead, he made up a story that God wouldn't *let* him re-translate the plates as a punishment for having been so careless.[11]

Even though his cover story is false, Smith acknowledged culpability in losing books of scripture. In fact, according to Doctrine and Covenants, he was specifically instructed to repent or lose his alleged ability to translate: "But remember, God is merciful; therefore, repent of that which thou hast done which is contrary to the commandment which I gave you, and thou art still chosen, and art again called to the work; Except thou do this, thou shalt be delivered up and become as other men, and have no more gift. And when thou deliveredst up that which God had given thee

---

[11] The typical LDS explanation is as follows: Joseph Smith chose not to re-translate the lost pages because he feared exposure. That is, had he produced a second copy, those who had "stolen" the first copy would alter it, produce it and exclaim, "See, Smith is a false prophet, for he cannot 'translate' the same material twice!"

sight and power to translate, thou deliveredst up that which was sacred into the hands of a wicked man" (D&C 3:10-12).

For the Christian's part, we may be absolutely confident that we have all the Scripture God intended us to have. We have the Lord's promise: "The grass withereth, the flower fadeth: but the word of our God shall stand for ever" (Is. 40:8). Christ himself asserts: "Heaven and earth shall pass away, but my words shall not pass away" (Matt. 24:35). Not even Jesus would change Scripture: "Verily I say unto you, Till heaven and earth pass, one jot or one tittle [the smallest letter or part of a letter] shall in no wise pass from the law, till all be fulfilled" (Matt. 5:18).

To consciously, deliberately alter the text of a book of Scripture and then pass that book off to others as God's inspired word is among the gravest sins imaginable. The book of Revelation closes with very somber warnings to whoever would dare to tamper with its text: "I testify unto every man that heareth the words of the prophecy of this book, If any man shall add unto these things, God shall add unto him the plagues that are written in this book: And if any man shall take away from the words of the book of this prophecy, God shall take away his part out of the book of life, and out of the holy city, and from the things which are written in this book" (Rev. 22:18-19).

This warning applies to every other book of divinely inspired Scripture. Yet Smith dared to make his "Inspired Version" of the Bible—actually a doctored version of the King James Bible. Not competent in biblical languages, the Mormon founder produced the Joseph Smith Translation through meditation and, he said, direct inspiration, having no contact with original-language versions. He simply read a biblical passage and "corrected, revised, altered, added to, and deleted from the King James Version" (*Mormon Doctrine*, 383), producing a new Bible supportive of the theology he at that time espoused.[12]

---

[12] For example, Smith gives his work divine approbation in his additions to Genesis 50: "And that seer will I bless, and they that seek to destroy him shall be confounded; for this promise I give unto you; for I will remember you from generation to generation; and his name shall be called Joseph, and it shall be

Opinions on the completeness of the Joseph Smith Translation vary. Smith certainly did not restore any of the "lost books" that supposedly belonged in the Christian canon. (He could not even restore the lost books of his own canon!) Nevertheless, the Reorganized Church of Jesus Christ of Latter Day Saints publishes and uses this version as their only Bible. The larger Utah Church merely incorporates the JST in footnotes and an appendix to the KJV text. Its leaders maintain the "inspired translation" made by Smith was not completed, so it should not be accorded the same status as the other scriptures Smith produced.

It's no surprise that Mormon scholars disagree on this point since Smith himself seemed to think that he *had* done all the reconstructive work that was necessary on the Bible. Doctrine and Covenants presents the Lord counseling Smith on January 10, 1832: "[I]t is expedient to continue the work of translation until it be finished" (D&C 73:4).

A year later, Smith wrote in his journal, "I completed the translation and review of the New Testament, on the 2nd of February, 1833."

In a letter dated July 2, 1833, he wrote, "We this day finished the translation of the scriptures, for which we return our gratitude to our heavenly Father."[13]

Yet succeeding Mormon prophets and theologians have declared just the opposite. Young, Fielding Smith and McConkie stated that Smith's version was never completed and therefore is not used as primary scripture by their church.[14] Of course, to anyone who recognizes the problems with Smith's claim to being a prophet, the "Inspired Version" of the Bible has no weight

---

after the name of his father; and he shall be like unto you; for the thing which the Lord shall bring forth by his hand shall bring my people unto salvation" (v. 33). Mormon scholars have determined that Joseph added 12,650 words to Genesis, changed 693 verses in the rest of the Old Testament and 1,453 in the New Testament. See John Widtsoe, *Evidences and Reconciliations*, 354.

[13] See B. H. Roberts, *Comprehensive History of the Church* 1:247–248.

[14] McConkie, however, praises it as "the best source of biblical knowledge." See *A New Witness for the Articles of Faith*, 397.

whatsoever. The changes Smith made are unsupportable from a standpoint of objective scholarship. The effort was undertaken to eliminate problem passages in the authentic Christian Scripture to keep them from being used against Mormon doctrines.

We must look to Smith's later writings (and the works of his successors and other LDS theologians) for an exposition of peculiarly Mormon tenets.

Chief among the writings introducing the new, distinctive and essential Mormon elements is the Doctrine and Covenants, which purports to be a record of revelations Smith and a few others received directly from Christ. Most of the 138 chapters were written before Smith's death in 1844. Two general purposes for the revelations were, first, to "give further witness of the Resurrection of Jesus Christ," and, second, proclaim that "he is still involved in the affairs of mankind."[15]

Of course, we are compelled to ask: What other word do Christians need? The four Gospels, Paul and the Church throughout the ages give reasoned, faithful testimony that Jesus Christ, the Redeemer, rose bodily from the dead on the third day, that he ascended body and soul to heaven, from whence he shall come again. Further, we remember in every age and place the Lord's promise always to be involved with us, to be present as both Lord and Friend: "Lo, I am with you alway, even unto the end of the world" (Matt. 28:20). Why would Smith's further revelations have anything substantive to contribute? They would be, at best, ignored by non-Mormons and, at worst, taken as evidence of Mormons' callous disregard for the sacred and complete nature of the revelation already given, and they would do little to convince Mormons of Christ's resurrection, for they already believed in it.

Smith's reasons for bringing forth the various revelations in the D&C had a more immediate purpose. The teachings of the Book of Mormon could not support his ever-changing theology. Additional divine approbation would be needed to persuade the

---

[15] See Robert J. Woodford, "The Remarkable Doctrine and Covenants," *Ensign*, January 1997, 42–49.

members of such novelties as temples, eternal families, polygamy, eternal progression, three heavens, missionary work among the dead, the Word of Wisdom and priesthood keys.

Smith also gave a great deal of commonplace counsel, mundane direction and outright false prophecies under the guise of heavenly orders. Consider the following:

- In Doctrine & Covenants 47, the Lord appointed John Whitmer to be church historian—at least for a while, since Smith later deposed him.

- In Doctrine & Covenants 57, Christ "appointed and consecrated" the land of Missouri for the gathering of Mormons. Later they had to be transferred to what would become Utah.

- In Doctrine & Covenants 87, Smith predicted that a number of "wars" would soon break out, "beginning at the rebellion of South Carolina" (87:1), which would lead to "war [being] poured out upon all nations, beginning at this place" (v. 2). "[T]he Southern States shall be divided against the Northern States" (v. 3), there will be a slave rebellion (v. 4), famine, plague, earthquakes, thunder, and lightning, "until the consumption decreed hath made a full end of all nations" (v. 6). Mormons often trumpet this as a prophecy of the Civil War, but needless to say, that conflict did not escalate into a World War, there was not a slave rebellion and no consumption making "a full end of all nations."[16]

---

[16] The idea of predicting a Civil War in the U.S. itself was a rather safe prediction. Political pundits had been predicting one for some time. In 1820, Thomas Jefferson predicted that the Missouri Compromise would be "the knell of the Union" and lead eventually to Civil War. Smith made this prediction in December 1832, on the heels of the Nullification Crisis, when South Carolina had nullified two federal laws within its borders, had been brought to the brink of military conflict with the federal government and was openly talking of secession. In making the "prophecy" of D&C 87, Smith drew on

- In Doctrine & Covenants 114, David Patten was instructed by the Lord to prepare himself for a mission in the spring of 1839. Too bad Patten died in the winter of 1838.

- In Doctrine & Covenants 119, Jesus Christ required all surplus property owned by Mormons to be given to their bishops. When most members failed to obey, "the Lord withdrew it for a time, and gave instead the law of tithing to the whole Church" (D&C, 238). Perhaps this is true religious democracy: God is permitted to rule, but only with the consent of his people. When beliefs or practices become burdensome, a new revelation is received, rescinding the previous.

- In Doctrine & Covenants 129, he instructed Mormons on how they could distinguish angels from devils—when you shake hands with an angel, you feel his hand; you don't feel the hand of a demon.

Mormon prophets have not been hesitant in changing the actual text of the revelations contained in Doctrine & Covenants. First published as the *Book of Commandments* in 1833, the D&C was republished in 1835. Many of the words first spoken by Christ to Smith and recorded in the 1833 book were changed, deleted or added to in the 1835 book.[17]

For example, mention has been made of the early Mormons' refusal to abide by the law of consecration, calling for a complete consecration of all possessions to the work of the church. In the 1833 *Book of Commandments*, Christ commands members, "If thou lovest me, thou shalt serve me and keep all my commandments; and behold, thou shalt consecrate all thy properties, that thou hast unto me" (44:26).

---

the popular political talk of the day, made a prediction that hundreds were making on purely non-supernatural grounds and amplified it to apocalyptic proportions, which then failed to appear.

[17] Tanners, *Major Problems of Mormonism*, 106–121.

The 1835 printing changes the Lord's revelation to read, "If thou lovest me thou shalt serve me and keep all my commandments; and behold, thou wilt remember the poor and consecrate of thy properties for their support, that which thou has to impart unto them" (D&C 42:29-30).

Note that the early, recalcitrant Mormons, by their refusal to consecrate *all* their property to the Lord, forced Smith into rewriting a revelation which he claimed, at first, to have been from Almighty God himself.

A second example is typical of much Mormon redacting. That is, when a teaching or view is seen as simply too unorthodox to justify, the teaching is buried, even expunged. (Given the mass production of written, audio and video materials today, however, the Mormon church cannot as comfortably cover up its previous mistakes. Rather, today's tactic is to say, "That was in the past" or "That was then, this is now" or "We look toward the future, not the past.")

In the *Book of Commandments*, chapter 7, Christ is speaking to Cowdery. He had asked the Lord for a gift similar to Smith's that he might translate ancient records. The Lord answers, "Remember this is your gift. Now this is not all, for you have another gift, which is the gift of working with the rod: behold it has told you things: behold there is no other power save God, that can cause this rod of nature to work in your hands, for it is the work of God; and therefore whatsoever you shall ask me to tell you by that means, that will I grant unto you, that you shall know" (7:3).

Like Smith, Cowdery had been involved with the occult practice of divining with rods. Sensitive to possible reproach for showing Christ approving Cowdery's superstitious experimentation, Smith's revised Doctrine and Covenants removed all references to the witching rod: "Now this is not all thy gift, for you have another gift, which is the gift of Aaron: behold it has told you many things: behold there is no other power save the power of God, that can cause this gift of Aaron to be with you. Therefore, doubt not, for it is the gift of God, and you shall hold it in your hands and do marvelous works; and no power shall be able to take it away out of your hands, for it is the work of God; therefore whatsoever you shall ask me to tell you by that means, that will I grant unto you, and you shall have knowledge concerning it" (D&C 8:7-9).

References to the rod, originally spoken by God himself, were removed in Smith's reworking of the divine words. Moreover, the "prophet" saw fit to add a 32-word phrase somehow omitted in the original pronouncement.[18]

When you have a changeable, "progressive" God, you get changeable, "progressive" revelations. Truth is constantly changing, divorced from history, determined by subjective feelings, and made to conform to what the Mormon church views as expedient.

Another Mormon work, The Pearl of Great Price, is composed of five sections: The Book of Moses; Joseph Smith—Matthew; Joseph Smith—History; the Book of Abraham; and the Articles of Faith. The Book of Moses is an extract from Smith's rewriting of the first several chapters of Genesis. In it, we learn that all things were first created *spiritually* before they were naturally found on the earth (3:5). Satan and Jesus had plans to redeem the world, presenting them to the Father, who chose Christ's. With his own plan rejected, Satan, Christ's brother, led a rebellion of one-third of the premortal spirits. He and they were ultimately cast out (4:1-4). God taught Adam and Eve the gospel of his Son and gave them the Holy Ghost (5:8-9). The first parents rejoiced in their transgression: Eve said, "Were it not for our transgressions we never should have known good and evil, and the joy of our redemption, and the eternal life which God giveth unto all the obedient" (5:11).

The name of Jesus Christ and the gospel were revealed to Adam, who accepted Christian baptism (6:51-53). The text concludes with Noah's preparations for the flood.

Joseph Smith—Matthew contains Smith's reworking of Mat-

---

[18] For these and other examples of changes made to supposed divine revelations, see the Tanners' *Major Problems in Mormonism*, 11ff.

thew 23:39 and chapter 24. It represents a portion of Smith's "Inspired Version," though at most it adds verbosity, and not clarity, to the canonical text.

In the seventy-five verses of Joseph Smith—History, we read Smith's account of his search for the correct religion, his first encounters with the angel Moroni, his vision of the Father and the Son, his persecution at the hands of Christian skeptics, his discovery and translation of the golden plates containing the long-buried Book of Mormon and his reception of the Mormon Aaronic priesthood at the hands of the resurrected John the Baptist. By church decree, Mormons must believe all this to be objective, historical fact.[19]

The most controversial portion of the Pearl of Great Price is the Book of Abraham. Its five chapters and three facsimiles were translated and reproduced by Smith from ancient Egyptian papyri. Michael Chandler had arrived in Kirtland, Ohio, in July, 1835, and displayed four Egyptian mummies and some other ancient curios, including writing fragments. Thinking that Smith, the prophet and seer, would be able to translate the documents, some of the Mormon brethren bought the entire exhibit for $2,400. Smith agreed he could translate the work, but it would take time. Skeptics who had denied the Book of Mormon would now have to acknowledge Smith's divine skills.[20]

---

[19] In fact, no independent, verifiable evidence exists to prove even one of these claims.

[20] Charles M. Lawson, . . . *By His Own Hand Upon Papyrus: A New Look at the Joseph Smith Papyri*, 12–14. In discussing Smith's translation of the papyrus, some have stated—incorrectly—that Egyptian could not be read at the time. In actuality, the Rosetta Stone (discovered in 1799) had already allowed Jean François Champollion and a group of other scholars to completely decipher the hieroglyphic script by 1822. Indeed, Champollion's *Summary of the Hieroglyphic System of the Ancient Egyptians* had been published in 1824. Whether Smith knew this or felt safe translating a text in a supposedly untranslatable language is another subject. It may be reasonably surmised that he did not expect anybody to check his translation in a scholarly, scientific manner, as later happened.

To the astonishment and delight of the faithful, Smith "commenced the translation of some of the characters or hieroglyphics, and much to our joy found that one of the rolls contained the writings of Abraham, another the writings of Joseph of Egypt, etc. . . ."[21] Cowdery, W. W. Phelps, and Warren Parrish served as Smith's scribes as he brought forth yet another ancient scripture, this much older than the Book of Mormon or the Old Testament. The work was supposedly in the hand of Abraham himself and gave an account of his sojourn in Egypt. The Book of Abraham either introduced new teachings or verified truths already expounded by Smith. Mormons learned that Abraham had held the high priesthood of the Lord (1:2); that he was saved by Jehovah from being sacrificed on a pagan altar (1:12–15); that he kept a journal of creation and the movements of the heavenly bodies (1:28; 3:2ff); that God commanded Abraham to lie and call Sarai his sister (2:23–24). Abraham also learned of the pre-existence of all things (3:22), the council of the gods and their plan for man (4 and 5), and the dwelling place of God—near the great star Kolob (3:16).

In bringing forth the Book of Abraham, Smith copied three illustrations he said were on the original papyri. He provided divine interpretations. In one, Abraham is stretched on an altar of sacrifice with an idolatrous priest standing over him with a blade. An angel of the Lord, in the form of a bird, hovers nearby. Under the altar are figures Smith identified as false Egyptian gods (28). The second figure portrays the star Kolob and God on a throne, the keywords of the Mormon priesthood and other symbols which "cannot be revealed unto the world; but is to be had in the Holy Temple of God" (36–37).[22] The final illustration is of Abraham on Pharaoh's throne, crowned with the priesthood and discussing astronomy in the king's court (41).

Some time after Smith's death, the Mormon church lost posses-

---

[21] *History of the Church* 2:236.

[22] Though I went to the temple at least weekly, I recall no such signs other than the eye. The others may have been removed or not included in later Mormon temples.

sion of the papyri, which were believed destroyed in the Chicago fire of 1871. Then, in 1967, the Mormon church made the dramatic announcement that a collection of manuscripts were found in New York's Metropolitan Museum of Art. Glued to the back of some of the papyri were maps of Kirtland and architects' rendering of a temple plan. There was no doubt these were the Smith papyri. Though not representing all the writings Smith had purchased from Chandler, the existing copies were sent to several competent Egyptologists. Each came to the same independent conclusion: The papyri were part of a pagan text called *The Book of Breathings*, which gave instructions on the proper preparation of a body for burial. There was no mention of Abraham or his faith. For example, facsimile number 3, which Smith had claimed was Abraham on Pharaoh's throne, is in fact "the Goddess Maat[23] leading Pharaoh before Osiris.[24] . . . Smith has turned the goddess into a king and Osiris into Abraham."[25] Egyptologist Richard A. Parker wrote: "The explanations [of the facsimiles] are completely wrong insofar as any interpretation of the Egyptian original is concerned."[26]

Mormon scholar Edward H. Ashment, former Coordinator for Translation Services for the Mormon church and an Egyptologist, concluded, "[B]elievers will have to continue to 'wait upon the Lord' for their convictions of the historicity of the Book of Abraham."[27]

It seems that a subjective testimony is the only recourse a faithful Mormon can have in the face of universal scholarly dismissal of Smith's "translation." Ashment concluded, "[A]pologia can

---

[23] Maat was an Egyptian concept/deity representing order, stability, justice.
[24] The Egyptian god of the underworld, before whom the dead were judged.
[25] Thus said Oxford scholar A. H. Sayce as early as 1912; quoted in F. S. Spalding, *Joseph Smith, Jr., As A Translator*, 23.
[26] Quoted in *The Case Against Mormonism*, vol. 2, 133. Parker, of Brown University, and John A. Wilson and Klaus Baer, of the University of Chicago, independently concluded that the papyri dated to between 200 and 100 B.C.
[27] Edward H. Ashment, "The Use of Egyptian magical Papyri to Authenticate the Book of Abraham," 9.

present 'faithful history' that is not historically rigorous to an unsuspecting audience. Unfortunately, everyone loses: apologists are not taken seriously by their colleagues in the academic world; church members are misinformed; and embarrassment may ultimately come to the church."[28]

In other words: Mormon apologists should not even pretend that there is any historical credibility to Smith's translation. So pretending only further harms and embarrasses the Mormon church.

The Pearl of Great Price's final section is the Articles of Faith, thirteen statements of belief held by the Church of Jesus Christ of Latter-day Saints. (See appendix III.)

Neither the Doctrine and Covenants nor the Pearl of Great Price is used much in Mormon proselytizing, and with good reason. The D&C is replete with "revelations" repugnant to first-time hearers of the Mormon gospel. And the Pearl of Great Price, with its councils of gods, eternal intelligences, and mythological origins, is too fantastical for historically minded Christians. Latter-day Saints use what has been termed a "layered" approach to truth,[29] presenting the most bland and inoffensive of their doctrines first, in order to "hook" the hearer. Only much later does the convert learn "the rest of the story."

---

[28] Ibid., 9–10.
[29] Latayne C. Scott, "Mormonism and the Question of Truth," *Christian Research Journal*, Summer 1992, 24ff.

33. Continuing Mormon Revelations

Closely aligned with the Mormon notion that the Bible is incomplete is the claim that God continues to give new public revelation throughout every age. Such "continuous revelation" supplies for the alleged deficiencies of the Old and New Testaments. In fact, this belief is one of the key planks of Mormon theology: "Continuous revelation is indeed the very lifeblood of the gospel of the living Lord and Savior, Jesus Christ. . . ."[1]

Catholics and other Christians, believing God's definitive Word to have been revealed once for all in Jesus Christ, are wicked and can be damned for holding to finished revelations only. General Authority George Reynolds noted in 1885, "The principle of continuous revelation is one which finds great opposition from the wicked whenever it is taught."[2]

One hundred years later, Apostle James E. Faust echoed the sentiment and passed judgment, saying, "[S]ome have died spiritually by exclusively following prophets who have long been dead."[3]

Ongoing revelation comes, Mormons believe, in various ways. On the simplest level, an individual may receive guidance from the Lord about a choice facing him. Or, as the head of a family, a father may be given instruction from God for the proper governing of his wife and children. Bishops receive revelation to help in running their wards and members. A member blessed with a revelation may use it only for himself or his charges. No one has the right to declare God's word to any member enjoying a superior position in the Mormon hierarchy. This is what Catholics would refer to as "private revelation"—that is, revelation that is

---
[1] *The Teachings of Spencer W. Kimball*, 443.
[2] *Journal of Discourses* 26:163.
[3] "Continuous Revelation," *Ensign*, November 1989, 9.

binding only on its particular recipients, not on all God's people. Catholics acknowledge that such revelation is still given in the world, since it does not claim to complete, correct or add to "the faith which was once delivered unto the saints" (Jude 3; cf. *Catechism of the Catholic Church* 67). Catholics do not agree with all points of Mormon thought regarding this kind of revelation; they certainly do not believe that private revelation is available on the scale Mormons claim. (The Mormon faith essentially promises private revelation to every individual, such as through the "burning of the bosom" regarding the Book of Mormon's truthfulness.) Nevertheless, we will focus here on what Catholic terminology refers to as "public revelation"—that is, revelation that is claimed to be binding not only on its particular recipients but also on all of God's people.

The Mormon prophet, the "President of the Church," is the only man on earth who possesses "all the keys" of authority and who can receive and proclaim revelation binding on the whole church without any to overrule him. This is *not* analogous to papal infallibility. Like magisterial infallibility in general, papal infallibility does not provide new revelation or new doctrines. It allows the pope, or the magisterium in union with him, to infallibly rule on whether or not a given doctrine is contained or implied in the revelation that has been passed down from Christ and the apostles. It does not allow the pope or his brother bishops to receive *new*, hitherto unrevealed doctrines from God. No such new teachings are needed, since the faith has already been delivered once for all. The charism of infallibility merely helps us keep from going astray as we (meaning the Catholic Church as a whole) meditate upon, interpret and implement the faith delivered to us by Jesus.

Mormon prophets and other leaders, by contrast, claim to receive revelations from their God on any matter, big or small, religious or secular.[4] Such a "key" has been avowed by Mormon

---

[4] James E. Faust, in the article cited, lists some current revelations: "The use of modern technology, such as films, computers, and satellite broadcasts . . . new ways to conduct missionary work . . . the location and building of temples . . ." (9–10).

prophets for the past century and a half. Ezra Taft Benson, in a February 26, 1980, speech at BYU, declared, "The Prophet can receive revelation on any matter—temporal or spiritual" (10). Moreover, according to Benson, "The Prophet is not required to have any particular earthly training or credentials to speak on any subject or act on any matter at any time" (6).

Indeed, according to seventh Mormon president Heber J. Grant, "To supply such inspired guidance is a main function of the president of the Church."[5]

Mormons find biblical support for modern-day prophets and revelation in Amos 3:7: "Surely the Lord God will do nothing, but he revealeth his secret unto his servants the prophets."

Mormons argue that this verse shows that the Lord must have a prophet on earth today (who, of course, is identified as the Mormon prophet). But Mormons cannot use this verse in this manner. Amos was in the process of prophesying disaster befalling the Northern kingdom of Israel. This was the context for his saying that God doesn't (from today's perspective: *didn't*) do anything without telling the prophets first so that they could announce it to the people. But do Mormon prophets claim to be informed about every calamity, every war, every disaster that impacts their sphere? Do they announce it beforehand to the Mormon people so they can repent and avoid it, as the biblical prophets did? Do they announce them as disasters brought on the Mormon people because of their sins—or do they announce no calamity at all and praise the Mormon people for their superior uprightness? Again, Mormons can't have it both ways. If they want to apply Amos 3:7 to the present day, then they are going to have to accept the biblical model for prophecy and how prophets function with respect to God's people. If they don't want to accept this, then they will have to say Amos 3:7 does not apply to today.

Each Old Testament prophet received partial revelation from God that he then preached to the people. Hebrews 1:1 states,

---

[5] *Gospel Standards*, vii. Elder Faust groups these men with the "prophetic oracles who have tuned in over the centuries to the 'celestial transmitting station,' with a responsibility to relay the Lord's word to others" (8).

"In times past, God spoke in fragmentary and varied ways to our fathers through the prophets. . . ." That there was to be a consummate and complete revelation, one needing no replication or supplement, is certain from the remainder of the verse: "in this, the final age, he has spoken to us through his Son, whom he has made heir of all things. . . ." (NAB). Here the fragmentary revelation of the past is compared with the complete and final revelation through the Son. Jesus Christ, God's supreme Word made flesh, embodied the fullness of divine communication. He who is the way, the truth and the life provides for no continuous, corrective or contradictory revelation. He is the same yesterday, today and forever.

One way new Mormon revelation is given and new scripture is produced is via pronouncements from the First Presidency of the Church and the general authorities gathered twice annually for general conferences. The messages are printed in the Mormon church's monthly magazine, *Ensign*, and studied in congregational and classroom settings. The printed talks of the general authorities are considered "scripture."

Combining the hypothesis of continuous revelation with the notion that the printed words of their leaders are scripture, Mormons can look to *Ensign*, the weekly "Church News" section of the Salt Lake *Deseret News*, semiannual sessions of general conferences and other authoritative pronouncements as embodying the developing, up-to-the-minute will of the Lord. This heavenly will is not static; it is fluid, malleable and expedience-oriented, changing in accord with the changing demands of men.

Oddly, though the general conference speeches of Mormon leaders are regarded as scripture in some sense, they are not added to the standard, canonical works of Mormon scripture. Since Smith's day, few "revelations" have been canonized and added to the bound text of Mormon scripture. One was a vision received by President Joseph F. Smith on October 3, 1918, concerning Christ's visit to the souls of the dead. The revelation was unanimously accepted by the Mormon leadership and printed as Section 138 of the Doctrine and Covenants. Two further revelations, called Official Declaration—1 and Official Declaration—2, have been appended to the end of Doctrine and Covenants but have not been included in the numbered sequence of sections, perhaps because they directly contradict previous sections.

Polygamy is unambiguously condemned in the Book of Mormon, which calls it "whoredoms" (Jacob 2:26–27). But thirteen years after the Book of Mormon was first printed, a revelation to Smith was recorded in the Doctrine and Covenants, proclaiming polygamy "a new and an everlasting covenant." All those "who have this law revealed unto them must obey" it. "No one can reject this covenant and be permitted to enter" into the Lord's glory (D&C 132:4–6). Jesus Christ, through Smith's mouth, commanded his handmaid, Emma Smith, "to abide and cleave unto my servant Joseph, and to none else. But if she will not abide this commandment she shall be destroyed, saith the Lord; for I am the Lord thy God, and will destroy her if she abide not in my law" (D&C 132:54).[6]

Section 132 of the D&C did not place a limit to the number of wives a Mormon man might have, and plural marriage (Mormons prefer this term to "polygamy," just as they prefer "plural gods" to "polytheism") was encouraged Mormon practice for the next four and a half decades, until 1890, when then-President Wilford Woodruff announced "in the most solemn manner" his advice to Latter-day Saints "to refrain from contracting any marriage forbidden by the law of the land" (Official Declaration—1). This so-called "Manifesto" was revealed to him by the Lord, Woodruff maintained, in order to thwart the Saints' persecution by an inflexible federal government. (See pages 292–293 of the D&C.) God apparently decided to change his rules rather than stand up to the

---

[6] By most accounts, Emma went along grudgingly as her husband obeyed the everlasting law and added several more wives. The official church position that Smith reluctantly took additional wives only after being threatened by a sword-wielding angel is brought into question by reports that the young prophet actively anticipated the printed revelation as early as 1831. See B. H. Roberts' introduction to *History of the Church* 5:29.

U.S. government—a far cry from the martyrdom in the cause of righteousness to which he called the early Christians faced with the might of the Roman Empire.

From a Mormon perspective, though, it's no surprise that God should flip-flop so easily. According to Mormons, continuous revelation from the Lord first allowed polygamy in the cases of Abraham, David, Solomon and other biblical men. He apparently disallowed it through the lips of the Book of Mormon prophet Jacob, and again through Jesus Christ. Its practice was restored by Smith, then again rescinded several years later. Current Mormon practice forbids plural marriage and excommunicates anyone involved with it. One of the questions asked of those applying for advancement or blessing in the church deals with their possible sympathy for Mormon "fundamentalists"—embarrassing apostate groups who revere Smith as a prophet and accept the Book of Mormon but deny the authority of the LDS church to change the revelation on "the everlasting covenant" of plural marriage and who insist on practicing it in their own circles.

It is anticipated that God will flip-flop again. Polygamy is still a requirement for godhood, and there will not only be polygamous marriages in the afterlife, but on earth, in the future, as well. Mormons anticipate there will be further revelation from God through the Mormon prophet on plural marriage. The "holy practice will commence again after the Second Coming of the Son of Man and the ushering in of the millennium."[7] The government presumably will not be threatening the Mormon church then, so it will be safe for God to reintroduce the practice.

Mormons have made a change also in another area: their treatment of blacks. The books of Moses and Abraham provide the "scriptural" basis for Mormonism's historical denial of the priesthood to blacks. Moses 6:8 reads, "For behold, the Lord shall curse the land with much heat, and the barrenness thereof shall go forth forever; and there was a blackness came upon all the children of Canaan, that they were despised among all people."

---

[7] *Mormon Doctrine*, 578.

The inferiority of those having a black skin is underlined in Abraham 1:26, where we read that the Egyptian pharaoh had received several blessings from Noah, who nevertheless "cursed him as pertaining to the Priesthood."

Similarly, the Book of Mormon explained the origin of the dark-skinned Native Americans. Though originally white Hebrews who had migrated to the Americas, they broke with their more righteous brethren, bringing upon themselves the divine curse of a dark skin.[8] When the evil "Lamanites" repented, however, the Book of Mormon notes that "their curse was taken from them, and their skin became white like unto the [righteous] Nephites" (3 Nephi 2:15). What's more, in the last days, when the American Indians are expected to be converted en masse to the Mormon gospel, "many generations shall not pass away among them, save they shall be a white and delightsome people" (2 Nephi 30:6).[9]

There's no lack of LDS commentary on the status of the black race. Traditionally, leaders have attributed a black skin to misbehavior in the pre-existence. McConkie taught, "Those who were less valiant in pre-existence and who thereby had certain spiritual restrictions imposed upon them during mortality are known to us as the *negroes*. Such spirits are sent to earth through the lineage of Cain, the mark put upon him for his rebellion against God and his murder of Abel being a black skin."[10]

In this, the Mormon apostle echoed the constant teachings of the LDS prophets, clearly set forth by Young, who wrote, "You see some classes of the human family that are black, uncouth, uncomely, disagreeable and low in their habits, wild, and seemingly deprived of nearly all the blessings of the intelligence that is

---

[8] See 1 Nephi 12:23; 2 Nephi 5:21; Jacob 3:3-5; Alma 3:6; Mormon 5:15-18.

[9] In the 1981 edition of the Book of Mormon, this last verse has been changed to read, "they shall be a pure and delightsome people." See also Jacob 3:8; 3 Nephi 2:14-15; Alma 23:18.

[10] *Mormon Doctrine*, 1958 ed., 476-477.

generally bestowed upon mankind. The first man that committed the odious crime of killing one of his brethren will be cursed the longest of any one of the children of Adam. Cain slew his brother. Cain might have been killed, and that would have put a termination to that line of human beings. This was not to be, and the Lord put a mark upon him, which is the flat nose and black skin. Trace mankind down to after the flood, and then another curse is pronounced upon the same race—that they should be the 'servant of servants;' and they will be, until that curse is removed; and the Abolitionists cannot help it, nor in the least alter that decree. How long is that race to endure the dreadful curse that is upon them? That curse will remain upon them, and they never can hold the Priesthood or share in it until all the other descendants of Adam have received the promises and enjoyed the blessings of the Priesthood and the keys thereof. Until the last ones of the residue of Adam's children are brought up to that favourable position, the children of Cain cannot receive the first ordinances of the Priesthood. They were the first that were cursed, and they will be the last from whom the curse will be removed."[11]

Young's declaration about the mark of Cain is, of course, nonsense. The idea that the human race was hanging by the thread of Cain is not only an affront to God's providence but also manifestly contradicted by the biblical text. Adam and Eve had other sons and daughters (5:4), notably Seth (4:25), and the mark was put on Cain to keep him from being killed by other, future family members, who might seek revenge for the murder of Abel. The mark thus was not a mark of shame but a mark of protection: God would wreak seven-fold vengeance on anyone who killed Cain (4:15). We are not told what the mark was, but from parallels later in the Bible, it was most likely a mark on his forehead (Ezek. 9:4-6; Rev. 7:3, 9:4, 14:1).

Nevertheless, Mormon leaders continued to proclaim the original Mormon ideology regarding the mark of Cain. Fielding Smith

---

[11] *Journal of Discourses* 7:290-291.

also quoted Woodruff's citation of Young's comment: "Any man having one drop of the seed of Cain in him cannot receive the Priesthood; but the day will come when all that race will be redeemed and possess all the blessings which we now have."[12]

That day, according to Young and other Mormon leaders, would come only at the end times. But in 1978, a revelation led President Kimball to announce a new policy: All worthy men, regardless of race, would be candidates for the priesthood. As before, this turnabout in Mormon doctrine was brought on by societal factors—principally by the increasing lack of tolerance for racial discrimination and by the spread of Mormonism in Brazil, where a large proportion of the population is racially mixed, having the "one drop" of Negro blood that would deny them the Mormon priesthood. Thus to avoid social stigmatization at home and to make new converts abroad, the Mormon God decided it was time for another "revelation."

Apparently, opening the priesthood to all worthy males, regardless of color, and opening the temples to all members who qualify, came in part from the expansion of the Mormon church into many nations. President Kimball noted that his prophetic predecessors had promised that at some time the priesthood would be extended to persons of color. By revelation, the Lord had "confirmed that the long-promised day has come when every faithful, worthy man in the Church may receive the holy priesthood . . . without regard for race or color." He concluded: "We declare with soberness that the Lord has now made known his will. . . ." Thus Official Declaration—2 was added to the end of the Doctrine and Covenants.

Young had just as clearly revealed the Lord's intention to withhold the priesthood from blacks until all divinely chosen white males had been brought into the church. Since the Mormon church continues to seek converts from among all races of people, it would seem that the full quota of elect white males has not yet

---

[12] *The Way to Perfection*, 106.

been achieved. The prohibition of the priesthood to blacks nevertheless has been repealed. Perhaps this decision was what Benson had in mind when he delivered his famous "Fourteen Fundamentals in Following the Prophet" speech a year and a half after the Official Declaration—2 was made public. His third point was: "The living prophet is more important to us than a dead prophet." And, "Beware of those who would pit the dead prophets against the living prophets, for the living prophets always take precedence" (4–5).

In *Mormon Doctrine*, McConkie wrote, "Negroes in this life are denied the priesthood; under no circumstances can they hold this delegation of authority from the Almighty. (Abraham 1:20–27.) The gospel message of salvation is not carried affirmatively to them. . . ." (476–477).[13]

However, a monograph published by former Mormons Jerald and Sandra Tanner in March, 1980, contains a talk by McConkie, in which he then stated, "Forget everything that I have said, or what President Brigham Young or President George Q. Cannon or whomsoever [sic] has said in days past that is contrary to the present revelation. We spoke with a limited understanding and without the light and knowledge that now has come into the world. . . . It doesn't make a particle of difference what anybody ever said about the Negro matter before the first day of June of this year (1978). It is a new day and a new arrangement. . . ." (no page number).

Under the rubric of "forget everything we ever said; today's a new day," the Mormon leadership considers itself excused from explaining, let alone justifying, conflicting and contradictory God-

---

[13] A revised edition was published in 1966. Twelve years later, McConkie found it necessary to back away from the traditional LDS position. Nevertheless, all subsequent editions of *Mormon Doctrine* bear the 1966 copyright, with no indication of further revision, and the text of the 1978 revelation about blacks appears in books ostensibly written in 1966. McConkie died in 1985; perhaps his best-known work will now remain in final form.

given decrees. Since the Mormon God continues to change, it should come as no surprise that his mind does too. Mormon prophets have the job of keeping members informed on God's current opinions.

During an interview on "60 Minutes" on Easter Sunday 1996, President Hinckley, when questioned about the Mormon church's previous ban on blacks in the priesthood, replied, "It's behind us. Look, that's behind us."

If such things are behind the church now, it is because of the changes in society. And who led those changes? The members, white and black, of Catholic and Protestant churches in the United States. It was the Mormon church that was "behind the times," being dragged along the path of racial reconciliation by all those "apostate" Christians. Rather than being the moral leader on such matters, the Mormon church was the moral caboose of the American religious scene, refusing full participation to African-Americans until the eve of the 1980s.

Moreover, Hinckley was engaging in wishful thinking by declaring that the racial issue is behind the Mormon church. While blacks may be allowed to hold the Mormon priesthood today, nothing has been done to overturn the supposed revelations concerning *why* blacks have darker skin. It still is "unrepealed" Mormon doctrine that people are born black because of misdeeds—or, at least, lack of valor—in their previous existence in the spirit world. The current Mormon strategy is to dismiss this fact, to sweep it under the rug and simply say, "Look, that's behind us." But this strategy won't work forever. Such a glaringly racist statement cannot remain "on the books" indefinitely, especially in the Information Age, without becoming a major embarrassment to the Mormon church. In his "60 Minutes" interview, Hinckley admonished the listeners not to worry about such insignificant vagaries of history, echoing a theme expounded by other Mormon leaders aware of the damaging facts in their church's past. Boyd K. Packer, current Acting President of the Quorum of the Twelve, is a zealous defender of Mormon orthodoxy. In an address published in

Brigham Young University Studies, Summer 1981, President Packer noted that even the study and telling of factual Mormon history can damage members' faith.

"In an effort to be objective, impartial, and scholarly," he said, "a writer or a teacher may unwittingly be giving equal time to the adversary. . . . Some things that are true are not very useful."[14]

With a God who continually changes his mind, who knows what the future theological shape of Mormonism may be? Perhaps with sufficient time and desire to be accepted in the mainstream, Christian world, the Mormon doctrine of God may be revised in an orthodox direction.

It's happened with other groups. The Worldwide Church of God, founded by Herbert W. Armstrong, originally held beliefs about God every bit as unorthodox as Mormonism's. Yet after Armstrong died, its leaders re-evaluated what Scripture teaches concerning the Godhead and found the historic Christian understanding true. Mormons have additional scriptures to deal with, but they also have the possibility of future "revelations" to deal with the inconvenient scriptures.

---

[14] 259ff.

Conclusion

November 1, 1995. The doorbell rang at 8:30 p.m., just after my wife and I had returned home from All Saints' Day Mass. The couple at the door were directors of a Mormon church department with offices in the Joseph Smith Memorial Building in Salt Lake City. This husband and wife had met us when we first became Mormons and moved to Utah. They became, in a sense, our "patrons," introducing us to the Mormon church and many of its most important members. Through their efforts, we had met with President Gordon B. Hinckley soon after arriving in Salt Lake and were sealed in the temple by him a year later.

It had been five months since we had left Mormonism and Utah. Our address was a post office box, so we had no idea how the couple found us, since we had not given anyone our home address. They had come to the house earlier in the day, but we had been out. Our neighbor had confirmed they had found the right house, so they waited until evening to come back and try again. Though surprised by their sudden appearance, we were pleased to see these friends and invited them in for what we hoped would be a pleasant visit. They stayed about fifteen minutes. After some small talk, they delivered a message from President Hinckley: He and the general authorities were deeply disturbed by the tapes I had made for Catholic Answers, a lay apologetics ministry based in San Diego. In the tapes, I had explained my experiences as a Mormon and the reasons for my return to the Catholic Church. The Mormon hierarchy was particularly distressed that I would speak about the temple rituals and other beliefs better left unrevealed to the uninitiated. Moreover, our visitors told us, the Mormon church was enjoying good rapport with the Catholic Church, and my work could put in jeopardy that irenic relationship.

I pointed out to them that the Mormon church targets Catholics for conversion. Brazil, Mexico, and the Philippines, for example, have seen massive numbers of (nominal?) Catholics fall away to the Mormon gospel. It's naive for Mormon leaders to expect no response from Catholics, like myself, who have been to "Zion" and, disillusioned, returned home to Rome. That's how our visit ended.

As I reflect on my experience in Mormonism, now that I have been back in the Catholic Church for several years, I sometimes ask myself how I would fill in the blank in the following sentence: "I _____ my having been a Mormon." A number of terms could fit: "am astounded by," "am ashamed of," "repent of," "regret." I am surely astounded by having converted to Mormonism. The facts presented in this book provide the basis for my dismay. How could I have believed these teachings? How could I have believed in many gods? That Jesus is inferior to the Father? That the Father has a body of flesh and bones and was once a sinful man who made good? That I could become as great some day as God is now? Not all these doctrines had been equally palatable to me, but I assumed that I would grow in confidence regarding the more wild, unhistorical ones as I studied more. I can say I am ashamed of having been a Mormon, of having given so much time, tithe, and energy to an organization I mistakenly believed totally pro-life and pro-family. More than anything else, I was mortified when I discovered the Mormon church's permissive stand on abortion. This is not to say Mormons commit abortion enthusiastically on a wide scale, but their church officially allows abortion for a wide variety of reasons. To me, this is both irrational and immoral.

I regret the time I spent in Mormonism because I lived for a year and a half without the Eucharist and other sacraments, without prayer to both Christ directly and through the intercession of the Blessed Mother and the saints, without the guidance of the Catholic faith, and with no effective spiritual nurture.

Of course, I have fully repented of having bought into Mormonism, because I now know that what I did was a grave, objective evil. Though my conscience seemed to "clear" me of any unworthy motives for conversion, I accept full responsibility for my lack of prudence, my insular thinking, and the scandal I caused.

CONCLUSION 487

For all these I have repented. And I expect ongoing repentance for my spiritual, emotional, and moral weaknesses. My actions continue to have repercussions. As long as these last, so does my contrition.

But these terms do not completely fill in the blank. My time in the Mormon church brought me into contact with many individual Mormons who wholeheartedly sought to serve the Lord as they understood him. They were sincere and took their responsibilities as Mormons seriously. Though they were gravely theologically misled by the organization Joseph Smith started, they were still good people, and many of them had never known anything except Mormonism. It is my prayer that these good people will come to know the truth of Christ as God intends it and as historic Christianity has understood it, that they will eventually see through the theological haze of Mormonism and be reunited with the Church *Christ*, not Smith, founded. And with God's grace, many of them will.

For those who do not perceive the errors of Mormonism in this life, however, there is still hope. As Catholics, we're not burdened by the fear that often grips our Protestant Fundamentalist friends, who believe they must work frantically to save Mormons from otherwise certain damnation. To them, the fact that many Mormons sincerely try to serve God matters not at all. All Latter-day Saints will go to hell unless they become "born-again" Protestants. While it is certainly true that those Mormons, like those of any group, who willfully blind themselves to God's truth cannot be saved, God will be merciful to those who, through no fault of their own, fail to discover him and his true Church in this life. I thus pray and expect to be reunited in heaven with many people I knew on earth as Mormons. We'll all be in the same heaven, of course—the heaven of the one, true, Triune God, where all will be united in the fullness of Catholic truth as they see God for what he is—the infinite, unchanging, omnipotent, and omniscient Creator and God, not just of this world, but of all that exists.

Then those who were Mormons in this life will recognize the

true grandeur and glory of God, who called the worlds into existence from nothingness and who sustains them in existence by his will. Then those Mormons who sincerely sought to follow Jesus will finally come to know the truth of Christ, which will set them free from the errors of Smith.

In the meantime, we as Catholics must redouble our efforts to reach not only Mormons for Christ, but the rest of the world as well. We must emulate the dedication and commitment that Mormons and others (including our own Catholic forebears) have shown in promoting missionary work.

This book has presented only fragments of Catholic truth—those most relevant to the situation of Mormons. The Catholic texts cited provide a more thorough and structured presentation of historic Christianity, whose eternal truth, unchanging, abiding and available to all throughout twenty centuries, is taught fully only in the Catholic Church.

If Mormonism and other groups who are hampered by an appalling and incoherent theology can through zeal alone take their message to the masses, imagine *how much more* the Catholic Church can do by redoubling its evangelistic efforts and calling its members to recommit themselves to the joyous and energetic preaching of the pure Christian teaching that only the Catholic Church possesses. That can truly guard souls against the dangers of groups like Mormonism, and that's my prayer, as it was the prayer of the apostle Peter:

> *Therefore, dear friends, since you already know this, be on your guard so that you may not be carried away by the error of lawless men and fall from your own secure position* [2 Pet. 3:17, NIV].

Appendices

Appendices

APPENDIX ONE

Key Mormon Figures

Sometimes it seems you cannot tell the players without a scorecard. This is certainly true with the history of the Mormon church and the large number of people who have occupied positions in it.

Members of the Smith Family

Joseph Smith, Jr. (1805-1844; founder and first prophet of the LDS church)

Joseph Smith, Sr. (1771-1840; father of the founder of the LDS church; one of "The Eight" witnesses to the Book of Mormon; became an apostle but not a prophet)

Lucy Mack Smith (1775-1856; mother of the first prophet)

Hyrum Smith (1800-1844; brother to Joseph; was killed with him on June 27, 1844)

Emma Hale Smith (1804-1879; first wife of Joseph; rejected Brigham Young's leadership)

Joseph Smith III (1832-1914; the prophet's oldest son; first prophet of the RLDS church; until the mid-1990s, the RLDS church was led by a direct descendant of Joseph Smith, Jr.)

Joseph F. Smith (1838-1918; son of Hyrum Smith; sixth LDS president)

Joseph Fielding Smith (1876-1972; son of Joseph F.; church historian, tenth LDS president)

Prophets

The highest position in the Mormon church is that of prophet. Thus far, there have been fifteen prophets. The dates given below are for the individual's term as prophet.

Joseph Smith, Jr. (1832–1844; wrote Book of Mormon; founded Mormon church; later introduced polytheism and polygamy)

Brigham Young (1847–1877; moved Mormons to the Utah territory, founded Salt Lake City)

John Taylor (1880–1887; went on the lam due to federal monogamy laws)

Wilford Woodruff (1889–1898; dedicated the Salt Lake temple, reversed polygamy)

Lorenzo Snow (1898–1901; emphasized tithing)

Joseph F. Smith (1901–1918; nephew of Joseph Smith, Jr.; had a vision of the dead that is now in Mormon scripture)

Heber J. Grant (1918–1945; increased LDS church's social programs during the Great Depression)

George Albert Smith (1945–1951; carried on charitable enterprises after Second World War)

David O. McKay (1951–1970; emphasized Mormon proselytizing)

Joseph Fielding Smith (1970–1972; LDS church historian and son of Joseph F. Smith)

Harold B. Lee (1972–1973; presided over developments in the LDS church's welfare and priesthood programs)

Spencer W. Kimball (1973–1985; reversed ban on Negroes and on those with Negro ancestry holding Mormon priesthood)

Ezra Taft Benson (1985–1994; Eisenhower's Secretary of Agriculture; promoted study of the Book of Mormon)

Howard W. Hunter (1994–1995; strong emphasis on temple attendance)

Gordon B. Hinckley (1995–present; former counselor in the First Presidency; international emphasis)

Apostles

Some important Mormons belong to the Quorum of the Twelve and hold the title "apostle." New prophets are elevated from these men. All of the prophets have been apostles first. However, some apostles have played an important role in Mormon history and theology even if they did not go on to become prophet. Among them are:

Orson Pratt (apostle from 1835–1881; excommunicated for few months in 1842)

James E. Talmage (1911–1933)

John A. Widtsoe (1921–1952)

LeGrand Richards (1952–1983)

Bruce R. McConkie (1972–1985)

Boyd K. Packer (1970–present)

Theologians

Perhaps the most influential non-apostle theologian is B. H. Roberts, who was a member of the Quorum of the Seventy and who lived from 1877 to 1933.

Book of Mormon Witnesses

The majority of the eleven witnesses of the Book of Mormon either left Joseph Smith or were excommunicated. All the remaining had died before the power struggle after Smith's death.

THE THREE WITNESSES

Oliver Cowdery (made apostle in 1829; excommunicated in 1838; rebaptized in 1848; died in 1850); David Whitmer (excommunicated in 1838; began his own sect); Martin Harris (excommunicated in 1837; rebaptized in 1842; drifted away after 1847 and joined several other sects; rebaptized in 1870)

THE EIGHT WITNESSES

Christian Whitmer (died in 1835); Jacob Whitmer (apostatized in 1838); Peter Whitmer, Jr. (died in 1835); John Whitmer (excommunicated in 1838; the four Whitmers were David Whitmer's brothers); Hiram Page (apostatized in 1838; married to Whitmers' sister); Joseph Smith, Sr. (1771–1839; father of Mormon church founder); Hyrum Smith (1800–1844; brother of Joseph Smith, Jr. and patriarch of the church); Samuel H. Smith (1808–1844; brother of Joseph and Hyrum Smith)

APPENDIX TWO

Joseph Smith's Vision Accounts

The following is a selection of accounts Joseph Smith gave concerning supernatural visions he claimed to have received. In the following, the spelling, punctuation, and grammar is that given in the originals.

A. *1832 Ledger Account of the First Vision*

I felt to mourn for my own Sins and for the Sins of the world for I learned in the Scriptures that God was the same yesterday to day and forever that he was no respecter to persons for he was God for I looked upon the sun the glorious luminary of the earth and also the moon rolling in their magesty through the heavens and also the Stars Shining in their courses and the earth also upon which I stood and the beast of the field and the fowls of heaven and the fish of the waters and also man walking forth upon the face of the earth in magesty and in the Strength of beauty whose power and intiligence in governing the things which are so exceding great and marvilous even in the likeness of him who created him them and when I considered upon these things my heart exclaimed well hath the wise man Said ~~the~~ it is a fool that Saith in his heart there is no God my heart exclaimed all all these bear testimony and bespeak an omnipotent and omnipreasant power a being who makith Laws and decreeeth and bindeth all things in their bounds who filleth Eternity who was and is and will be fron all Eternity to Eternity and when I considered all these things and that that being Seeketh such to worship him as worship him in spirit and in truth therefore I cried unto the Lord for mercy for there was none else to whom I could go and ~~to~~ obtain mercy and the Lord heard my cry in the wilderness and while in the attitude of calling upon the Lord in the 16th year of my age a piller of ~~fire~~ light above the brightness of the Sun at noon day come down from above and rested upon me and I was filld with the Spirit of God and he Spake unto me Saying Joseph my Son thy Sins are forgiven thee, go thy way walk in my Statutes and keep my commandments behold I am the Lord of glory I was crucifyed for the world that all those who believe on my name may have Eternal life behold the world lieth in sin and at this time and none doeth good no not one they have turned asside from the Gospel and keep not my commandments. . . .[1]

B. *1835 Newspaper Account of an Angelic Visitation*

In my last [letter], published in the 3d No. of the Advocate I apologized for the brief manner in which I should be obliged to give, in many instances, the history of this church. Since then yours of Christmas [i.e., your letter from Christmas] has been received. It was not my wish to be understood that I could not give the leading items of every important occurrence, at least so far as would affect my duty to my fellowmen, in such as contained important information upon the subject of doctrine and would render it intelligibly plain; but as there are, in a great house, many vessels, so in the history of a work of this magnitude, many items which would be interesting to those who follow, are forgotten. . . .

You will recollect that I mentioned the time of a religious excitement, in Palmyra and vicinity to have been in the 15th year of our brother J. Smith Jr's age—that was an error in the type—it should have been the 17th.—You will please remember this correction, as it will be necessary for the full understanding of what will follow in time. This would bring the date down to the year 1823. . . .

[During this religious excitement] our brother was urged forward and strengthened in the determination to know for himself of the certainty and reality of pure and holy religion.—And it is only necessary for me to say, that while this excitement continued, he continued to call upon the Lord in secret for a full manifestation of

---

[1] Milton V. Backman, Jr., *Joseph Smith's First Vision* (Salt Lake City: Bookcraft, 1980), 156–157.

divine approbation, and for, to him, the all important information, if a Supreme being did exist, to have an assurance that he was to accept him. . . .

On the evening of the 21st of September, 1823, previous to retiring to rest, our brother's mind was unusually wrought up on the subject which had so long agitated his mind—his heart was drawn out in fervent prayer, and his whole soul was so lost to every thing of a temporal nature, that earth, to him, had lost its claims, and all he desired was to be prepared in heart to commune with some kind of messenger who could communicate to him the desired information of his acceptance with God.

At length the family retired, and he, as usual, bent his way, though in silence, where other might have rested their weary frames "locked fast in sleep's embrace;" but repose had fled, and accustomed slumber had spread her refreshing hand over others beside him—he continued still to pray—his heart, though once hard and obdurate, was softened, and that mind which had often fitted, like the "wild bird of passage," had settled upon a determined basis not to be decoyed or driven from its purpose.

In this situation hours passed unnumbered—how many or how few I know not, neither is he able to inform me; but supposes it must have been eleven or twelve, and perhaps later, as the noise and bustle of the family, in retiring, had long since ceased.—While continuing in prayer for a manifestation in some way that his sins were forgiven; endeavoring to exercise faith in the scriptures, on a sudden a light like that of day, only of a purer and far more glorious appearance and brightness, burst into the room.—Indeed, to use his own description, the first sight was as though the house was filled with a consuming and unquenchable fire. This sudden appearance of a light so bright, as must naturally be expected, occasioned a shock or sensation, visible to the extremities of the body. It was, however, followed with a calmness and serenity of mind, and an overwhelming rapture and joy that surpassed understanding, and in a moment a personage stood before him.

Notwithstanding the room was previously filled with light above the brightness of the sun, as I have before described, yet there seemed to be an additional glory surrounding or accompanying this personage, which shone wit an increased degree of brilliancy, of which he was in the midst; and though his countenanc was as lightening, yet it was of a pleasing, innocent and glorious appearance, so much so, that every fear was banished from the heart, and nothing but calmness pervaded the soul.

It is no easy task to describe the appearance of a messenger from the skies—indeed, I doubt there being an individual clothed with perishable clay, who is capable to do this work. . . .

But it may be well to relate the particulars as far as given [by Smith]—The stature of this personage was a little above the common size of men in this age; his garment was perfectly white, and had the appearance of being without seam.

Though fear was banished from his heart, yet his surprise was no less when he heard him declare himself to be a messenger sent by commandment of the Lord, to deliver a special message, and to witness to him that his sins were forgiven, and that his prayers were heard; and that the scriptures might be fulfilled, which say— "God has chosen the foolish things of the world to confound the things which are mighty . . . Therefore, says the Lord, I will proceed to do a marvelous work among this people, even a marvelous work and a wonder; the wisdom of the wise shall perish, and the understanding of their prudent shall be hid; for according to his covenant which he made with his ancient saints, his people, the house of Israel, must come to a knowledge of the gospel, and own that Messiah whom their fathers rejected, and with them the fulness of the Gentiles be gathered in, to rejoice in one fold under one Shepherd."

"This cannot be brought about until first certain preparatory things are accomplished, for so has the Lord purposed in his own mind. He has therefore chosen you as an instrument in his hand to bring light that which shall perform his act, his strange act, and bring to pass a marvelous work and a wonder. Wherever sound of it shall go it shall cause the ears of men to tingle, and wherever it shall be proclaimed, the pure of heart shall rejoice, while those who draw near to God with their mouths, and honor him with their lips, while their hearts are far from him, will seek its overthrow, and the destruction of those by whose hands it is carried. Therefore, marvel not if your name is made a derision, and had as a by-word among such, if you are the instrument in bringing it, by the gift of God, to the knowledge of the people."

He then proceeded and gave a general account of the promises made to the fathers, and also gave a history of the aborigines of this country, and said they were literal descendants of Abraham. He represented them as once being an enlightened and intelligent people, possessing a correct knowledge of the gospel, and the plan of restoration and redemption. He said this history was written and deposited not far from that place, and that it was our brother's privilege, if obedient to the commandments of the Lord, to obtain, and translate the same by the means of the Urim and Thummim, which were deposited for that purpose with the record.

"Yet," said he, "the scripture must be fulfilled before it is translated, which says that the words of a book. Which were sealed, were presented to the learned; for thus has God determined to leave men without excuse, and to show the meek that his arm is not shortened that it cannot save."

A part of the book was sealed, and was not to be opened yet. The sealed part, said he, contains the same revelation which was given to John upon the isle of Patmos, and when the people of the Lord are prepared, and found worthy, then it will be unfolded unto them.

On the subject of bringing to light the unsealed part of this record, it may be proper to say, that our brother was expressly informed, that it must be done with an eye single to the glory of God; if this consideration did not wholly characterize all his proceedings in relation to it, the adversary of truth would overcome him, or at least prevent his making that proficiency in the glorious work which he otherwise would.

While describing the place where the record was deposited, he gave a minute relation of it, and the vision of his mind being opened at the same time, he was permitted to view it critically; and previously being acquainted with the place, he was able to follow the direction of the vision, afterward, according to the voice of the angel, and obtain the book.[2]

---

[2] Oliver Cowdery, *Latter Day Saints' Messenger and Advocate*, Feb. 1835, vol. 1, no. 5, 78–80.

C. 1835 Diary Account of the First Vision

A pillar of fire appeared above my head; which presently rested down upon me, and filled me with unspeakable joy. A personage appeared in the midst of this pillar of flame, which was spread all around and yet nothing consumed. Another personage soon appeared like unto the first: he said unto me thy sins are forgiven the. He testified also unto me that Jesus Christ is the son of God. I saw many angels in this vision. I was about 14 years old when I received this first communication.[3]

D. 1838 "Official" Account of the First Vision

Some time in the second year after our removal to Manchester, there was in the place where we lived an unusual excitement on the subject of religion. It commenced with the Methodists, but soon became general among all the sects in that region of country. Indeed, the whole district of country seemed affected by it, and great multitudes united themselves to the different religious parties, which created no small stir and division amongst the people, some crying, "Lo, here!" and others, "Lo, there!" Some were contending for the Methodist faith, some for the Presbyterian, and some for the Baptist. . . .

In the midst of this war of words and tumult of opinions, I often said to myself: What is to be done? Who of all these parties are right; or, are they all wrong together? If any one of them be right, which is it, and how shall I know it? While I was laboring under the extreme difficulties caused by the contests of these parties of religionists, I was one day reading the Epistle of James, first chapter and fifth verse, which reads: If any of you lack wisdom, let him ask of God, that giveth to all men liberally, and upbraideth not; and it shall be given him. . . .

At length I came to the conclusion that I must either remain in darkness and confusion, or else I must do as James directs, that is,

---

[3] Joseph Smith's Diary, 1835–1836, 24; quoted in *Dialogue: A Journal of Mormon Thought*, Spring 1971, 87.

ask of God. I at length came to the determination to "ask of God," concluding that if he gave wisdom to them that lacked wisdom, and would give liberally, and not upbraid, I might venture. So, in accordance with this, my determination to ask of God, I retired to the woods to make the attempt. It was on the morning of a beautiful, clear day, early in the spring of eighteen hundred and twenty. It was the first time in my life that I had made such an attempt, for amidst all my anxieties I had never as yet made the attempt to pray vocally.

After I had retired to the place where I had previously designed to go, having looked around me, and finding myself alone, I kneeled down and began to offer up the desires of my heart to God. I had scarcely done so, when immediately I was seized upon by some power which entirely overcame me, and had such an astonishing influence over me as to bind my tongue so that I could not speak. Thick darkness gathered around me, and it seemed to me for a time as if I were doomed to sudden destruction.

But, exerting all my powers to call upon God to deliver me out of the power of this enemy which had seized upon me, and at the very moment when I was ready to sink into despair and abandon myself to destruction—not to an imaginary ruin, but to the power of some actual being from the unseen world, who had such marvelous power as I had never before felt in any being—just at this moment of great alarm, I saw a pillar of light exactly over my head, above the brightness of the sun, which descended gradually until it fell upon me.

It no sooner appeared than I found myself delivered from the enemy which held me bound. When the light rested upon me I saw two Personages, whose brightness and glory defy all description, standing above me in the air. One of them spake unto me, calling me by name and said, pointing to the other—This is My Beloved Son. Hear Him!

My object in going to inquire of the Lord was to know which of all the sects was right, that I might know which to join. No sooner, therefore, did I get possession of myself, so as to be able to speak, than I asked the Personages who stood above me in the light, which of all the sects was right (for at this time it had never entered into my heart that all were wrong)—which I should join.

I was answered that I must join none of them, for they were

all wrong; and the Personage who addressed me said that all their creeds were an abomination in his sight; that those professors were all corrupt; that: "they draw near to me with their lips, but their hearts are far from me, they teach for doctrines the commandments of men, having a form of godliness, but they deny the power thereof" [Joseph Smith—History 1:5–19].

APPENDIX THREE

"The Articles of Faith"

These "Articles of Faith" are part of the Mormon scripture known as the Pearl of Great Price. Written by Joseph Smith, they were published March 1, 1842.

1. We believe in God, the Eternal Father, and in His Son, Jesus Christ, and in the Holy Ghost.
2. We believe that men will be punished for their own sins, and not for Adam's transgression.
3. We believe that through the atonement of Christ, all mankind may be saved, by obedience to the laws and ordinances of the Gospel.
4. We believe that the first principles and ordinances of the Gospel are: first, Faith in the Lord Jesus Christ; second, Repentance; third, Baptism by immersion for the remission of sins; fourth, Laying on of hands for the gift of the Holy Ghost.
5. We believe that a man must be called of God, by prophecy, and by the laying on of hands by those who are in authority, to preach the Gospel and administer in the ordinances thereof.
6. We believe in the same organization that existed in the Primitive Church, namely, apostles, prophets, pastors, teachers, evangelists, and so forth.
7. We believe in the gift of tongues, prophecy, revelation, visions, healing, interpretation of tongues, and so forth.
8. We believe the Bible to be the word of God as far as it is translated correctly; we also believe the Book of Mormon to be the word of God.
9. We believe all that God has revealed, all that He does now reveal, and we believe that He will yet reveal many great and important things pertaining to the Kingdom of God.
10. We believe in the literal gathering of Israel and in the restoration of the Ten Tribes; that Zion (the New Jerusalem) will be

built upon the American continent; that Christ will reign personally upon the earth; and, that the earth will be renewed and receive its paradisiacal glory.

11. We claim the privilege of worshiping Almighty God according to the dictates of our own conscience, and allow all men the same privilege, let them worship how, where, or what they may.

12. We believe in being subject to kings, presidents, rulers, and magistrates, in obeying, honoring, and sustaining the law.

13. We believe in being honest, true, chaste, benevolent, virtuous, and in doing good to all men; indeed, we may say that we follow the admonition of Paul—We believe all things, we hope all things, we have endured many things, and hope to be able to endure all things. If there is anything virtuous, lovely, or of good report or praiseworthy, we seek after these things.

— JOSEPH SMITH

APPENDIX FOUR

Patriarchal Blessing

On April 4, 1994, I drove to the home of our stake's patriarch to receive my patriarchal blessing. When I received it, I was seated in a chair with the patriarch standing in back of me, his hands resting upon my head. He taped his words so that, later, he could transcribe them and send copies to me and to church headquarters.

> Isaiah Michael Bennett, in humility and with love I place my hands upon your head to give you a patriarchal blessing. I do so by virtue and authority of the holy Melchizedek priesthood and by the right vested in me as patriarch of the Taylorsville, Utah, North Central Stake of Zion. I give you this blessing to help you have a greater understanding and knowledge of the blessings, powers, and the responsibilities which come to those who bear the priesthood of God and to help you find a way to use this great power to bless the lives of others. I give you this blessing as a personal source of spiritual guidance and instruction from the Lord which will lead you on the path to earthly happiness and eternal glory.
>
> Brother Bennett, you belong to the House of Israel through the tribe of Ephraim. Through this great heritage you are entitled to all the blessings promised to Abraham, Isaac, and Jacob and to become the elect of God.
>
> Brother Bennett, you are a spiritual child of the King of heaven. Our Heavenly Father, through his love for you, has blessed you with many talents with which to carry on your life. You were blessed with a calm and determined spirit to look for the good in life and to find the way to truth. You were gently guided by the hand of our Father in heaven to prepare you for service in his royal army, to help spread his gospel, and to stand with and for the church to help stem the tide of evil which abounds around us.

Brother Bennett, I bless you with the continued desire to know and understand the powers and blessings of the priesthood of God. Priesthood carries with it the right to receive things of God; it carries with it the responsibility to instruct; it holds the authority to govern; and it grants the power to bless and heal. To those who learn how to worthily develop this power comes the promise of eternal life. Your confidence will wax strong in the presence of deity and you go forth helping others by cheering, blessing, and comforting them. I bless you with the gift to reach into hearts and change lives by opening the doors and windows of understanding to those who need the gospel. I bless you with the gift of discernment. Through this gift you will be able to keep yourself and your loved ones from evil and harm. The gift of the Holy Ghost will bring you comfort and guidance. I bless you with the gift of prophecy. Be wise in your use of this marvelous gift. It is not given to you to see events that are frightening or to make you fearful of things to come. It is the gift to give you guidance and to help you prepare to go forth in life. In his own time, and according to his will and your worthiness, our Father in heaven will grant you the authority to use the gift of prophecy in behalf of others. Be not impatient in its use, but cultivate it in wisdom.

Brother Bennett, lean not to your own understanding, but trust in the Lord. Humble prayer and diligent study of the scriptures are the two greatest sources of spiritual insight and guidance. Living the Word of Wisdom will bring you health and strength and it will be a shield and a protection to you spiritually and physically. Following the counsel of the prophets will bring you peace and joy. As you conduct your self in this upright pattern of living, our Heavenly Father will grant you many blessings. You will have the privilege of taking your wife to the Temple of the Most High God to be sealed to each other for time and all eternity. You will have the privilege of receiving children and teaching them the gospel. Bring your children up righteously to fulfill honorable missions in our Father in heaven's kingdom. Your wife will be the queen in your home with you as its patriarch. You will have the blessing and privilege of doing research for the dead. Go back into the history of your family to prepare the way for them to partake of the great plan of salvation by completing their temple ordinances. The Lord will bless you and you will feel his love encircle your life.

Brother Bennett, the key to eternal life is living faithfully and obediently the commandments of God to the end of mortality. As you so live, I seal you up against the power of the destroyer to come forth on the morning of the resurrection of the just to stand before the judgment seat of God to receive your celestial blessings and glory. You will go forth into eternity to be a builder of worlds, kingdoms and principalities to reign over them in love and power and glory. These blessings I humbly seal upon you in the name of Jesus Christ our Redeemer. Amen.

APPENDIX FIVE

Resignation Letter

Barbara and I mailed the following letter to our former Mormon bishop (Sandy, Utah) after we had determined to leave The Church of Jesus Christ of Latter-day Saints and return to the Catholic Church. He responded by asking us to meet with him and other authorities. We refused, since our purpose was firm and our reasons were clearly stated in the letter. After another similar letter to the bishop, we were informed that our names had been removed from church membership rolls.

June 1, 1995

Dear Bishop Bolander:

During the past month, Barbara and I have been reflecting upon certain aspects of the Mormon church's teachings and practices. Throughout the time leading up to our baptism, we studied and discussed various principles and mores with our missionaries, priesthood authorities and others. We felt we understood the doctrines; we certainly respected the way of life of the members. I had had my fill of anti-Mormon literature, and felt that I could give adequate responses to most of the objections. For the rest—that would come in time.

As both Barbara and I were well-rooted in Catholic morality and spirituality, we had believed that the Mormon church would feel, to a great extent, very similar. Mormon emphasis on the family and respect for life mirrored our own deeply held convictions on the sanctity of all human life, from conception through natural death. In addition, we were continually assured that our temple experiences, when we were finally granted permission to attend, would be the most moving of spiritual experiences. Those who had had both experiences compared the temple endowment to a Catholic high Mass. But these two areas, and others, now present us with deep concerns.

It was not until we had been members of the church for several months that we discovered the LDS church's position on abortion. We had understood that the church was totally opposed to all deliberate killing of the unborn, seeing it as an intrinsic evil. Presidents Benson and Kimball used such terms as "unborn humans" and "child" in describing the victims of abortion. They and other general authorities variously describe the act of abortion as "crime," "calamity," "serious sin," "most revolting and sinful practice," "heinous." It is, as they say, "one of the most serious sins," a "damnable practice" "emphasized by Satan." This is akin to the Catholic teaching, at least thus far. This is what we knew, at the time of our baptism, to be the Mormon church's position on abortion. Abortion is sinful because it is the deliberate taking of the life of an unborn child (both innocent and defenseless, by any definition.) It was not until much later that we heard the full truth.

As President Kimball has stated, and as the present president of the church teaches (see the General Handbook of Instructions), "abortion is permissible," albeit in "exceptional situations." These circumstances, in which an abortion may be committed (after serious prayer and consultation with authorities), include the catch-all category of the mother's health. Not one of the reasons given for allowing the permissibility of abortion—rape, incest, serious birth defect, danger to mother's life or health—reaches back to the core: the abortion kills a "human," "child," "baby." The circumstances surrounding the baby's conception or gestation deprive him or her of neither humanity nor innocence.

That is the position of the Roman Catholic Church. It seems perhaps that Church alone holds to and teaches that position, while at the same time using all its resources to provide true Christian help and guidance to those involved. Once I had learned of the Mormon church's true position on abortion, I tried to find teachings that would indicate that the church's position had changed (as so many other of its positions have throughout its history). But I looked and studied and consulted in vain. That loophole remains, unreasonable and untenable. Barbara and I have felt confusion and embarrassment, and have determined that our testimony cannot bear this serious contradiction.

In addition, we are concerned about the "spirit" of Mormon worship, particularly in the temples.

We believe we were well prepared to attend the temple; our recommends and their renewal would indicate that the priesthood authorities believed the same. Members and leaders of each ward we had lived in promised that, unlike the Sunday block meetings, the temple would be a special and spiritual experience, filled with quiet reverence and focused on Christ. We were counting on this, for we dearly missed the holy and devout spirit of the Catholic Mass and services. But the temple was a great disappointment. While it did not present the gruesome rituals some anti-Mormon literature talks about, it seemed to us to be merely superficial and repetitive. We found nothing particularly Christ-centered. And, although some of the more rabidly anti-Christian and specifically anti-Catholic passages have been recently removed, the temple presentation still makes it clear that all doctrines but Mormon are serving Satan's purposes. (No wonder that such writers as Bruce R. McConkie and his son, Joseph Fielding, cavalierly toss about the term "apostate" in referring to orthodox Christianity. Or that Dallin Oaks could make such unfortunate and inopportune comments at the recent general conference.) The beauty of the various temples we have attended, together with the quieter atmosphere, white clothing, courteous workers and professional video presentations do not, for us, constitute true spirituality. While Mormons place great emphasis on "feeling the Spirit," we assumed that, given our proper motivation and open heart, we would also "feel of the Spirit." And we sincerely tried to delve into the temple ritual. We attended endowments between fifteen and twenty times. We visited six temples. We prayed and fasted for a right disposition. We brought with us the strongest testimonies we could. But we did not find "the Spirit" or Christ. Instead, we were disappointed with vacuous experiences time and again. We took seriously and lived up to all the covenants we made in the temple. We know that the temple rituals are meant, except for the participant's first time, to be applied to the deceased for whom they are being assigned. But our hearts are no longer in any of it. Displace or remove one piece of doctrine, and the Mormon church is no longer believable. For us, it was the abortion issue and the temple experience that impelled us to look more deeply into the rest of the church.

We find personal confusion and embarrassment over the Mormon church's permitting abortion in certain instances; we find that our own spirits have begun to dry with the lack of a spiritual sustenance so strongly promised yet so ineffectually delivered.

We have prayed about and reflected upon all this. When we received Mormon baptism, we did so in good conscience and sincerely. We lived up to all our covenants as best we could. We are grateful to all the good members of the Mormon church who helped us over the past eighteen months. We admire many of them for their strong faith and righteous lives. But we no longer can be a part of the LDS church. While we do not feel that we made a mistake in becoming members, we know that it would be a grave mistake for us to remain members. Please remove our names from the membership of the church. We renounce any ordinations, offices or positions we may have been given.

Through the power of the Spirit of the Lord, and by his kind and patient mercy, Barbara and I are returning to full membership in the Roman Catholic Church, which we now can testify, more strongly than ever, is Christ's true and only Church on earth, possessing the eternal priesthood and all authority, a firm and constant witness to the holiness and inviolability of all human life, the center and spring of all things spiritual.

Yours very truly,

Isaiah Bennett and Barbara Bennett

Bibliography

There's not much written about Mormonism from a Catholic perspective. I could find only three short books, two of which are seriously deficient. *Mormonism: The Prophet, the Book and the Cult*, by Peter Bartley, contains allegations similar to those made by some rabid anti-Mormon Protestants, belying its credibility. *A Tale of Two Cities: A Comparison Between the Mormon and the Catholic Religious Experiences*, by Rev. William Taylor, is the work of a self-described "post-Vatican II" Catholic. Its treatment of Mormon belief is brief; its presentation of "Catholic reality" is a politically correct depiction of large segments of the "American Catholic Church."

One other Catholic work is *A Christian Looks at Mormonism*, by Rev. William J. Mitchell. Father Mitchell's short book (55 pages) is in outline form and presents over forty topics with excerpts from Mormon writings and a brief critique. The work was first published in 1977.

Jerald and Sandra Tanner, former Mormons (though both left the LDS church before receiving their temple endowments), are well-known suppliers of information critical of the LDS church. Much of their material is copies of primary sources inaccessible to most researchers. In this, their service is unparalleled. Their major work is *Mormonism—Shadow or Reality?* first published twenty-five years ago and constantly updated. Other titles are listed in the bibliography. Their work is closely typed, mimeographed pages, packed with original research and bound with plastic covers. Their work is available from Utah Lighthouse Ministry, Salt Lake City, Utah. One word of caution: the Tanners are now Fundamentalist Protestants, members of The Christian and Missionary Alliance. Their *sola scriptura* bias occasionally shows up in their analyses.

Perhaps the most energetic apologetics work done by Mormons is that from Foundation for Ancient Research and Mormon Studies (FARMS), based in Provo, Utah.

Mormon Works Cited from Electronic Texts

References from the following works by LDS authors were taken from *LDS Collectors Library* CD-ROM, copyright 1995, Infobases, Inc.

Ballard, Melvin J. *Three Degrees of Glory: A Discourse by Melvin J. Ballard.* (22 September 1922, Ogden, Utah.) Salt Lake City: Magazine Printing Company, 1955.

Benson, Ezra Taft. *Teachings of Ezra Taft Benson.* Salt Lake City: Bookcraft, 1988.

The Book of Mormon. Translated by Joseph Smith, Jr. Salt Lake City: The Church of Jesus Christ of Latter-day Saints, 1981.

Brigham Young University Studies. Edited by Clinton F. Larson, et al. 20 vols. Provo, Utah: Brigham Young University Press, 1959–1980 (70 issues).

Clark, James R., ed. *Messages of the First Presidency of The Church of Jesus Christ of Latter-day Saints* [1833–1915]. 6 vols. Salt Lake City: Bookcraft, 1965.

Collected Discourses. Edited by Brian H. Stuy. 5 vols. Burbank, California, and Woodlands Hills, Utah: B.H.S. Publishing, 1987–1992.

Conference Reports of The Church of Jesus Christ of Latter-day Saints. Salt Lake City: The Church of Jesus Christ of Latter-day Saints, 1899–1970.

The Doctrine and Covenants of The Church of Jesus Christ of Latter-day Saints. Salt Lake City: The Church of Jesus Christ of Latter-day Saints, 1981.

Elders' Journal of the Church of Latter Day Saints. Edited by Joseph Smith, Jr., Kirtland, Ohio, and Far West, Missouri: October 1837 to August 1838.

The Evening and Morning Star. Edited by William W. Phelps and Oliver Cowdery. 2 vols. Independence, Missouri, and Kirtland, Ohio: June 1832 to September 1834.

Grant, Heber J. *Gospel Standards.* Compiled by G. Homer Durham. Salt Lake City: The Improvement Era, 1943.

The Holy Bible, Authorized King James Version.

Hymns of The Church of Jesus Christ of Latter-day Saints. Excerpts. Salt Lake City: The Church of Jesus Christ of Latter-day Saints, 1985.

The Improvement Era. Reports of Addresses Given in October 1949, April 1957, October 1960 and October 1970 General Conferences of The Church of Jesus Christ of Latter-day Saints. Salt Lake City: The Church of Jesus Christ of Latter-day Saints, November 1949, June 1957, December 1960, December 1970.

Jenson, Andrew. *Church Chronology.* Excerpts, 2nd ed. Salt Lake City: Deseret News, 1914.

Joseph Smith's "New Translation" of the Bible. Independence, Missouri: Herald Publishing House, 1970.

Journal of Book of Mormon Studies, FARMS, 3 vols., Provo, Utah, 1992–1994.

Journal of Discourses. Edited by George D. Watt, et al. 26 vols. Liverpool: F. D. Richards, et al., 1854–1886.

Kimball, Spencer W. *The Miracle of Forgiveness.* Salt Lake City: Bookcraft, 1969.

———. *Teachings of Spencer W. Kimball.* Compiled by Edward L. Kimball. Salt Lake City: Bookcraft, 1982.

Kirkham, Francis W. *A New Witness for Christ in America.* 2 vols. Salt Lake City: Utah Printing Co. 1959–1960.

The Latter Day Saints' Messenger and Advocate. Edited by Oliver Cowdery, et al. 3 vols. Kirtland, Ohio: F. G. Williams & Co., et al., October 1834 to August 1837.

Lectures on Faith. Compiled by Nels B. Lundwall. Salt Lake City: Bookcraft, n.d.

Ludlow, Daniel H., ed. *The Encyclopedia of Mormonism*. 4 vols. New York: Macmillan Publishing, 1992.

Maxwell, Neal A. *Meek and Lowly*. Salt Lake City: Deseret Book, 1987.

———. *Not My Will, But Thine*. Salt Lake City: Bookcraft, 1988.

———. *Notwithstanding my Weakness*. Salt Lake City: Deseret Book, 1981.

———. *Plain and Precious Things*. Salt Lake City: Deseret Book, 1983.

———. *Wherefore, Ye Must Press Forward*. Salt Lake City: Bookcraft, 1990.

———. *A Wonderful Flood of Light*. Salt Lake City: Bookcraft, 1990.

McConkie, Bruce R. *Doctrinal New Testament Commentary: The Gospels*. vol. 1. Salt Lake City: Bookcraft, 1966.

———. *Doctrinal New Testament Commentary: Colossians–Revelation*. vol. 3. Salt Lake City: Bookcraft, 1973.

———. *Mormon Doctrine*. 2nd ed., rev. Salt Lake City: Bookcraft, 1966.

———. *The Mortal Messiah*. The Messiah Series, vols. 2–5. Salt Lake City: Deseret Book, 1979–1982.

———. *A New Witness for the Articles of Faith*. Salt Lake City: Deseret Book, 1985.

McKay, David O. *Gospel Ideals*. Compiled by G. Homer Durham. Salt Lake City: The Improvement Era, 1953.

Nibley, Hugh. *Approaching Zion*. The Collected Works of Hugh Nibley, vol. 9. Salt Lake City: Deseret Book, and Provo, Utah: Foundation for Ancient Research and Mormon Studies, 1986.

———. *Enoch the Prophet*. The Collected Works of Hugh Nibley, vol. 2. Salt Lake City: Deseret Book, and Provo, Utah: Foundation for Ancient Research and Mormon Studies, 1986.

Otten, L. G. and C. M. Caldwell. *Sacred Truths of the Doctrine and Covenants*. 2 vols. Springville, Utah: LEMB, 1982.

The Pearl of Great Price. Salt Lake City: The Church of Jesus Christ of Latter-day Saints, 1981.

Pratt, Parley P. *Key to the Science of Theology*. 10th ed. Salt Lake City: Deseret Book, 1948.

Review of Books on the Book of Mormon, FARMS, 6 vols. Provo, Utah, 1989–1994.

Richards, LeGrand. *A Marvelous Work and a Wonder*. Salt Lake City: Deseret Book, 1976.

Roberts, B. H. *Comprehensive History of The Church of Jesus Christ of Latter-day Saints*. 6 vols. 1930. Reprint. Orem, Utah: Sonos Publishing Inc., 1991.

———. *Outlines of Ecclesiastical History: A Text Book*. 6th ed. Salt Lake City: The Church of Jesus Christ of Latter-day Saints, 1950.

Smith, Joseph F. *Gospel Doctrine*. Compiled by John A. Widtsoe. Salt Lake City: Deseret Book, 1919.

Smith, Joseph Fielding. *Answers to Gospel Questions*. Vols. 1–4. Salt Lake City: Deseret Press, 1957–1963.

———. *Doctrines of Salvation: Sermons and Writings of Joseph Fielding Smith*. 3 vols. Edited by Bruce R. McConkie. Salt Lake City: Bookcraft, 1954–1956.

———. *Teachings of the Prophet Joseph Smith*. Salt Lake City: Deseret Book Press, 1938.

———. *The Way to Perfection: Short Discourses on Gospel Themes*. 9th ed. Salt Lake City: Genealogical Society of The Church of Jesus Christ of Latter-day Saints, 1951.

Smith, Joseph. *History of The Church of Jesus Christ of Latter-day Saints*. Edited by B. H. Roberts. 2nd ed., rev. 7 vols. Salt Lake City: Deseret Book, 1980.

Smith, Lucy Mack. *History of Joseph Smith, By His Mother, Lucy Mack Smith*. Edited by Preston Nibley. Salt Lake City: Bookcraft, 1954.

Snow, Lorenzo. *Teachings of Lorenzo Snow*. Compiled by Clyde J. Williams. Salt Lake City: Bookcraft, 1984.

Talmage, James E. *The House of the Lord: A Study of Holy Sanctuaries, Ancient and Modern*. 1912 ed., reprint. Salt Lake City: Bookcraft, 1962.

———. *Jesus the Christ*. 15th ed., rev. Salt Lake City: The Church of Jesus Christ of Latter-day Saints, 1977.

———. *A Study of the Articles of Faith*. 12th ed., rev. Salt Lake City: The Church of Jesus Christ of Latter-day Saints, 1978.

Taylor, John. *The Gospel Kingdom*. Edited by G. Homer Durham. 3rd ed. Salt Lake City: Bookcraft, 1944.

Times and Seasons. Edited by Ebenezer Robinson, et al. 6 vols. Commerce, Illinois, and Nauvoo, Illinois, 1839–1846.

Widtsoe, John A. *Evidences and Reconciliations*. 3 vols. 1943–1951. Reprint (3 vols. in 1). Compiled by G. Homer Durham. Salt Lake City: Bookcraft, 1960.

Young, Brigham. *Discourses of Brigham Young*. Compiled by John A. Widtsoe. Salt Lake City: Deseret Book, 1978.

Other Mormon Works

Achieving a Celestial Marriage. Salt Lake City: The Church of Jesus Christ of Latter-day Saints, 1992.

BIBLIOGRAPHY

Alexander, Thomas G. "The Reconstruction of Mormon Doctrine: From Joseph Smith to Progressive Theology," *Sunstone*, July-August 1980.

Allen, James B. "The Significance of Joseph Smith's 'First Vision' in Mormon History," in *The New Mormon History*, edited by D. Michael Quinn. Salt Lake City: Signature, 1992.

Ballard, M. Russell. *Our Search for Happiness*. Salt Lake City: Deseret Book, 1993.

Barrett, William E. *The Restored Church*. Salt Lake City: Deseret Book, 1974.

Bennion, Lowell L. *An Introduction to the Gospel*. Salt Lake City: Deseret Sunday School Union Board, 1955.

Benson, Ezra Taft. "Fourteen Fundamentals in Following the Prophets," BYU Devotional, February 2, 1980. Published by Utah Lighthouse Ministry.

Buerger, David John. *The Mysteries of Godliness: A History of Mormon Temple Worship*. Salt Lake City: Smith Research Associates. 1994.

Burton, Rulon T. *We Believe*. Salt Lake City: Tabernacle Books, 1994.

Clark, J. Reuben. *Conference Report*, April 1954.

Doctrines of the Gospel Student Manual. Salt Lake City: The Church of Jesus Christ of Latter-day Saints, 1986.

Faust, James E. "Continuous Revelation," *Ensign*, November 1989.

Gorton, H. Clay. *The Language of the Lord*. Bountiful, Ut.: Horizon Publishers, 1993.

Gospel Principles. Salt Lake City: The Church of Jesus Christ of Latter-day Saints, 1978, 1979, 1988, 1992.

Hale, Van. "Defining the Contemporary Mormon Concept of God," in *Line Upon Line*, edited by Gary James Bergera. Salt Lake City: Signature, 1989.

Hale, Van. "The Origin of the Human Spirit in Early Mormon Thought," in *Line Upon Line*, edited by Gary James Bergera. Salt Lake City: Signature, 1989.

Harrison, Grant Von. *The Conversion Power of the Book of Mormon*. Orem, Ut.: Accord Publishing, 1988.

Hinckley, Gordon B. "Stay the Course—Keep the Faith," *Ensign*, November 1995.

———. "This Is the Work of the Master," *Ensign*, May 1995.

Horsley, A. Burt. *Peter and the Popes*. Religious Studies Center, Brigham Young University, 1989.

Hunter, Howard W. *Conference Report*, October 1968.

Hutchinson, Anthony A. "The Word of God is Enough: The Book of Mormon as Nineteenth-Century Scripture," in *New Approaches to the Book of Mormon*, edited by Brent Lee Metcalfe. Salt Lake City: Signature, 1993.

Jackson, Kent P. "Early Signs of the Apostasy," *Ensign*, December 1984.

Jessee, Dean. *The Personal Writings of Joseph Smith*. Salt Lake City: Deseret Book, 1989.

The Life and Teachings of Jesus and His Apostles, second edition revised. Salt Lake City: The Church of Jesus Christ of Latter-day Saints, 1978.

Ludlow, Daniel H. *A Companion to Your Study of the Book of Mormon*. Salt Lake City: Deseret Book, 1978.

Ludlow, Victor L. *Principles and Practices of the Restored Gospel*. Salt Lake City: Deseret Book, 1992.

Madsen, Truman. *Eternal Man*. Salt Lake City: Deseret Book, 1970.

Marston, Keith. *Missionary Pal.* Salt Lake City: n.p., 1987.

Maxwell, Neal A. "By the Grace and Power of God," *Ensign.* January 1997.

McConkie, Bruce R. *Mormon Doctrine.* Salt Lake City: Bookcraft, 1958.

———. "Our Relationship with the Lord." BYU Devotional, March 2, 1982. Monograph reproduced by Utah Lighthouse Ministry.

McConkie, Joseph Fielding. *Here We Stand.* Salt Lake City: Deseret Book, 1995.

McMurrin, Sterling M. *The Theological Foundations of the Mormon Religion.* Salt Lake City: University of Utah Press, 1965.

Matheny, Deanne G. "Does the Shoe Fit?: A Critique of the Limited Tehuantepec Geography," in *New Approaches to the Book of Mormon*, edited by Brent Lee Metcalfe. Salt Lake City: Signature, 1993.

Metcalfe, Brent Lee. "The Priority of Mosiah," in *New Approaches to the Book of Mormon*, edited by Brent Lee Metcalfe. Salt Lake City: Signature, 1993.

Millet, Robert L. "The Eternal Gospel," *Ensign*, June 1996.

Monson, Thomas S. *Conference Report*, October 1965.

———. "The Sustaining of Church Officers," *Ensign*, November 1995.

1995-1996 Church Almanac. Salt Lake City: Deseret News, 1994.

Oaks, Dallin H. "Apostasy and Restoration," *Ensign*, May 1995.

———. "The Historicity of the Book of Mormon." FARMS Dinner Address, October 29, 1993. Monograph.

Ostler, Blake T. "The Idea of Preexistence in Mormon Thought," in *Line Upon Line*, edited by Gary James Bergera. Salt Lake City: Signature, 1989.

Packer, Boyd K. "Address at the Fifth Annual Church Educational System Religious Educators Symposium," *Brigham Young University Studies*. Summer 1981.

Palmer, David A. "The Land of the Nephites," *Review of Books on the Book of Mormon*. Volume 2, 1990.

Parry, Donald W. "Hebrew Literary Patterns in the Book of Mormon," *Ensign*, October 1989.

Peterson, Daniel C. and Stephen D. Ricks. *Offenders for a Word*. Salt Lake City: Aspen Books, 1992.

Peterson, Daniel C. Book review of *Mormonism*, by Kurt Van Gorden, in *FARMS Review of Books*. Volume 8, Number 1, 1996.

Petersen, Mark D. *Isaiah for Today*. Salt Lake City: Deseret Book, 1981.

Pratt, Orson. *The Seer*. Salt Lake City: Seagull, 1993.

Quinn, D. Michael. *Early Mormonism and the Magical World View*. Salt Lake City: Signature, 1987.

———. *The Mormon Hierarchy: Origins of Power*. Salt Lake City: Signature, 1994.

Richards, LeGrand. *Conference Report*, October 1959.

———. *Conference Report*, April 1972.

Ricks, Stephen D. "Translation of the Book of Mormon: Interpreting the Evidence," in *Journal of Book of Mormon Studies*. Fall 1993.

Roberts, B. H. *The Falling Away*. Salt Lake City: Deseret News Press, 1931.

———. *The Mormon Doctrine of Deity*. 1903. Reprint. Bountiful, Ut.: Horizon, n.d.

———. *Studies of the Book of Mormon*. Salt Lake City: Signature, 1992.

Robson, Kent E. "Omnipotence, Omnipresence, and Omniscience in Mormon Theology," in *Line Upon Line*, edited by Gary James Bergera. Salt Lake City: Signature, 1989.

Skinner, Andrew C. "Apostasy, Restoration, and Lessons in Faith," *Ensign*, December 1995.

Smith, Joseph. *Lectures in Faith*. Salt Lake City: Deseret Book, 1985.

Sorenson, John L. *An Ancient American Setting for the Book of Mormon*. Salt Lake City: Deseret Book, 1985.

Spalding, F. S. *Joseph Smith, Jr., As A Translator*. Available reprinted in *Why Egyptologists Reject the Book of Abraham*, Salt Lake City, Utah Lighthouse Bookstore.

Sperry, Sidney B. *Were There Two Cumorahs?* FARMS reprint, 1964.

A Sure Foundation. Salt Lake City: Deseret Book, 1988.

Talmage, James E. *The Great Apostasy*. Salt Lake City: Seagull, 1993.

Welch, John W. "Chiasmus in the Book of Mormon." FARMS reprint, 1969.

Whitmer, David. *An Address to All Believers in Christ*. 1887. Photographic reprint by Utah Lighthouse Ministry.

Winwood, Richard I. *Be Not Deceived*. Salt Lake City: Richard I. Winwood, 1995.

Woodford, Robert J. "The Remarkable Doctrine and Covenants," *Ensign*, January 1997.

Critiques of Mormonism

Ashment, Edward H. "The Use of Egyptian Magical Papyri to Authenticate the Book of Abraham." N.p., n.d.

Beckwith, Francis J. and Stephen E. Parrish. *The Mormon Concept of God: A Philosophical Analysis*. Lewiston: The Edwin Mellen Press, 1991.

Brodie, Fawn M. *No Man Knows My History*, second edition. New York: Vintage Books, 1995.

Coe, Michael. "Mormons and Archeology: An Outside View," *Dialogue*, Summer 1973.

Lawson, Charles M. . . . *By His Own Hand Upon Papyrus: A New Look at the Joseph Smith Papyri*, revised edition. Grand Rapids, Mich.: Institute for Religious Research, 1992.

"Legacy: A Distorted View of Mormon History," *Salt Lake City Messenger*, May 1995.

Madrid, Patrick. "In Search of the 'Great Apostasy,'" *This Rock*, October 1992.

Marquardt, H. Michael and Wesley P. Walters. *Inventing Mormonism*. Salt Lake City: Smith Research Associates, 1994.

Scott, Latayne. "Mormonism and the Question of Truth," in *Christian Research Journal*, Summer 1992.

Sillitoe, Linda and Allen D. Roberts. *Salamander: The Story of the Mormon Forgery Murders*, second edition. Salt Lake City: Signature, 1989.

Tanner, Jerald and Sandra. *Answering Mormon Scholars*, vol. 1. Salt Lake City: Utah Lighthouse Ministry, 1994.

———. *The Case Against Mormonism*, volume 2. Salt Lake City: Utah Lighthouse Ministry, 1968.

———. *Evolution of the Temple Ceremony: 1842–1990*. Salt Lake City: Utah Lighthouse Ministry, 1990.

———. *Major Problems with Mormonism*. Salt Lake City: Utah Lighthouse Ministry, 1989.

———. *Mormonism—Shadow or Reality?*, fifth edition. Salt Lake City: Utah Lighthouse Ministry, 1987.

———. *3913 Changes in the Book of Mormon*. Salt Lake City: Utah Lighthouse Ministry, n.d.

Walters, Wesley P. *New Light on Mormon Origins from the Palmyra (N.Y.) Revival*. N.p., 1990.

Other Works Cited

Akin, James. "Is the Soul Inherited or Created," *This Rock*, June 1993.

The American Almanac: Statistical Abstract of the United States. Austin, Tex.: 1996.

Anderson, Vern. "Mormon Publisher Willing to Shake the 'Sacred Tree'." *Albuquerque Journal*, July 27, 1991.

Aquinas, St. Thomas. *Light of Faith*. Manchester, N.H.: Sophia Institute Press, 1993.

Baker, Kenneth, S.J. *Fundamentals of Catholicism*, 3 volumes. San Francisco: Ignatius Press, 1982, 1985.

Bloom, Harold. *The American Religion: The Emergence of the Post-Christian Nation*. New York: Simon and Schuster, 1992.

Bokenkotter, Thomas. *A Concise History of the Catholic Church*, revised and expanded edition. New York: Doubleday, 1990.

Bruce, F. F. *The New Testament Documents: Are They Reliable?*, fifth revised edition. Downers Grove, Ill.: InterVarsity Press, 1960

Catechism of the Catholic Church. New York: Doubleday, 199

Dever, William G. "Archaeology and the Bible," *Biblical Archaeology Review*, May-June 1990.

DiBerardino, Angelo, ed. *Encyclopedia of the Early Church*, 2 volumes. New York: Oxford University Press, 1992.

Dupont, Jacques. *Mariage et Divorce dans l'Evangile: Mathieu 19,3–12 et ses parallèles*. Bruges: Desclée, 1959.

Dyer, George J. *Limbo: Unsettled Question*. New York: Sheed and Ward, 1964.

Fisher, Helen, ed. *Gale State Rankings Reporter*, second edition, 1995. Detroit: Gale Research, 1995.

Flannery, Austin, O.P., general ed. *Vatican Council II: The Conciliar and Post-Conciliar Documents*, revised edition. Boston: St. Paul Editions, 1988.

Fraser, Gordon H. *Sects of Latter-day Saints*. Hubbard, Ore.: Gordon H. Fraser, 1978.

Fuller, Reginald C., et al. *A New Catholic Commentary on Holy Scripture*, revised edition. Camden, N.J.: Thomas Nelson and Sons, 1969.

George, Leonard. *Crimes of Perception*. New York: Paragon House, 1995.

Gottlieb, Robert and Peter Wiley. *America's Saints: The Rise of Mormon Power*. New York: Harcourt, Brace, Jovanovich, 1986.

Graham, Henry G. *Where We Got the Bible*. Rockford, Ill.: TAN, 1939.

John Paul II. "Christ's Divine Life Fully Humanizes Us," *Angelus Address*. February 23, 1997.

―――. *The Gospel of Life*. New York: Random House, 1995.

―――. "Reclaim Every Human Being's Right to Life," *Address to the Pontifical Academy for Life*. February 14, 1997.

Jurgens, William A. *The Faith of the Early Fathers*, 3 volumes. Collegeville, Minn.: The Liturgical Press, 1970–1979.

Keating, Karl. "Baptism: Immersion Only?" San Diego: Catholic Answers, n.d.

―――. *Catholicism and Fundamentalism*. San Francisco: Ignatius Press, 1988.

Kelly, J. N. D. *Early Christian Doctrines*, revised edition. San Francisco: HarperCollins, 1978.

Kreeft, Peter. *Everything You Ever Wanted to Know About Heaven.* San Francisco: Ignatius Press, 1990.

Kreeft, Peter and Ronald K. Tacelli. *Handbook of Christian Apologetics.* Downers Grove, Ill.: InterVarsity Press, 1994.

Latourette, Kenneth Scott. *A History of Christianity, Volume I to A.D. 1500.* New York: Harper and Row, 1975.

Lietzmann, Hans. *A History of the Early Church*, volumes 1-4. Cleveland: Meridian Books, 1953.

Madden, Charles, O.F.M. Conv. *Freemasonry.* Rockford, Ill.: TAN, 1995.

Maritain, Jacques. *On the Church of Christ.* Notre Dame, Ind.: University of Notre Dame Press, 1973.

McKenzie, John L. "Aspects of Old Testament Thought," in *The New Jerusalem Biblical Commentary*, edited by Raymond E. Brown, et al. Englewood Cliffs, N.J.: Prentice Hall, 1990.

Melton, J. Gordon, ed. *The Encyclopedia of American Religions*, 3 volumes. Tarrytown, N.Y.: Triumph Books, 1991.

Mirus, Jeffrey A., ed. *Reasons for Hope*, revised edition. Front Royal, Va.: Christendom College Press, 1982.

Most, William G. *Catholic Apologetics Today.* Rockford, Ill.: TAN, 1986.

The Navarre Bible. Dublin: Four Courts Press, 1988, 1990, 1992

Neuner, J., S.J. and J. Dupuis, S.J. *The Christian Faith.* New York: Alba House, 1982.

Newman, John Henry. *Conscience, Consensus, and the Development of Doctrine.* New York: Doubleday, 1992.

———. *Parochial and Plain Sermons.* San Francisco: Ignatius Press, 1987.

O'Grady, Joan. *Early Christian Heresies.* New York: Barnes and Noble Books, 1985.

Orlandis, José. *A Short History of the Catholic Church*. Dublin: Four Courts Press, 1993.

Ott, Ludwig. *Fundamentals of Catholic Dogma*, fourth edition. Rockford, Ill.: TAN, 1960.

Poulet, Charles. *A History of the Catholic Church*. St. Louis: B. Herder, 1934.

Roberts, Alexander and James Donaldson, editors. *Ante-Nicene Fathers*, 10 volumes. Peabody, Mass.: Hendrickson, 1994.

Schaff, Philip, ed. *Nicene and Post-Nicene Fathers*, first series, 14 volumes. Peabody, Mass.: Hendrickson, 1994

Schaff, Philip and Henry Wace, eds. *Nicene and Post Nicene Fathers*, second series, 14 volumes. Peabody, Mass.. 1994

Schönborn, Christoph. *From Death to Life: The Christian Journey*. San Francisco: Ignatius Press, 1995.

Sheed, Frank. *Theology for Beginners*. Ann Arbor, Mich.: Servant, 1981.

———. *Theology and Sanity*. San Francisco: Ignatius Press, 1993.

Shupe, Anson. *The Darker Side of Virtue*. Buffalo, N.Y.: Prometheus Books, 1991.

Spirago, Francis. *The Catechism Explained*. Rockford, Ill.: TAN, 1921.

Turley, Robert. *Victims: The LDS Church and the Mark Hofmann Case*. Urbana, Ill.: The University of Illinois Press, 1992

Scriptural Index

Christian Scriptures

OLD TESTAMENT

GENESIS
1:26	255
1:26a	254
1:26–27	262, 267
1:27	262
2:1	365
2:4	283
2:7	317
2:17	338
6:1–2	359
9:6	267
14:18–20	93
15:2	93
27:20	283
37:9–11	188
48:5	287
49:4	286
49:5–7	287
50	462

EXODUS
3:6–7	283
4:22	287
18:11–12	93
19:6	93–94
19:21–22	93
19:24	93
20:2–3	299
28:1	93
28:30	401
30:34–38	210
33:11	267, 268, 269
33:20	268, 274
34:14	299

NUMBERS
11:18	267
12:6–8	267, 268
16	94
18:21	63
21:14	458
23:19	270
30:2	267

DEUTERONOMY
4:24	270
6:4	283, 314
6:16	284
10:17	283
10:20	284
11:11	365
18:10–11	403
18:9–12	422
19:15	424

21:15–17	286
32:4	270
32:39	314

JOSHUA

9:14	267

1 SAMUEL

8:21	267
14:41–42	401
17:50	445

2 SAMUEL

7:22	314
22:25	267

1 CHRONICLES

5:1	287
16:17	167
23:13	94

2 CHRONICLES

26:16–21	94, 197
33:6	422

EZRA

2:61–63	95

JOB

1:6	327
5:8	96
10:8–12	147
10:21	446
33:4	317
35:5	365
38:4, 7	328
42:2	320

PSALMS

2:7	331
3:18	96
7:14	96
8:2	96
12:7	328
20:9	340
22:10	147
33:18	267
45:6–7	283
51:5	340
51:11	319
51:17	93
82	255, 258, 259
82:1	254
82:6	258, 346
85:10	269
89:27	286
90:2	318
91:4	270
95:6	299
98:1	267, 270
102:25	317
103:19	365
104:30	317
107:22	93
110:1	284
110:4	93, 96, 98
110:4b	96
119:90	229
139:7	319

ISAIAH

5:20	266
7:14	291
8:19	422
9:1–2	169
9:6	283

9:6–7	232	**EZEKIEL**	
24:1	167	9:4–6	480
24:3	167	37:15–17	418
24:3–5	167	37:16	419
29:4	421	37:22	420
29:8	168		
29:11–12	422, 424	**DANIEL**	
29:13	168	2:30	96–97
29:13–14	168	2:44	33
29:14	424	4:17	96
40:3	283	5	446
40:8	462	7	189
42:8	314	7:2–3	190
43:10–11	314–315	7:4–8	189
44:24	315	7:13–14	233
44:5, 14, 21–22	315	7:17	190
44:6, 8	314	7:21	190–191
45:5, 6, 14, 18, 21, 22	315	7:25	190
45:8	365	7:26	191
46:9	315	9:3	204
55:11	228		
59:1–3a	169	**HOSEA**	
59:20	169	11:9	270
60:2	168		
		JOEL	
		1:13	204
JEREMIAH		2:10	365
1:5	147, 326		
4:23	365	**AMOS**	
6:26	204	3:7	475
17:9	340, 430	8:11–12	169
23:23–24	319	8:13–14	170
31:9	287		
32:18	283	**OBADIAH**	
32:37–41	232	1:21	129
LAMENTATIONS		**MICAH**	
2:18	267	3:5–7	170

SCRIPTURAL INDEX

NAHUM

1:3	267

MALACHI

1:7	94
1:12	94

2:10	329
3–4	445
4:1	445
4:2	445

NEW TESTAMENT

MATTHEW

1:18	291
1:22–23	292
1:23	227
2:11	298
3:16–17	256, 258, 316
3:17	390
4:9	176
5:12	348
5:18	462
5:48	347–348
6:16–18	204
6:9	365
7:15	166, 172
7:24	229
10:2	235
10:7	233
15:8	168
15:19	430
16:18	53, 85, 192, 227, 234
17:5	390
18:20	319
18:21	236
21:43	172
21:45	173
22:30	370–371
23:15	183
23:27–28	141
23:39	469
24	41
24:35	462
26:26	75
27:19	427
28:18	320
28:19–20	244
28:20	41, 192, 244, 464
28:20b	227

MARK

1:9–11	316
3:2	235
3:27	230
7:4	213
8:29	236
12:25	206

LUKE

1:8	97
1:32–33	230
1:34–35	291
1:37	320
1:41	147
2:11	317
2:52	296

3:21–22	316	14:16	228, 243
6:14	235	14:16, 26	228
10:1	55	14:18	243
10:16	382, 427	14:26	243, 319
10:7–8	63	15:26	243
10:16	382	16:13	228
12:33	365	16:7	243, 309
12:41	236	17:3	315
12:50	213	17:5	331
14:28–30	229	20:28	283, 298, 316–317
16:19–31	359	21:15–17	53, 235
20:34–36	91, 133	21:18–24	247
21:19	455		
21:20–21	189	ACTS	
22:32	53	1:13	235
23:43	355	1:15–23	236
24:39	271	1:20–26	54
24:49	228	1:21–22a	54
		1:22b	54–55
JOHN		1:6	173
1:2	317	2:14	236
1:3	317	2:38	196
1:18	275	2:41	213, 236
1:31–34	316	3:6–7	236
3:5	77	4:8–12	236
:30	346	5:3–4	316
4.24	271, 275	6	100
6:51–57	77	6:1–	56, 01
6:69	236, 319	6:3	10
7:28	318	7:55–56	258
9:38	298	9:1–16	54
10:11	231	9:17–18	213
10:16	399, 425	10:44–49	236
10:30	258	10:47–48	213
10:34	258	11:27	53
10:34–36	346	11:30	105
14:2	376	13:1	53
14:6	318	13:33	331

14:14	54	2:10-11	319
14:23	105	2:9	370
15:32	53	3:11	230
16:15	212	5:9	458
16:33	212	7:1-2	206
17:11	429	7:5-6	207
17:28-29	346	7:7-9	207
17:29	328	7:11	150
18:8	212	7:19	95
20:28	231	7:27-28	207
20:30	173	7:32-35	208
26:26	444	7:36-38	208
		7:38	208
ROMANS		7:39-40	208
1:1	54	8:4	315
2:11	426	8:4b	261
2:5	376	8:4-6	261
3:8	145	8:5	259, 264
4:17	327	8:5-6	346
5:12	338	8:7-10	95
5:14	340	9:1	54
5:18	340	9:1-2	55
5:19	340	9:1-14	63
6:3	213	9:14	63
6:3-4	196	9:26-27	203
7:23	340-341	10:1-5	330
8:18	377	10:17	94
8:28	17, 343	10:18	94
8:29	287	10:21	94-95
10:12	317	12:28	53
12:1	94	12:28-30	107
12:2	147	12:7, 11	320
12:5	231	13:11	342
13:1	287	14:40	97
15:16	95	15:29	116
		15:35	363
1 CORINTHIANS		15:40-42	363
1:16	212	15:44	329

15:44–46	330	2:17	94
15:46	330	4:3	239
16:1–4	56	4:14–18	56
		4:18	94

2 CORINTHIANS

3:17	317	COLOSSIANS	
4:17	370	1:15	272, 331
6:2	359	1:15–17	288
9:1–5	56	1:16	317
12:2	365	1:16–17	290
12:12	55	1:18	231, 288
13:1	424	2:9	282
		2:11–12	72

GALATIANS

1:6–9	174	2:2–3	319
1:8	432, 452	2:5	97
1:15–16	54	2:9	291
1:18	236	2:9–10	320
2:10	56		
3:20	315	1 THESSALONIANS	
5:17	340	4:17	176
6:6–10	376		
		2 THESSALONIANS	

EPHESIANS		2:1–4	175
:3	228	2:7–8	175
:22	231, 319	2:8	267
:8–22	319	2:9	176
2:19–20	244	2:12	176
2.20	53	2:15	430
4:6	315		
4:11	53, 58, 106	1 TIMOTHY	
4:11–14	174	1:3	180
5:29	231	1:3–5	178
		1:4	184
		1:6	243
PHILIPPIANS		1:6–7	177–178
2:6	273	1:13	243
2:6–7	273	1:17	272, 316
2:6–8	282	2:4	244

2:5	316	1:8	316
3:1–7	105	1:8–9	283
3:8–11	101	3:1	94
3:15	230, 383	4:15	281, 291, 319
4:1–4	178–179	5:6	97
4:7	184	5:10	98
5:18	63	6:20	98
		7:3	94, 97, 99
2 Timothy		7:5	93
1:15	180, 182	7:11	93
1:16–18	180	7:12	94
1:18	180	7:12–16	98
2:3–4	206	7:12–16a	99
2:6	63	7:15–17	94
3:1–5	182, 184	7:17	94, 98
3:1–9	184	7:19	94
3:5	182	7:21	98
3:1–5	182, 184	9:14	318
3:6–9	183	9:27	359
4:1–2	243	11:10	230
4:2	177	12:2	287
4:3	147	12:9	329
4:3–4	147, 184	13:5	94
4:5	102		
4:6	181	James	
4:9–15	181	1:2–4	429
4:10	239	1:5	429
4:16–17	182	3:1	106
4:19	180	3:2	348
4:21	239	4.8 10	205
Titus		1 Peter	
1:14	184	2:5	94
		2:6	230
Hebrews		2:9	94
1:1	175	3:18	359
1:3	273	3:18–20	358
1:5–6	298	3:20–21	196

CHRISTIAN SCRIPTURES

3:21	77, 213	5:6	349
4:5–6	358	5:10	94
4:6	359–360	7:3	480
		8:3–4	210
2 Peter	187	9:4	480
2:1–3	185	11:3	205
3:3	186–187	12:1–5	187
		12:7	333
1 John		12:13–16	188
1:7	453	12:17	188, 189
4:4	230	13:1–2	189
4:12	275	13:4	191
5:6	318	13:7	189–191
		13:18	190
Jude		14:1	480
3	425	14:6	191
3–4	186	14:6–10	192
18	187	15:4	318
25	316	20:2	188
		20:1–4	361
Revelation		21:4	368
1:6	94	21:7	349
1:8	318	21:10	348
3:7	318	21:21	349
3:21	348	22:18–19	462

Mormon Scriptures

THE BOOK OF MORMON

1 NEPHI

3:3, 20	445
5:12–13	445
12:23	31, 479
13:15	31
13:26–27	457
13:5, 6	161
13:7–8	442
19:6	398
19:10, 21	445
20:1	453
22:15	445
22:24	445

2 NEPHI

1:14	446
2:25	336
2:33–34	336
5:15	439
5:21	31, 479
12:7	441
13:23	438
25:13	445
25:23	69, 453
25:26	296
26:4	445
26:9	445
27:12–13	412
29:6, 8	458
30:6	31, 44
31:13–14, 17	453

JACOB

2:23–24	26
2:26–27	477
3:3–5	479
3:8	479
3:8–9	31
5	442
7:27	446

JAROM

1:8	440

WORDS OF MORMON

5	398

MOSIAH

2:19	397, 445
3:19	397, 445
3:34	397, 445
3:5–8	453
4:22	397, 445
4:24	397, 445
4:9	451
7:27	453
8:10	439
8:17	458
9:16	439
10:5	438
11:15	442
13:18	439
15:1–5	453
15:3–5	314

ALMA

1:29	438
3:6	479

MORMON SCRIPTURES

4:6	438	3 Nephi	
10:2–3	446	2:14–15	31, 479
11	439	2:15	479
11:7	442	10:18	426
11:22–29	451	11:25	79
11:38–40	453	20:3–7	446
11:7	442		
16:6	435		
17:36	445	Mormon	
18:5	314	1:13, 16	248
18:9	440	5:15	400
18:27–28	314	5:15–18	479
22:8–11	314	9:32–33	398
22:9–11	451		
23:18	479	Ether	
34:36	450	2:3	34
40:12–14	356	9:17	438
43:22	435	10:24	438
51:26	435		
56:25	435		
		Moroni	
Helaman		4:3	74
3:8	435	5:2	75
6:13	438	8:14	211
6:31	439	8:18	451
8:19–20	445	10:3–4	428–429

DOCTRINE & COVENANTS

Doctrine & Covenants		20:1	49
1:29	407	20:8	407
3:12	415	20:8–9	396, 450
3:12–15	405	20:9	410
8:7–9	468	20:37	79
5:14	417	20:73	79
7:1–4, 8	246	21:4–5	51
17	124, 413	27:2	75

42:12	396	107:74	60
42:29–30	467	107:91–92	458
59:6	141	107:98	58
73:4	463	115:3	49
76:103	373	115:3–4	49
76:24	332	121:26, 28, 32	262
76:28–30	448	130:22	46, 275, 306
76:55	366	131:1–5	366
76:72, 75–76	372	131:7–8	289
76:79	372	132:2	29
76:89	373	132:4–6	477
76:89–98	448	132:19	366–367
77:2	290	132:54	477
88:119	124	138:53, 56	333
93:3	289		
93:29	324	OFFICIAL DECLARATION—1	
101:4	27		38, 43, 477
103:9	129		
107:13–14	81		
107:22	53	OFFICIAL DECLARATION—2	
107:25	55		43, 477, 481–482

PEARL OF GREAT PRICE

MOSES		1:26–27	31
3:5	290, 333	1:28	470
5:11	336	2:23–24	470
6:8	478	3	451
6:51	333	3:2ff	470
6:64–66	85	3:16	470
7:8, 12, 22	31	3:22	325, 470
		3:22ff	31
ABRAHAM		3:24	289
1:2	470	3:26	289
1:12–15	470	3:28	470
1:20	482	3:36–37	470
1:26	479	4	451, 470

5	470	1:22–23	387
4:26–27	262	1:27	389
4:27	262	1:27–54	401
		1:34–35, 42	390
Joseph Smith—Matthew		1:53, 59	390
468		1:56	403
		1:59ff	24
		1:61	405
Joseph Smith—History		1:65	123
1:3–34	23	1:68ff	414
1:5	388		
1:14	389	**Articles of Faith**	
1:17	390	2	336
1:5–19	502	6	50
1:19	22, 182	8	381
1:21–22	23, 392	10	367
1:21–26	388	11	163

Mormon Writings Not Held to be Scripture

History of the Church		**Journal of Discourses**	
1:11	401	1:50	36
1:51–53	413	1:62–63	334
1:54–55	413	1:346	301
2:79	432	2:137	357
2:236	470	2:171	391
3:231–232	5	2:210	302
3:307	417	2:268	293
3:381	58	2:288	445
4:461	396, 449	2:338	304
4:552	136	2:345–346	264
5:423	403	4:219	222
5:556	292	4:90	62
6:408–409	159	5:180	307
6:475	451	6:120	345

6:176	219	13:78	391
7:164	418	14:171–172	368
7:289	356	16:46	313
7:290–291	480	18:213	129
7:324	51	18:329	391
10:5	367	20:167	391
10:109	35	22:333–334	355
11:122–128	35	26:163	473

Subject Index

Aaronic priesthood, 81–82, 95–96, 102
Abortion, changing Mormon position on, 141–149
Adam-God doctrine, 36, 40, 42
Administering to the Sick, 73, 107
African descent, persons of, *see* Racist Mormon teachings
Alcohol, 26, 76, 111
Alger, Fanny, 29, 414
American Indians, *see* Lamanites, Nephites, Racist Mormon teachings
Anointing of the Sick, 107
Apostasy, *see* Great Apostasy
Apostolic succession, 240–244
"Articles of Faith," 472, 503–504
Asceticism, 203–205

Baptism for the Dead, 115–120
Baptism, immersion, 212–214
Baptism, infant, 211–212
Baptism, Mormon, 76–79, 87–89
Benson, Ezra Taft, 44
Bible, Mormon view of, 456–4
Bishops, biblical, 102–103, 105–106
Bishops, Mormon, 60, 82, 102–103
Blacks, *see* Racist Mormon teachings

Blessings, Mormon, 86–87
"Book of Abraham," 469–472
"Book of Mormon," 23–25
  "Coming forth" of, 400–404
  "Translation" of, 404–409
  archaeological and geographical problems with, 432–444
  changes in, 449
  contradicts current Mormon theology, 449–455
  on baptism, 454
  on the Eucharist, 454–455
  on original sin, 454
  portion of destroyed by Martin Harris's wife, 405, 460–462
  praying concerning, 428–431
  relation to King James Version of Bible, 397, 444–446
  relation to *View of the Hebrews*, 409–411
  style of, 444–449
  summary of, 397–400
"Book of Moses," 468
"Burning in the bosom," 428

Caffeine, 70, 76
Catholic Church, Mormon teaching on, 161–164, 215–225
Celestial kingdom, 366–368
Celibacy, 205–208
Chiasmus, 446–448

SUBJECT INDEX

Church and state, separation of, 195–199
Church, indefectability (permanence) of, 226–233
Clergy, paid vs. unpaid, 60–63
Confirmation, Mormon, 80, 107
Constantine, Emperor, 195–199
Cowdery, Oliver, 414–416
Creation, Mormon stories about, 125, 323–326
Crusades, 216–220

Deacons,
   biblical, 100–101, 104
   Mormon, 81, 100–101
Death, see Spirit world
"Deseret," meaning of, 34
Divorce, Mormon position on, 149–150
"Doctrine and Covenants," 27, 464–468

Early Church Fathers, polytheism and, 350–351
Early Church, persecution of, 193–194
Eight Witnesses, 417–418
Elders
   biblical, 102–103, 105–106
   Mormon, 83, 102–103
Elohim, 282–284
Eternal progression, 344–352
Eucharist, Mormon, see "The Sacrament'
Eucharistic sacrifice, 211

Fall of man, Mormon view of, 336–343

Familiar spirits, 421–422
Families in heaven, 369–371
First Presidency, 53–54
First Vision, 21–23
   evaluation of, 388–395
   versions of, 384–388, 495–502
Freemasonry, see Masonry

Galileo, 223–225
"Garments," 122–123
General conferences, speeches at as scripture, 476
"Gentiles," Mormon use of term, 111
Gestures, Mormon Temple, 125–126
Glory, three degrees of, see Three degrees of glory
God the Father,
   as Elohim, not Jehovah, 282–284
   physical body of, 267–279
   physical impregnation of Mary, 291–294
   wives of, 42
God, Mormon view 311–312
Golden plates, 24–25, 4 406
Grant, Heber J., 40
Great Apostasy, concept of, 159 160
   historical arguments concerning, 193–199
   impossibility of, 226–233
   incomplete by Mormon admission, 245–249
   New Testament and, 172–192
   Old Testament and, 166–171

SUBJECT INDEX

Handclasps, Mormon, 125–126
Harris, Martin, 413–416
"Heavenly Father," see God the Father
"Heavenly Mother," 42, 285–286, 294
Henotheism, 311–312
High priests, Mormon, 103–104
Hinckley, Gordon B.,
   60 Minutes interview, 483
   San Francisco Chronicle interview, 45–46
Hoffman cover-up, 152–153
Hoffman, Mark, 152–153
Holy Ghost,
   Catholic view of, 310
   Mormon view of, 303–310
Holy Spirit, see Holy Ghost
Hunter, Howard W., 44

Incense, 210–211
Indefectability of the Church, 226–233
Inquisition, 220–223
Intermediate state, see Spirit world

Jack Mormons, 111
Jehovah, 282–284
Jesus Christ,
   as Jehovah, not Elohim, 282–284
   as polygamist, husband, and father, 300–302
   Christian teaching on, 280–282
   physical conception of, 291–294
   pre-existence of, 285–289
   resurrection of, 294–295
   subordination of, 295–300
John, apostle, immortality of, 245–248
"Joseph Smith—History," 469
"Joseph Smith—Matthew," 468
Joseph Smith Translation, 274, 462–463

Kimball, Spencer W., 42–44
"King Follet Discourse," 32, 276–277
King James Version,
   Mormon use of, 457–458
   Smith's "Inspired Version" of, 462–464

Lamanites, 44, 398–400, 407, 432–433, 436, 438, 479
Lee, Harold B., 42
Lord's Supper, see "The Sacrament"
Lost Tribes, 399
Lying, 208–209

Marriages, Mormon, 89–91
Mary, Virgin, physically impregnated by God the Father, 291–294
Masonry, Mormon connection to, 135–139
Matter, spirits made of, 289–291
McKay, David O., 41
Meat, 26, 76, 179–180, 260–261
Melchizedek priesthood, 82–83, 99–100
Millennium, 361–362
Monogamy

SUBJECT INDEX

legislation, 35–39
  reintroduction of, 38–39
Monotheism, biblical teaching of, 314–316
Mormon church,
  founding of, 26
  general authorities of, 51–59
  organization of, 49–63
  President and Prophet of, 474–476
  regional and local authorities, 59–63
Mormonism, stages of, 21–46
Mountain Meadows Massacre, 35

NAACP, 43
Naming of an Infant, 72
National Geographic Society, 434
Native Americans, *see* Lamanites, Nephites, Racist Mormon teachings
Nauvoo Expositor, 33
Negroes, *see* Racist Mormon teachings
Nephites, 245, 247–248, 398–401, 406, 425, 432–436, 438–438, 441–442, 445–446, 453, 479

"Official Declaration—1," 476–477
"Official Declaration—2," 476, 481
"Order" of Melchizedek, 96–99
Ordinances
  Catholic "changes in," 209–210
  classification of, 70–71
  Mormon, 64–107
Ordination, Mormon, 91–107
Original sin, Mormon denial of, 336–343
"Other sheep," 425–427

Paganism, charges of, 164–165, 195–202
Patriarchal and Paternal Blessings, 72–73, 505–507
"Pearl of Great Price," 468–472
Penance, sacrament of, 107
Peter, apostle, role of, 234–237
Philosophy, Ancient, 200–202
Plural gods, *see* Polytheism
Plural marriage, *see* Polygamy
Polygamy, 29–31, 477–478
Polytheism,
  condemned in Mormon scriptures, 261–262
  Mormon, 31–32, 253–254, 263–266
  verses misused by Mormons, 254–261
Popes, authority of, 234–240
Pre-existence of man, 323–335
Presiding Bishopric, 56–57
Priesthood
  biblical, 93–95
  Christian, 94–95
  Mormon, 95–96
  ordinations, Mormon, 80–83
Priests, Mormon, 82
Prophets,
  biblical, 475–476
  Prophets, Mormon, 51–53

Quorum of the Seventy, 55–56

SUBJECT INDEX

Quorum of the Twelve Apostles, 54-55

Racist Mormon teachings, 31, 35, 41-44, 334-335, 479-482
"Reformed Egyptian," 24-25, 405-408, 423
Revelations,
  continuing, Catholic view of, 473-474
  continuing Mormon, 473-484
Rewards in heaven, 376-377

"The Sacrament," (Mormon communion), 73-75, 107
Sacramentals vs. Ordinances, 86
Sacraments vs. Ordinances, 85
Sacraments, Mormon, see Ordinances
Salvation, Mormon view of, 353-354
Sheep, see Other sheep
Smith,
  Emma Hale, 24
  George Albert, 41
  Joseph F., 40
  Joseph Fielding, 42
  Joseph,
    "Inspired Version" of the Bible, 462-464
    affair with Fanny Alger, 29, 414
    affiliates with Methodist church, 403-404
    death of, 33
    false prophecies of, 465-466
    money digging, 24, 402-403
    peep stone, 24, 402

Smithsonian Institute, 434
Snow, Lorenzo, 39
"Sons of perdition," 375
Spirit world, 354-356
  Mormon missionaries in, 357-360
Stages of Mormonism, 21-46
"Stakes," 59
"Standard works," Mormon, 381
"Sticks" of Judah and Joseph, 418-421
Subjectivism, Mormon, 428-431

Taylor, John, 36
Teachers,
  biblical, 106-107
  Mormon, 81-82, 102
"Telestial kingdom," 373-375
Temple
  Endowment, 121-131
  Sealings, 132-134
  Square, 108-111
Temples, Mormon, 108-111, 112-139
"Terrestrial kingdom," 372-373
Three degrees of glory, 363-365
  see also Celestial kingdom, Telestial kingdom, Terrestrial kingdom
Three Nephites, immortality of, 245, 247-248
Three Witnesses, 412-416
Tobacco, 26, 76, 111
Trinity, biblical basis of, 313-320

Underwear, Mormon, see "Garments"

Urim and Thummim, 23, 245, 362, 401, 405, 407–408, 410, 499
Utah,
    admission to statehood, 36
    child abuse rate, 152
    crime rate, 152–153
    divorce rate, 149
    Mormon settlement of, 34
    substance abuse rate, 151
    suicide rate, 152

View of the Hebrews, 409–411
Virgin Birth, 291–294

"Wards," 59
Whitmer, David, 416
Woodruff, Wilford, 37
"Word of Wisdom," 26–27

Young, Brigham, 33–36